Hodges' Scout

WAR / SOCIETY / CULTURE

Michael Fellman, *Series Founder*

Hodges' Scout

A Lost Patrol of the French and Indian War

Len Travers

JOHNS HOPKINS UNIVERSITY PRESS   BALTIMORE

© 2015 Johns Hopkins University Press
All rights reserved. Published 2015
Printed in the United States of America on acid-free paper

Johns Hopkins Paperback edition, 2019
9 8 7 6 5 4 3 2 1

Johns Hopkins University Press
2715 North Charles Street
Baltimore, Maryland 21218-4363
www.press.jhu.edu

The Library of Congress has cataloged the hardcover edition of this book as follows:

Travers, Len, 1952–
  Hodges' Scout : a lost patrol of the French and Indian War / Len Travers.
    pages cm. — (War/society/culture)
  Includes bibliographical references and index.
    ISBN 978-1-4214-1805-6 (hardcover : acid-free paper) — ISBN 1-4214-1805-3
(hardcover : acid-free paper) — ISBN 978-1-4214-1806-3 (electronic) — ISBN
1-4214-1806-1 (electronic) 1. New York (State)—History—French and Indian War,
1754–1763—Reconnaissance operations. 2. United States—History—French and
Indian War, 1754–1763—Reconnaissance operations. 3. Hodges, Joseph, 1714–
1756. 4. Combat patrols—New York (State)—Lake George Region—History—18th
century. 5. Indian captivities—New York (State)—Lake George Region—History—
18th century. 6. Massacres—New York (State)—Lake George Region—History—
18th century. 7. Soldiers—New York (State)—Lake George Region—History—18th
century. 8. Prisoners of war—New York (State)—Lake George Region—History—
18th century. 9. New York (State)—History—French and Indian War, 1754–1763—
Prisoners and prisons. 10. United States—History—French and Indian War,
1754–1763—Prisoners and prisons. I. Title.
  E199.T73 2015
  940.2'534—dc23   2015004325

A catalog record for this book is available from the British Library.

ISBN-13: 978-1-4214-2898-7
ISBN-10: 1-4214-2898-9

*Special discounts are available for bulk purchases of this book. For more information, please
contact Special Sales at 410-516-6936 or specialsales@press.jhu.edu.*

Johns Hopkins University Press uses environmentally friendly book materials,
including recycled text paper that is composed of at least 30 percent post-consumer
waste, whenever possible.

For Carolyn, who knows why

And some there be, which have no memorial; who are perished,
as though they had never been; and are become as though they had
never been born. . . .

Ecclesiasticus 44:9

Contents

Acknowledgments

This has been a particularly absorbing investigation for me, and I need to thank those who helped me to complete it. A fellowship at the Massachusetts Historical Society made it possible for me to spend a long time with General John Winslow's papers from the 1756 campaign, which proved invaluable to telling this story; my thanks to Conrad Wright, Peter Drummey, and the top-notch staff of the MHS library. Likewise, the folks at the Massachusetts Archives at Columbia Point helped me to find essential materials there and were always willing to bring forth original documents when the ancient microfilms were simply too difficult to read. I pestered the librarians and town clerks' staffs at Middleborough, Norton, Taunton, Lexington, and numerous other Massachusetts towns for nuggets of local history and always found them gracious and helpful. The same goes for the good people at the several Registries of Probate and Deeds I visited.

Several friends and colleagues read or heard portions of the manuscript and offered valuable advice. Laurel Ulrich gave some kind words of support when this project was in its infancy, years ago. I doubt that she remembers the occasion, but her words have stayed with me since that time. Brian Glyn Williams gave early and enthusiastic encouragement and advice toward publishing; in fact, all of my colleagues in the History Department at UMass Dartmouth have been wonderfully supportive about the project since its inception. I am glad to be able, finally, to show them the result; they are among the very best teacher-historians I have known, and it has been an honor and pleasure to work with them. I am indebted to former U.S. Army Captain Victor Duphily for his insights on combat situations and psychology. His Honor John G. New also offered a thoughtful critique, especially regarding Jonathan Barnes' court-martial. Mae Ngai, at Columbia University, and my former mentor at UMass Dartmouth, Dr. James Hijiya, also gave encouragement.

In the course of writing this book I had the opportunity to present portions of the work to very collegial groups of both academic and public historians; in all cases I received helpful advice and searching questions that sent me back to the sources. Members of the Boston Area Seminar for Early American History, hosted by the Massachusetts Historical Society, read an early draft of chapter 11 and offered a lively discussion on the subject of renegades. Colin Calloway provided thoughtful and challenging commentary on that occasion. Attendees of the Annual War College for the French and Indian War at Fort Ticonderoga heard my presentation on the fate of Hodges' Scout; my thanks to Beth Hill, president and CEO, and Richard Strum, director of education, for the opportunity to speak to such a dedicated and well-informed group. While there, I met Stephen Brumwell, who generously shared with me his copies of official papers relating to the court-martial of Jonathan Barnes. Walt Powell offered me another such occasion to speak at the annual conference of the Braddock's Road Association, at Jumonville, Pennsylvania; special thanks to R. Patrick Murphy for sending me that great passage from the Book of Ecclesiasticus.

Dr. Maria A. Liston shared with me her thoughts concerning the human remains and other artifacts she had studied at Fort William Henry and alerted me to the possibility that the remains of Captain Hodges may yet be found in undisturbed ground nearby. My French is about as rusty as is possible, so I am grateful to Claire Travers and Michelle Cheyne for help with some translations. Early in this project I knew that maps would be critical for the finished work. Die Hoxie took my crude sketches and transformed them into cartographic works of art.

A number of people at Johns Hopkins University Press have given their time and talents to making this book a sight better than it could have been without them. My sincere thanks to Bob Brugger, who sent the e-mail every author wants to read: "Sounds Interesting; send me the manuscript." Since then, he, Kathryn Marguy, Julie McCarthy, and others unknown to me have had a hand in shepherding my original manuscript into the form you have now; earnest thanks to you all. Joanne Allen, the most careful and supportive copy-editor I have encountered, has saved me from countless gaffes; if any remain, they are of a sort not in her bailiwick, but mine to answer for.

I now know that Gregory Evans Dowd was the anonymous reader of this manuscript in its early form. I cannot thank him sufficiently for the kind words of support he offered at a critical time, and I hope I have sufficiently addressed the caveats to which he alerted me. We have never met, but I have long admired his work, so his input was a very pleasant surprise when it came. Likewise, it was a great treat to get John Buxton's artwork for the book's cover. While it depicts an ambush scenario from a somewhat earlier time, the sense of drama and foreboding it conveys convinced me I had to have it, and John graciously gave his permission.

I fear that there may be others whose names should probably appear here but are omitted; for that, the fault is all mine. I must plead absent-mindedness, but not ingratitude, and beg your pardons.

Of course, my greatest support in this undertaking has been Carolyn Freeman Travers, first reader, ruthless critic, chief morale officer, and indexer extraordinaire, who has patiently (I hope) put up with my long disappearances into the study to write and rethink. She inspired this project, in that she warned me long ago that she could never love a man who could write only *one* book. She has all my love and thanks.

Hodges' Scout

Prologue

Recovering Lost Lives

In September 1756 a company of Massachusetts Colony soldiers, nearly fifty men, on a routine reconnaissance, or *scout,* was all but obliterated by French and Indian enemies near the shore of Lake George, in New York Colony. The incident became known at the time simply as Hodges' Scout, named for the unfortunate company's commander, Captain Joseph Hodges. Today, only a few specialists are aware of the incident; no modern history of the French and Indian War even mentions it. The omission is understandable. In terms of numbers, the loss of Hodges' command was hardly of significant consequence to the conflict. Additionally, Hodges and his men died at the beginning of a long and brutal war, one that would see much in the way of high drama and make household names for British, Canadian, and American history: James Wolfe; the Marquis de Montcalm; George Washington.

The history of warfare is like that. It tends to elevate a few individuals and relegates hosts of others to obscurity. Historians are wont to write of wars as aggregate experiences: "generals" decide, "armies" move, "soldiers" clash, "casualties" mount, "the dead" are buried. Likewise, "captives" are taken—and then largely ignored. But in all of these cases, and on the home front as well, war was—and still is—felt and understood by its participants at a deeply personal level. Although largely forgotten, the story of Hodges' Scout can tell us much about this particular war as ordinary young men— those without whom wars cannot be fought—actually experienced it and, for those who survived, remembered it. The narrative that follows assumes that the lives and experiences of ordinary men and women in war are as instructive, and as compelling, as those of the "great." And in this case, as it happens, the great were never very far removed from the ordinary. In the course of this story we will see that Captain Hodges and his men, obscure as they were, rubbed elbows (albeit briefly) with some of the best-known individuals of the war on both sides.

The setting for this story is the French and Indian War, the American theater of a European conflict known as the Seven Years War. It was the fourth in a series of imperial conflicts, chiefly between Britain and France and their allies, for domination in Europe and over their expanding overseas empires. The first of these wars began in 1689; when peace came, the antagonists began preparing for the next. Typically, fighting began in Europe and spread outward to include conflict among the European colonies and Native American nations. Officially the Seven Years War began in 1756, but it had erupted in North America two years earlier and spread to Europe. It would end with British victory in 1763. In America the war's conclusion ushered in a new world order, not only for the British colonists but also for the French-speaking inhabitants of Canada and for Native American peoples halfway across the continent.

It was a war in which British red-coated regulars and American colonial soldiers made common cause against a traditional foe. When the French and Indian War began, the American Revolution was two decades in the future and almost unimaginable. No one in 1756 seriously contemplated an independent America. And when the war ended, grateful colonists would boast of their British heritage. They celebrated the great British triumph that culminated with victories at the walls of Quebec and Montreal, victories in which they had participated. They lit bonfires, rang bells, shot off fireworks, and "All acknowledge[d] their Subjection to his Majesty," the young king George III.[1] They felt part of an empire—powerful, Protestant, wealthy, and enlightened. The Boston minister Jonathan Mayhew concluded a sermon extolling America's bright future under Britain's protective wing with the words "Oh happy country! happy kingdom!"[2] The patriotic revels did not last long. Almost immediately following the victory, the first in a string of measures by Britain designed to stabilize its burgeoning empire began to tear at the colonists' confidence in a shared British interest.

What follows is not a new chronicle of the war and its place in American history. That mission has been very ably undertaken by eminent historians in recent years. It is, however, a story about the war; a story drawn from that war. It is the story of a relatively small group of men—young men, for the most part—who became casualties early in the conflict. The stories of those who died with Captain Hodges, and of those who lived to tell of it, form the heart of this account. Theirs are stories worth retrieving, as the experiences of war, for the common soldier, are largely made up of events that never command public attention. And in the stories surrounding the circumstances of Hodges' Scout the reader will discover facets of this war not usually addressed in standard chronicles.

History begins implicitly with questions. The most basic are, what happened? and why? I hail from, and still live in, southeastern Massachusetts, from whence also came many of Hodges' men. I first learned about Hodges' Scout obliquely, as so often happens, while looking for something else in local records. References to the event in nineteenth-century town histories were vague and, as I discovered, seriously flawed. Curious, I began to follow the trails of evidence and found that survivors had left clues to a much more complex, varied, and fascinating human story—stories, really—than simply about an underreported scrape in the woods. Theirs were accounts of high hopes and frustration, of warfare in an unfamiliar environment, of a frightful, bloody encounter, of harrowing captivities and then, for the survivors, a difficult homecoming. So the question that came to this historian's mind was, why had I never heard of Hodges' Scout before?

But there were other questions. What had brought these specific men to that place on that day? Most of them were volunteers—what had motivated them to be there? What did they think about their service? What did it mean to them? As the records of Hodges' men will reveal, a number of imperatives, alone or in combination, prompted young New England men (and some not so young) to leave their secure coastal towns and enlist in provincial regiments, to become soldiers of empire in an international conflict they only partially understood. Some of Hodges' men survived the massacre but endured long captivity, some for the duration of the war. Their stories illustrate the variety of experiences awaiting the more—or less—fortunate victims of defeat in this hybrid war of European armies in wilderness environments. The story of these men, captives among the French and Native inhabitants of New France, is part of the story of Hodges' Scout.

The war was fought on many fronts; indeed it was a world war, but for New Englanders like the men of Hodges' Scout the vital theater was the Lake George–Lake Champlain corridor, which stretched between Albany to the south and French-held Montreal to the north. With a population pool many times larger than that of their enemies, the British colonial (or *provincial*, to use the contemporary term) forces always outnumbered their French, Canadian, and Native opponents and could command far greater resources. And yet, for years the progress of provincial armies, even when stiffened with British regular soldiers, was stymied in this region; indeed, the Anglo-Americans suffered a number of serious reverses. The sheer size of the campaign theater, and the logistics necessary to operate in it, proved a challenge for colonial governments with meager treasuries, unaccustomed to long-term, large-scale operations. Additionally, provincial soldiers, although generally sturdy and healthy compared with their European contemporaries, were not professional soldiers, and there were limits to what could be expected from men largely unacquainted with the military mentality and army discipline. As we will see, these factors played a part in determining what happened to Hodges' Scout, and why.

Part I of this book is largely an anatomy of disaster. Answering the question how Hodges' men came to grief requires that we survey the events and circumstances that brought Captain Hodges and his company to northern New York. The opening chapter begins with the central event, the destruction of Hodges' command. Subsequent chapters step backward to trace the war's progress up to that point and the recruitment of a provincial army for a campaign that all hoped would end the war. As the recruits arrived at the front, difficulties in carrying out the plan adversely affected Hodges' men directly. From often conflicting accounts, I attempt to determine, as fully as possible, what actually happened to Hodges' Scout. This is an exercise in historical forensics, employing both what I feel can be stated with authority, based on surviving records, and what I feel may be reasonably inferred from those records. A second, closely related question is, why did things go so terribly wrong for these men? We will see that the answer to this is complex, an amalgam of individual decisions, "standard operating procedures," circumstances, and plain bad luck.

Part II is dedicated to telling the stories of the survivors of Hodges' Scout, prisoners of a feared and obdurate enemy. For this a surprising number of clues survive, in documents ranging from town and provincial records, to French correspondence and memoirs, to the minutes of a British court-martial, to the words of survivors themselves, and to a family story, an oral history fortuitously recorded a century after the event. The captives' accounts demonstrate some of the wide-ranging experiences of prisoners of war at this time and help to fathom some of the remaining questions regarding the circumstances of Hodges' Scout. No less captives of the war in their own way, the families of the missing also had to endure uncertainty and hardships as they anxiously waited to learn the fates of their fathers, sons, husbands, and brothers.

Just as I do not attempt a chronicle of the entire war, neither do I attempt to give equal time to all the major combatants. I focus my attention on the fate of a discrete group of American provincials. This involves building a considerable context for their activities and stories, and this context includes British officers and soldiers, Canadian *habitants*, Native American warriors, and French officials. But this book is not *about* them. That would be a much larger book.

Some clarification of terms used in this book is in order. Unless otherwise distinguished, *French* refers to both the metropolitan French and the white inhabitants of Canada. For that matter, by *Canada* I mean that part of northern New France comprising the St. Lawrence River basin, the Great Lakes region, and all points north of those. I use *Indian, Native American,* and *Native* interchangeably, though I am aware of the lingering controversy surrounding those terms. Somewhat more specifically, I distinguish generally recognized regional, cultural, and language groups, such as *Algonquian* or *Iroquois,* and where I or my sources identify particular nations or people, such as Ottawas and Wabenakis, I so name them in the text. I use the term *British* to describe soldiers and officials from the British Isles, but not with regard to the colonists: neither the latter nor the former seem to have considered the inhabitants of the British colonies to quite fit that description. For those inhabitants, then, I use *colonists* or *Americans,* while realizing that they did not generally use those terms, often referring to themselves instead as *English.* When writing of armed American colonists serving in colony regiments, I employ an adjective they did accept: *provincial.* Lastly, in cases in which the reference is to a joint British and provincial effort, I use the term *Anglo-American.*

In the following pages I frequently quote from my sources in order to let original "voices" be heard. In those quotations, I retain the original spelling, vocabulary, punctuation, and abbreviations unless changes are necessary for the sake of clarity.

1   HODGES' SCOUT

1

"Kill'd or taken"

"We have Lost forty five men"

The nights at the south end of Lake George had become downright chilly by mid-September 1756. Winter came early to these parts; in less than five weeks one soldier would report the ground to be frozen hard. But on the nineteenth of the month, and for a few days thereafter, summer returned with a vengeance. The day had dawned warm and still, and by early afternoon a hot sun had driven the temperature to ninety degrees or more. Samuel Greenleaf, a lieutenant in Jonathan Bagley's regiment of Massachusetts provincial soldiers, inwardly cursed the heat, for although it was a Sunday, "all hands [were] Order[ed] to work this day" on the never-ending labor that had recently been christened Fort William Henry.[1] Greenleaf and thousands of other New England men had spent the summer clearing ground, digging foundations and entrenchments, and hauling massive timbers. They had fired bricks, made quicklime for mortar, transported innumerable tons of food and supplies, and done the thousand and one other tasks necessary to raise the low, star-shaped stronghold on the edge of the lake in what seemed to them like the middle of nowhere.

Elsewhere in the compound, Ensign Josiah Thacher, until six months earlier a farmer from Yarmouth, on Cape Cod, also discovered that there would be no rest for the weary. He had returned to the fort on Friday from a two-day patrol, or *scout,* as they were called, with fifty of his fellow soldiers and then exchanged his musket for a spade or pickaxe or crowbar and resumed the unglamorous work of construction. Scouting the woods for signs of the enemy, with all its potential dangers and discomforts, had certain advantages over the work he was now doing, he concluded. The mosquitoes that had plagued them earlier in the summer were fewer now, and the unbroken canopy of forest provided continual shade that would be welcome on this day.

The scouts had become routine affairs. The lake, a thirty-mile-long gash through the mountainous Adirondack range, was the first leg of a vital water route to the heart of New France, and the fort they were building was to be the jumping-off point for operations in that direction. But they knew that the French, the Canadians, and their Native allies had been watching their every move. For more than a month now, to prevent surprise attacks on the fort, the provincials had sent company-size scouts, armed reconnaissance, down both sides of the lake to detect or interdict enemy activity. Thacher had been on one of these, on the west side of the lake, and as usual, they had found no sign of the enemy.[2] Perhaps he thought there were none to be found nearby in any case; it was late in the season to begin a campaign, and that would be as true for the French as it was for the British and their provincial auxiliaries. He had seen another such scout go out the previous day to cover the same ground; it was likely to prove as fruitless as his.

It was not supposed to have been like this. The New England army that converged upon northern New York Colony in the spring of 1756 was the largest provincial force ever assembled in North America, and its goal was nothing less than the capture of the French fortress at Crown Point on Lake Champlain. Some even dreamed of racing northward on the lake after that victory to threaten Montreal itself. This was the second year of fighting in the contested frontiers between French Canada and the northern British colonies. The previous year's campaign had seen hard fighting, with a disaster for Anglo-American arms in the Ohio country and a bloody victory, of sorts, on these very grounds. Provincial governors and British army generals had been determined to go on the offensive this year, and the campaign had begun with good hopes for success and high spirits among the men who had enlisted in the provincial armies. Yet here they were, no closer to their objectives than they had been a year earlier, the campaign season running out, the fort unfinished, too many men sick, and little indication of any forward movement. The bright promise of spring had dissolved, replaced by a fatalistic disappointment bordering on depression. The crushing labor of the summer, the enervating heat, the bad food, the fears of ambush by an enemy they never saw but were certain was all about them, the isolation, the realization that there would be neither military glory nor plunder to take home, the seeming purposelessness of it all—it was enough to dispirit even professional soldiers, and these young, inexperienced New England men were anything but that. Meanwhile, the number of graves in the fort's cemetery grew ominously.

The worst of it was, as Greenleaf complained, that there was "no Rum." The soldiers' daily allowance of watered-down rum was one of the few perks of the service, but it was not simply a concession to an alcoholic soldiery. Spirits of some sort, in moderation, were widely considered necessary to working people's health, especially in hot weather. Now even that sovereign talisman against disease was gone, just as sickness was on the rise in the camp.

It was in the midafternoon, when the heat and the noxious smells of the camp were at their height, that the wounded man staggered into the compound, his shirt wet with sweat and stained dark red with his own blood. Shot through the shoulder, exhausted and dangerously dehydrated, when he was able to get his breath he gasped out grim news: the scout that Ensign Thacher had seen leave the previous day, commanded by Captain Joseph Hodges, had been ambushed and overwhelmed by a large force of French and Indians. The wounded man, twenty-two-year-old Private Robert Wilson of Lexington, had somehow broken through the melee and run for all he was worth back to the fort. Terror had given him wings. The site Wilson described was eleven miles distant, near the lake's shore. He feared that Hodges' command "could not escape" and that "the whole Scout would be Cut of[f]." For all he knew, he was the only one to escape alive.[3]

The news brought a quick response from John Winslow, the general commanding the provincial troops at the fort. Private Wilson had covered the distance to the fort in about three hours; Winslow could not possibly get help there so quickly, but he did what he could. The entire fort was put on high alert. He sent three hundred men under Major Richard Saltonstall to retrace the overland route northward down the lake; they might intercept the enemy force if it was continuing on toward the fort, and pick up any survivors fleeing in their direction, but they could hardly be expected to arrive at the site of the action before dark. The general was counting on the fort's flotilla to bring more immediate support to Hodges' men, if it was not already too late. Scores of the New England men had been busy over the summer building vessels for the projected campaign, and now these were pressed into service. Ensign Thacher boarded the armed sloop *Loudoun*, which, accompanied by two whaleboats and a bateau, made sail or rowed for the site. They were to "Cover our party and Bring them of[f] if the Enemy were too much for them."[4]

The late afternoon breeze failed, however, and the sun was well behind the mountains by the time the waterborne relief force approached the general area the wounded man had described. They watched the shore and listened for the sound of firing but heard nothing, saw nothing. At length someone spotted a man at the edge of the lake waving frantically but silently, no doubt stealing fearful looks over his shoulder as he did so. One of the whaleboats was sent inshore to retrieve him; relieved at his rescue, he explained that he had escaped from the scene of the fighting, now only a mile and a half off. The woods were ominously quiet, and had been for hours. He feared that "few or none were taken alive." Guided by this second survivor, the boats soon reached their objective. Covered by the sloop's six-pounder cannon and eight swivel guns, Ensign Thacher and about twenty-five others landed the whaleboats to investigate.

A scene of horror greeted them. Three scalped heads, impaled upon stakes, gaped at the would-be rescuers, marking the spot where ten corpses, frightfully mangled, lay stiff on the ground, their gore blackening in the warm air. Someone in the landing party was able to identify one of the mutilated grotesques as Captain Hodges.[5] There were likely more of these nearby, but the men on the shore were disinclined to search much further. The light was rapidly fading, and whoever had done this might still be nearby, might be watching them even now, waiting for them to separate themselves from the sloop's protective artillery. If fifty men had been swallowed up by the enemy's force, half that number would hardly fare better. And if there were any survivors nearby, they would have heard or seen the relief force's arrival and come forward or called out. They had seen enough. Some of the men were given the revolting duty of retrieving the corpses and placing them, and the heads, in the bateau, which was then towed by one of the whaleboats through the darkness, arriving back at the fort about ten o'clock.

Three hours earlier, Major Saltonstall and the three hundred men sent by land had returned to the fort with three more survivors, including the lieutenant who had been Hodges' second in command. Like the other two men who had escaped, they thought themselves the only likely survivors of the fighting. The lieutenant told a story of sudden ambush, futile resistance, and a quick collapse of Hodges' command in the face of a "Vast Superior

Number" of the enemy—three times their strength, he reckoned. With almost no one in the scout left alive, the lieutenant went on, he and one other soldier had taken to their heels and "hid under the Edge of the Mountain till all was Quiate" before making for the fort and safety. In short, it was a massacre, lasting, he thought, a mere two minutes at most. Accepting the likelihood that no more survivors were coming his way, and with night coming on, Major Saltonstall had decided to head for home.[6]

That evening, and the next day, General Winslow wrote reports of the disaster for Lord Loudoun, the general commanding British regular forces in America, and for the colonial governors. He admitted that he did not as yet have all the facts, but the evidence and survivors' accounts all pointed to the likelihood that "the greatest part" of Hodges' command had been "cut off," a contemporary euphemism for *slaughtered,* and that "few or none were taken alive." Nor could Winslow or anyone else identify with much certainty the dead who were brought in. Captain Hodges' remains had been identified somehow, but the other nine, stripped and butchered, were not named in any dispatches (and some, as we will see, were misidentified). But Winslow would not write off the rest completely. All that was "Certain," he wrote, was that "we have Lost forty five men either killed or taken." For there was always hope: the recovery party had not searched thoroughly; perhaps there were no other bodies to find. And unless more were found, or other confirmation came, one could not assume that all those unaccounted for had been slain. An anonymous reporter writing the day after chose to interpret the lack of information optimistically, offering vaguely that "we hear most of the others are fallen into the Enemys Hands." For the vast majority of the missing, however, their places on the muster rolls, taken at the end of the year, simply carried the words "kill'd or taken."[7]

Few today have heard of Hodges' Scout, and with reason. In a war already replete with disasters on a far more dramatic scale, and with many more to come, the loss of a single company of men, while tragic, could not hold the public's attention for very long. The destruction of Hodges' company that day had no real military impact, involved no illustrious personages (at least not directly), and was soon overshadowed by events that are more the stuff of military history. Not even a roster of the slain survives, though it is possible to reconstruct our own. If it was remembered at all, it was as an emblem of the dangers to English colonists of wilderness warfare, and of their limited competence at it, against which more successful, lucky—and rare—figures such as Robert Rogers, leader of the celebrated Rogers' Rangers, could stand out as American masters of the Indians' own game.

At the time, however, Hodges' Scout was a shocking affair. In terms of the *proportion* of white men lost in a woods engagement, it was almost unmatched since the darkest days of King Philip's War in the previous century. Not even the disastrous Battle on Snowshoes in 1758 or the Pyrrhic raid on St. Francis the following year (both involving Rogers' Rangers) came close to producing the 90 percent losses suffered by Hodges' band. It also had elements of the mysterious about it, for as General Winslow discovered, the stories told by the survivors of the lost command did not match. The man picked up at the water's edge by the boat crews insisted that "the action Continued for more than half an hour, and that Our men behaved Bravely till Quite Over powered." The company's lieutenant, who admitted that he had "hid under the Edge of the Mountain," had said it was all over in two minutes. If this other soldier's version was more accurate, then the lieutenant, the unit's second in command, had not stayed around for the ensuing twenty-eight. Winslow, clearly disturbed by the implications of these conflicting narratives, pledged to "make Enquiries strictly into these matters." If he ever did, the resolution of his inquiry has not turned up.[8]

In addition to trying to understand what exactly had happened to Hodges' command, for Winslow there was the lingering uncertainty regarding additional survivors. As ferocious as wilderness warfare could be, Native war bands did not normally kill everyone who fell into their hands, preferring to take some captive when practicable. Only ten bodies had actually been found. Some of the missing might yet have been alive, prisoners of the French or of the Indians. But unless word came from another source, no one could be certain that such was the case. And if some were still alive, then who were they, and who were among the slain? How could relatives of the missing know whether to mourn or to hope?

In fact, there *were* survivors, though no one on the Anglo-American side would be sure of that for the better part of a year.

The Captain's White Gloves

Back at Fort William Henry, General Winslow wrote his reports, someone penned an account for the newspapers in Boston, and comrades of the dead and missing wrote to the folks back home. Burial details dug fresh graves for Hodges and the other recovered corpses, and work at the fort went on through the last heat wave of the season. One last office for the dead had to be performed: making an inventory of their effects, presumably so that they could be returned to families or otherwise disposed of. For the common soldiers these likely were simple enough, a few articles of clothing and some personal items. The value of the inventoried possessions of ten Massachusetts men (privates and noncommissioned officers) killed in a skirmish in 1758 averaged a shade over £7 11s. in "Old Tenor."[9] Private Simon Wheeler's possessions were typical:

Itum one Coat at	2 - 10 - 0
It one Cotton Shirt at	1 - 10 - 0
It one pair of Indin Stockins	0 - 18 - 0
It one Knife and gimblet	0 - 07 - 0
It one Rasor	0 - 05 - 0
It one pair of trousers and Handkercheif	0 - 15 - 0
It half a pound of tobacco and Bottel	0 - 05 - 0
It one Napsack and hatch[et?]	0 - 10 - 0
	[£]7 - 0 - 0 Total[10]

In contrast to these, the inventory of Captain Hodges' belongings at Fort William Henry was more extensive and elaborate. He had clearly prepared for the campaign in terms of clothing: at the time of his death he still had in his chest a great coat, another of homespun, a "pair of Red Everlasting [tough woolen] Breeches," one flannel shirt, and "2 pair of Yarn Stockings." But in addition to these very sensible and utilitarian items, there was "1 white Shirt" valued at £3, one "camblet" coat (a wool-and-cotton blend meant to resemble an expensive weave of camel's hair and silk) worth £5, and a brown wig. To finish the look, Hodges had a tricornered hat, valued at only slightly less than the camblet coat, and "1 pair white Gloves." Interestingly, he had left behind on his last mission a "Hanger," a short, curved cutting sword. Altogether, Hodges' inventory, including "Sundrys," amounted to a small fortune in soldiers' terms: £31 6s. 6d.[11] Half of the value, however, was made up of what we might call "luxury" wearing apparel, a pricey ensemble of "white" shirt, faux-exotic coat, brown wig (hardly a necessary item on campaign), fine hat (as opposed to whatever he was wearing when he died)—and those white gloves.

We have to imagine Hodges in such an outfit, perhaps with the red breeches and the hanger (valued at £2 5s., it was suitable as an officer's side-arm), and wonder why he had brought these items nearly three hundred miles from his home in Massachusetts? What had he expected this war to be like? Had he imagined himself wearing that outfit as a victorious New England army accepted the surrender of Crown Point, or even of Montreal? What compulsions had brought Captain Hodges and his men to this disputed place in the wilderness, to end their war very differently, surely, from what they had imagined?

2

Captain Hodges' Company

Imperial War

The war that brought Captain Hodges, his ill-fated men, and thousands of other New Englanders to the New York frontier in 1756 had begun more than two years earlier, and hundreds of miles away. For more than sixty years, French and northern English colonists, supported by Native American allies, had sparred in a series of conflicts given various names but which Americans eventually styled the French and Indian Wars. These conflicts roughly coincided with periods of open warfare in Europe in which the main protagonists were France and Great Britain. The first such was the War of the League of Augsburg (1689–97). Called King William's War in America, it was fought largely in northern New York Colony, along with a failed attempt by New England forces to capture Quebec. The next, known locally as Queen Anne's War (in Europe, the War of the Spanish Succession), was longer, lasting from 1702 to 1713, with the theater of war shifting to the New England frontier and Nova Scotia. Even in the absence of official states of war, both the colonies and their parent states were either recovering from the last conflict, preparing for the next, or, in America, engaged in more low-level conflicts with Native peoples. The third imperial war, known in European history as the War of the Austrian Succession (and in America simply as King George's War), ended in 1748, but few doubted that the peace was little more than an intermission. In North America, French officials in Canada, British colonial governors, and American Indian nations jockeyed for advantage in what was clearly the next flashpoint on that continent, the Ohio River valley.

Fully aware that American colonial settlers and land speculators intended to assert their trans-Appalachian claims, French officials in Canada moved first to establish a foothold. French soldiers and civilian workers built new forts south of Lake Erie, claiming the Ohio River for France and driving out American settlers. Though vastly outnumbered by American colonists, the French could generally count on Native Americans in the region to support their far less demanding program. This placed trading posts, the occasional fort, but few settlers on their land, and always through negotiation and compensation. What followed is a fairly well known story: in the winter of 1753–54 Virginia's governor sent a militia colonel named George Washington to demand that the French depart from the Ohio country. Politely rebuffed, Washington returned in the spring with a larger force. In the meantime the French had been busy, establishing yet another new fort, Duquesne, at the strategic forks of the Ohio River (modern Pittsburgh). Learning of a small French detachment nearby, Washington, spurred on by Native allies, ambushed them, killing more than a dozen and capturing most of the rest. Rightly fearing a forceful response, Washington and nearly four hundred men took shelter in a hastily built and poorly situated fort. Following a brief siege by a superior force of French and Indians, Washington surrendered. After signing a controversial capitulation and giving up hostages, he was allowed to return with the rest of his men to Virginia.

Had Washington been more successful, or at least more circumspect, the contest over the Ohio country might have remained a strictly colonial affair. As it was, pugnacious British politicians were determined to show the French and, for that matter, the Americans how eviction was properly done. The year 1755 brought two regiments of British regular soldiers—redcoats—to Virginia, the first such commitment in a century and a half of colonization. American units joined the regulars to form an army of sixteen hundred men, led by the British general Edward Braddock, bound for the forks of the Ohio (fig. 2.1). Meanwhile, two large-scale, all-colonial efforts were afoot. The first was aimed at ending French influence in Nova Scotia for good. That campaign, in which the Massachusetts general John Winslow participated, resulted in the infamous Grand Dérangement, the expulsion of most of the Acadian population. The second, championed by Massachusetts governor William Shirley, intended both to threaten the French Fort Niagara, at the west end of Lake Ontario, and to capture Fort St. Frederick, at Crown Point on Lake Champlain. The expedition against Fort Duquesne resulted in a

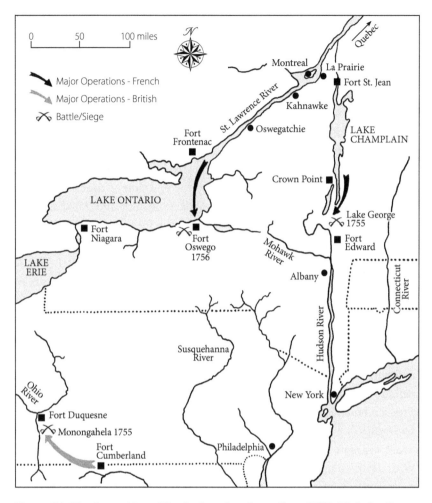

Figure 2.1. The Seven Years War in America: Operations 1755–56, Lake Champlain to Ohio River. Map by Die Hoxie

spectacular disaster. On July 9, and within only a few miles of his objective, General Braddock's advance force was attacked by an inferior number of Indians with some French. After several hours of chaotic fighting in the unfamiliar woodland environment, the Anglo-American force collapsed in rout, with more than 60 percent casualties, including a mortally wounded Braddock. Washington, who had been attached to Braddock's staff, helped conduct the pitiful retreat.

Two months later the colonial forces in northern New York were very nearly handed another catastrophe. By late August a fifteen-hundred-man army of New England and New York provincials commanded by New York's Indian commissioner, William Johnson, had gathered at the south end of Lake St. Sacrement, which Johnson rather optimistically rechristened Lake George.[1] The campaign season was drawing to a close, but there was still hope of attacking Crown Point. The French, however, decided to run out the clock with a preemptive attack on the provincial army. A similar-sized force of French regulars, Canadian militia, and allied Indian warriors had pushed south from Johnson's objective, first to the junction of the lakes, known by the Native name Ticonderoga,[2] then via South Bay and Wood Creek to a position behind Johnson's advance camp. The French commander Baron Dieskau's intention was to destroy the supplies and boats Johnson needed at the Great Carrying Place[3] on the Hudson River. Unfortunately for his plans, though, the Indians with him, who made up nearly half his force, refused to assault the fort the provincials had built to protect the landing there (Fort Lyman, renamed Fort Edward the next year). Frustrated, Dieskau led his men down the road to attack Johnson directly at Lake George.

The battle that resulted on September 8 was a bloody, seesaw affair, larger and only slightly less sanguinary than Braddock's destruction two months earlier. Hearing that Fort Lyman was threatened, Johnson dispatched a thousand men back along the road to protect the fort. They were ambushed by Dieskau's Native allies in what became known as the Bloody Morning Scout and sent reeling back to their hastily fortified camp at the lake shore. With nowhere to run, the badly shaken provincials, along with hundreds of untried men who had been left at the camp, readied themselves for the continuation of the attack. If they broke now, with their backs to the lake, if the French-Indian force cracked the provincials' crude defenses, Braddock's defeat would look like a draw by comparison. Fortunately for the provincials, Johnson's position was good, and he had cannon, which kept the Indians and militia at a respectful distance and tore bloody lanes through the regulars' assault on the camp. Dieskau was wounded and captured, the attack petered out, and the French-Indian force retreated to Crown Point, much to the relief of the provincials.[4] The French and the Indians could claim victory in the morning's ambush, the provincials for their desperate defense in the afternoon. Already the new conflict in America had produced two ferocious battles, larger than any previously recorded on the continent, with hundreds of dead and wounded, thousands of civilians displaced—all without any declaration of war.

More regulars arrived in early 1756, commanded by the prickly John Campbell, Earl of Loudoun. No diplomat, Loudoun quickly alienated the colonial governors and their military establishment, demanding control over the money and men he expected the legislatures to tamely vote him. Months of invaluable time were wasted in this fruitless infighting. Before this, Governor Shirley, placed in overall command of North American forces after Braddock's death, had been busy raising two new regular regiments in America for his projected attack on Fort Niagara, positioning them at a forward base at Oswego. The New England legislatures, prodded by Shirley's promises of British reimbursement, voted funds for a provincial army to take the field and finish the job at Crown Point, opening the way to Montreal. It is at this point that Joseph Hodges and the men who followed him enter our story.

Raising a Provincial Army

Massachusetts' share was to be three thousand soldiers. These were to be drawn from the commonwealth's considerable supply of men available for military service. Since the early seventeenth century, all able-bodied white men in Massachusetts between the ages of sixteen and sixty had been enrolled in the colony's militia (blacks and Indians were largely prohibited from militia service). Organized at the town level, the militia was primarily a local-defense organ, instituted for the purpose of repelling attack by foreign powers or by the indigenous peoples. For offensive operations, such as those in the Pequot War (1636–37) or King Philip's War (1675–77), colonial commanders formed temporary, ad hoc task forces made up of volunteers (often with some conscripts) raised from the town companies. If reinforcements or replacements were needed, these too were drawn from the town militias. Thus, by the eighteenth century, the militia system of Massachusetts (and New England generally) represented "a combination of home guard, draft board, and rear-echelon supply network."[5]

To tap this manpower reserve for the 1756 Crown Point campaign, Massachusetts had in place a system that was in effect a patronage chain flowing from the governor, a royal appointee, to prominent men at the local level. The chief organizational unit was the regiment, to be commanded by a colonel. The governor granted commissions for this rank to men of his choice, ideally because of real military acumen, but rewards for past services, or for future political support, could also be factors. Governor Shirley granted six such commissions in the first months of the year. The colonels were then given blank commissions for up to ten company commanders (captains) of *their* choosing. These were usually town militia captains or other well-known persons in the community who, through a sense of duty, desire for prestige, or other motives, sought officer status in one of the provincial regiments. Being "well known" was vital, for it was the captains' responsibility to get sufficient recruits from the militias of nearby towns, and their commissions depended upon their persuasive talents. Notions of what constituted company strength varied, but it was generally considered to be about fifty men, including officers, sergeants, and corporals. Thus a Massachusetts regiment was expected to comprise about five hundred men, but much was contingent on the colonel's prestige and the various captains' legwork: no men, no commissions. Richard Gridley, of Boston, received one of the coveted colonel's commissions from the governor. He, in turn, gave one of his blank company commissions to Joseph Hodges, of Norton, a small town in the southeastern part of the colony.

In many ways, Hodges was typical of the company commanders who did the work of filling out the regimental rosters. Provincial officers as a whole were older, considerably better off, and more active in church and local government than the rank-and-file soldier, though not strikingly different in occupation.[6] Hodges was no exception to this pattern. His ancestors had been among the founding families of the Plymouth Colony town of Taunton and lived in the northern part of the town. When that tract split off in 1710 to form the new town of Norton, the Hodges family retained their prominent place in local affairs. Joseph Hodges' father, Joseph Sr., was a deacon of the church, six times a selectman, four times an assessor, and once a member of the General Court (the legislature) at Boston. He had clearly done well in his worldly estate, for at his death he bequeathed to his youngest son "my new dwelling House and Barne and farme wherein I now dwell," explaining that he had previously set up his three older sons fittingly as well.[7] Joseph Jr. evidently tried to continue the family legacy of service, holding the offices of tithingman and assessor, though he would not match his father's record. The younger Hodges was never a deacon, but he was active in the church, perhaps feeling a special responsibility as the first child baptized in the new town, in 1714, once the church had gathered. When the South

Precinct of Norton elected to build a new meeting house in 1751, Joseph Jr. was among those who pledged to help collect building materials, making a "promise to Gitt 2 Beems, forty-two feet Long, twelve and ten Inches square; and four lock-tenant's Posts, to be 26 feet Long, 10 inches square; to be Good white-oake timber, well Hewed; at 19 lb. 10s. old tenner, to be Paid out of my rates," all of which entitled him to a prominent pew toward the front of the finished meeting house. His dwelling, one of fewer than three hundred in the town of about nineteen hundred souls, stood a half mile up the road from his father's, in a remote but busy part of town called Crooked Meadow. In addition to decent farmland, nearby cedar swamps and easily dammed streams provided the water power and materials for grist, saw, and shingle mills; Hodges was part owner of a sawmill his father had built. Although he died well before the stage in life his father had reached, his will suggests that like the elder Hodges, he had built a very comfortable estate.[8]

In one respect, though, Hodges stood out from other company officers. At forty-one he was considerably older than the average for that group (thirty-two years); in fact he was one of the oldest Massachusetts officers in service that year. Forty-one is hardly ancient by modern standards, and Hodges the farmer and mill owner was likely an active and vigorous specimen. Still, soldiering is typically a younger man's calling, and one has to wonder what moved a middle-aged man to leave his wife, son, two daughters, house, farm, and all he had worked for to face the risks and uncertainties of a war that so far had not gone well for his side. None of his three younger brothers enlisted, though all were of age.

It happens that Hodges' father had bequeathed another legacy to his eldest son: military service. The elder Hodges, with the rank of major, had commanded a company of men raised for the New England expedition against Louisbourg in 1745. Age had not held him back: he was fifty-seven at the time, older, indeed, than the expedition's commander, Sir William Pepperell, and he claimed in the will he made out in February of that year that he was "in very good health of Boddy and of a sound mind [and] memory, blessed be God for it." Louisbourg, a fortified town on the Cape Breton coast, guarded the approaches to the Gulf of St. Lawrence and posed a serious military threat to New England's security. The investment, siege, and capture of the town was the most celebrated accomplishment of arms of which New England could yet boast. An amateur colonial army, fired by a crusading zeal against the Catholic French and hopes for plunder, sailed northeastward in the spring of 1745 with a train of cannon capable of breaching Louisbourg's formidable stone walls. Aided by an understrength French garrison, good luck, and the timely assistance of a squadron of Royal Navy vessels, the provincial army forced the town's surrender at the end of June. (To the disgust of many, the fortress was handed back to France after the war.) New England casualties during the siege were light, but disease set in shortly afterward, especially among the garrison left to occupy their prize. Scores of soldiers and civilians succumbed to illness; one of these was Major Hodges. According to family history, the major died aboard a vessel returning home.[9]

Among the major's personal possessions itemized in his will, and the first one mentioned, was "my Silver-Hilted Sword." This obviously prized possession, which family tradition maintained had been "taken from a French Officer" (which would indicate service prior to 1745), was likely of the court-sword variety, a light, very quick weapon with a stilettolike point and finely decorated guards for the hand. It was a sword favored by gentlemen not only for defense but for display, made to be worn and seen by all. Rare indeed was the colonial farmer, of whatever standing in his locality, who possessed such a piece. And the *way* it had been acquired—taken from the enemy—only added to its considerable pecuniary value. In short, it was an heirloom, a family trophy, and Major Hodges had willed it to his eldest son, the newly coined Captain Hodges. Just why Joseph Jr. had not also gone to Louisbourg (he was thirty at the time) or gone instead of his aging father (if the old man could have been prevented from going) is not clear, but it does not appear that he had any military experience before signing up for the 1756 campaign.[10] But he had that sword to remind him of his father's accomplishments, his sense of duty to God and to New England, and his father's death in that service. If Captain Hodges was at all like the sons of veterans everywhere, he may have felt a strong sense of obligation to follow in his father's footsteps. At forty-one he was still far younger than the major had been on his last campaign, and who knew whether another such opportunity for military achievement would ever come? In any event, he sought, and received, a captain's commission.

But with so many officer candidates available, and with no military experience, how did he get it? In the absence of surviving correspondence it is impossible to be certain, but the colonel from whom the commission came, Richard Gridley, had been a lieutenant colonel in charge of the New England artillery at Louisbourg, which makes it likely that Gridley had known Major Hodges. At the very least, the younger Hodges could have called upon the decade-old connection in soliciting his captaincy.

In the months between February, when he received his commission, and May, when he marched his company westward, Hodges went to work finding the men for his company. Timing was, as in all things, vital. In order to get his company on the rolls in time to begin active service in April or May, he had to start recruiting in late winter and March. Fortunately, this was when New England town militias typically held their first (and sometimes only) musters of the year, before spring planting consumed every farmer's time and attention. Hodges (and perhaps his prospective lieutenants) had to show up at these musters and make a pitch to the assembled men to persuade them to join the company he was building and commit themselves to a campaign year of service. Of course, every other captain in every other regiment was doing the same thing, and often their "hunting grounds" overlapped in the scramble to fill out their companies.

In his quest for recruits, Hodges was aided by two factors that by the end of the war had placed nearly every third eligible man in the colony in a provincial regiment, if only for a year. The first factor was a sizeable pool of men available for service. Beginning with the founding generation, New England men and women generally lived longer lives than settlers in other European colonies, longer on average than those they had left behind in the British Isles. Food supply and the lack of urban disease environments (except in Boston) account largely for the difference, but the effect was that married couples survived long enough to have more children, who in turn were more likely to survive to adulthood, marry, and produce children themselves. The result of such successful families by the mid-eighteenth century was a population that doubled every few decades, producing more sons than could easily be provided with land or livings as they approached majority. The oldest sons stood to inherit the most from their parents' estates (as did Hodges), while the second, third, and fourth sons might have to put off marriage and fiscal independence for years while they and their parents worked to obtain a "competency" for them. As Fred Anderson has demonstrated, these extra sons were not poor, but they were in a state of dependency.[11] This does not mean that eldest sons avoided service, however. John Con, of Haverhill, who would march with Hodges on his ill-fated scout, was one such; just seventeen, he could not have expected to receive his competency for some years yet. In the event, he would get it two years later, when his father died, but by that time the young heir would be in no position to take immediate advantage of it.

In most cases there were sufficient volunteers from the population centers and inland farming towns, but ambitious colonels from the coastal areas could find their recruiting efforts thwarted by local circumstances. After three frustrating months, Colonel Thomas Winslow, of Harwich, on Cape Cod, was forced to admit to Governor Shirley that he was unable to raise the men for the regiment he had been awarded. He had received his warrant for recruiting on April 15, and

> immediately sent my Warrants to the several Cap^{ts}. in my Regiment, but on their return Made out no more than 21 Men, which was all y^t could then be obtained, The men being apprised of what was Coming betook ymselves to Sea, some Whaling, and some a fishing (as they are Mostly seafaring men.) That ye Officers had not opportunity to warn them [i.e., notify them to make themselves available], So y^t in Some Companies which Consisted of 80^{ty} or so soldiers, not more than Six appeared.[12]

There would be no Winslow's Regiment that year, nor indeed for the rest of the war.

The second factor aiding Hodges was economic. Military service compensated Massachusetts recruits with that rarest of colonial commodities, hard cash, and in amounts that were generous by the standards of the day. Fred Anderson reckoned that a Massachusetts private's monthly pay in 1756 was £1 12s. in the colony's currency, in sterling value nearly double that of a British redcoat. Together with a subsistence allowance for the march to the front (8p per day) and an enlistment bounty of £1 16s. upon signing, the rank and file of Hodges' company could anticipate about £15 for the campaign, much the same as a laborer might earn in a year—but this was for a shorter period, and in real money. Commissioned and noncommissioned officers earned more, of course. The money the rank and file received would not make a young man economically independent, but it could certainly help: £15 might buy as many as thirty acres of land (unbroken) in the old towns surrounding Boston. Inland, toward the Connecticut River, it might purchase five times that number. There was one catch: the men would not receive their full wages until the end of the campaign, when their total days of service could be accurately tallied. But that was not too great a hardship; if they were careful not to incur too many unnecessary expenses on campaign (e.g., paying sutlers' high prices or gambling), the men would return home with money to help struggling families or to prepare for their own independence. Bounties paid upon enlistment surely sweetened the deal, as well as sealed it. On March 17, 1756, one Elijah Gary agreed to "serve His Majesty King George the Second, in a Company of Foot, under the Command of Joseph Hodges as Captain . . . and I do acknowledg I have received Six Dollars as bounty Money, according to the act of the General Court."[13] And there was always the possibility of plunder: the customs of war permitted a kind of systematized looting of captured enemy assets, to be divided among the victorious soldiers according to their rank. All in all, "from the private's perspective, military service was a reasonably profitable proposition."[14]

Some of the men in Hodges' Scout, perhaps most, were there for the money, at least in part. Eighteen-year-old Moses Emerson's father was a Haverhill shoemaker, one of the most poorly paid professions in colonial America. Moses was only three when his father died. His mother did not remarry for another seven years; how she made ends meet with five minor children to provide for is anyone's guess, but surely it was challenging. Moses eventually chose a guardian and was working as a farm laborer in 1756;[15] for him, enlistment surely meant opportunity and perhaps adventure. Similar considerations may have motivated Jonathan Barnes, of Boston. His mother died when he was a child; when he was six years old his father remarried and started a new family. The elder Barnes seems not to have been successful. By 1756 he had taken his family to nearby Malden, his second wife's hometown, but Jonathan remained in Boston, working for a blacksmith—a decent arrangement, which his father must have regarded as a success. Nevertheless, nineteen years old and on his own, Jonathan enlisted for the Crown Point expedition. He did not die with Hodges, but he would never see Boston or his family again.

Some clearly needed the money more than others. John Erwin, of Dunstable, had a "very poor and . . . aged" mother who evidently depended on her eighteen-year-old son for her support; she felt forced at one point to draw his wages from the colony's treasury before he returned home.[16] Ebenezer Pratt, of Bridgewater, also eighteen, had "no Relation but a Mother, who is a widow, not able to earn her own living." He was indentured as a servant to a local farmer when the war began, and the wages due for his military service would ultimately go to his master. But only the wages: Massachu-setts law guaranteed to servants who signed up the substantial enlistment bonus plus any lawful plunder or scalp bounties earned in the campaign. Pratt saw that in terms of finances, service in a provincial regiment easily beat his present working arrangement and would benefit both himself and his mother when he returned—if he returned.[17] It is also possible that Pratt, along with other servants enlisted that year, did not get much choice in the matter. Responding to a query from the Provincial Council of Pennsylvania concerning the propriety of enlisting servants, William Shirley assured them:

> My own Government of Massachusetts Bay is so far from thinking it a Hardship that indented Servants should be allowed to inlist, that they not only chearfully consent to that, but have even impressed a great number of indented Servants for the Expedition against Crown Point; and it is the constant Practice to im-press them as well as other inhabitants for garrisoning our Frontier Forts, where they often remain several Years; nor is it uncommon in other Governments to do the same.[18]

Pratt's master, who would surely have found use for his servant's cash wages, might have been the instigator of his enlistment; the rolls do not say. Per-haps both parties regarded the arrangement as beneficial.

One of Hodges' men may have been particularly needy. John Lewis was forty-three when he joined his Woburn company—older even than Hodges. He must have been well regarded by his neighbor-soldiers, for they made him a sergeant. Or perhaps they felt sorry for him; his family does not ap-pear to have been a fortunate one. He married late, at age thirty-two, sug-gesting that he could not provide for a family before that time. When his father died in 1755, in his will he named his son-in-law, rather than one of his own sons, his executor. John and his brother both received only twenty shillings (though perhaps they had already received their portions when they married), while his sister and brother-in-law got all the lands and meadows. When John died, or was presumed dead, the value of his inventory amounted to only £22 18s.—a paltry sum—£9 12s. of which was the wages due him. It appears that he did not own any land. His debts exceeded his estate by £7. A sergeant's wages would have gone far toward maintaining solvency, at least.[19]

The mere availability of manpower and the promise of cash wages were not the only considerations that moved men to enlist, however. If Captain

Hodges served out of a colonial American sense of noblesse oblige, others might do so too. Jeremiah Lincoln, scion of a prominent Hingham family that would produce a general during the Revolution, received a commission as ensign. Revealing the expectations of the times, the commission referred to the twenty-two-year-old as a "gentleman" (although he may have had a trade as a blacksmith), an honorary title Lincoln also used in his correspondence. That title and the rank it conferred on him would be of immense benefit to him soon enough.

War has always provided aspiring men with opportunities to improve their social, political, and economic conditions, but for many in Hodges' command, their motives for enlisting may have stemmed largely from a sense of self-realization, that near-universal desire in young men to test and "prove" themselves, both for their own satisfaction and for the approval of others. Few provincial soldiers wrote directly on this topic in the records that survive; their upbringing would likely have discouraged such introspection as vanity, or they may simply have lacked the awareness or the language to do so, cloaking myriad competing impulses under the mantle of duty. In later years, some veterans were able to express their motives, as did one Rufus Putnam, who served in 1756, but, luckily for him, not with Hodges. By 1758 Putnam had enlisted in two previous campaigns, but in his memoir he confessed that he was reluctant to volunteer for another. At last he signed up, in part out of feelings of guilt, as he saw so many others enlisting. "I have heard that some men say they liked to fight as well as they liked to eat," Putnam remembered. "I never had any such feelings; so far as I am able to judge for myself, it was pride and a wish to excel, or at least to be behind none, that influenced me, at that period of my life, to be amongst the foremost on all occasions."[20]

The phrase "at that period of my life" is undoubtedly the key to understanding the complex mix of motives that prodded the vast majority of New England men to enlist. Of all those whose ages were recorded on surviving Massachusetts muster rolls in 1756, numbering nearly twenty-four hundred, fully one-quarter were under the age of twenty, and more than half were under twenty-five.[21] As it does young men and women today, military service offered the eighteenth-century recruit steady pay, social recognition, and a sense of accomplishment or self-worth, in some combination or other. Who can say whether John Con, who stood to inherit a competency in time; or Jonathan Barnes, who did not; or the aspiring gentleman Jeremiah

Lincoln was not motivated in good part by a hope to be, at least for a time, something more than what birth or fortune had made him? Even the middle-aged, down-on-his-luck John Lewis may have seen in the Crown Point expedition a chance not only for economic relief but also for personal redemption: assurance that he was not, in fact, a failure.

Military service is often regarded in both anthropology and literature as a "coming of age" experience; so it may have been for Andrew Allen of Gloucester. The age he gave to his mustering officer—sixteen (the minimum age for enlistment)—may have been a lie. Allen's father had recently died, and a neighbor, George Riggs, had been given the guardianship of Andrew, "a minor upward of fourteen years of age," in early 1755.[22] Of legal age or not, Andrew would have to have prevailed upon his guardian to agree to his enlistment. Andrew had no trade—unusually, no occupation was attributed to him on the muster roll—and rather than be apprenticed or put out to farm labor, the boy may have chosen the adult world of a military campaign to establish his status as an independent male. We can get some sense of the process of a boy moving haltingly into the world of men from another recollection. Like Andrew Allen, John Wood, of Woburn, was just sixteen in 1756, young but technically just old enough to enlist. A "traditionary" local story recorded a century later relates how he showed up at nearby Concord on a day when a recruiting officer was busily signing up local men for the campaign. When the older men had been disposed of, the officer turned to Wood, who had been standing by sheepishly, and asked him what he wanted. "To enlist, Sir, if you will accept me," the boy answered. "To enlist!" exclaimed the officer. "Why, do you think you can kill an Indian?" "I don't know about that, Sir," Wood replied, "but I think I can fire a bullet into an oak stump as far as any man." According to the story, the officer "at length took down his age, measured him, and going through all the other ceremonies of enlistment, dismissed him to the company in which he was to serve." One wonders whether the officer went through all the "ceremonies" purposely, to give the boy time to reconsider his decision.[23] John Wood and Andrew Allen may stand for the scores of very young men who elected to test their manhood as early as possible—perhaps even before strictly permissible. But while Wood survived to tell of his experience, Allen did not.

And what do we make of the motives of William Merry, who hailed from the same town as Captain Hodges? He was thirty-three, considerably older than most of the youths with whom he marched but a decade younger than his captain or John Lewis. Of all the men who went on Hodges' Scout, he may have had the most military experience. Certainly he was among the luckiest. In 1747, during the previous war (known to the colonists as King George's), Merry had been with other New England soldiers in Grand Pré, Nova Scotia. On the night of February 10 the Yankee force, commanded by Arthur Noble, was caught off guard by French and Canadian attackers. After taking some losses in the initial attack (including Colonel Noble), the soldiers took shelter in a large stone house in the village. Unable to take this stronghold, the French agreed the next day to a ceasefire, then to terms that permitted the colonial soldiers to retreat. When the Seven Years War broke out, Merry enlisted again, and this time was sent west rather than down East. According to a sworn statement, he was present at the desperate 1755 fighting at Lake George. So he was even, with one defeat and one victory, and himself none the worse for it. But there is reason to suspect that money had something to do with his actions. He had married a widow a year after his return from Grand Pré, and she had borne him three children, the oldest only seven when he went to war again. His stepson Henry Smith joined a new redcoat regiment raised in America, the 50th (known as Shirley's Regiment, after the Massachusetts governor), so he was no longer available for household labor. Merry, like so many others, may have reenlisted to support a family. Since the horror of the previous year's battle obviously did not dissuade him, perhaps he, like the sort Rufus Putnam described, enjoyed the prospect of fighting. If so, he would get another chance.[24]

Preparations

In early May the newly formed companies began to gather throughout eastern Massachusetts. They met chiefly at the taverns in village centers; next to the meeting houses, the taverns were centers of both civic and social life. There, in the public spaces that accommodated churchgoers, travelers, and local militia musters, the recruits assembled as units for the first time, took stock of their commissioned officers, and elected their sergeants and corporals. The officers and non-coms called the rolls, noted delinquents, and made at least a cursory inspection of the equipment the men were supposed to have brought. The orderly book of a regiment raised later in the war gives us some idea of what was expected: "You are to inform the Men, That they must be furnished with a good Coat, Waistcoat and Breeches suitable for the Campaign, also three good Shirts, two good pair of Stockings two pair of Shoes and a Hat. . . . That you influence the Men as much as you can for them to carry their own Arms, also to do your Endeavour to obtain all public Arms."[25]

Two points are worth noting. First, the order suggests the lack of uniforms available for provincial units, even late in the war. Despite the ideal of blue uniform coat with red facings prescribed by the Massachusetts legislature, few units appear to have actually achieved this standard. Provincial armies were notorious for their motley (and to British eyes, unsoldierly) appearance. The second point concerns the firearms the men were expected to use. Many were to be given British muskets, bayonets, and cartridge boxes upon reaching Albany, the administrative nerve center for the campaign, but to make sure there were enough of these for everybody, the men were encouraged to bring their own arms. There were some advantages to this, at least in theory. All members of the town militias were required by law to have or "find" their own firearms, and surely familiarity with one's weapon was desirable in a soldier. If the men brought their own guns and these were lost or destroyed in the service, they could be compensated for the loss, often for more than the gun was worth. The drawback to this scheme was that personal arms varied considerably in age, caliber, state of repair, and suitability for service: fowling pieces and antique muskets unable to mount bayonets, while adequate for militia requirements, were next to useless on the battlefield. In the event, a good many Massachusetts men left for the front unarmed, to be issued their weapons in New York Colony. Gridley's Regiment, which included Hodges' company, was more fortunate, if that is the right word; they received 510 Long Land Pattern muskets, the famed "Brown Bess," with accessories,[26] as they were preparing to march. They may have felt more like soldiers for that, but now they had to lug their ten-pound weapons all the way to New York. Hodges signed off on 48 of them for his company on May 5.[27]

Mustering the regiments also gave company commanders an opportunity to weed out those who were clearly incapable, whether from sickness, physical disability, age, or status, of standing up to the rigors of the campaign to come. One hopeful who presumably had been healthy enough when he first enlisted was by May found "By the Dr. not fit for Duty."[28] Emanuel Clark, not strictly qualified to enlist, managed to stay on the rolls, only to demonstrate his unsuitability halfway through the campaign, when he was "Confined for sleeping on his Post, which the Prisoner Confessed, but as he appears to the Court to be Creasey and About 70 Years Old The Court are of the Opinion that he is unfitt for any Service In the Soldiery Way and therefore Ought to be Dismiss the service."[29]

Once the entire regiment was mustered, if companies were still short of men, the colonel could obtain a warrant to "press" the non-forthcoming into service. Fewer than 10 percent of the recruits in 1756 had to be raised in this manner, and they were theoretically to be drawn from the "idle elements," but even here there was an escape route for those who were emphatically unwilling to serve—and who could afford it. From the time of King Philip's War, New England men pressed into service had been allowed to hire substitutes to go in their places. In 1756 Massachusetts law required those wishing to legally dodge the draft to pay a £5 fine to the commonwealth for the privilege, and to hire a suitable replacement could cost another £10 (potential replacements learned that they could hold out for far more as the war continued). Since the fine and the cost of hiring a substitute amounted to a laboring man's yearly income, hiring a substitute clearly was beyond many men's capacity. Even so, in 1756 the Massachusetts regiments included 247 "hired" men.[30] Abner Barrows, of Middleborough, who enlisted in 1756 but was disinclined to serve the following year, nevertheless confided to his diary: "This Day Engaged to go in his majestes Servise for Caleb Wellimson," a man in his forties who wanted to go to war even less than did Barrows.[31] The eighteen-year-old Thomas Pulling, of Rochester, who would die the following September with Hodges, was also a "hired" man.[32] Money was probably the decisive factor in hiring oneself out as a substitute. Fred Anderson found that as a rule hired recruits tended to be less motivated and less willing to take risks and thus more likely to desert before the end of the campaign.[33] Such a one was the "whalefisherman" Samuel Hunter, of Dartmouth, "about 28," who allowed himself to be hired in the place of another man pressed for Thacher's regiment. Hunter, who possessed a specialist's skills, pursued a notoriously independent lifestyle, and killed the biggest animals on earth for a living, could have had little to prove in the army. When he deserted in the fall of 1756, he naturally forfeited the pay he was due, but he would have had the draftee's money in hand long before that.[34] Thomas Winslow, the would-be colonel who had had his own difficulties recruiting seafaring men, might have predicted such an outcome.

As the day approached for marching orders, those with families or possessing estates worth anything significant had to consider that this was war, after all, and they might not return. The conscientious used the opportunity to make or update their wills. Captain Hodges, who had both family and estate, on May 1, 1756, put his signature to a will he had prepared against his departure. The document (in which he styled himself "Gentleman") asserted his "good state of Bodily health" and "sound disposing mind, and memory," and added, by way of explanation, "But as I am going into his Majistes service, think it proper to settle my Estate." It was a good thing he did.[35] Those who neglected this always solemn duty did their families no favors. Obadiah Eddy, of Norton, thirty-four, long considered to have been killed with Captain Hodges, in fact died in camp near the end of the campaign season. He left no will, and for years afterward his widow had to make frequent reports to the court of probate justifying her expenditures for clothing and other necessities for their five children. Joshua Sprague, of Abington, likewise "died Intestate," and his wife, Elizabeth, was not finally confirmed in her widow's portion until 1764, nearly eight years after Joshua's death and three years after the fighting ended in Canada.[36]

One last, vital ritual remained before the companies marched for the rendezvous points for their regiments, and that was to be reminded that the enterprise upon which the men embarked was the Lord's business, as well as that of their colony and king. Although religion probably was not uppermost in the soldiers' minds or motives, the war against the Catholic French in Canada and their converted Native allies retained some quality of a religious crusade.[37] The ideal New England soldier, at least in the clergy's conception, was mindful that he fought not chiefly for pay or plunder but to crush the enemies of God. To that end, ministers presented special sermons to the assembled companies, who were, as the title of one such sermon suggests, "directed and encouraged" to conduct themselves as befitted Christian soldiers "when going on a just and important, tho' difficult, enterprize, against their enemies." The content of these clerical pep talks was largely formulaic, comprising a rationalization of the war effort, statements of the "duty of all to be ready" for inevitable sacrifices and the need for discipline, and, above all, a statement of "the importance of God's presence with an army. . . and the grounds on which it may be expected." Didactic as such lectures may sound to the modern ear, the provincial soldiers seemed generally to appreciate the exhortations to duty and the clergy's explicit blessings of their service. The Reverend John Ballantine's sermon to a Westfield company, for example, was so well received that it was printed and "made publick at the desire of the hearers."[38]

One sermon in particular gave practical military advice that came far too late to be of use to Hodges and his men. In Pembroke, Gad Hitchcock, who would one day deliver an anti-British Election Day sermon attended by General Thomas Gage, referred in his text to 1 Samuel 30:1–20. The biblical story relates how King David pursued and overtook barbarian raiders who had abducted Israelite women and children, including one of David's wives. Interpreting freely but plausibly, Hitchcock told his listeners that "this battle, very probably, was conducted . . . not unlike the Wilderness Skirmishings of our Indians: for it appears, David took them on Surprise, and made the On-set while they were spread abroad." David's men were victorious, killing and scattering the foe and recovering all the captives and loot. "And Accordingly," Hitchock reasonably concluded,

> the Souldier should not be unacquainted with the Methods of War that are practiced by the Enemy, nor unable to play the Man, and fight skillfully, either in the Wilderness or in the Field—The Regular Method of fighting is, indeed, only, or chiefly practiced among the civilized Nations of Europe, and accordingly this only need be taught there; but 'tis far otherwise with us in this Continent: We have here to encounter both Regular Bodies, who can keep rank, with their horrid Artillery, in the open Field, and the Irregular Salvages, with their peevish treacherous Musquetry in the Wilderness.

The lesson for the latter-day Israelites was clear: "'Tis therefore necessary for the *American Souldier*, to be variously accomplished, as that he may dare to face either the one or the other."[39]

Over the Hills and Far Away

At last, beginning in late April and May, the regiments marched. For the thousands of newly minted provincial soldiers, just getting to the New York theater was an adventure. Simply gathering and marching with hundreds and thousands of other young men was outside almost everyone's experience. They had to cover more than two hundred miles, through countryside most of them had never seen and over mountains that seemed to eastern residents amazingly steep and high. Along the way they bivouacked near taverns, whose keepers stood to make a good deal of business from the colony government for accommodating the men and supplying them with food and drink. If time permitted, company commanders sometimes drilled the men in the use of their weapons (though considering the paucity of muskets among some companies on the march, these drills must have been conducted in pantomime, or with sticks standing in for firearms). Seth Metcalf, of Rutland, recalled a rare occurrence for provincial units: when his company arrived in Brookfield, "We Exersiesed the fier lock" three days in a row. Few of the diaries or orderly books that remain from this time suggest as much practice.[40] Abner Barrows, who also marched in Gridley's Regiment in 1756, reached western Massachusetts and observed "two Companys thair Who shot at marcks a Good Spell," though whether this was an official company exercise or a friendly competition is not clear. Probably the latter, for "at Length thair Came a man out of the house," a local, who "Borrowd a gon of one of the men that Was Loded" and, whatever the mark was in fact, instead blasted a hole through Samuel Hunter's pack as it hung on a fence. The bullet tore through Hunter's carefully packed coat, jacket, and trousers "in many pleaces which almost Spiled them." It was perhaps fortunate for the bat-sighted miscreant that the whaler turned soldier had left the tools of his trade behind. As it was, the erring marksman was arrested, tried by a hastily convened court-martial, and sentenced to be stripped, flogged ten lashes, and fined four dollars (which one hopes went to Hunter for his loss).[41]

Carelessness with weapons was a significant danger for the recruits, and rare is the New England soldier's journal that does not mention at least one such accident, often with serious results. While the men may have been familiar enough with their own firearms used for hunting and fowling—and the degree to which eighteenth-century, eastern colonists actually engaged in these practices is controversial—handling muskets safely, in formations with scores of other men, for protracted periods, required far more training than provincial units actually received. What is known today as "muzzle discipline," simply being aware at all times of the direction in which one's weapon is pointed, appears to have been lacking, and inattention to other firearms basics made for potentially dangerous conditions. Jacob Gould, a private in Hodges' regiment, was court-martialed for a "Breach of Orders," firing his musket in camp. Gould beat the charge when he was "found to be Ignorant of his Piece being Loaded."[42] Under the circumstances, accidents were practically inevitable. Along the march, Nathan Cary, of Gridley's Regiment, was "Badly Wounded by a musket Ball by a Chance shot from on[e] of our province men." The one-ounce lead bullet "went through his body, but we hope he will git well." Cary recovered but was unfit for further duty; he was discharged and paid off the following month.[43] Edward Cobb's military career almost ended about the same time when "by accident [he] was wounded in one of his legs by a fellow Soldier Carelessly discharging his Gun." And on another occasion over the same route, in 1757, one Jedediah Winslow "was Shot and wounded by An Axident through the hip and [the] Ball was Cut out By the Docter."[44] And this was before they had come anywhere near an enemy.

The last obstacles on their march to the frontier were those parts of the Appalachian Mountains chain known today as the Berkshire and Taconic Ridges, but to the provincials generally known as the Wilderness Woods. Once they left the Connecticut River valley, the hills rose steeply and abruptly, some to heights well over two thousand feet. With only rough, rocky trails through the range, the men struggled to carry their packs, weapons, and supplies, which up to that point had been carried in wagons. Few of the easterners had ever seen such geography, much less hiked it, and the surviving journals that mention this portion of the march agree that the going was tough. Abner Barrows described the going as "Ex trodeney bad. . . . over hills and hols and Swamps Exciding Bad travling." When after several days of this they arrived at the settlement of Pantoosuck (soon to be renamed Pittsfield), they were astonished to learn that they had covered only thirty-five miles since leaving Northampton on the Connecticut River; it had "Semed to us above 60 mil[e]s."[45]

But finally, after two to three weeks' travel, the men of Hodges' company, and much of the provincial army, had reached the Hudson River valley, had been issued the arms with which they were to fight their way into Canada, and were on their way north. Their next objective was the south end of Lake George, which would be the springboard for their invasion and where they had heard there was a new fort.

3

General Winslow's Dilemma

"Upon a Vigourous attack Depends our Fate"

The place they were going had become, along with the forks of the Ohio River, a major front of the current war (fig. 3.1). Albany, the northernmost English colonial town, situated on the Hudson River, and Montreal, the colonial nerve center of French Canada, lay some 225 wilderness miles apart. If the Appalachian Mountains had run uninterrupted through New York province into New England, that distance might have seemed impenetrable enough to both sides, and the war, assuming there were one, would largely have bypassed the region. As it was, of course, there were two major routes through the mountain chain: up the Mohawk River valley westward to Lake Ontario; and north via Lakes George and Champlain—both claimed by the French—to the St. Lawrence River. Over both routes, most of the way was by water. From Albany a traveler could follow the Hudson River north to the Great Carrying Place, below the falls of the river, debark, and follow a fifteen-mile trail to the head of Lake George. From there that traveler could paddle or sail another 30 miles to the north end of the lake, disembark again, this time hiking a mile past the cascading series of falls called La Chute, and take to the water a third time on Lake Champlain. From there it was 180 miles or so to the French settlements on the Richelieu River, all by water, and then a short distance overland to Montreal. An optimist might see in this geography opportunities for peaceful trade among English, French, and Native peoples, and indeed there were. But realists also saw economic competition, rival claims, and, in the event of war, a ready-made military highway that could make those 225 miles seem uncomfortably short.

In 1755 the English colonists of New York and New England were deter-

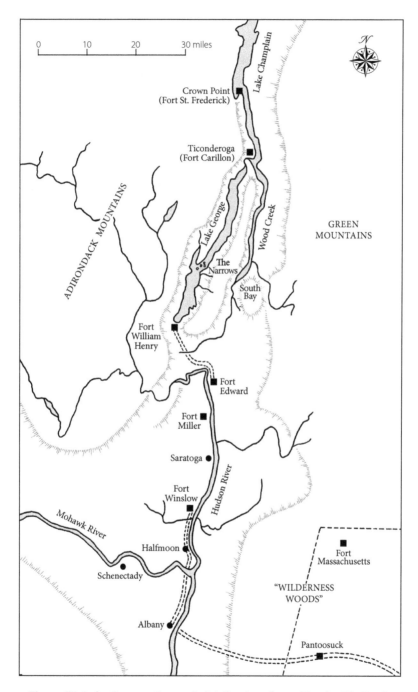

0   10   20   30 miles

N

Crown Point
(Fort St. Frederick)

Lake Champlain

Ticonderoga
(Fort Carillon)

ADIRONDACK MOUNTAINS

Lake George

Wood Creek

GREEN
MOUNTAINS

The
Narrows

South
Bay

Fort
William
Henry

Fort
Edward

Fort
Miller

Saratoga

Hudson River

Fort
Winslow

Mohawk River

Halfmoon

Schenectady

Fort
Massachusetts

"WILDERNESS
WOODS"

Albany

Pantoosuck

Figure 3.1. Lake George–Crown Point theater of war. Map by Die Hoxie

mined to do something about that. The plan, championed by Massachusetts governor William Shirley, was to push aggressively through the Mohawk River valley (with the permission and cooperation of the Six Nations), to establish a British presence at Oswego on Lake Ontario, and also northward, to neutralize the French Fort St. Frederick on Lake Champlain. This latter place, situated at what the British and Americans called Crown Point, had been a thorn in the side of the northern New England settlements for decades. The stone-faced fortification, with its intimidating four-story artillery tower, commanded a narrow point on the lake and not only placed a physical claim on the water highway (which the Anglo-Americans had not yet done) but also served as the jump-off point for numerous French and Indian raids into the northern settlements. The English wanted it gone, but as described in the previous chapter, the campaign in 1755 had fizzled out because of delays and the disruption caused by the carnage of September 8. Following that battle, William Johnson's battered army was in no condition to pursue: his provincials had received quite a shock, suffering some 20 percent casualties, including the wounded Johnson. "To my great Mortification," Johnson wrote to William Shirley, "I must confess to you, that Notwithstanding the Providential repulse we gave the Enemy, Our Troops are . . . far from being invigorated thereby or filled with any Additional Ardor for pursuing the Main Plan. . . . The resolute and obstinate Attack made upon our Breast work in the Face of our Cannon seems to have given our Troops a dread of the Enemy."[1] Instead, both sides licked their wounds and prepared for the next year's campaign. At both ends of Lake George, they began to dig in.

The man Governor Shirley appointed to finish the job was fifty-three-year-old General John Winslow, a native of Massachusetts and scion of one of the first English families in New England (fig. 3.2). His great grandfather Edward had come to America in the famed *Mayflower* in 1620,[2] and both the Pilgrim and his son Josiah had served as governor of the colony. General John, the current patriarch of the family, had already proved himself a willing and reasonably competent commander in the present war. Two years earlier, while young George Washington was blundering about in western Pennsylvania, Winslow had been given command of a provincial task force sent into the Maine wilderness. His mission was to root out suspected French encroachments in what was then claimed as Massachusetts land. No enemies were found, but in the next year he was the lieutenant colonel of a provincial regiment sent to help take Fort Beausejour in Nova Scotia and

Figure 3.2. General John Winslow, by Joseph Blackburn, ca. 1756. Courtesy of Pilgrim Hall Museum, Plymouth, Massachusetts

then to assist with the expulsion of the French-speaking Acadians. He appears to have been reluctant to take on the latter task, complaining that rounding up and transporting the unfortunate *habitants* was "Very Disagreable to my natural make & Temper." Perhaps so; he nevertheless carried out his disagreeable orders. By the end of 1755 he had helped expel more than fifteen hundred Acadians to English colonies as far south as Georgia.

Winslow's current assignment—to command the provincial army gathering in northern New York—was more to his liking. If successful, his force would strike one of the major blows against the French planned for the campaign year. With both British regulars and colonial troops available (many of the redcoat ranks filled by American volunteers), the general plan was to push against sensitive French areas in four different places. In the Ohio country, provincial soldiers, supported by more British regulars, would again descend on Fort Duquesne; regulars would also move out from Oswego against the French forts near the mouth of Lake Ontario. An all-provincial army had the task of taking Crown Point, while a fourth force was to make a feint against Quebec.[3] The smaller French and Indian armies would be unable to counter every threat in theaters hundreds of miles apart; victory was all but certain somewhere—and with luck, everywhere.

The new fort at the south end of Lake George was to be the launch point for Winslow's campaign. The Battle of Lake George the previous September had demonstrated that *both* sides could use the lakes as military highways, and both French and American provincials began building fortifications at their respective ends of Lake George to forestall quick invasion. The French effort was named Fort Carillon (often called Ticonderoga by the Anglo-Americans), placed where the waters of Lake George entered Lake Champlain via La Chute. The fort guarded the approaches to Crown Point from both Lake George and Wood Creek, which snaked southwest some twenty miles, roughly paralleling Lake George. For their part, the American provincials began work on Fort William Henry as soon as it became apparent that offensive operations for 1755 had been shelved. The need for a fort in this wilderness, sixty-five miles from Albany, was clear: preparations for the 1756 campaign required a safe forward base where troops could gather, collect and store supplies, and prepare boats to carry them all northward. From a defensive point of view, the fort was more necessary than ever: since the provincials had built a military road from the Great Carrying Place to the head of the lake, that road now had to be protected to ensure that the other side did not use it first.

While a second fort, Fort Edward, was being finished at the Hudson end of the military road, Captain William Eyre, a British army regular, laid out and supervised the initial construction of Fort William Henry in the fall of 1755. What he designed was a European-style, square structure with arrowhead-shaped bastions at the corners. Barracks built within the walls were meant to hold a garrison of five hundred men. This was to be no crude, stockade-style enclosure; it had to withstand the possibility of a sizeable attack by enemies equipped with artillery. Accordingly, Eyre designed a strong earthen fort, "in the manner the French build," with walls thirty feet thick at the base, and sides nearly four hundred feet long, including the bastions. Such a sturdy, elaborate structure, as the historian Ian K. Steele so aptly explained, was "constructed primarily with shovels. . . . [It was] a gigantic sandbox of pine logs outside and inside."[4] Except on the side facing the lake, the fort was surrounded by a protective dry ditch. Axes were the other necessary tools: hundreds of trees had to be felled, cut to length, and notched to interlock with the other logs in the structure.[5] In addition to the fort proper, the provincials also made a supporting fortified camp on high ground nearby, also involving earthworks and ditches. It was an enormous amount of work, but despite the lateness of the season, increasing sickness among the troops, and poor discipline, the fort was sufficiently completed by mid-November 1755 to be functional, if far from comfortable. A garrison of several hundred provincials was left to hold it over the winter. So for the 1756 campaign, General Winslow had his forward base. He also had an obstacle not present in the previous year's effort: Fort William Henry's counterpart at the other end of the lake, the French Fort Carillon. In between was a thirty-mile no man's land of thick forest and steep defiles. Crown Point seemed farther away than ever.

Nevertheless, English hopes for success that year were high. A large and motivated provincial army was gathering, arms and redcoats from Britain had been dedicated to the effort, and logistical difficulties, it was hoped, had been ameliorated with experience. And there was a further geographic advantage the provincials would enjoy: spring came earlier to New York than to Canada, meaning that French reinforcement of Crown Point and Carillon would be delayed by persistent ice and muddy roads, while the Anglo-American armies could begin moving sooner. A head start of a couple of weeks could make all the difference in the campaign, permitting an overwhelming descent on Carillon from Fort William Henry if all were ready. Speed was the key.

And that was where Winslow's troubles began: virtually nothing was ready for a springtime launch to the campaign, and nothing seemed to happen speedily subsequently. Just assembling the provincial army proved to be a problem. Winslow arrived in Albany on May 24 to survey the Massachusetts men who had arrived and were encamped there, "and to my great surprize [I] find them fall Vastly short of the Number Intended by the Province." A quick look at the rolls of those present and correct showed that on average there were "no more then Forty men to a Company which for the 62 Companys makes Only 2480 men" at hand. Additionally, Colonel Richard Gridley's vital artillery train was somehow missing about a hundred men. Winslow estimated that in all he was 920 men—27 percent—short of the number he should have, and where the rest were nobody knew. And that was just one colony's levy: "should the Other Governments fall as much short in proportion as Ours we shall be in danger of being Out Numbered in the Field." To Spencer Phipps, the acting governor of Massachusetts, Winslow urged all speed in making up the missing numbers of men, "for upon a Vigourous attack Depends our Fate." If he had the men, and quickly, Winslow wrote, Crown Point could be theirs within two months of mission launch. In the meantime, he wanted the men moved upriver from Albany to Halfmoon, "that our men may be Out of the Way of Debauching and at their Duty."[6]

"It allmost makes me Creasy"

Winslow was also disturbed by difficulties that were becoming clear for the first time. His manpower shortages were made more serious by the very need to keep his men supplied, "Especially If It be Considered that It will take us, out of the whole Force, 1500 Men to man the Boats and Battoes, and for our Forts and Guards for Provisions, sick Included, 1000." The lifeline of the army that was to gather at Fort William Henry stretched seventy miles to Albany, by land, water, and then land again. Depending on where they originated, supplies might be loaded onto boats or wagons and unloaded four or more times before reaching their destination. Boats needed men to row them, wagons needed men to drive them, and both needed constant maintenance. Pick-up points for supplies, such as Halfmoon, Stillwater, Saratoga, and Fort Miller, needed protection, and that meant more men, especially if fortifications were built. With all these soldiers siphoned off for the necessary but essentially static function of keeping the supply line open, Winslow feared, "we shall have But a small Army to Attack our Enemy."[7]

Indeed, conveyance upriver was inefficient and inadequate. Winslow complained: "We have been sadly put to for want of Battoes to Transport our stores." These thirty-foot, shallow-draft, flat-bottomed boats were ideal for moving heavy supplies on inland waterways, but there were simply not enough of them on the river to handle the unprecedented volume of freight needed for the campaign. The lack of proper conveyance led not only to delays but to the waste of precious supplies. General Winslow was "greatly surprized on my Arrival" to discover "a Vast Quantity of Provisions of all species, rum not accepted [excepted], Lying upon the Beach exposed both to Rain and sun." Some shipmasters hired to bring the supplies from New England or New York apparently found no one to receive them and no place to put them when they arrived. Then as now, time was money, and the skippers simply dumped their cargo on a convenient strand. Disgusted, Winslow feared that "It will Turn out to bad account: not Only great Wastage but also Loss." It would have been better, he wrote, "if store houses Could not have been hired or Built," to have detained the vessels they came in—most likely sloops and schooners—and used them as floating warehouses until land transport could have been arranged.[8]

Waste came by other means as well. Jonathan Bagley, commanding at Fort William Henry, informed Winslow in early June that he had found the tents stored at the fort over the winter "very Bad, but few if any fitt for service." They had been stored properly enough when the army had marched off the previous December, but the garrison soldiers had only one blanket apiece, and no beds had been built in the barracks yet, so they had used the tents to lie on and cover themselves through the long, frigid winter.[9]

Shortages of manpower and materiel would be much of the story for the waning spring months. Ordering a count of the provincial forces at his disposal in early June, Winslow found his overall returns somewhat better— 3,940 men in all—but these were scattered up and down the way to Lake George: only 489 at Fort William Henry; 293 at Fort Edward (these were minimal garrison strengths); 306 at Stillwater, midway between Albany and Fort Edward; and 1,424 at Halfmoon, forty-five miles from where they needed to be. The remaining 1,428, as Winslow predicted, were on various detached duties.[10] The general moved men northward as quickly as they came in, and by mid-June they were arriving in better numbers: by June 19, Forts William Henry and Edward had increased their complements to 738 and 762, respectively, and Winslow had nearly 6,000 men in his theater, though more than a third of them were still at Halfmoon and Albany.[11]

This was still not enough. Winslow could read a calendar as well as anyone and fumed at the delays forced upon him. To New York governor Charles Hardy he complained that he "Could wish we ware Forwarder, both in men and Our Transportation of Provisions to the Lake, the Delay of both which, Gives me some uneasiness as the sumer is spending and Our Enemys Strengthning themselves against us."[12] Writing to the Massachusetts Council of War, in Boston, after the most recent head count, Winslow acknowledged that the provisions for the campaign were coming along but said that he "Could heartily wish that we Ware In Equal forwardness with regard to our men; that is not the Case as we are wanting, as you will See by the returns, above Eleven hundred from Our Province[. I] am Supprised that we should be the most behidehand of all [and] God Knows the Consequence of this delay." Winslow felt that he knew the consequence: he reminded the council that "It will be allmost as fatal to do nothing as to be Defeated, and should I miscarry for want of men Gentlemen, Consider what an appearance Our Province will make In History for the Great Ommition, and how the Lives of so many Good men will be accounted for. This I have Opened to you that some Measures may be taken that we may have Our Numbers, Sacredly Promised."[13]

Winslow had never been given such a chance to distinguish himself as this campaign offered. With the other thrusts at New France being directed by British regular officers, success on this front would assure Winslow a place in New England history equal to that of William Pepperell, the Massachusetts general who had taken the French stronghold of Louisbourg in the last war, for which he had been knighted. Aggressive action was called for, and Winslow assured the Council of War that "it is vastly Disageeable to me to be On the Defensive only, and my Temper Ill brooks being Idle." With none of the other British operations any more forward than his, he feared he might have "the Biggest part of the Force of Canada to Dispute with" if the delays continued. If he could get sufficient supply for just fifty days, he confided to Governor Hardy, he would "Go forward" by the end of the month "If not prevented By Absolute Orders."[14] To Winslow's nudging, the Massachusetts Council of War rather unhelpfully replied that it was indeed regrettable that their colony, "who were first in the undertaking should be the last of all In Collecting their Number," but that "what is the Occasion of It we can't tell." They suggested that "the Blame lays at the several Colonels doors who had Orders to raise [the men]," and then upon "some Others"—just who they did not say—"for not calling them to a strict account." At any rate, they denied that it was their problem.[15]

In the event, Winslow would never get his fifty days' worth of provisions. At the approved daily allowance of a pound of meat and a pound of bread per soldier, plus peas, beans, and rice in smaller proportions, six thousand men required at least six tons of food each day, all of which had to be transported to wherever they were. Wagons, and horses to pull them, needed to be hired or purchased, and these had to be brought by water to Fort Edward for use over the road to Fort William Henry. The horses in turn needed tons of grain and fodder, and these too had to be brought by boat. Colonel Bagley, at Fort William Henry, had the unenviable task of not only finishing and improving the fort's defenses, keeping out scouts, and building boats, wharves, and warehouses; he also had to accommodate the soldiers as they came in, feed them and their animals, and assemble provisions for the big push. "When I consider," he wrote, unburdening himself to his general, "how many Tons of provisions and Artillery we have to Carry it allmost makes me Creasy [crazy]; as to Building Gundaloes and Battoes to Carry the Dead Weight Its allmost Endless."[16] In late June, Winslow, passing through Fort Edward, told Colonel John Choate that there were insufficient stores of oats on hand to keep the wagons moving, but he said that if necessary he would substitute peas from the soldiers' stores and even their "Campain samp and Indian meal[, which] is on hand unbounded." The general's frustration trickled down the supply bureaucracy; John Ashley, at Fort Hardy (Saratoga), whined that he was "misrepresented" in being described as not doing all he could to expedite wagon teams: "I am Informed [I am] stiled a Damd Rascal and Ought to be put in Irons &c."[17]

Winslow also had to be concerned with water transport at the Lake George end of the supply line. For the army to move against Fort Carillon, there would have to be sufficient water carriage for the thousands of men he brought as well as for their supplies, food, cannon, and ammunition. As was the case everywhere, there were delays and shortages here. Many of the men who reached Fort William Henry in May and June were put to work building boats of various sizes and complexity. Lighters—broad-beamed, thirty-three-ton sloop-rigged vessels with six-foot holds—would be needed to carry both men and freight, but hundreds of men could travel in light, fast whaleboats. These double-ended open boats, developed for southern New England's specialized fishery, could be both rowed and sailed and were light enough to be easily carried over portages by their crews. Connecticut had sent some to the lake, where they proved to be excellently adapted to reconnaissance and general transport. Winslow wanted more of them constructed at the fort, but as he was realizing by now, nothing connected with this campaign went smoothly. Whaleboats in New England were made largely from cedar, and as Jonathan Bagley informed his general from Fort William Henry, "Suitable stuff for the Boards is Exceeding scarce and hard to gett, we are obliged to goe a great Way down the Lake for It and [it is] Bad at Best." But perhaps most needed were tools for the men: Winslow complained to an associate that "the Business [of boatbuilding] is Delayed and Can't go on for want of Carpenters tools." Bagley agreed, adding that not only tools but hardware for the boats were lacking. "Never was any man plagued as I am, the Carpenters fretting and Driving to gett the work done but Its hard making Brick without straw." Weeks later Bagley wrote to give Winslow some good news: one of the lighters had been launched, but it needed sails before it could go anywhere, as well as swivel guns for armament. And as for gunpowder for those guns, Bagley reported that out of 380 half-barrels at the fort, 102 were spoiled or defective, "fit only for salutes."[18] Nevertheless, Bagley promised to "leave no stone unturned; every wheel shall go that rum and Human flesh can Turn, but Tools are exceedingly much Wanted."[19]

The delays and shortages proved to be decisive in terms of blighting Winslow's hopes for a Champlain-corridor blitzkrieg. By May the ice in the St. Lawrence had broken up, restoring Canada's contact with France and permitting men and supplies to reach Crown Point and Fort Carillon from Montreal. By early June, an American prisoner later reported, some six hundred French regulars, recently arrived from France, had reached Carillon, along with an equal number of Canadian troops, augmenting the five-hundred-man garrison there. By late July the number of men there had reached thirty-five hundred. By that time Winslow, still without his full complement of men, would have had to strip his forts and supply depots down to skeleton crews to gather an invasion force to top that number, especially as he could expect the French to be fighting from fortified positions.[20] And Winslow did not dare do anything so rash, for it soon became clear that the campaign's vital supply line was uncomfortably, even embarrassingly vulnerable.

"The Enemy are Lurking about us every Day"

About the same time that Captain Hodges' company was settling in at Halfmoon, the enemy they had come to fight was making its presence known in the region. On May 27 a party of twenty-eight men went out from Fort Edward to find eight oxen that had gone astray. Three miles from the fort, "One of the Party heard a Rustling in the Bushes that he Imagined an Enemy and fired his Gun, which frightened the Party so that they ran to the Fort as fast as they Could." Some in the group thought the noise had only been "wild beasts," but they were not about to be left behind to be proved wrong. The fort's commander sent out a Lieutenant Brooks and twelve men (presumably all who could or would go) to try to find either the oxen or any sign of an enemy nearby. They did not even get as far as had the first group when the woods before them suddenly erupted in gunfire. Several men fell instantly, including Brooks, and three were wounded, "on which most of them retreated with precipitation." Only five made it back, however, so others had been killed or made prisoners or were lost in the woods. The survivors insisted that they had been attacked by "near two hundred of the Enemy," though how they arrived at that figure is unclear.[21] The next morning a party of fifty set out from the fort to find and bury the dead. They discovered three corpses, "among whom was Lieu^t Brooks who was Miserably butchered." Brooks had had his mouth split open, "his Tongue Cut Out, his Belly Cut open, and his Bowels taken Out, and some of them put Into his Mouth." The fort commander, lacking sufficient men to counter such a large mobile force (if it was that large), could do little more. "Tis hard," he lamented, "to be thus Treated at Our Own Door and not have men Enough to Avenge It." He warned that without a reinforcement, "the Waggons beeing stopped on every Alarum will Intirely Disconcert the whole Affair."[22]

At nearly the same time, Colonel Bagley, having recently arrived at Fort William Henry with men and provisions, was finding not all as secure as could be wished. Although he had lent some of his men to help scour the woods about Fort Edward for two days, one of his captains "Judged it not Safe" to march a detachment that way "untill the Woods was Rambled." Obligingly, Bagley sent one hundred men under an experienced New Hampshire officer named Robert Rogers to scout the road ahead of the nervous captain, and beyond that toward Wood Creek. The following day, Bagley sent out a second party, led by Ebenezer Poor, "to Cover Rogers." It was a prudent move, for eight miles from the fort Poor's command "fell in with a large Party" of the enemy, possibly the same force that had butchered the unfortunate Lieutenant Brooks. This time the provincials did not panic, and after trading several volleys, the marauders broke off. Poor's men pursued them into a swamp, at which point the skirmish petered out. Back at the fort, though, Bagley reported frequent harassment of his work parties: "The Carpenters cannot go Out 100 rods from the fort . . . to Cut Timber for the Lighters, Flatt Bottomed Boats &c." without a hundred armed men to protect them.[23]

Raids kept Winslow's gathering forces off-balance at the other end of the supply line too, and at various points in between. At Halfmoon, where Winslow had moved the bulk of his army from Albany, a member of a twenty-man scout on the east side of the river claimed to have discovered "a Considerable Number of french and Indines." In response, the camp commander dispatched a force of two hundred men to interdict the reported enemy, but they saw no sign of them. Annoyed by their fruitless, day-long search, and convinced that the man who had brought the news had been jumping at shadows, they subjected the unfortunate fellow to some ritual humiliation. They "pickt up a Dears horn, Got Som hair tied to it [and] Dresed it up in form of Scalp," then "maid him Carry it Round the Camp," followed by "a grait Number of Solders . . . with Wooden Swords and Staves." The rumor made men jumpy nevertheless; the following night, two sentries fired at something moving outside the camp, only to discover that it was "a parcel of Swine."[24]

Or was it? The next day, June 4, on the east side of the river across from Halfmoon, just where the lone scout had reported detecting the enemy two days earlier, a small number of Connecticut and New York soldiers were attacked by a "Large Party of French and Indians." The raiders "Began by Firing singly and at Last they Began to fire twenty at a time," suggesting a deliberate tactic to confuse the men, fix them in place, and then annihilate them with heavy, repeated volleys. The attackers were eventually driven off by the camp's cannon, or so said the camp commander, but the damage seems to have been done: the party on the east side of the river had not come in by nightfall, and "I fear [many of them] are Cutt of[f] [i.e., killed]." It was perhaps worse than that. One who had been present was fearful that "all Our Provision Boats who went off from here This Morning will be Cut off as we have not men Enough here to Defend this Place or to allow Guards Sufficient to Guard them On the River."[25]

Adding yet more insult to injury, the elusive raiders even struck at the campaign's nerve center a week later. Eleazar Fitch wrote hurriedly from Albany to General Winslow at Halfmoon that at ten thirty in the morning, in broad daylight, "a Party of near fifty French and Indians had the Impudence to Come Down to the River Oposite to this City and Captivate Two men." Charlotte Brown, who had crossed the Atlantic with the British forces to serve as matron for their general hospital, wrote in her journal that "All the Town [was] alarmed" by the kidnappings, which had occurred "not half a mile of[f]." The next day, "A Girl [was] taken by the Indians just out of Town." On June 14, Brown "Receiv'd an Invitation to go a Mile out of Town with Col'n Glasier and Miss Miller," but these were not normal times, and the party was "obliged to have a Guard with us for fear of the Indians."[26]

Bands of French and Indian raiders seemed to be everywhere throughout June and July, killing soldiers and picking up prisoners whenever someone let down his guard. Fort Massachusetts, in the northwest corner of that colony, had been part of the frontier bulwark against Indian raids in the last war. Since then the frontier had moved on to the north and west, or so many assumed. But on June 7, Indians ambushed a patrol from the garrison only a half mile from the fort, killing and scalping two of them. Since then, the fort's commander reported, "the Enemy are Lurking about us every Day." At the same time that Indians were taking captives around Albany and putting the town on high alert, Robert Rogers' scouts "Heard 24 Guns on the West Side of Lake George which we supposed to be a Scout of French and Indians clearing Out y^r Guns"—a bold violation of the common-sense rules of guerrilla warfare that reflected contempt for their Anglo-American opponents. Indians were also spotted near Stillwater on July 1.[27]

These depredations by irregular forces, minor in tactical terms, had strategic consequences and highlighted weak points in the provincial offensive efforts. They disrupted the efforts of an amateur army trying to sort out the already complicated issues of an offensive campaign. They threatened the logistics lifeline of the army, not so much by capturing or destroying supplies as by interrupting their already irregular flow. The boldness of their raids, reaching deep into the colonial settlements, was both infuriating and demoralizing, and the provincials' inability to protect every point along the army's march, to say nothing of unprepared settlements, underscored their impotence to neutralize the threat. Such, of course, was the intention of these raids: to keep the provincial army in this theater off-balance, fearful, and uncertain. Lines of supply and vital depots needed to be protected, and doing so sapped Winslow's offensive strength. And the men taken from their regiments and assigned to guard boats and wagons often did not understand or care about their jobs. Henry Babcock, who had informed Winslow of Indian sightings at Stillwater, "Thought proper to Inform you . . . that the Guards that Comes with the Teams" were not only too few but woefully slack. They tended to go on ahead of the slow-moving wagons, which followed too far behind "with only a few [guards] In the Front; they scarce have any rear or Flanque Guards." On another occasion, Babcock reported that "the waggons . . . came in full half an hour before the Guards." Such poor practices were invitations to disaster. Even in the absence of constant raiding, which the French and Indians were unable to manage, the knowledge of their elusive enemy's capability and the unpredictability of their attacks nonetheless had lasting effects. When men imagined Indians "Lurking about us every Day"; when sentries at Stillwater "were very sure they heard the Enemy Walk round them in the night"; when boat handlers and wagon masters would not move without heavy escort; indeed, when the ordinary social life in Albany was disturbed, and people visiting neighbors required armed guards, then the raiders demonstrated their strategic value far beyond their numbers and the actual damage they inflicted. They frustrated Winslow's designs, spreading terror and producing operational paralysis.[28]

"I have not men to scout"

Winslow had no choice but to take detachments from his regiments and assign them to securing his supply lines, but he took proactive measures as well. He was thoroughly aware of the need for ranging companies for the army, though he had initially imagined them as scouts to screen his *advancing* army, not as interdiction forces to protect it. But the need was clear, and frequently seconded by his subordinates. When a redcoat company that had been at Fort William Henry was ordered south, Colonel Jonathan Bagley was "Obliged to send One hundred of the Yorkers and Capt Rogers Company to Guard Or Escort the Regulars down to Fort Edward." Without those escorts the redcoats, in march formation on the narrow military road, would simply have been too vulnerable; indeed, they had to pass by the very spot where the previous year the Battle of Lake George had begun with a bloody ambush on the road. But more than that, Bagley complained that he had little sense of security, rarely knowing exactly what might be hiding beyond the tree line from day to day: "I have not men to scout which I judge would be very Necessary, and the Carpenters Work is retarded for want of Guards to goe over the Lake to Cut and haul Timber Plank Logs &c." Jehosaphat Starr, at Fort Winslow (Stillwater), wanted fifty-seven Massachusetts men to protect his boats.[29] Bagley thought that the greatest danger came from the "back door" of Wood Creek and South Bay and that the "Greatest protection to the Convoys of provisions from Albany . . . would be to keep out Large scouts of 100 or 150 Men Constantly Recovering the Woods from South Bay and so Down aCross Wood Creek so that no party of the Enemy can be out but that our Scouts may Discover them by their Tracks every Day and keep the Course Clear."[30] It was sound policy but easier said than done; those 100 to 150 men would have to come from somewhere.

The issue of raising ranger companies, bodies of men whose primary function was to conduct irregular warfare and reconnaissance, had surfaced early in the campaign year. William Shirley enthusiastically endorsed their deployment, and in April of the year, while pressing Winslow to make all haste in moving troops westward, also urged him to "get Three Companys of Rangers raised as soon as Possible" from his levies, insisting that it was "Necessary for His Majestys Service" and even suggesting a number of experienced officers to raise them. Such men were to have extra monetary inducements for enlistment, such as "A Good Hunting Coat, Vest and Breeches, a pair of Indian Stockings, shoes, and a Hatchett," and "£5. stg. [sterling] for Each Indian scalp" they acquired in the service. Shirley had in mind something on the order of Robert Rogers' company of New Hampshire rangers, which had performed well for Sir William Johnson the previous year and was shortly to become famous for its exploits.

Curiously, Winslow baulked at Shirley's proposal, opining that "It would be of Ill Consequence to have Such Compnys taken from the men Raised by the Provinces and Colonies." He explained first that the provincial companies at that time were understrength to begin with and that the officers who raised them would not take kindly to having their most able men recruited from their companies. He also objected that since clear monetary and prestige benefits accompanied the ranging service, "a Door should be Open to every Individual to be of that Number" rather than to only a select few. Indeed, he argued that "the Service will be better Performed" this way, "for as ambition and money are the springs that Actuate mankinde . . . was the Honour and reward open to all, all would Industriously strive to Meritt both." Making distinctions among people as famously egalitarian as were New Englanders "Tends to Raise Divisions" among them and so "Ought Carefully to be Avoided." Instead, Winslow proposed that "as often as a Party for Scouting is judged Necessary," some "aproved and Experienced officers" would raise an appropriate number of volunteers from available provincial companies. These should be "of the best and most able Bodyed men" available, Winslow conceded, but "for their Encouragement" they were to have "some Extra Pay or reward for their Service, part Certain and part Depending on their Success." By changing the roster on each occasion to include as many volunteers as came forward, "we shall soon come to know our best men and those that are Most fit for the Duty." Dedicated ranging companies, Winslow reminded Shirley, were expensive, and not as versatile as provincial companies, but if they were desired nevertheless, then they should be separately raised for the purpose and paid for.[31]

Winslow's reasons may seem penny-wise and pound-foolish to modern readers convinced of the utility of special forces. He may seem to have placed a great deal of confidence in the ability of the "invisible hand" of the market to supply the functions of dedicated ranger companies, but Winslow understood something of the temper of his army and was justifiably concerned with propping up their notoriously delicate morale. Also, in his previous campaign in Nova Scotia, Winslow had not had to deal with persistent guerrilla resistance, so the expedient he proposed may have seemed sufficient to him. Still, had the discussion with Shirley continued, the Massachusetts governor might have pointed out some drawbacks to Winslow's scheme. Permitting any soldier, however motivated, to volunteer for ranging service, while laudably democratic, sidestepped the issue of aptitude to the demands of the service. Not everyone who wants to join a team has the talent for it. If scouting companies were raised in the manner Winslow described, they would be composed of men who had not otherwise worked or trained together; each and every scout would become a shakedown mission, an exercise in trial and error in which there would always be personnel inadequate to the task. When not on an actual mission, the men would return to their respective companies and regiments, and to their accustomed fatigues; there would be no opportunity for the specialized training that might turn even raw material into competent woodsmen. In the event, though, Winslow had his way, not on the merits of his argument, but because Shirley was replaced in late June as commander in chief by the British general James Abercromby, who was in turn only holding the place for John Campbell, Earl of Loudoun, who would not arrive on the scene until late July. In the meantime, Winslow had a free hand to implement his preference with regard to rangers.

So in response to the raid near Albany on June 11, and with rumors of a "large body" of Indians still in the area, Winslow wrote orders for Major Samuel Thaxter, a provincial officer from Hingham, to

> take upon you the Command of the Party this day raised for a Scout Consisting of three Captains three Lieu[ts] three Ensigns and One hundred and fifty non Commission officers and private men and with them to Examine the Woods and by all means to make Discovery wither there be any signs of French or Indians

and If you should be so happy as to meet with a Party you to use your Endeavers to Captivate or Distroy them, and In your Rout[e] you are to take In your way and Call at Fort Massachusetts Enquire how matters are there and you will take Especial Care not to be Surprpised in your March and to Do everything you Judge Necessary for the Good of the Service for the Distruction of the Enemy and Preservation of the Kings subjects and return In seven Days.

Winslow confided to another his desire that "Some Day may favour us with an Opportunity to be up with Those Sculkers."[32]

If that was his hope, there are some curious elements to Thaxter's instructions, not the least of which is that by the time Winslow's secretary wrote them, the raiders would have been long gone. But in addition to that, the orders reveal an ad hoc quality as to purpose and method that often characterized the directions given provincial scouting units. Apparently, Thaxter was to pick up the enemy's track, but he was not specifically ordered to follow it or to locate the enemy; indeed, a direct confrontation with the enemy was only imagined *if* Thaxter's men were "so happy" as to bump into them. Also, strangely, Thaxter's orders required him to take his relatively large force out of the area entirely, to Fort Massachusetts, forty miles to the south and east, to "Enquire how matters are there," a task that surely could have been performed as well, and more quickly, by a much smaller group of men.

Thaxter's report, dutifully submitted by the major seven days later, reveals much about the requirements of a reconnaissance in force and how much the eastern provincial soldiers had yet to learn. After marching north to Stillwater, Thaxter's men crossed to the east side of the Hudson, which makes sense if the major was hoping to intercept the French and Indian raiders on their return to Carillon. However, Thaxter immediately "proceeded On my way towards Fort Massachusetts," meeting with "nothing Remarkeable." The next morning, after marching about five miles, men at the rear of Thaxter's column realized that they were being followed by two Frenchmen and one Indian—at least that was all they saw. "The rear of the Scout . . . fired three Guns at them to no purpose," following which Thaxter sent a captain and fifty men after the intruders "to see If he could come up with them but he returned without Success." Frustrated, the men marched on until noon, when they stopped to dine and then were halted by a thunderstorm that lasted through the night "by which our Bread was Greatly

Damaged and the men were very wett." They stayed where they were until the next morning, despite the possibility that the enemy who had been tracking them, and could easily have continued to do so, might have been part of that "large body" they were supposed to be looking for. As they made ready to take up the march again, "One Sam Carpenter of the Connecticut Forces . . . had the Rhumitizm so bad that he Could not March," and his fellows had to carry him on a hastily made litter the rest of the day. The traveling was hard, and the next day another man, "Sick of the Plurisie," had to be carried. Coming to a field where someone's horses grazed, Thaxter ordered a halt, while some of his men caught two of the beasts to carry the sick men. Even this moment of relative calm turned tragic when one of the men, wishing to examine the major's pistol, accidentally shot John Martin (who was from Hodges' company) with it, wounding him seriously. Now Thaxter had three men unable to fight, two of whom were too badly off to ride, meaning that eight more men had to be designated to carry them. Fifteen miles short of Fort Massachusetts, "we discovered Where the Enemy had been and burnt a house and Barn and Killed a number of Cattle." There was no sign of the former occupants. Finally reaching the fort, Thaxter learned details of the recent enemy activity in the area and rested his men in the fort that night. The next day they buried John Martin, who had endured an agonizing couple of days being carried through the woods only to expire in the morning. Thaxter had to borrow 150 pounds of bread for his hungry men before setting out for the return trip to Halfmoon. They made much better time, arriving two days later, though not soon enough for some: they were six miles from the Hudson River crossing when Thaxter called another halt, but "three of my men Contrary to Order Left the Scout and went away by themselves." Reaching the camp at Halfmoon about sunset, Thaxter immediately had the men arrested and confined.[33]

Thaxter's scout was in several ways a test of Winslow's scouting philosophy, and the results the major reported ought to have given the general reasons to reconsider. As per his orders, the volunteers for Thaxter's command were drawn from at least seven different companies, representing three different colonies. In his report of the slaughter of Lieutenant Brooks and his men only two weeks earlier, Colonel Whiting admitted that, apart from Brooks, he had no idea who the dead men were, since "the officers had no list of them; the Party were strangers to him and one Another."[34] Thaxter at least had a roster for his scout—an unusual circumstance in the historical record—but his men were every bit as unknown to one another. Some may have been chosen for their experience in the forest; if so, they surely had more experience than their commander, whose home was a seaport town. But the scout as a whole was unable to prevent being shadowed for at least part of the way by the enemy or to ambush the men tracking them. Thaxter's men were clearly unprepared for foul weather: rain and a hailstorm brought them to a dead halt for some eighteen hours, and the food they had brought was both unsuitable and inadequate and could not be kept from spoiling. Some of the men clearly should not have been allowed to go in the first place, and their subsequent incapacity endangered their fellows, who could hardly have abandoned them. Thaxter himself had contributed indirectly to his casualties, since it was his pistol, casually lent to satisfy a subordinate's curiosity, that mortally wounded one of his men—and incidentally gave away their position to any enemy that might have been nearby. And then there were disciplinary problems, in three cases amounting to desertion in the field. In his report of the scout, Thaxter concluded that two men had "Beheav'd bad," six others were likewise "bad," and one more a "Bad fellow." All told, it was probably fortunate that Thaxter's men did not find the enemy they were looking for.[35]

Instead, an unfortunate lieutenant named Grant did. Grant was dispatched with thirteen men, including one Indian, to Fort Massachusetts to aid and retrieve the sick men Thaxter had left there. Just short of their destination they were "shott upon by a great Number of Indians," whose fire killed several outright. In the melee that followed, the Indian of Grant's party, who had been bringing up the rear, was the only one to escape. Days later, when a large provincial scout came upon the scene, they found eight bodies "most Inhumanly Butchered." Stuck into the back of one of them, "which we supposed to be Lieut Grant," one of the attackers had left a tomahawk—a calling card for whoever found the corpse.[36]

The inadequacy of provincial scouting, in which Captain Hodges' men took part, was borne out in another report Winslow received. About the same time that Thaxter's command was lurching toward Fort Massachusetts, a much smaller scout from Fort Edward was ten miles out when the men "heard a Tree fall, which made them Listen, and then they heard a Great Number of Axes going and . . . People talking." Just who these workers were, their number, or what they were doing, the scout never learned, "as the Woods were very thick," but the author of the report opined vaguely that "by their taulk and Noise they Believe [there were] a great Number." After the scout had "Tarried as Long as they Dared they Crept away and sett out to return Back," having learned next to nothing, even though the "taulk and Noise" and the thick woods had offered them favorable conditions for re- connoitering the enemy. Near sunset, as they came within five miles of the fort, they "discovered another Party" near the wagon road to Fort William Henry. This time they did somewhat better, waiting until dark, when they "Crept up and Veiwed them as well as they Could." They counted six camp- fires, and by the light they could see people walking around them, but again the report contained no specifics as to identity or numbers. The author of the report complained, "I have but 309 private men here fitt for Duty [and] Cannot with Prudence send out a sufficient Party to Encounter those Impu- dent fellows who I Suppose Designe to strike a fatal stroke On our Provisions very soon." Impudent indeed: that very morning, the report continued, "we Discovered some Tracks . . . where they Came last night within about forty Rods of the Fort." The report finished with a plea for more men, "both to Maintain the Garrison and also to Give those Villians a Dressing."[37] Winslow would have liked that too, but in late June he was forced to admit in a letter to Governor Hardy, "We have Scouts Daily out who Discover the Enemy but have not as yett been able to Obtain [i.e., capture] a single Person."[38]

Winslow, along with the rest of his army, had as a counterexample the activities of Robert Rogers, who was making a name for himself and his in- dependent company of rangers for their bold penetrations of the no man's land. Already that year, Rogers and his men had visited Crown Point three times, reconnoitering the French fort, burning outbuildings, slaughtering precious cattle, and taking prisoners for interrogation. Fort Carillon, so much on General Winslow's mind these days, received the rangers' attention on four occasions, with Rogers once "approaching so near as to see . . . sen- tries on the ramparts" and at another time ambushing a French detachment to obtain a prisoner.[39] He rarely commanded numbers equal to those of some of the large enemy raiding parties sent south from Crown Point and Carillon, but he and the men he had performed many of the same opera- tional functions as his French and Indian counterparts: intelligence gather- ing and disruption of the enemy. Rogers received a great many accolades then, and has since, because his achievements contrasted so sharply with the rather less productive efforts of scouts drawn from the provincial ranks.

The success of Rogers' men, of course, lay partly in personnel selection and leadership. Most rangers, at least early in the war, were experienced woodsmen, and Rogers was young, ambitious, and aggressive. But Rogers' company also enjoyed a consistency of mission, especially when they became an independent company in the spring of 1756 under the auspices of William Shirley, then still in command of British forces in America. Shirley's general orders specifically encouraged Rogers to, in Rogers' words, "use my best endeavours to distress the French and their allies, by sacking, burning, and destroying their houses, barns, barracks, canoes, battoes, &c. and by killing their cattle of every kind; and at all times to way-lay, attack, and destroy their convoys of provisions by land and water, in any part of the country where I could find them."[40] In other words, Rogers was to do what the French and Indians had been doing in the Lake George theater. To be fair, Winslow had enough on his plate just keeping the campaign moving, and achieving local security was difficult enough, but more than once over the rest of the campaign he must have longed for the independent companies that Shirley had proposed and he had rebuffed. By early July Fort Edward had the reinforcement requested, and Winslow had high hopes for a scout "of two hundred and fifty men sent to reconoitre South Bay," some twenty miles away. Instead, he was exasperated to learn "that they are returned without doing that Duty, which a good Deal surprises me, as our Fortune Depends on Intelligence, and sufficient number can be spared, I should think, for that purpose."[41] He could not seem to understand why his scout-raising policies had produced so little result. Responding shamefacedly from Fort Edward, Colonels David Wooster and Timothy Ruggles reported that they had sent out another, smaller scout to do the job "and shall Continue the same Scouting, till Our people gett a good Acquaintance with the Country, which it seems notwithstanding all pretentions is not yett Obtained."[42]

Meanwhile, Winslow did his best to raise the men needed, move them north, and keep the supplies coming, all the while trying to keep his British superiors from interfering with his operations. He might have comforted himself, perversely, with the knowledge that the other elements of the year's grand strategy—directed by British army commanders—were no farther advanced than his own. Getting a jump on the French at Carillon was obviously no longer in the cards, but there was still the chance that the enemy, unable to adequately defend three (or four) fronts, had not reinforced the Lake George front too strongly. The only thing to do was to push forward and hope for the best.

4

"Ye very bane of New England Men"

"Poor Doggs"

It was not until the end of July 1756 that Winslow's army was ready to begin shifting its weight from the camps at Halfmoon, Stillwater, and Saratoga to Fort Edward and Fort William Henry, a positive step in more ways than one. Until the twentieth century, an army on the march was generally healthier than one forced to remain static—in garrison, in camp, besieging, or being besieged. Before World War I, armies generally lost far more men to illness than to the enemy. Certainly eighteenth-century people had little understanding of sanitation generally. In the close confines of the camp, town, or fort, diseases such as dysentery and typhoid fever could easily spread, placing hundreds or thousands of men in makeshift hospitals to recover or die. If particularly virulent diseases such as diphtheria or smallpox penetrated the army's lines, as they so easily could, they could wreck an army in weeks, ending a campaign as effectively as any climactic battle. Winslow's slowly gathering army managed to avoid such horrors for the first half of the summer; indeed, Jonathan Bagley wrote from Fort William Henry on July 6 to report that it was "a time of General Health in the Garrison, the people in high Spirits." Only eleven days later, however, the picture had changed; after relating the fatigues the garrison had been put to in preparation for the campaign, Bagley told his general that "the feaver and flux [dysentery] for this week past prevails." Even the surgeon's mate was sick, leaving the surgeon "more than he can do."[1]

There were other signs that sickness was working its inevitable way into the provincial army, though perhaps to no greater degree than might be expected. In a return of army strength that crossed Winslow's desk on June

19, the category "Invalids" appeared for the first time, with 207 out of a total of 5,971 men listed in that condition.[2] As long as that proportion—less than 4 percent—did not increase alarmingly, there was no need for serious concern. The trouble was that it did increase, and alarmingly, as the summer progressed. Back at Fort William Henry, Colonel Bagley grew more worried: by mid-July the men were "allmost worne out and are very sickly," and now even the surgeon, Dr. Otis, had the fever. Phineas Lyman, at Fort Edward, wrote to General Winslow that "our men are more sickley then when you left us," and at Albany so many bateau men had sickened "that we can hardly gett Our Fodder along for the Waggons' horses, and that must be done or all will fail." By July 26 the number of invalids in the army had more than trebled since the June return, to more than 10 percent of Winslow's men, prompting the general to admit to William Shirley that "we in the Army have a great many men Down with fluxes, [and a] few with fevers." Winslow thought the men would recover eventually, "yett these Distempers weaken us."[3]

The men's work load exhausted them, which did nothing to improve their general health. Soldiers are never simply fighters, of course, and it was expected from the beginning that the provincial troops would also be laborers. As early as May 10, the Committee of War urged Winslow to employ some of the men marching westward in "Assisting In the Transport of Provisions & c. . . . and for the Soldiers Encouragement the Court have allowed two shillings a day to Each man for his Extra service in Building and Refitting Battoes Lighters and Other Extra Work." Carpenters, smiths, and boat builders were encouraged to use their skills for the army, so long as they did not "Impose on the Province as to the Time taken up in Such Services"—a caveat that could be broadly interpreted. The committee also suggested drafting coopers out of the regiments "to take Care of the Casks, as they are from Time to Time Transported," a prudent safeguard no doubt, but one that also revealed how military service could be part of a patronage system. The committeeman writing the recommendation added, "& If you will allow us to mention a young man (Isaac Fowles) In Capt Benjs William's Comp. as One of Them, It will Greatly Relieve his distressed Parents As well as Gratifie us of the Comm^tee."[4] There was surely much to do to keep the campaign moving: boats, and wharves to accommodate them, had to be built at the lake; roads needed to be improved and mended to handle the heavy traffic; barracks and storehouses for supplies needed finishing; the fortified camp on the high ground near Fort William Henry required earthworks; clay pits had to be dug to furnish the material for bricks—all to be done by the men of the provincial regiments, whether specialists or not.

As the summer advanced, it was hot work in the open sun, occasionally fatal. July 8 must have been a particularly awful day, for "there were thre[e] men dyed with the he[a]t for it was very hot."[5] The farm boys who made up the majority of Winslow's soldiers were certainly no strangers to hard labor, but farm work was seasonal in nature, and measured: farmers and artisans could pace themselves, resting frequently as needed. The work required along this military road, by comparison, was heavy and relentless. Jehosaphat Starr reported complaints from Fort Winslow's commander that his soldiers, between their labors, guarding boats, and mounting guard, were "allmost worn Out," and if he did not get more men soon, "the Boats must Lay still for I Dayly see the Grumbling among the few men he has and the Great pains he takes to keep the Boats going." In mid-June, Jonathan Bagley, at Fort William Henry, explained that he was "Obliged to keep two hundred men dayly mending roads," and a month later he wrote that he "must realy Confess I have almost wore the men here Intirely out (poor Doggs)." Bagley was keeping long hours himself, asking his reader in a postscript to "Excuse blotts and Erasem[ts] for I am half a Sleep."[6] Also, the grumbling Jehosaphat Starr noticed was spreading: building roads and fortifications was not what this voluntary army had signed up for. Instead of moving against the enemies of God and Anglo-American civilization, it began to look to Massachusetts men as though they were there to build forts to protect New York. The men wanted to be soldiers, not forced labor. Officers desirous of keeping up company strength contributed inadvertently (one hopes) to the delays Winslow and the army were experiencing. At Fort Miller, on the upper Hudson, Hezekiah Gates reported that he was having difficulty getting men to volunteer for work on the bateaux, or to stay with it for long, because "the officers Discourag[e] them by Calling them Cowards and Otherways."[7] Whether they were digging, rowing, or just marching, throughout the army dirt and dust clung to sweaty clothes and bodies, and since few of the men had brought many changes of clothes with them, their garments began to rot. Thomas Moody, a provincial soldier subjected to just such a grueling regimen, asked himself, as surely others did too, "Well . . . how do you like Soldiering now?"[8]

Under these pressures, it is small wonder that discipline, such as it was in provincial units, may have begun to slip. Up to this point in the campaign, camp infractions had been relatively few, minor in nature, and probably underreported. In the record for late July and August, however, instances of indiscipline, some of them serious, appear more frequently. Unauthorized discharges of weapons continued to be a problem—one such instance involved William Drake, of Hodges' company—but there were also signs that the soldiers were becoming frustrated enough to take defiant action. Desertion was always a problem, for volunteer armies especially, but such instances tended to be infrequent, and individually specific, as in the case of the whaler Samuel Hunter. More serious was the case of a soldier confined "for threatning to Desert to the French," but such cases could be dealt with readily. Mass desertion, however, was a particularly worrisome and delicate situation, for these could snowball if not effectively countered, and the only means at hand to stop them was other volunteer soldiers, who might be more sympathetic to the deserters than to the officers who ordered them out against their fellows. Such was the case when, on July 28, "One Serjant, 2 Corps. and about forty Privates took upon them to March off In Open Day light," allegedly over the issue of their pay. They were "brought back"—by what means is not clear—but the "unhappy affair" was an indication that the general enthusiasm that had marked the beginning of the campaign was dissipating.[9]

Nor did the officers always set shining examples for the men. At a provincial court-martial in mid-August, Captain Joseph Johnson was found guilty of disobeying orders, and it was recommended that he be broken in rank. He had not had his men ready to march one morning at dawn as ordered, and had answered his superior "In a very Indifferent manner" that he would get to it in his own good time. A Lieutenant Mercer refused orders to go from Fort Edward to Fort William Henry; he felt that he had been assiduous in his duties, while another lieutenant had been slack, and said that "he would not Do any more Duty" until the other lieutenant pulled his own weight. Mercer demanded to know "wether the Government sent up Officers here for Others to do their Duty." He too was broken. Another lieutenant was lucky to be merely reprimanded for refusing to help a captain struggling to move a cannon, challenging him to "show his Authority." The lieutenant's defense was that he "should have helped [the captain] had he asked him Civily." A Captain Hammond was cashiered outright for dereliction of his duty. He had been given leave to stay temporarily in Albany on account of lameness, but unfortunately for him, several witnesses had seen him up and about the town. The court considered his excuse, that he was awaiting conveyance for his baggage, exceedingly lame indeed.[10] If their officers were blasé, surly, insubordinate, or shirkers, the men could hardly be blamed if they became so too. Nor could they take heart when their officers were clearly, even dangerously incompetent. When the officer of the day at Fort William Henry made his rounds and reached the guard under the command of Ensign John Miller, he found "no sentry at the Guard Door, nor any Other Person that Challenged the Rounds, nor Did the Officer know the Parole, but told him the Adjutant had not given him the Parole, and Did not know he should know It." Miller could only plead, accurately it appears, "that he was Young In the service and Knew no better."[11]

With all the work needed, there was little time for training the men in skills beyond the few they already had. There was apparently no designated area at the Halfmoon camp even for target practice, and any casual efforts were discouraged for reasons both pecuniary and of policy. For one thing, stores of powder and shot were not sufficient early in the campaign to warrant much live-fire practice.[12] Among the "Rules for Regulating the Camp" issued at Halfmoon on May 30 was an order against discharging weapons on pain of punishment. Surely this was in part a safety precaution common in most armies, and especially necessary among the accident-prone provincials. But the shortages plaguing the campaign seem evident in the further instruction that violators would also have deducted "Two Pence for every Charge of Powder and Ball Expended, to be paid by the Commanding Officer of Each Company and stopt out of the soldier's Pay." A better impression comes from General Winslow's orders for a field day a month later, on which occasion "each man may Discharge his Peice at a mark"—once—"and Orders to be given that they don't fire any more On their Parril." To save lead, the targets were on a large box of sand, so that the bullets could be recovered for reuse![13] Another reason for the general shooting ban was that with all the recent raids and alarms, the sounds of gunfire could be easily misinterpreted. Major Henry Babcock, commanding at Stillwater, found himself apologizing to Winslow for following his general's lead. "Honoured Sr," he began, "I was Informed . . . that you had given all the Troops Liberty at half moon to fire at Mark—agreable to that I gave Leave to all the Troops here to Fire at mark, not Imagining it was ever possible that small Armes Could be heard so far." But apparently they could, and we can imagine the reaction at

Halfmoon from Babcock's obvious embarrassment "that I have occasioned all this Trouble I am Sr. your most Obed^t. most Obliged and very humble servant."[14] As comic as these occurrences may seem to the modern reader, the continued lack of training did the would-be soldiers no favors.[15]

More serious than the dearth of firearms proficiency, perhaps, was the problem of unit cohesion. The habit of detaching platoons or companies of men from their regiments for extended work details, guarding wagons, poling bateaux, and scouting scattered large segments of the provincial contingents and defeated one of the purposes of regimental organization. The practice began early in the campaign, such as when a meeting of field officers in Albany, in order to secure the area around Fort Edward, decided to take detachments of men from several different regiments instead of simply assigning one of the regiments the task. In mid-June a scout of fifty men returned from Stillwater to the camp at Halfmoon "that was Detacht out of the several Regimts" there. The officer in charge at Stillwater had been reluctant to let them go, "as this place is short of men," and he asked for another detail to guard the boats. Labor gangs were put together in similar fashion. An officer reported from Fort Hardy in mid-June that the work "allways since I have been here hath Been Conducted by Detachments out of every Company here according to their Numbers fitt for Duty without regard to any Particular Province."[16] And as we have seen, General Winslow's peculiar philosophy regarding the many scouting missions he needed to assure local security meant that the polyglot makeup of the scout described above was typical. Juggling detachments from available regiments probably seemed the easiest solution to the myriad little emergencies that cropped up incessantly, but it meant that provincial regiments, seasonal organizations to begin with, rarely had the opportunity to forge anything approaching a sense of identity or unity of purpose or even to have the experience of working together consistently. For that matter, they rarely had full complements together at one time, further hampering training.

With sickness nibbling away at his army, and with many more men engaged in building projects, security, and reconnaissance, the "sharp end" of Winslow's spear was looking rather blunt. Most of his army was still well back from the jump-off point of Fort William Henry, in part for the very good reason that with preparations at the fort a long way from completion, it was easier to keep the army supplied when it was close to Albany. But sooner or later the army must move, or all the efforts made thus far would be in vain. That Winslow was eager to push on was never doubted by those who knew him. On June 9 Governor Stephen Hopkins, of Rhode Island (who twenty years later would sign the Declaration of Independence), had written to the general to caution him. He understood Winslow's impatience at the maddening delays but urged him not to "risque the main Cause without so much strength . . . for a Defeat would be almost as fatal to your Constituents as to you." It was good advice, but it only reminded Winslow that he was missing large numbers of men who ought to have been present and accounted for. To his previous appeal to the Massachusetts Council of War to hurry along the eleven hundred men (nearly a third of the colony's promised levy) missing from his army, he received the unhelpful response that the shortfall he had described was simply "Impossible."[17]

Standoff

What Winslow needed at least as much as men and material was knowledge of the enemy and his intentions, and he was getting little enough of that as well. Scouting missions performed by Winslow's provincials were dedicated to protecting his operations from assaults by the enemy; he had only Robert Rogers' company and about forty "Stockbridge" Indians led by Lieutenant (later Captain) Jacob Cheeksaunkun available for long-range reconnaissance purposes. For all the attention Rogers and his men were enjoying in the newspapers, and the acclaim heaped on them by admirers, he brought home only limited bits of information, and these helped Winslow form only a weak impression of what lay at the other end of the lake. Rogers had scouted Fort Carillon twice that year in the winter, when neither side could consider offensive movements, and only three times since May. He could rarely get close enough to the fort to accurately estimate French troop strength, though it was evident that the enemy was increasing in numbers and busily improving its defenses. Most of his scouting trips consisted in making observations from a distance, burning nearby houses and barns, and destroying cattle before skedaddling back to Fort William Henry, the hornets sufficiently aroused behind him. The best intelligence would come from prisoners nabbed in these raids, and a scout was considered particularly successful if it managed to carry away one or several captives.[18]

To be fair, Rogers and the Stockbridge Indians could only do so much. Rogers himself never had more than fifty-seven men for his forays, on one occasion only a dozen. Lieutenant Cheeksaunkun likewise might go out with only a handful of men at a time; they were in no position to challenge the large bands of French and Indians, frequently in the hundreds, that moved to and fro about the French lines and could respond decisively if they had even a hint that enemy rangers were in the vicinity. Cheeksaunkun reported one occasion on which he had to cut short his reconnaissance near Crown Point on account of the swarms of Indian scouts in the woods; his men were spotted, and they were hotly pursued for miles before finally losing their pursuers. With their advantage in numbers, the French and Indian woodsmen were largely able to keep nosey enemy scouts at a respectful distance.

So, what information Winslow received from his ranging companies was disappointingly infrequent and short on details. Better or verifying intelligence came from French prisoners, and only the rangers could bring these in. From one of these, an officer taken by Rogers in May, Winslow learned that "they have 4 French Regiments in Canada, one of which was at Ticonderoga and the other three were ordered to Fort Frontenac," supporting Rogers' round-figure estimate of one thousand men at the fort (which would include the garrison and laborers). The report must also have given Winslow some hope: if it was accurate, then three-quarters of the French regular troops in Canada, from whom he had the most to fear, would be far away if he could make his move on Carillon soon. But Winslow had to think again when only weeks later Rogers returned from a subsequent scout of the fort to report that (from the distance of half a mile) he now estimated that there were three thousand men there—this at a time when Winslow had barely fifteen hundred men at Forts Edward and William Henry. The picture was more confused by mid-July, even though Rogers had managed to bring back seven captives from Lake Champlain. These proved to be "raw country men, just impressed from St. John's," who gave vague statements about reinforcements and rumors of having six thousand soldiers at Ticonderoga— someday. "We got very little intelligence from them," was the general conclusion.[19] Even more perplexing were Rogers' insistence that the French were "strongly fortified at both Forts [Carillon and Crown Point]" and his now wildly inflated estimate of nine thousand troops at Carillon alone—enough to steamroll the Anglo-American forces all the way back to Albany.[20] Even if the French numbered half that, Winslow clearly could not launch his operation until the balance of force was more in his favor—if that ever occurred.

Operations in the Oswego sector were paralyzed too. From there the supply chain ran 170 miles to Albany, straight through the homeland of the

Six Nations; only the good offices of Sir William Johnson, and the relations he had built over decades with them, had secured their assent to this violation of their long-held neutrality. The garrison at Oswego suffered many of the same evils as those on the Lake George front. In the spring there had been "terrible" sickness, "men dying every day." At the same time "there were continual parties of Indians lurking round them," with little remedy for it. The arrival of the 50th and 51st Regiments in early June did little to change the situation. By late June Winslow had received news that the forts had been attacked by from six hundred to seven hundred Indians, who killed men guarding the fort's whaleboats and boldly strode out from the woods to take potshots at the fort and dare the garrison to come out and do something about it.[21] The strategic plan for 1756 had called for offensive operations from Oswego against the French forts on the lake; with half the summer gone and the garrison semi-besieged, that seemed an increasingly unlikely scenario.

The game seemed to change dramatically for the better in the last week of July, and this time the intelligence was fresh, detailed, and from people in a position to know: three French deserters from Carillon itself. At least one of them, Thomas St. Law, was a soldier in the "Canadian Colony Troops," that is, the *troupes de la marine,* so called because the French colonies in America were under the jurisdiction of the Ministry of Marine. St. Law had come to Canada two years earlier and had been part of Carillon's garrison for half that time. He was forthcoming, as deserters are wont to be, and told his interrogators that there were about 3,500 men at the fort (much closer to Rogers' earlier estimates), of which 1,200 were regulars recently arrived from France, and 112 Indians (an interestingly precise number). There were 400 men at the "advance guard" at the north end of Lake George, guarding the only feasible landing sites along that steeply vertical shore (Rogers had accurately assessed this defensive outpost also). A mere 80 to 100 men garrisoned Crown Point. There seemed to be no immediate plan to attack the English forts. The most St. Law could say was that he had heard of a 600-man raid to go somewhere and do something; it had been *discussed* for a long time, he said, but there had been no signs of it yet. There was additional scuttlebutt to the effect that 1,500 more men were expected from France that year, but how and where they would be disposed was anyone's guess. There was talk of a reinforcement of both French and Indians for Carillon, "but where they were to come from they could not tell." The other deserters, questioned separately, confirmed St. Law's story.[22]

There was more. The fort had twelve cannons mounted, but not yet its bigger ones, which threw fearsome eighteen-pound cannonballs. Moreover, they assured their listeners, "the fortifications at Ticonderoga were not far advanced." The west wall was "the height of ten pieces of timber," but "the parts towards the narrows of Wood Creek anybody could leap over"—so much for Rogers' "strongly fortified." The ground surrounding the fort had been cleared of trees to a distance of only about a quarter mile. Provisions at the fort were low—perhaps two months' worth—and of poor quality. "Their pork and flower were very bad," they reported; the men lived mostly on peas, of which they did seem to have plenty. Most encouraging, perhaps, was the news that the soldiers "were very sickly. . . . [a] great many of them ill of the scurvy which raged amongst them." One more valuable piece of information was "that they were surprised to see our army so far advanced."[23]

Mixed though the message was, it was the best news Winslow had had for some time. Those twelve hundred French regulars were certainly a concern, but the great bulk of the force at Carillon would be colony troops and Canadian militia—no better, perhaps, than his own provincials, and many of the enemy were sick with a seriously debilitating disease. The reported number of French-aligned Indians on hand could be managed by his own rangers and provincial scouts, and there were apparently no French reserves at Crown Point. Winslow had some forty-six hundred men at Forts William Henry and Edward; if he could get more of the men promised him, and move them north quickly, he would have numerical superiority at least, perhaps a thousand or more men than the French, and of course he would not be bringing his sick men along. Surprise would be on his side; the French deserters intimated that the enemy was not expecting an attack anytime soon. If the four-hundred-man advance guard at the bottom of Lake George could be overwhelmed quickly and the landing sites secured, he would be able to march his army the two short miles to the unfinished fort. His men would be safe from Carillon's cannon until the last quarter mile of cleared ground. The French would have to fight him, for the fort could only hold five hundred or so. If his men showed spirit and Providence favored them, Carillon might be theirs within a week, start to finish—certainly before much help could arrive from Canada. And with only a skeleton garrison at Crown Point . . .

At least it was an opportunity such as might not come again, a window that might be open for only a short time. Winslow was at Fort Edward when he read the deserters' story, and he did not hesitate. "Upon hearing this information [he] sent out a chosen [command] of 300 on a scout" to head off a rumored raiding party and to get more confirmation if possible.[24] In the meantime he gave orders to move more of his army toward the lake; Winslow wrote Colonel Bagley to inform him that he was sending a thousand men from Fort Edward his way, both to increase security in the area and to forward the mission. Winslow had his tail up; his men were going to "Curb the Insolence of the French" at last. Additional cannon had been sent to Fort William Henry recently, and their passage over the raw, rutted military road had nearly destroyed their carriages, but they had been quickly repaired, "the wheels allmost made new." When Winslow reached Fort William Henry, he was miffed to find that military discipline at the lake was slack, noting that "Divers Soldiers and Others, take Freedom without Liberty, to go a fishing, and for other uses Improve [i.e., use] the Boats and Battauxs Belonging to the Army, by reason of which many of them are lost and Damaged."[25] The general also griped at the continued shortage of manpower, noting ruefully that the Massachusetts contingent was still "shamefully short of Our Numbers." Nonetheless, he wrote hopefully on July 28 that "if the boats are in forwardnes I hope In One Fortnights time [we] shall attempt the other end of the Lake."[26]

Alas, it proved a vain hope. The logistical difficulties that had retarded the operation since the spring plagued it yet. As Winslow's last remark suggests, the boats necessary to transport his army and cover his proposed landing still lacked essential materials not locally available. After viewing the progress at the lake days later, Winslow concluded that "Water Carriage is the thing we most want" to put the plan into effect, and apparently it was not the absence of hulls that was the holdup. Rather, wrote Winslow, the larger vessels—gondolas and lighters—needed more cordage than had been sent. Worse—and this must have given Winslow fits—the necessary sails had not yet even been ordered! To save time, Winslow begged that sufficient canvas be sent directly to the lake, to be fabricated there. Taking no chances, Winslow, displaying his maritime savvy, warned the suppliers not to be stingy: the sails would be large, and cheap material would only split under the pressure of the wind. The boats also needed more blocks, pumps, and other hardware. Betraying his state of mind, in a postscript he added, "Dispatch is the Life of the Cause,"[27] but he could hardly expect to get everything ready before mid-August, and by that time the situation at Carillon might have changed dramatically, the window of opportunity shut for good. In desperation, Winslow even ordered his rangers to look for any place along the lake where a road might be cut to bring his artillery to Ticonderoga. They gamely looked (although anyone familiar with the geography of the lake might doubt how seriously they tried) but had to give their commander the disappointing facts: artillery and wagons simply could not go there by land, and the French guarded the only place where Winslow could disembark his army.[28] From Albany there was yet more unwelcome news: some of the munitions for the regular regiments had come in, but it was unclear whether any provincial units could have them, and anyway they would need "Suitable Waggons and Guards" to convey them, "for there is none in these Parts." If Winslow's army consumed what had already been sent them, "we see not how It will be in our powers to replace It."[29]

"Little better than dead Men"

At least the supply line was more secure. Winslow's scouting parties, the heavy guards placed at every transshipment point, and the armed escorts accompanying every wagon and boat were having their desired effect. The enemy raids along the Hudson corridor had trailed off in late June and July, but Indian bands about the upper forts could still be troublesome. On the very day that Winslow had decided to act on the deserters' information, two hired teamsters going out from Fort William Henry to bring in their grazing oxen were killed and scalped by Indians hidden some sixty rods from the fort; the Indians then killed the oxen they had used as bait and peppered the fort walls with bullets. Provincial soldiers responded, trading shots with the enemy and pursuing them about a mile, but as usually happened in such cases, "they Outrun Our Party and got off." Two additional men were wounded in the running skirmish.[30] It wasn't that Colonel Bagley, commanding at the fort, did not take reasonable countermeasures. He "constantly" kept small scouting parties out on both sides of the lake, but these could "make no Discovery but the Tracks of small Partys who are Plaguing us constantly." Bagley could not keep the frustration out of his reports to General Winslow. "What Vixes me most," he grumbled, was "that we Cann't Catch none of the sons of whores." He tried sending out, under cover of night, "skulking partys some distance from the Sentrys in the night to Ly

Still in the Bushes to Intercept [the Indians] when they Attempt to Catch our out Sentrys," but he had no luck there either; the clouds of deer flies and mosquitoes were "so pesky our people can't bear them and are obliged to return."[31] The probability that at any given moment dangerous, unseen enemies lurked just beyond the cleared ground was simply a fact of life at the forts. As the bulk of Winslow's army moved toward Fort William Henry, even a flock of sheep received an armed escort.[32]

The lack of transport, problematic logistics, and Indians were bad enough, but equally worrisome in August was an acceleration of disease casualties in Winslow's army. The Reverend John Graham, chaplain for the Connecticut troops, was receiving an education in the realities of spiritual mentoring among young men far from home. Much of the journal he wrote of his experiences is a litany of complaint about the "awfull growing wicked[ness] of the Camp," but at Fort Edward on August 10 he recorded that while other "things remain in much the same Situation," "the Sickness Encreases very fast, and deaths multiplied."[33] The situation only grew worse as the season progressed, so that by the twenty-second Winslow had to confess to Lord Loudoun that at Fort William Henry he found "the Camp Disorder Prevalent near a Third Part not fitt for Duty." Those who were the worst off found little comfort where they ought to have found the most. Winslow was shocked to hear that some of his officers had "stripped the Hospital of Bed, Sacks and Sheets, provided for the Sick" for the officers' own comfort, "so that the Sick really suffer." There may have been something to this charge, and worse. Investigating, Winslow discovered incompetence as well as downright theft. He wrote angrily that the sick were "not Only Suffering but Dying for Necessarys; [I] can't Conceive why those things are not forwarded or what service they Can be of If not used In season for the Preservation of mens Lives." Winslow's clerks told him that according to their records he should have "560 bb: [barrels] Chocolate, Quantitys of Vinegar, 4 Barrels of Limejuce [suggesting that scurvy had set in at both ends of the lake], Barrel of Tin Spout Cups, bedpans, Close Stool pans, &c none of which I can find ever Came to hand, neither Candles nor Soup [soap?] Issued." Winslow had no one to accuse, and just where the "neglect" had occurred he could not say, "but Surely It is no Jesting matter to Triffle with mens lives."[34]

Those who remained relatively healthy were being worn down quickly and themselves becoming candidates for the hospital. In mid-month Colonel Joseph Dwight described the toll being taken by the continuous security work and keeping the army supplied:

> We have had full Employ for our People to guard all the Roads from the half moon, Every Day to the Lake and keep out necessary Scouts, In so much that It has been Vastly Difficult to find men fit for the Duty of the Day that have not been 24 Hours already on hard Duty. We have never had less than 500 men upon the Road at a Time between the 2 upper forts for 6 or 8 weeks past and am sure we have never wasted an Hour of time Thro Idleness or Inattention to Business.

Dwight was sure, even if Winslow was not, that all this toil had succeeded in accomplishing its objective. According to his estimation, even 2 weeks earlier "We had Provisions at Fort W——m H——y sufficient for 8000 men 8 weeks to which daily additions have been making."[35]

By the end of the month, however, illness in the army and the inability to halt it had all but ended any serious hope of prosecuting the campaign. After an inspection of the fort, which British soldiers were scheduled to garrison that winter, Lieutenant Colonel Ralph Burton wrote to Lord Loudoun blasting the provincials' creation and the conditions pertaining there. "At Fort William Henry," he wrote, there were "about 2,500 men, 500 of them sick [a smaller proportion than even Winslow had admitted but still crippling], the greatest part of them what they call poorly." He reported that the sickness was lethal, writing that "they bury from five to eight daily, and officers in proportion."[36] Conditions were as bad, or worse, at Fort Edward, according to the surgeon Thomas Williams, and he saw the hand of God in it: "Divine Providence seems to frown on our present Expedition in sending a grievous sickness amongst our Troops & frequent death, whereby we are weakened dayly, burying 5 or 6 a day at this place for some days past." Similar to the conditions Winslow reported at Fort William Henry, there were, Williams reckoned, "not more than 2 thirds of our Army fit for service, & those extremely dispirited, & disheartened, not half the men they were when they came from home." The men's hopes for quick recovery were small, and "scarce any will be of future service this Campaign." Even those whose fevers broke, for whom the immediate dangers were past,

> seam to pine away & wither like a Cabbage plant, with ye heat of the sun, & I fear will die, as many others have, in a strange way, when apprehended to be getting

well; I think it must be for want of Fresh Air, warm Lodgings, proper nursing, and a suitable nutritious diet, as Vegetables, Milk, & roots, which they hanker after extremely. but those things are not to be had here.

Williams concluded that these conditions had in fact been predictable; they would "necessarily follow from long Encampments; it is ye very bane of New England Men, what their constitutions cannot bear, & indeed proves almost as bad to them as Ratsbane." And yet the work at both forts was unrelenting. Virtually every surviving journal of those soldiers present testifies to the unremitting labor: the struggle to finish and improve Fort William Henry; the efforts to make Fort Edward defensible in its own right. Williams reported that he had heard that General Winslow had begged the New England governments for a large number of replacements, and "large they must be if we go on with any probability of Success," wrote Williams, "for the Troops we have here are but little better than dead Men."[37]

For his part, Colonel Burton was sure what the "bane" of New England men was: they were, he observed, "Extremely indolent and dirty, to a degree." Depending on the wind, one might smell Fort William Henry long before ever catching sight of it. "The Fort stinks enough to cause infection," Burton complained, and the reason was not hard to find. "They have all their sick in [the fort], their Camp nastier than anything I could conceive, their Necessary Houses, Kitchens, Graves and places for slaughtering cattle, all mix through their Encampment."[38] In the sultry summer months especially, the smell of thousands of sweating, unwashed men, of the feces of both man and beast, of discarded and unburied entrails of slaughtered animals was overpowering even to denizens of the eighteenth century. Toxic too: in 1760 one Captain Jenks "recorded taking walks as long as 'five or six miles, in order to keep out of the smell of the camp'" to avoid infection.[39] Inside the fort itself the stench must have been gag-inducing, for that was where the hundreds of emaciated sick and dying were housed, stricken with lethal diarrhea, vomiting, and scurvy. The water from the fort's well, the most accessible source for the sick men, was "not fit for drinking."[40] Years later, even at a camp administered by the British army, a provincial soldier recorded his revulsion when he visited the hospital: "Of all the smells that ever I smelt there never was none that smelt so bad."[41] Fort William Henry had become a hellhole, a sweltering, noxious disease environment that bid fair to destroy Winslow's army.

Based on Burton's report, Loudoun decided that it was necessary to school his provincial counterpart on the fundamentals of camp hygiene. "Dirt and Filth, If there is any," he offered diplomatically, "should be Immediately Cleared Out of Camp, and none suffered to be In It for the future." The men's tents needed to be opened at least twice each week, weather permitting, and ideally struck down entirely, "In Order to dry the Ground under them." Slaughtering of cattle needed to be done in one designated area, and at "such a Distance from the Camp, as It may have no annoyance from the Putred Smells that come from thence, which are very harmful to the Mens healths; the Butchers should be Obliged to Bury all their Refuse that is sometimes Left rotting on the Ground, when they are not Carefully Lookt after." "Perticular Care" had to be taken regarding "your houses of Office [latrines], to remove them far in your rear as you Can." They needed to be filled up each week, and new ones dug, lest they "Infect the whole Air." This was especially important "If you are Troubled with fluxes, for nothing breeds more Infection than men going to houses of Office, where men with bad Fluxes have been." Lastly, the many burials taking place "should Likewise be removed at some distance from the Camp," not so much as a matter of hygiene as because "when there are [so] many it is better to bury them a Little further off, as it is a Disagreeable Sight, for those that remain, to see numbers of the Graves of their Companions."[42]

"A sad omen of what is comin"

With all of the difficulties and discouragements facing him, Winslow did not need the letter that arrived in mid-August from his former commander, William Shirley. In a long discourse, Shirley argued that Winslow ought to agree to accept help from the redcoat regiments at Loudoun's disposal, a joining of forces that Winslow had long resisted, with Shirley's support. Now Shirley was changing his tune, urging Winslow to face reality:

> The Enemy, we have reason to Think, are at least 3000, among which is a Considerable Body of Regular Troops, their works are strong, and you must Expect to find them Entrenched under Cover of their Cannon; your Provincials Consist, as you Observe of new raised Troops, of Different Governments, not well Disciplined, and Altogether unexperienced in every part of Regular Service; you can't reckon upon more then 6000 men fit for Duty among them, which without a Considerable Body of Regular Troops to Support them would not be Eaqual to

an attack of the French works, defended with so Strong a Body of Troops as they must have at Tionderoga [*sic*].

Unless Winslow acquired regulars of his own to take the lead in the operation, Shirley concluded, "I think Defeat and Ignominy are now Likely to be your Lott."[43]

It was sound advice, and Shirley was being realistic, but Winslow's disappointment is easy to imagine. After some soul-searching, however, he took up his pen to respond. "It has seldom hapened in the Course of many years," he wrote, "that I have differed In point of Judgement from your Excellency, which in some measure is now the Case." Winslow reminded Shirley that he himself had been instrumental in making the conquest of Crown Point an all-provincial operation. Winslow argued, with some reason, that if the colonies had waited until His Majesty's pleasure had been known, nothing would have been done, and the French would now control everything north of Albany. He also reiterated his position that a juncture with regulars, which would necessarily place the provincials under British army authority, would be disastrous; the New Englanders especially were too "Tenatious of their own Rights." Winslow believed that with luck and the promised reinforcements, his provincial army could still pull off an attack on Ticonderoga at least.[44]

Whatever the actual prospects for the Crown Point campaign might have been (and it is difficult to disagree with Shirley's assessment), the point became suddenly, dramatically, and decisively moot. While Winslow's army was stalled at the south end of Lake George, the French had made their move. Commanding 1,300 white-coated regulars recently arrived from France, some 1,500 colony troops and militia, and at least 250 Indians, the Marquis de Montcalm had pounced unexpectedly on Oswego and taken it in just a few days. Exploiting his advantage in water-borne transport, his mixed force, with all its supplies and artillery, had appeared before the British forts on August 11 after leaving Montreal just twenty days earlier. Completely surprised by the unexpected attack, the 1,100 or so men in the unfinished and poorly situated forts at Oswego stood little chance. After offering only weak resistance, the garrison surrendered on August 14. At a stroke, the Anglo-Americans' only toehold on the Great Lakes, along with its guns, stores, and vessels, was lost. Montcalm would not grant the garrison honors of war for what he considered an ineffectual and halfhearted defense; instead they were sent as prisoners of war to Montreal. The Indian troops looted the fort, killing and scalping from 30 to 100 sick and wounded in the hospital and taking some prisoners. The French destroyed the fort and everything they could not carry with them, then left the way they had come.[45]

The British and provincials' reaction was something like panic. A reinforcement of British regulars had reached a strategic carrying place about halfway to Oswego when they learned the news of its fall; without trying to establish whether the French were moving eastward to attack the Mohawk River valley settlements (they were not), the British commander ordered the storehouses at the carrying place burned, and then his force retreated toward Albany. As a result, rumors abounded of an unstoppable French force marching "full tilt" toward German Flats. When the word reached Albany on August 23, Charlotte Brown wrote in her journal, "Every one here in the greatest Distress for we expect the French will be at Albany soon."[46] At Fort Edward, Thomas Williams also heard the rumors and hoped they would prove untrue, "as the reverse would be such a terrible shock as the Country never felt." A Calvinist to his core, Williams feared that the fall of Oswego "may be a sad omen of what is comin upon poor sinful New England, perhaps a Reduction of it to ye French Power. . . . Indeed when we consider our Wickedness & y^t Pitch it is arrived to, we cant expect any thing, but to be severely chastised, 'till we are humbled for our Pride, & haugtiness, & become a reformed People."[47]

The reason for all this distress had to do, once again, with geography. Oswego's military significance for the Anglo-Americans lay in its potential to choke off communications between the French and their Ohio and Great Lakes forts and settlements. To that end, a long supply line to Oswego extended west from Albany through relatively flat lands and waterways. With Oswego in French hands, that same route pointed like a dagger in the opposite direction, toward a suddenly vulnerable-looking Albany. Lord Loudoun had been on the job in America barely a month, but he certainly understood that "This Post of *Albany* is a *material one*; here are our Magazines, here is the only Communication with the low Countries; here Centers the Communication with *Crown Point*; and here Centers the Communications with *Oswego*, and all the Country above this, on that Road; from whence we draw a great part of our Provisions; and from this, the People advanced, must be totally supplied." For all its strategic importance, however, Albany was "defenseless by its situation, and at present has only a rotten Stockade, which we are repairing, for at present we are not able to do more." Worse, the enemy could approach it by any of three routes: from the west via the Mohawk River valley, from the north via Lake George, and from Lake Champlain via South Bay and Wood Creek. Protecting Albany was vital; "here is the place where we have every thing to collect, and indeed almost every thing to get; the People of the Country to be brought to be Serviceable, which is not the case at present; and every thing to forward from hence."[48]

And although Loudoun would not have appreciated the significance, the loss of Oswego made British relations with the neutral Six Nations even worse. Against the better judgment of many of them, they had allowed the British to build the forts at Oswego and to pass freely through their lands to keep it supplied. The fall of Oswego was an embarrassment, to say the least, and made them liable to be treated by the French as openly hostile. A Six Nations delegation told a provincial officer at the head of the Mohawk River that "they must and should be gone"; that they had granted leave to Governor Shirley to occupy and build on the strategic carrying place, and only for a year, "upon his promising to come this Year with a Very great Army and Settle their Trade upon good and Advantageous footing so that they should not be imposed upon by any one and other pompous pretentions." The Six Nations had duly waited "two Seasons to see what great Feats we were capable of Doing; and found we were incapable of doing any thing." In contrast, the exasperated delegates observed, "the French were quite otherwise: . . . they told what they designed open & Boldly, and when they had done so they Effected it."[49]

Despite the grand design and high hopes for the campaign year, the British and provincial forces had been unable to seize and hold the initiative. Free to act, the French, the Canadians, and the Indians had done just that, and by taking Oswego they had turned the strategic situation upside down: now it was the Anglo-Americans who feared invasion, from an enemy who might attack they knew not where. "We are at present groping very much in the dark," complained Loudoun; "no Intelligence; no part of the Country reconnoitred; few Men to Act . . . . I must endeavor to remedy that total want of *Intelligence* in this Country; the distances are so great, and no way has never been tried, but by Indians, who are in no Shape to be relied on, that we really know nothing at present: And I am at a loss to Judge what Step the Enemy will take on this Success." Still new to his command and contemptuous of how the campaign had been managed so far, Loudoun would take no chances. On the same day he wrote to explain the local situation to his superiors across the Atlantic, he wrote to inform General Winslow of Oswego's fall, and of an end to Winslow's ambitions, "I must Necessarily for the present make an Alteration [in the Crown Point initiative]." Loudoun explained that because of the priority of defending Albany, he now had few men to support a push northward, so "if you, In proceeding to attack Tionderoga [sic] before we are Reinforced from New England, should meet with any Misfortune . . . It might not be in my Power to stop the Enemy's over Running the whole Country." He directed Winslow to think no more about attacking the French and instead to go over to the defensive.[50] Winslow faced the facts and did so, though reluctantly. The French and their Indian allies had wrecked the Anglo-American strategic plan for the year, and in doing so they had set in train the destruction of Captain Hodges and his men.

5

Slaughter

"Continual scouts"

The loss of Oswego had made clear that while forts protected, they also needed protecting. Accordingly, General Winslow "Ceased Preparation" for the campaign, instead ordering "all hands to Fortify and Intrench up to the Eyes" at Fort William Henry. His greatest concern was for Fort Edward, and he urged General Phineas Lyman there to "take the same method." If the French attacked in strength via Lake George, they would encounter an immediate check to their operation in the form of Fort William Henry and its entrenched garrison. Putting himself in his enemy's place, Winslow could readily see that Fort Edward was the greater threat to his position at the lake. If they chose, the French could transport their army entirely by water to the South Bay of Lake Champlain and up Wood Creek, landing unopposed (and probably undetected) only twenty-one miles from Fort Edward—just as they had done the year before. If Fort Edward were invested, Fort William Henry would be cut off; if Fort Edward fell, Fort William Henry would be untenable. Winslow knew that the former was "not so defensible" as the latter, and so he advised Lyman to "lett no time be Lost, for It is not unlikely you'l have a Viset from these Gentry, and It behoves us of all things to be prepared to Receive them Properly."[1]

Winslow might affect levity, but the situation was serious enough, especially as shortages continued to afflict the provincials' efforts. In an update penned days later, Winslow fumed to Lyman that his men should have finished the breastworks surrounding the camp at the lake but that they still lacked, of all things, entrenching tools. Winslow felt "Greatly Deceived In that Point By the store keeper, as I was told these things were forwarded here." Just as annoying to Winslow was the revelation that "we are at this place out of all small Stores" and that the Massachusetts contingent had not "more than a weeks allowance of Rum and Sugar." Lyman could do little to help; indeed, he had more immediate concerns, asking Winslow, "If you have any Cartridge paper suitable for Cartridges for small Armes please to Order some for we have not any."[2]

Fueling the renewed urgency at both forts was the near-absolute absence of specific intelligence regarding the enemy's strength, capability, and intentions. Winslow was "sadly off for Intelligence," he admitted, and there were scant means at hand for a remedy. Few Six Nations Indians were willing to openly back the seemingly feckless Anglo-Americans. The loss of Indian support meant that there would be no great numbers of forest-wise allies capable of pushing back or penetrating the screen so effectively put in place by their French-aligned counterparts. That was unfortunate, particularly as the Stockbridge Indians with the army, though few in number, had demonstrated their potential for gathering information. In July, two Stockbridge Indians had left Fort Edward to reconnoiter Crown Point, some fifty-five miles away. Reaching their destination, they had "Tarried One night on the High Land back of the Fort and in the Morning approach'd very near." Returning by way of the west side of Lake George, "about halfway to Fort William Henry. . . they Came aCross a Track of the Enemy traveling up near the side of the Lake." They had followed the trail until it was clear that the group had divided, upon which they made their way into Fort William Henry to report. The whole excursion had taken just six days.[3] About the same time, Lieutenant Cheeksaunkun had led twenty Indians and two white men to probe the environs of Fort Carillon. Before returning nine days later, they had twice observed the French fort, seeing there "a great many Tents . . . more In Number than we have at Fort William Henry and the Camp at Fort Edward," and counting eight storehouses, "a great many Barrels" on the shore, and "a Great Many Battaux." They had come back with two scalps, having ambushed some French soldiers near the advance guard. On this occasion, Cheeksaunkun had shown that English-allied Indians could also leave calling cards for the enemy to find: discovering that one of the men shot was not dead, "I immediately stuck my tom hawk Into the side of his head and there Left It."[4]

Cheeksaunkun's report of his scout may have left much to be desired from the English standpoint. "A Great Many" was hardly specific, and he would surely have done better to take a live prisoner, provided that had been possible. But apart from the imprecise language (and Rogers did not always do better), Cheeksaunkun's report was not a bad one, and his performance suggests the potential for far more effective raiding and intelligence-gathering if he had had anything like the numbers of his opponents. It was an indication of what the Anglo-Americans were missing by losing so much Native support. Then again, the whites were hampered by their own inability to recognize the potential for Native American reconnaissance and their unwillingness to appreciate what they did get. When Lord Loudoun complained of "that total want of *Intelligence* in this Country," he added (incorrectly) that no alternative had been explored "but by Indians, who are in no Shape to be relied on." Winslow the American shared the prejudice of Loudoun the Briton: at the end of August, when two Indians had come in from the north end of Lake Champlain reporting that they had seen one schooner on the lake and innumerable bateaux already built and being built, Winslow had sniffed, "But as this is Indian News, I Dont make much Dependence on It and Indeed am not fond of their Company in Camp being Suspicious of the whole Nation." This was unfortunate, because the substance of Cheeksaunkun's report was soon confirmed by others.[5] Cheeksaunkun and his men had made two more scouts to Ticonderoga by the first week of September.

Nor was Rogers' company of rangers able to fill the intelligence void. In mid-August, before the news of Oswego had reached the English, he led a scout via whaleboats to the outskirts of St. Jean, on the Richelieu River. There he captured a small family—"a man, woman, and girl of about ten years old"—and returned with them to Fort William Henry. The man was the only one of the three with information, but even his was vague enough. He told of some four thousand men at Ticonderoga and volunteered other information about the place, although he admitted "that he never was at Ticonderoga or at the advance guard." Apparently Rogers did not attempt to view Ticonderoga himself on this trip, so the intelligence was hardly definitive.[6] He returned to scout Ticonderoga only once more before mid-September, but without securing prisoners and still with no notion of the enemy's intentions. But at least he was trying, and his efforts had earned him not only frequent mention in American newspapers but apparently a nickname among his adversaries. The "Great Rogers," wrote William Williams, had come to be called by Indians "the Snipe because he can hide himself from them in the Grass." It is small wonder that Rogers later preferred "White Devil," a more menacing-sounding sobriquet.[7]

For the provincials, frustrated in their efforts to discover what the enemy was up to thirty miles away, but fearing the worst, scouting for local security took on a new urgency. Knowing the routes by which a French army must come, their best option, in addition to improving their forts' defenses, was to establish a system that would give them the earliest possible warning, interdict enemy scouts and raiders, and perhaps even harry an enemy's advance. At Fort Edward the task was straightforward: "We immediately agreed to set the whole body of men here to intrenching, and to settle particular officers and small partys of men to keep intelligence between South Bay, Wood Creek, and this Fort."[8] For Winslow, at the lake, the response to the new strategic situation was likewise clear. An enemy approach was at least theoretically possible on both the east and west sides of Lake George, despite its rocky and precipitous shoreline. Earlier in the summer, provincials at the fort had watched as, far out on the lake, a sizeable flotilla of French bateaux and canoes had come into view before turning into what is today Dunham Bay, about four miles north of the fort on the east side. Nothing, apparently, had come of this excursion (the boats, and the men they carried, were gone by the time provincials arrived on the scene), but it alerted the English to the possibility that the enemy was exploring landing sites nearby. Inlets there provided access to gaps through the mountains, which in turn led to more traversable ground approaching Fort William Henry from the south, cutting it off from Fort Edward. It was an unlikely route for a full-scale invasion, but it could not be ignored. On the west side there were also potential landing sites, and there the coast was not as broken up by inlets as on the east, permitting either friendly or enemy forces to move with greater speed and facility. There had been several known instances of enemy activity on the west side of the lake, and doubtless many more had gone undetected. Also, about eleven or twelve miles from the fort on the west side, there were excellent bays and coves where enemy scouts probably beached their canoes. It might be a good place to ambush the enemy (which the provincials as yet had been unable to do). Additionally, the area possessed points from which provincial scouts could observe enemy activity at the "first narrows" of the lake, where it jogs to the northeast past the commanding Shelving Rock.

Winslow had an additional option, of which he took full advantage. Any serious attack on Fort William Henry would have to come by water, and the provincial army had a decisive advantage there. The sloop-rigged lighters the provincials had been building all summer were sufficiently completed and furnished with cannon by September 2 for General Winslow himself to lead a reconnaissance by water down the lake, nearly to the French advance guard. Accompanied by 190 volunteers in whaleboats, the lighters swept unopposed down the lake, driving a smaller French vessel before them until they reached the "last narrows" (probably just past today's Heart Bay), beyond which it was not prudent to take the lighters. Firing a parting shot "at random," the flotilla returned, having lost one man, who had fallen overboard and drowned. The cruise convinced Winslow (and probably the French as well) that the provincial flotilla on the lake could counter any threat from the water. It also convinced him that, once again, he had not been as well served by his scouts as he would have liked; he had "no plan [map] of the Lake that I have yett seen In the Least like It."[9]

Practically speaking, the boats could not keep up a constant presence on the lake. What was needed on land, then, were relatively hefty-sized scouts, capable both of reconnaissance and of taking on similar-sized enemy units should they meet any. Winslow needed no prodding from Lord Loudoun to put such a plan into practice, though Loudoun prodded him anyway. It was at least comforting, perhaps, for Winslow to realize that the commander in chief and he thought so nearly alike in this regard. Loudoun ventured to advise that "in your Present Situation, what Occurs to be the most necessary point to Guard against, is the Enemys coming to you, by either side of the Lake, and in Case they Attempt It, you will have the same Advantage, in harrassing and Cutting them off In their March as they would have had of you, in going to them; and I think Proper Poasts should be secured for that Purpose, and Continual Scouting parties to bring you timely Notice."[10] In short order, provincial commanders at Fort William Henry worked out a routine for keeping out "Continual scouts" on both sides of the lake. These scouts were company-strength units of about fifty men, each commanded by a captain, a lieutenant, an ensign, and several noncommissioned officers, the rest being private soldiers. Consistent with Winslow's philosophy, the scouting companies were made up of volunteers from among the available regiments rather than men of any single company under their nominal captain. As we have seen, this was in part for practical reasons, as because of sickness and detached duties few original companies still had their full complement of men. Just how great the mixture of men might be for any given patrol we will see.[11]

As for the scouts' operation, that too became familiar. The scouts gathered in late afternoon or at dusk and marched out of the encampment, covering from one to several miles before bedding down for the night, at the same time setting an ambush for enemies who might pass their way. On the east side, the scout moved out the next morning, following the lakeshore as far as "East Bay" (probably today's Warner Bay), looking for signs of enemy landings. About midday they turned south-southwest, keeping to the back of the mountains to the east of Fort William Henry, presumably along the track an enemy would use to approach the fort. After camping for the night, the scout turned northwest for home base, finding the military road they had probably helped build a few miles south of the fort. On the west side, the scout left its camp/ambush site and headed northerly along the lakeshore until it reached the bays looking down the Narrows. After investigating, they camped for the night and spent the following day returning to Fort William Henry. Upon the return of these two scouts, two more went out to repeat the process.[12] If there was a potentially dangerous predictability in the routines just described, the scouts, each a reconnaissance in force, constituted a reasonable response to the likeliest enemy threats and were an integral part of the defenses of the fort the provincials had labored to build. At least a dozen such scouts, involving hundreds of men, were raised in the month following the bad news from Oswego. Robert Rogers has claimed the lion's share of popular attention with regard to scouting, but from the beginning of the 1756 campaign to its end, it was provincial volunteers, in far greater numbers, who performed the less glamorous but essential duty of providing local security.

Which is not to say that they were always good at it. On one scout commanded by David Darling, of Newport, Rhode Island, a nervous soldier fired at what he swore was "two men One with a laced hatt the Other an Indian." Darling, who apparently knew something about tracking, went to investigate, but when he got to the spot where the apparitions had been said to be, he "Could not Discover any Signes of the Enemy, for our People had been there before I came, and Trampled round the Place So I could not tell wether the Enemy had been there or no." Darling pushed on in the direction the "enemy" had supposedly run, but "Discovered no Tracks." Probably deciding that the shooter had made up the story to cover his ineptitude, Darling re-joined his men, but after they went through a swamp and over a ridge of land, a signal came down the line to halt. Three men now claimed to have seen an Indian. Ordering his men to stay put this time, Darling again investigated, but again "Could not Discover neither Indian nor Track." Then it began to rain heavily, and "the men told me they Could not keep their Peices Dry." Deciding that he could do nothing more with these men (who were either starting at shadows or fabricating reasons to return), Darling led them back to the fort.[13]

Men could become separated from their fellows and become lost in the unfamiliar forest primeval. It happened to two provincials on a patrol near South Bay who were on a flank of the scouting column. Whether they strayed away from the column or the column strayed away from them, they became disoriented and wandered the woods for two days "and had but half a biscuit all the time" before finding another patrol.[14] It could also happen to more experienced woodsmen. On a scout earlier in the summer, Samuel Eastman, one of Rogers' men, had left his fellows to retrieve a pack he had left not far behind. He became lost, and what should have been a two-day return trip to Fort William Henry stretched to five; when he finally made it back he was "almost famished for want of sustenance." Another of Rogers' company, John Hammer, was "Lost in the woods 23[d] of Aug[t]." near Crown Point, and whether he ever made it back is not clear.[15] Incidents like these and the terror of becoming hopelessly lost in a wilderness, to die of starvation or at the hands of Indians, made men inclined to stick close together.

Captain Hodges led at least two of these scouts before his final one. Indeed, Hodges stands out among his fellows in this regard. As at Fort Edward, the commanders of the scouts from Fort William Henry were "particular officers," volunteers who, owing either to their zeal or to their abilities, offered to lead other volunteers on these two-day expeditions. Of those who ventured out in the month between the fall of Oswego and September 19, only Hodges led more than one—three in fact. That he did so suggests that he took seriously what he saw as his duty and perhaps hoped for some action worthy of the son of Major Hodges. It may also suggest that Hodges was well liked among the rank and file, as he apparently had little trouble in raising the men.

Hodges' first foray, on August 25, followed the more or less standard pattern. Leaving just before dark, his scout went only a mile down the west side of the lake and encamped for the night, laying out an ambush. The next morning they made their way eleven more miles down the lake to the observation point and camped again, returning the next day. What is significant in Hodges' subsequent report is that he had some Indians with him, perhaps members of the Stockbridge company encouraged to join the scout to lend their particular expertise. Their presence turned out to be a concern and, later, an annoyance for Hodges. On the second day, as the scout headed toward the landing bays to the north, "two Indians being on the Flank Guard parted from the Scout" about halfway to the destination. Hodges had no idea what had happened to them but continued his mission, perhaps expecting the missing men to rejoin the main body later. They never did. When Hodges and his men returned to Fort William Henry, they "found the Two Indians that left us" already there.

Brief as it is, Hodges' report is worth considering on several counts. First, he mentions only a single "Flank Guard," suggesting that the body of the scout traveled close to the lakeshore, where the going was less steep. This appears to have been the pattern for these scouts, which would naturally have tended to follow the paths of least resistance. However, it also appears that Hodges prudently put experienced woodsmen on his left flank, to prevent the column from being surprised from the heights above them. Hodges was probably angered by the unheralded desertion of the Indians—certainly he made it an issue in his report—and like Winslow probably chalked it up to Indian disingenuousness and lack of reliability. It was how most whites regarded Native peoples. But there may be another explanation. From the Indian scouts' point of view, there may have seemed to be little point to these excursions, aimed as they were merely at inspection rather than at offensive effort. And given the provincial soldiers' relative inexperience in this environment, they may have made too much noise, marched too closely together, been entirely too inattentive to the potential dangers they faced. Traditionally, Natives joined war parties for the prospect of scalps, prisoners, prestige, and enemy loot and followed men whose skill and leadership they trusted. If none of those factors obtained, they were just as free to leave a war party. That may have been the case here.

Hodges' next scout, which left on September 9, suggests that some scout captains were learning their trade. This time Hodges' men made their overnight ambush two miles from the fort before proceeding eleven more miles the next day, indicating that they had pushed forward slightly to the entrance of Northwest Bay. Establishing a base camp, Hodges then "Sent out Scouts"—smaller parties or even individuals—to examine a number of spots for enemy activity. On September 11 they returned "and kept out Flank Guards all the way," also finding an abandoned bateau (one of those "misplaced" by the joyriding soldiers Winslow complained of), in which they sent home some of the party who had become sick. Hodges, warned to "be very Cautious not to be Surprized On your March," on this trip had decided to put out flankers for the return march, a prudent move since he was essentially retracing his steps—just the sort of practice that invited ambushes. By implication, however, he seems not to have deployed flankers for the initial march north, a point that would become significant when he led his men on his last scout a week later.[16]

In neither of Hodges' scouts, and in none of the other scouts on either side of the lake that month, was there any contact with an enemy, nor even a sign of one. None of the dusk-to-dawn ambushes netted a single victim, and nary a boat or canoe belonging to the French or Indians was found. Hodges concluded his scout reports with "made no Discovery of any Enemy," and those of other scout captains ended much the same: Nathaniel Fuller "Discovered nothing worthy of Remark," and Thomas Lorde "saw no signs of the Enemy In all my March, and nothing Remarkable happened." This was good news, of course; each day that no enemy was sighted meant more time to perfect the forts, time that Winslow's men used, among other things, to build a dam that would convert a morass east of the fort into a wide moat. But the lack of enemy activity was also puzzling, especially as everyone had expected the French, flush with victory and concentrating their forces rapidly by water, to make some appearance by now, at least to probe the forts' defenses. Winslow dared hope that his defensive scouting system was responsible; he had written shortly after Oswego's fall that "we of Late have kept the Enemy at home by keeping Out Continual scouts," and their sweep and frequency had only increased since then. But two days after Hodges' second scout came in, Winslow admitted that "the Scheems of the Enemy are Impenetrable to us, we do all in our power to Discover them, but gain but Little or Indeed no Knowledge of their Designs."[17] Perhaps the French could be stalled until it was too late in the campaign year to attack the forts. Perhaps they had given up that option already.

So by the third week of September there was less of a sense of urgency, or at least of immediate danger, at Fort William Henry than there had been four weeks earlier. The possibility of attack still existed, but in the absence of any hard evidence a routine of work, patrol, privation, and disease became the enemy for most of the provincial army. Already the nights, and even some of the days, were becoming chilly. "The Season becomes Cold for Camp Duty, and will Daily grow more so," Winslow warned the commissioners in Albany. The cold weather did nothing good for the sick, who still made up a quarter or more of the army. "Your Honor will Please to Excuse my not sending a return of the sick at this time," wrote the Ipswich surgeon John Calef, "for reason they are so many, and scattred about In Such a manner, as from Green Bush to Half Moon, which must render the return very Imperfect." Winslow sent away the worst cases, or those unlikely to recover in time to be serviceable, but kept the rest in hopes of their recovery—which probably made that eventuality less likely. Winslow begged the commissioners to "send us a Quantity of Vegetables for the Army Especially for the sick, this is a thing Greatly Wanted, and when the sick and Invalids are Removed there must be Carriages to Transport them, and Why! mayn't they Bring those things that may Save the Lives of the remains."[18]

Winslow knew that in addition to vegetables and wagons, the sick needed rum. Spirits were generally considered restorative libations, and in the northeastern colonies the spirit of choice was rum, distilled from molasses in Boston and Newport, most of it consumed regionally. In the tropics especially it was thought to keep people healthy, and in diluted form it was drunk with meals in New England. All believed that it possessed recuperative powers not only for the ill but also for the weak and fatigued; as such, it was essential for workingmen and soldiers. One of Winslow's commissaries reckoned that he had sent up from Albany 203 barrels of rum, enough for a full daily allowance for thirty-two hundred men for more than two months. The commissary remarked that he had sent Winslow all he had, "Except about 10 Barrel of Rum which was kept here for the use of the sick people."[19] As with all things, the provincial army ran short of this commodity too, and Winslow feared that the shortage affected progress on the fort as well as the health of the men: "We are at this Garrison, Though of the Province of Massachusetts, Intirely out of rum," he admitted to a British officer, "which makes our people Extreemly uneasy; should think It would be for the good of the Service that these waggons, and If Possible more be spared, should come with that Specia, as this is the Whetter both of saw and ax—Can't be done without and hope you will Indulge us."[20]

Hodges' Scout

On the morning of September 18, orders went out as usual for scouting parties, four of them this time. Captain Hodges was to visit the west side of the lake again, another officer was to visit the east side,[21] and none other than Robert Rogers, "the Snipe," was to take his men east toward Wood Creek. In addition to these routine patrols, Major Stephen Miller, "an Active young Gentleman," led a very Rogers-like, five-day expedition over the mountains to the west, to an area that it was said "some of the Enemys Hunters" frequented. Miller would be "in an untreaden Path" where the enemy "have never been molested that way." Each of the provincial captains was to have two subalterns, three noncommissioned officers, and forty-three privates. Each man was to take with him "two days Provisions and twenty rounds of powder and ball."[22] The companies were ordered to parade at four o'clock in the afternoon, in readiness for their evening departure. That gave Hodges the day to secure his volunteers, however that was done—presumably by this time everyone knew when such were needed and could come forward if they had a mind to go.

And why *would* anyone volunteer to go, putting their lives at risk, far away from the safety of the fort, since there was no material benefit for doing so, no extra pay, rations, or furloughs? Some, like Hodges, might go out of a desire to perform the function for which they had enlisted: to be soldiers rather than simply laborers with guns. Some may have liked the scouting service, with its adventure, semi-independence of action, and the possibility of excitement. Less appropriate motives may have moved others: to escape the unceasing toil, the sickness, the loathsome stink, that was Fort William Henry. As for danger, how could being on a scout with a full company of armed men be riskier than remaining in the disease environment about the fort, especially as there had been no sign of the enemy for a month? If the fort was not to be attacked, where was the "safety" in staying there another day if one could help it? With nothing to look forward to but unrelenting labor, infection, and the remote chance of being besieged by the French, there seemed little reason to stay at Fort William Henry. By comparison, a two-day hike in the woods might well have seemed the more reasonable course by far. In other words, many of the men offering themselves for the scouts were probably volunteering for all the wrong reasons.

At any rate, we know the names of most of the men who paraded that afternoon for Hodges' scout. One of Hodges' two officers was the twenty-

two-year-old ensign from Hingham, Massachusetts, Jeremiah Lincoln. Next
in rank was John Lewis, who hoped his sergeant's pay would keep his struggling family solvent another year. Two of Hodges' three corporals were
young men with good trades: Joseph Abbot, of Andover, was a joiner, and
Peleg Stevens, of Dartmouth, was a barber, whose training may well have
gone beyond cutting hair and shaving to include bloodletting and drawing
teeth. The ranks included the servants John Con and Azor Roundy. The laborers John Erwin, of Dunstable, and Ebenezer Pratt, of Bridgewater, both
thought of themselves as breadwinners for their widowed mothers. Jonathan Barnes, the fledgling blacksmith from Boston, and Moses Emerson, a
farm laborer from Bridgewater, probably expected their much-anticipated
soldier's pay to jump-start them on the way to economic independence. One
private, Isaac Foster, was taking no chances with the money he somehow
had already managed to acquire; perhaps not fully trusting his comrades at
the fort, he carried four dollars in his pocket. John Erwin later claimed that
he, at least, had not wanted to go but "with two more of my Company were
draughted out" for the mission. The Irish-born Robert Wilson, of Lexington, also may have had little choice, for he later wrote that he had been
"Detached out of Capt Lords Companey" to go with the scout.[23]

In all there were about forty-eight men in Hodges' command, including
the captain; as we will see, reports differed as to the exact number, and no
scout roster has yet surfaced. But from muster rolls drawn up in the following month, in which the status of soldiers enlisted in the spring was up-
dated, it becomes clear that Hodges' scout was a pastiche of men drawn from
as many as twenty-six different companies, representing at least five separate regiments.[24] Probably many of them, perhaps most, had been on scouts
previously, as had Sergeant Lewis, who had gone out with Captain Thaxter's
band two months earlier. William Merry, a veteran of the previous war and
a survivor of two battles with the French, probably had the most combat
experience in the group—certainly more than did his captain. But this particular grouping of men had never operated as a unit before, nor were the
scout's officers necessarily familiar to them, or to one another for that matter. Of the thirty-five members of the scout whose origins can be determined,
not a single man was from Hodges' original company, though one, William
Merry, was from the same town, and there were several from neighboring
towns who probably knew, or knew of, the captain. Why were there not more
from his own company? Were they sick or otherwise employed that day?

After parading the men, there must have been an inspection, even a cursory one, to make sure that everyone had what they needed for two days and nights in the field. Each man would have his musket, of course, the heavy but reliable Brown Bess with which they had been furnished four months ago; even their captain shouldered one this day. If the sergeant and corporals did their duty, they saw to it that the men's Crown-issued cartridge boxes contained the required twenty paper cartridges, each holding a pre-measured load of coarse gunpowder and a one-ounce, .75-caliber round bullet. Each man had also been given a bayonet in a leather scabbard, which would be fixed to the strap holding the cartridge box, but the men may have left these behind in favor of a belt axe (hatchet) or tomahawk, the hand weapon of choice for scouts and rangers, which doubled as a general camp tool. Captain Hodges had a hanger—a short, curved cutting sword—but he elected not to take it on this scout; like a bayonet, a sword did only one thing, and it was not handy to carry in the woods.[25] For food, the soldiers most likely packed the staple ration, hard biscuit, along with some smoked or dried beef, in knapsacks or rolled up in blankets. Water was kept in leather bottles or in canteens of wood or tin; so close to the lake, access to water would be no problem. And that was a good thing, for the air that evening was still and growing heavy—the cool days and chilly nights they had experienced recently, those heralds of autumn, could fool the hopeful into thinking the hot days of summer were over. If the men were wise, they probably carried an extra shirt, provided they had one, rolled up in their blankets, prepared for either eventuality.

The late afternoon shadows lengthened; with all in readiness, did Hodges delay the march until the sun dipped below the top of the mountain ridge to the west? Accounts of the next day suggest that Hodges aimed to camp at the two-mile mark he had reached on his last scout. Even with the sun out of sight there would easily have been enough daylight to cover that distance before the darkness closed in under the canopy of forest. There was no reason to change the routine; the two scouts that had come in from both sides of the lake the previous day "did not Discover anything" out of the ordinary. And so Hodges' last scout marched off the parade, perhaps in a column two abreast at first, past the fort, past the work parties, and past the outlying sentries, disappearing into the woods. Watching them go was Ensign Josiah Thacher, of Cape Cod. On another day he might have volunteered to go with Hodges, but he had returned just the previous afternoon from a scout and was likely glad to rest and let Ezekiel Webb, a lieutenant in his company, have a go. Webb, who had been on several such scouts already, was likely the scout's second-in-command.[26] Also watching was Corporal Samuel Henche, or Hencher, of Boston, who recognized a man from his company, the black-smith Jonathan Barnes, filing out with the rest. Henche's memory of this moment would be put to the test four and a half years later.

"Cut to Peaces in a Most Barboras manner"

The scout made its usual bivouac and ambush, with the usual une-ventful outcome, and set out the morning of the nineteenth for the landing areas some ten miles north. It was a Sunday, and it was soon clear that the day was going to be unexpectedly hot. Shielded by the mountains and the tall trees, the men would have been out of the hot sun, but they would also have been denied any light lake breezes. They followed what was by then a familiar, even well-trodden path along the lakeshore. Even a single person traveling through the forest leaves a trail of scuffed earth, overturned leaves, and trampled vegetation that is visible to a skilled tracker. Fifty men in sin-gle file (the standard and most natural march formation over rough terrain) will leave an obvious path. Fifty men traversing the same ground virtually every day for a month creates a "road"—so called in Winslow's letters and on maps—that a child could follow. Hodges' men took the accustomed way northward. The rocky, wooded ground rising sharply to their left precluded any easy alternatives and channeled them onto the narrow stretch of rela-tively flat ground by the water. If they kept intervals of three feet between them, their column would have stretched 150 feet; it could well have been longer. Hodges had used flankers on his two previous scouts, but not con-sistently, and it is not clear that he did so this time. Perhaps he intended to deploy them on the return trip, as he had done most recently. They were on familiar ground, on a mission with a predictable, oft-repeated outcome. There had been no serious alarm, or even news, for weeks, and no scouts on either side of the lake had detected anything amiss. The woods were quiet and shady, a welcome relief from the noise and toil they had left behind. Only those at the head of the column were likely to be very alert; the rest were more relaxed, perhaps with their muskets slung, thoughts far away, talkative. Careless.

For what happened next we have three secondhand accounts, surviving in official reports and journals, from three men who made it back to Fort

William Henry hours later. Let us take the first. At about three o'clock that afternoon Private Robert Wilson, shot through his shoulder, reached the fort.[27] He was weak, probably at the end of his endurance, from blood loss and his long run back in the midday heat. He could at least relinquish the gnawing terror of his ordeal, if not the pain. We can imagine him, holding his arm close to his body as he ran, hardly daring a backward glance lest he see the pursuer that would herald his death. He needed water, perhaps even to speak, and someone to dress his wound, but his news could not wait: that some three hours earlier Hodges' Scout had been "attacked by a vast Superior Number"; that he imagined Hodges' men "could not Escape"; that early in the fighting he, Wilson, had been hit and, whether ordered to or not, had "made the best of his way" out of the fray; that "he was afraid the whole scoute wold be Cut of[f]." He described the fight as occurring near the lakeshore, twelve miles distant.[28]

Three hours had passed since the fighting had begun, but General Winslow acted quickly on the information he had. Hodges and his men had been "attacked," had been "Beset by the French and Indians," but for all he knew, they were holding on, perhaps in a good position where they might fend off their attackers for a while. There were still hours of daylight left; help might get to them in time, especially if sent by water. Winslow ordered Major Richard Saltonstall to take three hundred men down the west-side path "to their relief," though he must have known that they could not reach Hodges before nightfall. The possibility existed that Hodges' men were conducting some kind of fighting retreat southward, but even if they were in rout, Saltonstall's men would be able to rescue them. If not, Saltonstall could push on for as long as he dared and hope to reach Hodges' position in the morning. Winslow pinned his hope on his boats, however; he sent one of the sloop-rigged lighters, diplomatically named the *Loudoun*, with its cannon and eight swivel guns, down the lake, accompanied by two whaleboats and a bateau. Their mission was to "Cover our party" with the boats' artillery "and Bring them off If the Enemy were too much for them." With the sun dipping in the sky, the boats' crews were hastily assembled, the sloop manned; with sails set to the light airs and with oars dipping, the flotilla made its agonizingly slow way down the lake and out of sight.

Darkness had come before Winslow received a situation update, and it was not good. Major Saltonstall and his men returned at nightfall; with them were three more survivors, including Lieutenant Webb, the scout's

second-in-command. The lieutenant's story, with which the others con-
curred, agreed in part with that of the wounded messenger but included
detail. They had indeed been attacked, "or Rather Ambushed" by overwhelming numbers of Indians—they estimated 150[29]—at about noontime
and been quickly overwhelmed. The enemy, Webb said, "had the Advantage
of the Ground" and "made the first fire," which killed some of the men outright. In response, "Our force drew up in Order and returned" fire, doing
little damage as the Indians facing them "flatted," that is, went prone as the
provincials squeezed off a ragged volley. As soon as they did so, "a Fresh
party of the Enemy rose and fired," felling more of Hodges' men. According
to the lieutenant, the provincials had nevertheless stood their ground, returning fire a second time, upon which "the Indians fired a very Large Volley" that left "almost none of Ours" standing. At that point, Webb and one
other man had scrambled up the slope of a mountain to their left "and hid
under the Edge of the Mountain till all was Quiate; and then made of[f]."
The two fugitives may have met the third survivor in their flight south, but
all eventually made contact with Saltonstall's reinforcement. The lieutenant
and the others "Imagine[d] they are all that Escaped." Saltonstall took them
at their word and returned to the fort. Webb was certain, he told Winslow,
"that the action Did not Continue above . . . two Minuts," if that.[30]

Winslow's fragile hopes for Hodges sank. Private Wilson's report had
suggested that Hodges' men were fighting a defensive battle, the result of a
"meeting engagement" that, though desperate, had still been in progress
when he made his break. He had given the impression, or at least Winslow
had received the impression, that rescue efforts were justified by a real possibility of success. What Lieutenant Webb now described was a classic and
exceedingly deadly ambush scenario. Hodges' men, probably in single-file
column, had blundered into a carefully prepared trap: a hidden line of Indian
musketmen had blocked their path and opened fire at the closest possible
range, with maximum effect. While the Indians were reloading, Hodges'
men had somehow formed a line facing this threat and returned fire in a
volley, which was about all they had been trained to do. Their opponents
had avoided the shot at the last moment, whereupon a second enemy force,
probably at a right angle to Hodges' newly formed line, had sprung from
their hidden positions and caught the provincials in flank, their musketry
adding to the casualties and the mounting confusion. Hodges' men had
managed to get off a second volley before the enemy, their muskets all now

reloaded, poured a crushing blast of crossfire into the exposed soldiers. The few survivors, "almost surrounded . . . were forced to give way and run off, and were closely pursued by the Indians," who had struck down all but the three who had made it back.

This was disaster, plain and simple. But how could Winslow have had such a different first impression from what the lieutenant related? Could Private Wilson have been so completely mistaken about the situation? He would have to have bolted from the scene almost immediately not to be aware that the fight was over in only two minutes, and even then . . . Something was not right, but Winslow had other things to think about. He would be anxious to hear word from the boats, but that could hardly happen for hours. He had to consider that at least part of the long-feared French invasion force might be just behind the large screen of Indians. He might have been annoyed that Major Saltonstall had brought all his considerable force of men back to the fort with him: despite the lieutenant's fears, there could well have been more forlorn stragglers making their way back in the dark, with no one to help bring them in; surely a squad of men could have conducted the three survivors to the fort safely. And surely a three-hundred-man ambush might have turned the tables on the enemy force if it had pushed its luck. Once again, provincial soldiers had proven inadequate against the enemy in his element. And neither Wilson nor Lieutenant Webb had mentioned Hodges or his actions specifically. Had he led his men into a trap? Had he been killed with the first shots, leaving his men leaderless?

Meanwhile, the fort's flotilla had made its way down the lake, looking and listening for some indication of where Hodges' men might be. They had only a vague notion: some twelve miles north on the west side of the lake, and near the shore. They might have learned from Wilson that the site was "Oposite to round Island" (almost certainly today's Dome Island), which would have put the fighting in the area of present-day Huddle Bay or Bolton Landing.[31] They might never have found the site but for a fortunate discovery: as the boats crept close to the land, cannon and swivel guns no doubt trained shoreward, they spied a man at the water's edge, signaling frantically. Warily, one of the whaleboats rowed to the shore and brought him off. He was Joshua Perry, of Hingham, a private, who had also escaped the melee.[32] He informed Captain Nixon, commanding the *Loudoun*, that he was too late to rescue anyone else but that they were a mile and a half from "the Place [where] the Engagem^t began." With Perry to guide them, the boats continued into the bay, and though the light was fading, the whaleboats and bateau, covered by the *Loudoun*'s guns, went ashore. Twenty-six men jumped out of the boats and into the shallows, nervously clutching their muskets and straining their eyes for any sign that they might be the next victims.

But the enemy had gone, leaving behind evidence of their handiwork. The boats' crews found ten corpses near the shore, including that of Captain Hodges, scalped and "Cut to Peaces in a Most Barboras manner." Three of the bodies had been decapitated, the skinned heads "stuck upon poles," and all had had "their limbs chopt & hackt to pieces." The grisly display had its desired effect: The men of the boats' crews had certainly seen death before, but not like this. They "ceast to make further search" and were ordered instead to carry the bodies and the heads to the bateau, the loathsome task given urgency by approaching darkness and the fear of sharing a similar fate if they stayed too long. One of the whaleboats took the bateau, with its grim contents, in tow, the rowing men, including the rescued Perry, no doubt grateful at least that with the darkness they could not see its contents. They reached Fort William Henry about ten o'clock that night.[33]

General Winslow heard Perry's report, and while it only confirmed the unhappy fate of Hodges' Scout, there was something materially different about this version. Perry insisted that while the scout might have been surprised by the enemy, it had been no walkover; in fact, "the action Continued for more than half an hour, and that Our men behaved Bravely till Quite Over powered." In short, this man "gave a very different acco^t: from the Lieu^t," and one that raised serious questions about the latter's conduct. Winslow may have had misgivings about Webb's story from the start; if he was to be believed, the provincials had, after the first shock of combat, coolly changed their column formation to form a line—in the woods—and fired a disciplined volley upon command, not once but twice, all the while taking casualties. It was the sort of performance every European-trained commander dreamed of, but was it likely? These men, so casually trained, so famously undisciplined, had never before worked together as a unit and barely knew the officers commanding them. Surprised as they had been by a much larger body of a terrifying enemy, would they even have responded to their officers' commands had they given any? And yet they supposedly had stood their ground until most were killed in place. Such a scene was possible, of course, but it was simply not consistent with experience.[34]

It always looks bad when one of the few survivors of a last-stand scenario is an officer, but if the scout had been carelessly led into a devastating ambush; if it had not been a battle but a slaughter that was over almost as soon as it had begun; and if there had been virtually no one left to command after the hailstorm of lead, the lieutenant could hardly be blamed for saving himself. If, on the other hand, Joshua Perry told the more accurate story, then Hodges' men had encountered a superior force and, unable to retreat, had gone to ground, taking up the best defensive position they could and holding it for as long as possible. That scenario is supported by the wounded Private Wilson's description of a battle still in progress when he made his escape. If Lieutenant Webb's story was true, both he and Wilson had escaped the carnage within two minutes of each other; yet Wilson had made it back to Fort William Henry at least three hours before the lieutenant. The discrepancy in the stories was disturbing. Winslow had to consider that Webb's story could have been a self-serving one that masked a less than stellar performance of his duty. If Perry's story, and not the lieutenant's, was true, then Webb had fled the fighting early, abandoned his men, and, as he had admitted, "hid under the Edge of the Mountain" for several hours "till all was Quiate." Winslow was troubled enough to promise, "as soon as I have Time," to "make Enquiries strictly into these matters." Upon one point Perry agreed with the lieutenant: "he Imagined few or none were taken alive." All that was "Certain," wrote Winslow, was that "we have lost forty five men either killed or taken."[35]

Dissecting Disaster

Two minutes or half an hour? We might doubt whether any of the eyewitnesses could relate the entire event objectively. People under extremes of stress are known to experience either time compression (an hour seeming to pass in mere minutes) or time expansion (the opposite effect). It is possible that the lieutenant, the other survivors, or all of them, inaccurately recalled the fighting's duration. Also, soldiers in combat tend to be narrowly focused on what is happening directly in front of them, and far less aware of what is transpiring to their right, left, or rear. Indeed, this well-known phenomenon is what makes the lieutenant's story all the more dubious: he was able to describe, in blow-by-blow sequence, the contours of the entire encounter with a certainty that should give us pause. Perhaps, in addition to the conflicting versions we have, modern studies in combat psychology may provide insights regarding what happened to Hodges' men.

First, all indications are that whether the encounter was a meeting engagement or an ambush, Hodges' men did not initiate the action; that they were fired upon first or at least that the first shots came unexpectedly from their front. If so, the first response for all was surprise, even shock, at which point the limbic (that is, the emotion-centered) portion of the brain gains ascendancy and a "fight, flight, or freeze" response results. Some of Hodges' men may have jumped for cover, but a considerable number almost certainly "froze" in place for several seconds or longer, making them easy targets for their opponents. Studies of twentieth-century combat situations, most notably those of General S. L. A. Marshall, John Keegan, and Dave Grossman, reveal that 30 percent of those killed in combat died "frozen," unable to take the action necessary to save their lives.[36] This "freeze" response, which in animals functions to avoid detection by predators, contributes to another, more controversial phenomenon. According to Marshall, only a distinct minority of soldiers in combat during the two twentieth-century world wars "would take any part with their weapons." In other words, whether overcome by fear or a reluctance to kill, they failed even to fire in the general direction of the enemy. Marshall's study suggested that 75–85 percent of combat soldiers in these wars failed in this regard.[37] His assertions are still disputed, but even if that percentage is halved, at least a third of Hodges' men may not have fired a shot in their defense.

For those who object that Marshall's study pertains only to the twentieth-century battlefield, where the sheer lethality of the environment was so much greater than its flintlock-era counterpart, there is a Marshall-like example from only the year before Hodges' Scout came to grief. In the first phase of the Battle of Lake George, in 1755, a thousand provincials and two hundred Indian allies were ambushed by hundreds of enemy Natives. Scores were killed in minutes, and scores more bolted for the camp three miles away. Seth Pomeroy, present at the battle, insisted that of those who maintained some kind of organized retreat, "there was not above 100 of our men y^t Fired at all."[38] The reader may not regard this response (or nonresponse) to danger as a rational solution. Exactly so: as Grossman explains, "When a man is frightened, he literally stops thinking with his forebrain (that is, with the mind of a human being) and begins to think with the midbrain (that is, with the portion of his brain that is essentially undistinguishable from that of an animal."[39]

Fight, flight, and freeze are only the three best-known responses available to those for whom the forebrain has shut down. To these Grossman adds a fourth: posturing. A fearful animal facing a dangerous adversary may attempt to intimidate its opponent with threatening behavior, such as stamping, roaring, or rearing to make itself appear larger. For some of the men of Hodges' command, posturing probably took the form of yelling or, unlike their frozen comrades, firing their weapons as rapidly as possible. The advent of firearms to warfare introduced not only a weapon of new destructive force; "gunpowder's superior *noise*, its superior *posturing* ability, made it ascendant on the battlefield." But posturing could also be an offensive weapon, as Indians had demonstrated to Europeans since their first conflicts. Hard on the sounds of the first fusillade, Hodges' men would have heard the whoops and piercing screams of their attackers, "verbal posturing" that inflated their numbers and induced the very limbic responses that made the provincials hesitate or waste their ammunition at the half-hidden enemy.[40] As eighteenth-century European armies knew, rigorous training, and the confidence it gave soldiers in themselves, in their weapons, and in their comrades, could at least mitigate these nonproductive responses to fear and make soldiers perform as desired. But training was exactly what the men of Hodges' Scout lacked. From the first shots, they were hopelessly in over their heads.

Casualties, of course—or the threat of them—are the key to breaking a unit's collective will to resist. If Hodges' Scout fell into an ambush, then it is likely that there were immediate casualties and that their numbers mounted steadily, as the enemy's superior firepower poured relentlessly on the confused company, scrambling for effective cover. Some at least returned fire, but as each enemy bullet found a target, the effect on those remaining was to amplify their fear. The historian Clifford J. Rogers argues that "*all* weapons are as important for their effects on those they do not hit as for their effects on those they do hit. Battles are won more by the psychological effects of weapons than by their physical impacts." However, "those psychological effects are the direct results of the physical ones, for it is primarily the sight of comrades wounded and killed that demoralizes." Rogers was actually writing about the effects of archery on the medieval battlefield. His argument is even stronger when one considers the fire, smoke, concussive noise, and shocking wounds generated by firearms.[41]

For all the casualties induced by musketry, much of the slaughter may have occurred when Hodges' unwounded men ultimately did break under the stress and attempt to escape. This was the case in most battles before and during this period, for the sight of men on one side turning their backs and fleeing has an immediate effect on both sides. A soldier becomes terrified when he is compelled to turn his back to his enemy. Up to that point, frightened soldiers may have been held in place by "a type of reverse ostrich syndrome," in which the mounting danger before them was "bearable only while the men continued to watch it."[42] Once that spell was broken, men ran, and then their sense of danger was significantly amplified by their inability to see it and by the terror of being struck down from behind. Typically, routing soldiers throw down anything that might encumber their flight,[43] especially their heavy weapons, which consequently instills them with the knowledge that they are completely defenseless—there is nothing to do but run. Lieutenant Webb's story admits that something like that happened, though in the case of only a small number of survivors. The actual proportion may have been greater: surely Webb and the four others who made it back to Fort William Henry were not the only ones who fled the action while "closely pursued by the Indians."

The sight of their enemy in flight led to a corresponding reaction among the Indians: pursuit. "There is a chase instinct in most animals," argues Grossman, which causes even the most nonaggressive species "to instinctively chase and pull down anything that runs." Humans are famously aggressive animals, especially when they perceive a clear advantage. A panicked, running enemy poses next to no threat; Indians who moments before had been firing muskets from behind cover now dropped their own firearms and, with knives and tomahawks drawn, set off to intercept and bring down the fleeing provincials. Clearly, some got away, but others were almost certainly killed from behind, as they had feared, by the more sure-footed woods runners. Wounded men who tried to run off simply made easier prey; even if their pursuers possessed any reluctance to kill a helpless enemy, the circumstances dictated against the victims, for the whole history of battle demonstrates that the "chase instinct in man . . . permits him to kill a fleeing enemy" without a second thought.[44]

So much for forensics. If the principles outlined above apply in any degree to the eighteenth century as they do to more recent wars, then Lieutenant Webb's account of what happened to Hodges' Scout simply does not seem credible, though he may have remembered aspects of it accurately enough: the suddenness of the attack; desperate attempts to restore order; fire coming from multiple directions; men falling and, finally, running in panic; the sense that it all happened quickly. Perhaps, though, in the light of the studies surveyed above, it is possible to reconcile somewhat the seemingly incompatible stories of the lieutenant and the private:

> The men walked the well-defined path confidently despite the lack of flankers further up the slope to their left. It had been an uneventful walk in the woods since the previous day, after an uneventful month. The trees protected them from the sun, but the air was still very warm, and after more than ten miles of walking they were thirsty. They thought of their comrades back at the fort, sweating over the innumerable tasks the officers always seemed to find for them; they were glad to be free of them for a couple of days.
>
> A ragged fusillade at the head of the column jolted them from their reveries. Demonic shrieks followed, leaving no mistake: Indians! Adrenaline set hearts to pounding, stomachs churning: the life-or-death situation of combat, once an abstraction, always safely in the future, was suddenly, unexpectedly, here and now. Men ducked instinctively. Some sought cover, while others, seemingly insensible to the danger, stood like statues, as if disbelieving. Officers were shouting orders, but others were shouting too, some cursing, some screaming in pain. Few men seemed to be acting together. Soon, though, men had come forward and formed something like a line facing the direction of the enemy's fire; they began to fire back. The thick white smoke from the guns on both sides, hanging in the still air, was obscuring visibility, and the enemy kept well hidden, exposing themselves only to make a shot, then disappearing again. How many? Hard to tell. Will we charge them? Keep firing? Who is giving orders? Suddenly a volley crashes in from the left—there are many more of them, and attacking the flank! Heavy slugs punch horrible wounds into flesh and bone; the sound of them striking comrades is sickening and horrifying. Those who remained rooted in place have been shot down. Some are cowering in terror, hugging their muskets but doing nothing with them. Others fire, reload, and fire again with maniacal rapidity, burning through their twenty cartridges in minutes. They take no aim, blazing blindly into the fog they have helped create. There is no line now, more of a circle or horseshoe formation, men huddling closer together instinctively. The fire coming from the enemy is almost ceaseless, as is the dreadful war-whoop. They clearly outnumber the provincials several times over and have all but sealed off any avenue of escape.
>
> Small groups seem to be resisting, sheltering their wounded. But finally—how long has it been?—the pressure is too much. Men who have fired off their ammunition throw down their muskets and run, desperate to escape what is now clearly a death

trap. Seeing them, others who have done little take their cue and follow. The Indians have been waiting for this. As long as the provincials kept up some fire, it was best to wait, pick men off when possible, scream like furies, and count on superior numbers to take their toll on the enemy. But with resistance collapsing, it is now time to bring the fight to an end. As soon as a few Indians set off in pursuit, more follow, lest they miss out on the spoils of war—plunder, scalps, perhaps prisoners—until the trickle becomes a torrent of musket- and tomahawk-wielding terror descending on the pitiful remnants of Hodges' command. Anyone brave enough to continue resisting dies, as do the wounded, whose scalps are worth more than their lives now. Sharp knives take trophies and decapitate bodies with dexterous strokes. Jubilant victors, their own adrenaline still working in them, hack at the dead men's arms and legs. Those who had pursued the fleeing men return, some empty-handed, others with captured guns and dripping scalps. It has been an easy but exhilarating victory. It was what they had come for. Acrid gun smoke hangs in the air as the Indians, the masters at this game, sing and give victory shouts.

At this remove, and with so few survivors' accounts, we cannot know with certainty what happened when the two forces met. The fantasia above, while plausible, may not describe the events any more accurately. Was it a battle or a massacre? Meeting engagement or carefully laid ambush? What was Captain Hodges' role in the fighting? Did the men put up any degree of effective resistance? Who was "kill'd," and who "taken"? To borrow an oft-used metaphor, what we have before us is a picture puzzle for which most of the pieces are missing. But as we will see, some of those missing pieces can be found, and with each one we gain a clearer impression of the original work. The pieces are men's lives, so in much of the rest of this book we will look for clues in the stories of survivors. Indeed, our focus will soon turn from what happened and why to recovering the experiences of men, and some women, caught up in the consequences of Hodges' Scout.

Rumors

Shortly after first light the next day, September 21, graves were opened at Fort William Henry for the recovered corpses. The Reverend Gideon Hawley was on hand for the solemnities. Hawley, like so many others at the post, would have preferred to be somewhere else. The 1749 Yale graduate had taken enthusiastically to missionary work and had provided religious instruction at Stockbridge for a year under the direction of the venerable

Jonathan Edwards, the famed New England divine. Consequently, Hawley undoubtedly knew some of the Stockbridge Indians serving with the army. In 1753 he had been given the opportunity to establish a new mission on the Susquehanna River in New York for Six Nations Indians, but when the war broke out it had been simply too dangerous to continue there. He had accepted a position with the army as chaplain to Gridley's regiment, but he was never very happy with the position and yearned to be back at his mission. Now he and other officers of the regiment were gathered outside of the entrenchments, where the bodies had been laid out prior to being carried in procession to the fort's sadly expanding graveyard. Hawley was understandably melancholic; it "affected" him, he confided, "to see ye horrid barbarities committed on ye bodies of those poor men who fell" with Hodges. The remains of the captain, "being a good officer tis s^d, lov'd while he lived & lamented now he is dead," rated a coffin, but as for the others, "we could not afford Coffins for y^m so y^t they were obliged to be exposed—No, so far from it y^t we could not allow y^m blankets to be wrapt in—ye legs & Arms all naked & besmeared with Blood appeared very gashfully." John Emory, a twenty-year-old soldier from another regiment and a veteran of previous scouts, viewed the bodies briefly and moved on, perhaps thinking that there, but for the grace of God, he well might lie.[45] After several more minutes, when all was ready, Colonel Gridley gave the order for the "porters" to take up Hodges' coffin and the mutilated corpses of the others and begin the procession.

But one last indignity awaited Hodges and his men. No sooner had the bearers begun when "a Gun without ye Camp was discharged wch was emmidiately seconded by another," upon which "the Drums beat to arms." The burial party literally put down what they were doing, and "we rush'd into camp," where "we were kept in a ruffle for some time." They soon learned that "a Couple of Lads" had gone to the swampy area near the fort to cut saplings for the brick kiln. A shot, the first that Hawley had heard, had rung out from the nearby woods but failed to hit either man. The hidden assailant was not to be denied, however, and though within gunshot of the garrison and only fifty yards from a nearby sentry, the Indian sprang from cover and charged the men with knife and tomahawk. Stunned and unarmed, the men bolted for the fort; sentries, mistaking the Indian for one of "our Mohawks" or perhaps not believing what was happening, hesitated. The attacker ran down one of the young men, struck him mortally, and "Scalp'd him on ye Spot." A sentry finally reacted, firing his musket without effect, and the Indian "went off without harm." It was a deed of incredible audacity, and it had the desired effect on Hawley, as it must have had on all who witnessed it: "How insolent, how daring is this—what have we not to fear from such an Enimy If numerous & successful?"[46]

"As soon as ye Camp was a little settled," continued Hawley, the funeral was resumed, this time without interruption. Hodges "had a Grave by Himself," but the others were put into a common grave and covered over. Hawley subsequently learned that the young man killed in sight of the garrison, in his way the last victim of Hodges' Scout, was John Emory, the one who minutes earlier had stopped to pay his respects to his comrades. He was actually buried before Hodges and his men, for his scalped body was "immediately bro't jerking" from "ye Place where he was kill'd to ye Burying Ground," having "died in the Arms of those who brought him in." "How sudden, how unexpected his Death!" mused Hawley. "How soon his Consignment to ye Place of Forgetfulness?"[47]

There were predictable alarms, stand-tos, and fevered preparations following the slaughter of Hodges' command. Everyone from John Winslow at the lake to Lord Loudoun at Albany was certain that this most recent disaster signaled the French advance that was universally expected and feared—what else could such a large force of the enemy, so close to the fort, portend? A ranger who had come across the tracks of those who had destroyed Hodges' command judged them to be three hundred in number, double the survivors' estimates.[48] For the following week, Winslow reported "small Partys of the Enemy Lurking about us," one of them even coming "so near us as that they Answered the Garrison, all is well." "It is a confounded thing," he admitted, "that we Cant give the shaberoons a Drubing and Daily meet with Loss." The general still could not seem to grasp what was behind his men's inability to thwart their elusive opponents: "Its Strainge to think," he mused, "how Vigilant they are, and that It has not been in our power to surprize any party of them."[49] Instead, adhering to his market policies regarding scouts, Winslow and his officers raised one hundred dollars among themselves as prize money for "scouts that brought In the best Intelligence."[50] But the French never came, and for the next month, and then the next, the customary patrols, some of them heavily reinforced, found no further sign of enemy activity on either side of the lake.

For the provincials at the forts, and for the red-coated regulars who would take their places over the winter, the Crown Point campaign, which had seemed to promise so much in the spring, had reached its sorry end. Even Winslow began to feel forgotten. Writing to Council of War secretary Samuel Willard in Boston on November 3, the general chided him because he had not heard anything official from that quarter in a while "and begin to Conclude with my self, that we were either given up for lost or a sett of men not worth regarding."[51] Conditions at the forts continued to be appalling, and the sick (and apparently some malingerers) were transferred down the Hudson to Albany on a near-regular basis; 264 went from Fort William Henry on October 19 alone.[52] Of 28 men in Abner Barrows' understrength company (part of the same regiment as was Hodges'), 3 died at the fort and 16 "Went sick in the Waggon," of which 2 more died subsequently. On September 30 Barrows' company received 17 replacements, 5 of whom died after little more than a month. Five more were left behind when the regiment returned home, too sick to move, and 2 deserted.[53] In three months, from late July to mid-October, 154 men of the Massachusetts provincial regiments died, and another 606 fell ill or were seriously injured. All told, more than a quarter of all Massachusetts provincials were casualties of illness or accident.[54] Only the men of Hodges' Scout and a handful of others killed in isolated incidents over the course of the campaign were actual combat casualties, and these must be added to the total. Those who survived the campaign marched out of Fort William Henry on November 11 and 12, bound for home. Winslow, his military career also at an end, characteristically looked for the silver lining in the effort and sacrifice of the previous half year. All the available intelligence, he insisted, had indicated that the French intended to invade northern New York, and "I Presume nothing Diverted them from that Resolution, but the Posture we were In to receive them. . . . So that on the whole Tho. we fail'd in the design of tak[g]. Crown Point, yett still have been Instruments under Providence of Great service to the Society."[55]

And what of the missing men of Hodges' Scout? In their companies' rosters surviving in the Massachusetts Archives, the designation "killed" or "kill'd or taken" appears alongside the names of thirty-three men in relation to September 19. Only four besides Hodges were identified positively in the rosters as dead—and this, as we will see, was premature in some cases. An additional dozen or so were listed as "dead" or "deceased" in the days following, though surely some, and perhaps all, of these fell to illness rather than to enemy action.

There is mystery implicit in the phrase "kill'd or taken." Ten mutilated bodies had been found the day of the fighting,[56] and of course there were the five who escaped, but what had become of the others? Many heard or assumed the worst. At Fort Edward, the surgeon Ammi Ruhamah Cutter received word that "Capt Hodge went out from Fort Wm Henry with 44 Men, who fell into an Ambush, and 'tis thought all are cut off [i.e., killed], save 4 who made their Escape." William Hervey heard on the night of September 19 that "Captain Hodges and his party had fallen in with an ambush," that four had escaped, and that "they were all but themselves, they imagined, either killed or taken." Three nights later, however, Hervey heard that "40 of the dead bodies of Captain Hodges' party were found on the spot."[57] In Albany, William Williams seemed to lay the blame for the slaughter squarely on Hodges: he had taken forty-seven men with him "upon the Scalping Design" but had "led his Men into such an Ambush of the Enemy as to lose himself & 43 of his Company." Others, including General Winslow, preferred not to write off the missing so easily, and a Boston newspaper claimed to "hear most of the others are fallen into the Enemys Hands."[58]

The pessimists must have felt justified when, on October 3, the Connecticut captain David Wooster led a scout down the west side of the lake and on the second day "came to the Place where Captain Hodges was defeated." There, probably guided by the smell of decaying flesh, they found "six dead Human Bodies," which, according to one in the scout, "ware almost Desolved"— rotted and torn apart by animals, presumably, though perhaps "helped" in this regard by human activity two weeks earlier. The fact that these remains had not been discovered by the boat crews on September 19 suggests that these men had been slain some distance from Hodges and the nine clustered about him and may indicate that in the final stages of the fighting groups of men had become isolated when their comrades had run for their lives. Wooster's men continued northward to what they called "Louden Harbour" and encamped for the night. Instead of returning to Fort William Henry as usual, though, they pressed on to Northwest Bay, at the southwest end of which they discovered two landing places the enemy had been using at about the time of Hodges' destruction. At one of the landings they also found what was left of one more of Hodges' men.[59] Had he run so far, and in the wrong direction, before being cut down? Wooster's report seemed to give little room for hope. If his men, who apparently had made a thorough search, had found all of the bodies that were still to be found in the area of the fighting, then only sixteen men had died more or less in place. The rest, except for the lucky five, may have been run down and killed like the man at the landing, their decomposing corpses scattered about in the woods, never to be found.

Or perhaps not. Late that same month Captain John Shepard, who had been taken by Indians near Fort Edward in August, escaped his captors and with three companions made his way back to Fort William Henry. They had news about the Oswego prisoners, French designs for the coming year, and disturbing indications that someone on the Anglo-American side was feeding sensitive information to the French. Almost as an afterthought, Shepard said that he had heard that an "insin Linkon and fourteen men that belonged to captain hoges Scout were brought into canada captive."[60] Was it true? For nearly a year there would be no confirmation of the rumor. Fortunately for our story, our next clue to the fate of Hodges' Scout comes from a source not available to the English at that time. On that same September day, standing only a few miles away from where Hodges' command was destroyed, swatting mosquitoes and fuming, was the most celebrated diarist of the war—writing in French.

6

Captain de Bougainville's
American Adventure

The Mathematician

Standing at the top of what is today's Shelving Rock Mountain, at the Narrows of Lake George, Louis Antoine de Bougainville had a splendid view southwesterly, up the lake to where the English fort lay. It was much too far away to see, but the young French captain could *feel* its presence in the heightened tension of the allied Indian war party about him. His vantage point brought the maps he had seen of this area to life. He could see clearly now how the archipelago of wooded islands below him—no longer mere dots on paper—interrupted the lake's more typical expanse, how a mountainous tongue of land three miles long jutted into the lake, creating Northwest Bay, an obscured "back-door" route for English scouts heading toward Ticonderoga. Mostly, he could plainly appreciate this strange theater of war, seemingly in the middle of nowhere: a "country of mountains [and] precipices" in which rattlesnakes reportedly hung in trees, waiting to drop on unwary passers-by, "entirely a tricky and dangerous country."[1] It was September 18, a warm autumn day, and de Bougainville's hike to this strategic overlook in full uniform had soaked his underclothes with his sweat. As he rested, perhaps enjoying the view, he had opportunity to reflect on the dazzling series of turns his life had taken in the last eight months.

To look at him, de Bougainville must have seemed as unlikely a person to be in this environment as one might imagine. Twenty-six years old, born to a comfortable, bourgeois family in the Chatelet neighborhood of Paris, he was short, pudgy, sleepy-eyed, and asthmatic. A bookish sort, Louis had produced a volume on integral calculus only two years earlier, with its sequel ready for press in 1755. The success of these works had won him an influential patron and admission to the prestigious Académie des Sciences. Although an officer, he had no active-duty experience whatever, much less exposure to combat. Yet here he was, in one of the most dangerous places in the world for a European and, for urban sorts like himself, an altogether unfamiliar and unsettling environment. But then the history of French Canada is replete with such extraordinary characters.[2]

De Bougainville had held a series of junior-officer positions in militia companies in France, but he probably regarded military affiliation as a stepping-stone to social advancement, not an end in itself. Nevertheless, his academic acumen brought him attention from officers in need of intelligent, hardworking staff, without which armies could not operate. Seventeen fifty-six began for him with his election to the Royal Society of London (a testament to his mathematical work), followed by a captain's commission the next month. Then, when Louis-Joseph de Montcalm, Marquis de Montcalm, was given the field command of French forces in Canada, de Bougainville was recommended to accompany him as aide-de-camp. Thus the diminutive scholar found himself embarked for Quebec in April, arriving five weeks later at the docks of the Lower Town. He would soon come to appreciate Montcalm's audacious generalship, while the general in turn found in de Bougainville an energetic and intelligent staff officer despite his lack of real military experience. Like so many of the American provincial soldiers at the other end of Lake George, de Bougainville began to keep a journal of his adventures in this strange new land.

Representatives of France's Indian allies in this as yet undeclared war were to be seen everywhere in Canada, but de Bougainville's first real encounter with them probably occurred in July—at least, that was when he first recorded his impression of them. The occasion was the arrival at Montreal of about forty Menominees from the far-off *pays d'en haut,* who had braved the smallpox that was breaking out, or rumored to be, among the French forts to fight the French king's enemies. The arrival, as de Bougainville learned, required elaborate ritual and diplomatic exchanges—much as would a treaty of alliance in Europe. The Menominees made their appearance in style, in five "great birch-bark canoes," bringing with them a half-dozen scalps and several prisoners for the festivities. They saluted the shore with "a discharge of guns and loud cries," which were answered by three cannon blasts from the town. Coming ashore, they marched to the governor's house in two files, between which walked the prisoners, each carrying "wands decorated with feathers." Ushered into the presence of Governor General Vaudreuil himself, the prisoners were made to sit on the ground, while the Menominee chief, or war captain, made a short speech that, with its "action and force," nevertheless surprised de Bougainville. The warriors then commenced to dance around the captives "in a manner more suited to terrify than to please." They were clad in breechclouts only, "the face and body painted, feathers on their heads . . . tomahawk and spear in their hand." The warriors, de Bougainville observed, were all "brawny" men, "large and of good appearance. . . . All the movements of their body mark the cadence with great exactness." He thought the performance resembled the "pyrrhic [dance] of the Greeks." What the cowering prisoners thought of it all he did not record. All in all, de Bougainville found it an "extraordinary spectacle."[3] He had heard much about the fighting abilities of the American natives, and watching these men, he could now imagine it.

"It is necessary to adjust to their ways"

So it was with anticipation, then mounting puzzlement, and finally frustration that de Bougainville came to observe wilderness warfare on the ground. After Oswego's surrender in August (which de Bougainville had helped to negotiate) and destruction, Montcalm's army had rushed back to Lake Champlain and Ticonderoga, using the water routes to full advantage. De Bougainville, along with the Guyenne regiment, made it to Ticonderoga on September 10, gratified to find the situation there stable. Between the reports of French-aligned Natives and the Anglo-American prisoners they frequently took (de Bougainville himself questioned one of them), the French commanders were well informed about the state of Fort William Henry and the paralysis of English operations in that sector. Encouraged by French successes, as many as six hundred Natives were on hand for some action, as were Canadian militia and officers of the *troupes de la marine*, colony soldiers experienced in woodlands warfare. Such an opportunity could not be wasted, and on the thirteenth a large council was held to determine what ought to be done.

French officers pushed for a two-pronged raid in force, one group to go by Lake George, the other by South Bay toward Fort Edward. De Bougainville now learned something else about France's "brawny" allies: they were not to be commanded. Because Native war parties operated by consensus and persuasion, he observed, "it is a long job to get them to make up their minds." Additionally, there were at least five nations of Indians at the council: Iroquois (of Kahnawake, long aligned with the French), Wabenakis, Chippewas, Ottawas, and those Menominees he had met in July (led by the famed partisan officer Joseph Marin). Reaching consensus among these, wrote de Bougainville, required "authority, brandy, equipment, food," and many long speeches. More accustomed to military decision making from the top down, de Bougainville found the process tedious, wasteful, and "very irksome."[4]

And it was not over. Apparently agreeing to the French initiative, the two war bands were set to leave the evening of the fourteenth, when "several Iroquois who for two days have been on a scout came back with seven deer they had killed. They invited their brothers to a feast, and behold, everything is off and the departure can wait." By the next day, the fifteenth, the plan had changed entirely, with the Indians insisting that they all go together, and by the Lake George route. The combined force of seven hundred warriors and Canadians was to leave that night, but de Bougainville wisely decided that he would believe it when he saw it, having concluded that "the caprice of an Indian is of all caprices the most capricious." Finally, as darkness fell on the sixteenth, four hundred Indians and one hundred Canadians, in thirty-four canoes, pushed off from Carillon's advance camp on Lake George and onto the flat waters of the lake. They made Sabbath Day Point, about eight miles distant, in the darkness and there rested while a lone canoe went ahead to reconnoiter passages through the Narrows.[5] De Bougainville was impatient with the pace and irked further by the fact, now evident, that the French "commander" of the force was only nominally so. The Indians, de Bougainville observed, "determine the route, the halts, the scouts, and the speed to make, and in this sort of warfare it is necessary to adjust to their ways." He soon learned that there was something to their ways after all. The scout canoe returned within a few hours, having spotted an English bateau prowling about the Narrows, obviously from Fort William Henry. It was moonlight, but the canoe stayed motionless in the shadow of trees by the shore, and the enemy bateau left without seeing it. If the alarm had been given, the raiding party's hopes for success would have been severely compromised.[6]

After a day of careful reconnoitering of the Narrows, on the night of the seventeenth the whole force moved to the sheltered north side of Shelving Rock, staying in the canoes until daybreak, then going ashore. A council met immediately, determining for security's sake not to make any fires or noise; de Bougainville noted, however, that "as soon as it broke up the Indians at once did both."[7] It was shortly after this that the French captain hiked to the summit of Shelving Rock for his bird's-eye view of the lake. He was beginning to think that nothing would come of this excursion after all. The Iroquois warriors made up the largest contingent of the war party and thus they made crucial decisions regarding what it would do and when; at the time, they seemed content to stay where they were another day at least. The Ottawas, Chippewas, and Menominees, who had traveled hundreds of miles to be there, were unhappy with that prospect. For the first time, de Bougainville noticed, there seemed to be "discord" among the Indians, a bad sign. But the prospects for action changed suddenly in the afternoon, when scouts reported seeing a canoe put in at "a point" on the opposite shore, where they also thought they had made out some huts or shelters.[8] Here, then, was a target: the men in the canoe could hardly be from anywhere but Fort William Henry, and the shelters suggested an observation post housing more than a few men. The crude huts, constructed near the shore, where they could easily be seen from a distance, also suggested incredible carelessness. Even the curiously lethargic Iroquois could not ignore this opportunity. As night fell, they dispatched two canoes to investigate more closely. Doubtless another council met in the meanwhile to determine the next course of action, for when the canoes returned around eleven o'clock, confirming the first report, the entire force "embarked at once, crossed the lake in complete silence,"[9] and sheltered in a small cove some three or four miles north of the target, there to catch a few hours of sleep (fig. 6.1).

Who were the men in that canoe, and what were they doing there? While armed bateaux frequently patrolled the Narrows—the Indian scouts had encountered one only two nights earlier—this does not appear to have been one on such a mission. They could have had nothing to do with Hodges' Scout, for as we have seen, about the time the canoe was spotted Captain Hodges was mustering his scout at the fort, and while the Indians were conducting their nocturnal investigation of the point, he and his men were bedded down in the woods almost ten miles away. The answer may rest in another of the many breaches of discipline that plagued General Winslow at Fort William Henry: at the end of July he had complained that "Divers Soldiers and Others, take Freedom without Liberty, to go a fishing, and for other uses Improve the Boats and Battauxs Belonging to the Army, by reason

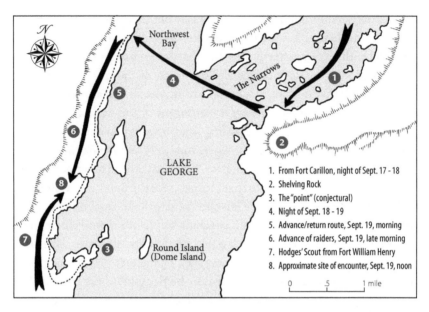

Figure 6.1. Indian and Canadian movements, Sept. 17–19, 1756. Map by Die Hoxie

of which many of them are lost and Damaged."[10] He issued orders to stop the practice, but as with so many such orders, it may have been more honored in the breach than in the observance. If so, the truant anglers had inadvertently doomed Hodges' men: their discovery had brought the entire force of French and Indians onto the northwest side of the lake and on a collision course with them.

"An hour before daybreak," as de Bougainville recalled, after leaving some men to guard their hidden boats, the attackers had moved through the woods "in several files" in order to hit the objective at first light. The French captain must have been nearly giddy with excitement: if his friends at home could but see him now! It was clearly going to be a warm day, and the Indians had stripped to their breechclouts and painted themselves in red and black. It became easier for de Bougainville to see them in the woods as the sky slowly brightened, a ghostly, almost silent procession of lethal menace bearing steadily down on an enemy whose force they could not know exactly but whom they certainly would overwhelm by numbers and surprise. Stealthily the column moved on the point, surrounding it. De Bougainville waited for the shots, the shouts, and the war cries that would signal the general attack.[11]

They never came. Whoever had been at the point must have left in the night or before daybreak; the disappointed attackers "found nothing except old fires smoldering in the roots of trees and a few abandoned huts." Disappointment quickly turned to anger and suspicion as the would-be attackers returned sullenly to their boats: why, some asked, had they not gone ashore in the night *south* of the point, to cut off the enemy's path of retreat? The Indians from the *pays d'en haut*, and apparently de Bougainville as well, began to suspect that the Kahnawake Iroquois, cousins of the Six Nations Iroquois aligning with the English, "had deceived us," that they had had no real stomach for this fight, that they may have deliberately given the quarry every opportunity to slip the trap. The charge was probably unfair, but the abortive attack had brought to a head the "discord" among the multinational Native contingent. At the rendezvous, another council was held, and the Iroquois were "deprived of command." Just how this was done, one would give a good deal to know, but de Bougainville does not say. A likely possibility is that Joseph Marin, soldier, fur trader, and woods fighter of renown, who was leading the Menominee contingent, was among those who took control of the situation. Next, "with a common accord 110 Indians, the most nimble of all the detachment," together with thirty of the "most active" Canadians, led by the aggressive Marin, struck out on foot southward toward Fort William Henry, determined not to return "until they had made a coup" of some sort. As it turned out, they would not have to go far: it was this carefully chosen, highly motivated group that encountered Hodges' Scout only hours later.[12]

Sadly for us, de Bougainville did not go with them to record the fighting that ensued. It was hardly the place for an inexperienced staff officer, and he probably felt that he had seen enough of wilderness "warfare" for the moment. About noon, he and two other French officers debarked from the landing place and made their way back to their advance camp at the north end of the lake, reaching Fort Carillon at seven that evening.

"It is an abominable way to make war"

Hours later, soldiers at the advance camp were startled to hear "a continuous fusillade" of musket fire out on the pitch-black lake. Flashes from the explosions gave them glimpses of a flotilla of canoes, evidently the same ones that had departed only a few days earlier, returning to the advance camp. As they neared the shore, the boats drifted, the firing ceased, and out of the darkness instead there came chilling wails from scores of throats. French soldiers new to America must have reckoned that some disaster had befallen the expedition. More experienced Canadian officers knew that that was not necessarily the case, but one thing was clear: there had been casualties. It was probably such an officer who knew the protocol and knew what to do next: a canoe went out from the camp, and the occupants were asked the reason for their grief. "Marin is dead," came the reply, "we are dead." In fact, only two Natives in the war party had been killed (ironically both of them Iroquois), and the illustrious Canadian was alive and well. As de Bougainville explained, it was traditional for a war party that had lost some of its members to declare that its captain was dead. The camp representatives offered ritual words of consolation, at which the war party erupted in death cries, indicating that they had indeed made the coup they had promised. Mourning gave way to triumph as the boats came to shore, the warriors and Canadians firing again in celebration.[13]

The warriors flourished twenty scalps they had taken.[14] According to de Bougainville, the Indians also had seventeen prisoners, but "they have already knocked several of them on the head."[15] To the French captain's horror, he discovered that it was quite usual for Indians to dispatch surrendered prisoners, particularly if they were mourning the loss of comrades in battle. He probably heard much worse, namely, how the exulting warriors had scalped and butchered the remains of Hodges and his men. Depending on the nationality of the triumphant warriors and the degree of their rage, mutilations of the fallen could vary considerably, going far beyond decapitation and the "chopt & hackt" limbs reported by Reverend Hawley. For example, the previous May, Lieutenant Brooks' corpse had been disemboweled. There may well also have been violence done to the dead's genitalia, these being chopped away or placed in the victims' mouths.[16]

Writers referring to Indian mutilation of the dead have long presumed that the practice was intended to cripple enemy combatants in the afterlife, and in the case of butchered arms and legs this makes some sense. But in targeting the male sex organs the perpetrators aimed at something more to do with the here and now: ritualized emasculation of the dead "manipulated . . . men's fears and flaunted their powerlessness to protect themselves."[17] Mutilation, whatever its putative effects in the spirit world, was carried out with more immediate purpose: mangled bodies of both men and women were left *in order to be found* by the enemy, to fill them with helpless rage, despair, and terror. And it worked: back at Fort William Henry Reverend Hawley, who had witnessed the ravaged corpses, mused, "Tho' tis true y^t tis little matter to persons after y^y are dead w^t becomes of y^r Bodies, yet I could not but be something affected tho' I always endeavor to be above these things and mix ye hardy principles of ye Soldier with those of ye Christian." At the other end of the lake, at nearly the same moment, de Bougainville was less philosophical. "The cruelties and the insolence of these barbarians is horrible," he stormed, "their souls are as black as pitch. It is an abominable way to make war." Worse, almost, was that the Canadians and even his French colleagues seemed to take it all in stride; there was no evident outrage such as he was experiencing. "The air one breathes here is contagious," he concluded, and he feared it made one "accustomed to callousness."[18]

The surviving prisoners were interrogated by the French, and de Bougainville, with some experience of his own, apparently took some part in the proceedings. From these wretched, frightened men they gained an accurate update on the situation at Fort William Henry. Most important to the French was whether an attack on their own position was imminent, as Fort Carillon and its defenses were far from finished. They soon learned they had nothing to fear from that quarter: the prisoners assured them that there were "not two thousand men at their fort, all militia, many sick, no plan for an offensive," and in fact they lived in "fear of being attacked," for Fort William Henry, like Carillon, was unfinished. The prisoners told their captors that there would be a thousand men at the fort over the winter, including several hundred regulars; that the English had had "some communication with our Iroquois" (the question of loyalty again); and the interesting detail that the British regulars did "not get along with the militia and Indians."[19]

The modern reader may find the survivors' willingness to divulge so much so quickly perplexing. We are accustomed to international conventions that require only that prisoners identify themselves to their captors, and we expect prisoners to resist revealing sensitive military information. De Bougainville provides no details about the methods of interrogation or whether coercion of some sort was applied. If we go by existing recorded interrogations of both French and Anglo-American prisoners, however, it does not appear that much pressure was needed. It may be that our standards for prisoner behavior did not apply in the eighteenth century and that captives saw no reason to be anything other than honest. Of course, other forces may have been at work: the conditions of incarceration (never very good at this time); promises of better treatment; threats of worse.

Very much in the favor of the French was the provincials' utter dread of being held by Indians, who likely had been the first interrogators. James Smith, taken the previous year during Braddock's disastrous campaign, was questioned initially by his Indian captors and "threatened with a cruel death if I did not tell the truth." He told them what they wanted to know, though he attempted to equivocate.[20] Prisoners of Indians looked upon the French as potential saviors, often assuming (incorrectly) that French officers wielded authority over "their" Native auxiliaries. The survivors of Hodges' Scout probably inferred from their questioning by French officers that they were now prisoners of the French and could expect relative safety and protection; relief and gratitude would make them open to persuasion. The French saw no reason to disabuse them of their hopes, and indeed their slightest hint that the prisoners would be "returned" to the Indians could be persuasive. But French officers were not above applying more direct threats. An American ranger captured years later was threatened with death by the commanding officer at Fort Carillon, but the French interpreter later confessed that "this was done only to terrify" the prisoner. Promises of reward might work where threats would not; this same prisoner was promised a hefty reward if he would agree to show the French general Rigaud where best to assault Fort William Henry's walls. When he refused, he was put in irons and eventually handed back to his Indian captors.[21]

If de Bougainville thought that the Native warriors, flushed with success and eager for more, would use the momentum gained by their coup to strike again at the demoralized foe, he was about to learn something else regarding France's allies in America. Early the morning of the twenty-first, the Ottawa warriors, "having four prisoners and about five hundred leagues to go to get home," decided to leave that evening. At midmorning the French held a council with the Iroquois, in part to perform the requisite condolence ceremonies for the loss of their two warriors. As the afternoon advanced, with temperatures approaching the mid-90s, it became clear to de Bougainville that "all of the Indians . . . want to leave, Iroquois, Abnakis, Hurons, Five Nations. Of 450 scarcely 30 will remain." It had been explained to him that "they have made a coup" and that it was now "necessary to seek their native hearth." It was almost unfathomable to the young captain; even more unbelievable was that "the Canadians feel the same way."[22] And accordingly, over the next few days the decisive and unprecedented Native presence on the Lake George front all but vanished. The captain-mathematician, along with most of General Montcalm's army, remained at Carillon until the end of October, their most important duty being to complete work on the fort and ensure its security for the winter, when it would be left with only a small garrison.

Some Answers, More Questions

De Bougainville often recorded the frustrations of his assignment in America, but from his journal it is clear that he also found people and experiences to fascinate him. His six-month adventure in this strange and violent land would stretch into years. He was present at Montcalm's first victory at Oswego, and he would be on hand for the final acts of the war in North America, at which time he will reenter our narrative briefly. He relates nothing more about the survivors of Hodges' Scout—for this we must look elsewhere—but his journal provides us with details and clues we would otherwise lack.

First, and obviously, the men of Hodges' Scout were not all killed, as those at Fort William Henry had feared. The Indians initially spared more than a third of them, which not only suggests the premium they placed on prisoners taken in battle but further discredits the version of events told by Lieutenant Webb, who claimed that nearly every one of Hodges' men had been killed or wounded and that "few or none were taken alive."[23] Second, de Bougainville confirms the actual number of warriors and Canadians who took part in the destruction of the provincials (140) and reveals that there were Native casualties as well: two killed outright and three wounded, indicating at least some effective resistance on the part of the provincials.[24] Those slain warriors perhaps explain the lone skeleton later found near the attackers' landing site. De Bougainville wrote that "several" of the captives had been killed by the time he saw them;[25] it seems that the Natives had vented their rage and loss on one unlucky victim before they set out onto the lake for their return. Two or perhaps more were apparently sacrificed at the French advance camp; this may have been what prompted de Bougainville's unusual outburst regarding wilderness warfare.

Lastly, de Bougainville's journal may help us to sort out another of the questions left from the provincial accounts. As de Bougainville described the encounter, the Indian-Canadian force "suddenly ran into" Hodges' men, rather than having set a trap for the unwary provincials.[26] Such a meeting engagement seems consistent with other circumstances he related: the impatience and determination of the picked group of attackers, who were bent on reaching Fort William Henry, and their belief that no enemies were near. It is easy to imagine them, in two or three columns abreast such as de Bougainville had observed, the column nearest the water taking the well-worn path,

> when almost at the same instant, perhaps turning a bend in the path, the lead men in two opposing columns suddenly spot enemy where they had hardly suspected any. They are very close. Instinctively they raise their weapons and fire, falling back or jumping quickly to cover in order to reload. The opponents begin to form lines and commence firing, each trying to determine the other's size and strength. But the other columns of Indians and Canadians keep moving forward, maintaining the higher ground and using the sounds of gunfire and yelling below them to find the flank and rear of Hodges' men. Convinced of their numerical superiority, the unengaged columns now descend into the fray, and their impact is decisive, turning whatever order there was among the provincials into chaos. The scout, about fifty men, collapses, with many dead and wounded, individuals and pockets of men surrendering, and some breaking through the trap and fleeing into the hills or southward along the lakeshore.

It could have happened this way, but questions remain. De Bougainville did not see the fighting, and it seems out of character for experienced Canadian officers like Marin, not to mention the Native warriors, to push blindly into unfamiliar territory without point men and flankers to protect against just this sort of action, which in different circumstances might have turned out as disastrously for them as it did for the provincial soldiers.

Be that as it may, it is not the end of our story. For the bound, terrified survivors of Hodges' Scout, it is just the beginning.

II CAPTIVES

7

Ensign Lincoln's Great Escape

The Return

On July 1, 1757, picket guards at Fort William Henry were startled when two emaciated figures stumbled out of the woods, waving and calling in weak voices for help. It is doubtful that anyone recognized them, especially in their condition, but one of the apparitions explained that he was Ensign Jeremiah Lincoln, of Hingham, twenty-three, a survivor of the disaster that had occurred nearby ten months earlier, which had since become known simply as Hodges' Scout. They had a story to tell: they had escaped from Montreal, 180 miles away, and had been traveling on foot for more than two weeks through wilderness and enemy country, with little or no food.

Safe at last, the two escapees were escorted to the fort for debriefing and, one hopes, a decent meal. Lincoln must have noticed some changes to the place since he had left it on that dreadful September day. For one thing, the fort was finished, as was the large fortified camp to the east, which held the bulk of the garrison, some fifteen hundred to sixteen hundred all told. For another, there were regulars in red coats, particularly at the fort, some with the blue facings of the Royal American Regiment, others sporting the distinctive orange lapels of Colonel Otway's (the 60th and 35th Foot, respectively). The tree line had been moved back even further, and there was visibly more order about the place, and less smell. There was a large garden to the west of the fort—Lincoln would have agreed that fresh vegetables would have been very welcome the previous year. Sadly, the fort's burying ground had also grown. Whether Lincoln and his companion were interviewed by British or provincial officers, or by both, is not known, but the fort's commander, George Munro, lieutenant colonel of the 35th, would have been very interested in what they had to say. They would have been able to bring the latest intelligence of conditions in Canada and possibly news of military movements, especially any coming his way. As Lincoln sat for his examiners, weary and hungry but relieved, it was an opportunity for him not only to be in service again, by telling what he knew, but also to relive, and reflect upon, the extraordinary events of the past year. And could anyone blame him if he also basked in some self-congratulation for coming through the most trying experience of his young life and for ending it with such a remarkable feat of daring and endurance?

Fort Carillon

Lincoln may have begun his reveries by recalling another interview, held under very different circumstances. That time it had been French officers, at another fort, and he had felt anything but reassured. Hardly twenty-four hours had elapsed since those terrible minutes in the woods. The horrors of seeing wounded comrades slaughtered, the dead scalped and butchered, and survivors like himself hustled roughly northward to a fate their imaginations could only dread were very fresh memories indeed. He was exhausted: the previous day they had marched nearly ten miles in the heat, fought a desperate, hopeless battle, and been forced to help paddle the canoes that took them northward into captivity. Their treatment at the hands of their captors had been pretty rough; they had been tied, perhaps with cords around their necks as well, and cuffed or kicked if they did not maintain a quick pace, or even if they did. At the French advance camp the prisoners suffered further abuse. They may have been forced to run a gauntlet, a common, easily organized ritual that allowed all present to share in a victory by beating the victims as they passed between two lines of stick-wielding Indians and Canadians. Then there were the executions (one before they had even embarked in the boats), so terrifying in their apparent randomness, though in fact these victims may have been singled out for reasons known only to the captors. There could have been very little sleep for the survivors that night. Daylight brought temporary relief when French officers had the captives brought to their fort, more than a mile away, for questioning, but the adrenaline that had sustained Lincoln the day before had left him drained of energy, and his Indian captors probably had given him very little to eat, if anything.

The French, who had some experience in these matters, knew their advantage in the interviews that followed. The Indians' treatment of the prisoners had rendered them weakened both physically and psychologically, as well as confused and fearful. It is likely that the French officers gave them some food and drink, perhaps even some wine or brandy to "fortify" them. Grateful, hopeful captives would be more willing to cooperate. We cannot know how much Lincoln told them (or whether he noticed a somewhat portly, sleepy-eyed young captain among them). Sadly, the records of these interviews have not yet been found; they may no longer exist. But as de Bougainville indicated, the prisoners collectively gave the French a very fair sense of the situation at the other end of the lake. Ensign Lincoln may have been cooperative, or it may simply have been French policy regarding captured officers, but he soon discovered that he, at least, would be a prisoner of the French, not of the Indians: General Montcalm himself had secured his "freedom" by paying Lincoln's captor two hundred livres.[1] He was to be sent to Montreal as soon as a boat traveling down Lake Champlain could accommodate. Lincoln's relief must have been palpable. His fellow survivors would have done almost anything to trade places with him. Fourteen of his fellow captives had survived the massacre and the frightful hours that followed.[2] All of them would begin their captivity as prisoners of their Indian captors, and some would remain in Indian hands for the duration of the war. Others, for better and for worse, found themselves held by Canadian masters or imprisoned. Most would eventually return to their homes; some would never return.[3]

While he awaited passage, Lincoln could observe, ruefully, that at last he could view Fort Carillon, just not in the way he had imagined. Undoubtedly he did not have free run of the place—he was still a prisoner, after all, and was likely lodged in the fort's guardhouse—but simply in coming and going he would be able to gather impressions. Today, visitors to the restored fort-museum see an impressive work of stone: solid, formidable, and bristling with large cannon. What Lincoln saw in 1756 was very different. Like Fort William Henry, Fort Carillon had begun life only the previous year, and also like its English counterpart, it was a work in progress of earth and timber (although with stone foundations), but much farther along than suggested by the most recent reports brought to General Winslow. It was in shape and design much like what Lincoln knew well: four-sided with arrowhead-shaped bastions at the corners, and thanks to the five hundred or so men assigned daily to the building of it, all but one of these were completed. He probably did not have an engineer's eye for the fort's location; otherwise he might have been critical, as de Bougainville was. In the French captain's opinion the fort was "badly oriented and . . . not far enough out" on the point over Lake Champlain to cover it, necessitating an additional, and to de Bougainville unnecessary, artillery redoubt there.[4]

Lincoln perhaps also observed, with grim satisfaction, that sickness was as much a problem at Carillon as at Fort William Henry. Scurvy was rife among the French, the bane not only of seamen but of all those deprived of fruits and vegetables for extended periods. Carillon's commander in early August reported four hundred men sick at the fort, and a deserter in late July had told his English hosts that two or three men died of scurvy each day. Such widespread illness had put a crimp in the building timetable, especially as it affected the always too few skilled workers. On the very day that Lincoln was interrogated, an officer at the fort wrote that "sickness is very prevalent which has considerably retarded the work." Still, he thought the fort would be "in a thoroughly effective condition by the end of October."[5]

After spending three days at Carillon, Lincoln recalled, he began his journey to Montreal, probably in the flotilla of bateaux or other vessels that left on the evening of the twenty-second, carrying the most seriously ill French and Canadians to the hospitals there.[6] They stopped briefly at Crown Point, where Lincoln got to see the campaign's objective, but again only imperfectly. After the bustling, sprawling complex that made up the fortifications and encampments at Carillon, the installation at Crown Point seemed comparatively quiet, even quaint. Above the fort there, dubbed St. Frederick, rose a curious, four-story artillery tower of stone that looked like a transplanted Renaissance hybrid, the product of an earlier generation—which indeed it was. With the French effort to make Carillon the new first defense against English invasion, Crown Point had become more of a transshipment point and now contained only a nominal garrison. From there Lincoln's flotilla rowed or sailed the length of Lake Champlain, which demonstrated to Lincoln the strategic importance of this waterway: the passage to Fort St. Jean, some ninety miles from Crown Point, could be covered in just two days, with an overnight bivouac at present-day Schuyler Island. The fort at St. Jean, built eight years before at the end of the last war, was less impressive, really a fortified depot (three weeks earlier de Bougainville had described it as "badly built, cost 96,000 francs, and is in bad condition. . . . could very easily be burned by a winter raiding party"), but it was the debarkation point, and

Figure 7.1. "An East View of Montreal in Canada. Drawn on the spot by Thomas Patten. Engraved by P. Canot." Engraving, ca. 1760–62. National Archives of Canada, C-2433

from there one had to walk or ride to the St. Lawrence—Lincoln probably walked. Compared with previous marches he had made, this one was easy; it was a mere seventeen miles to La Prairie, just upriver from Montreal, along a road that was remarkably flat (but which the fussy de Bougainville called "very bad" in September and "abominable" by the end of October). At La Prairie Lincoln's party, perhaps still accompanying the sick, again embarked in boats and floated down the wide river for about five miles, the Isle de Mont Real to the left, until the roofs and spires of Montreal came into view.[7]

Montreal

Lincoln's hometown of Hingham lies within the protected waters of Massachusetts Bay, in his time a half day's sail (the easiest way to go) from Boston. It is likely that he was familiar with that city, which at the time had the third largest population in the British colonies. Montreal presented him with something else altogether. It was a walled city, unlike anything in the British colonies, of perhaps five thousand souls, set snugly against the

St. Lawrence River, with the massive Mont Real, the city's namesake, rising dramatically behind it. As his boat touched at the busy riverfront, Lincoln must have received several distinct impressions that told him, in the words of William Henry Foster, that those who "passed from Indian hands into those of the French found themselves in yet another new world."[8] One impression was perhaps of sheer solidity. Just past the beach rose a masonry wall eighteen feet high with musketry loopholes near the top every six feet. Beyond that he could see the upper stories of stone buildings, some of them quite grand in appearance.[9]

Lincoln's second impression he could easily have gathered from the steeples of the city's churches and religious compounds, surmounted as they were by crucifixes—telltale signs of a people hostile to the Protestantism of Lincoln's New England. From his youth he had heard stories of the pressures Protestants endured from their captors to convert to the "popish" religion, an act that would surely signify his damnation if he ever weakened to that point.[10] With no hope of attending Protestant meetings, without a "proper" Bible (a King James or Geneva version) for comfort, Lincoln would have to rely on prayer and his earlier religious training not to betray his faith. Third, and perhaps most obvious, Lincoln was entering a world in which few of the inhabitants spoke his language. Of course he had heard French being spoken since his capture, but so far there had been interpreters and French officers to tell him what lay ahead. But now, as he passed, under guard, through one of the five gates along the river, he was bombarded with the language on all sides. It was surely disconcerting to realize that he would be nearly helpless to communicate in his new surroundings until he could learn at least some rudimentary French.

Lincoln's first lodging in Montreal was likely the prison, located according to one source on Rue Notre Dame, one of the city's two main avenues, near the intersection with Rue St. Lawrence.[11] If so, Lincoln may have passed through the gate facing the grand residence of Governor Vaudreuil, the same house where de Bougainville had witnessed the Menominee ritual. Passing the house on his left, Lincoln would have been led up a gently rising street at the top of which were the walled gardens and houses of the Jesuit establishment in the city. From there, the prison was only a short distance to the right. Lincoln would not have to stay there long.

Montreal, indeed all of French Canada, was experiencing an acute labor shortage. If he was a particularly astute observer, Lincoln might also have noticed a decided gender imbalance on his brief course through the town; if not, it soon became apparent to him. The war was making extraordinary demands on Canada's small white population (Massachusetts alone had four times the number). Concerted defense building in the Ohio River country and on Lake Champlain and the need for logistical support for French offensive operations (every bit as labor-intensive as those of the British) meant that much of the available male civilian labor had been hired or drafted for the war effort. The result, reported John Vela, a recent escapee, was that "Montreal. . . was almost drain'd of Male Inhabitants, they being forced away to the Reinforcement of Crown Point and Ticonderoga."[12] Sons and servants had left the city; many would be away throughout the winter, leaving children, the elderly, and especially women to carry on the necessary work of a busy urban center. In the countryside too, farms critical to sustaining the town dwellers, and now thousands of French regulars as well, were having to make do with many fewer workers.

One solution to this dilemma was to employ enemy prisoners. While the conventions of Europe forbade the forced labor of prisoners of war, especially upon military projects, no one frowned on the practice of releasing them into civilian hands in exchange for their labor. As a result, during the last two imperial wars in America "men designated as *prisonniers de la guerre* [i.e., military captives] were often leased or sold to individuals or traders."[13] It was a custom that in some ways was agreeable to all parties: French officials were relieved of having to feed, house, and guard the sometimes large numbers of prisoners; civilians received cheap, often skilled labor; and the prisoners enjoyed more freedom of movement and probably better living conditions than they would have had in overcrowded, pestilent jails. Europeans and European colonists had long familiarity with servitude, especially of the indentured variety, so the transition to bonded laborer must have been understandable enough, if demeaning for the majority of them. Nor was the prisoners' service to be free labor; would-be Canadian masters had to come up with the money to redeem a prisoner. John Vela reported that "he was sold to a baker at Montreal for Nine Pounds," the baker expecting to make back his investment with Vela's service. During the course of his stay, Lincoln may well have met another newcomer to Montreal, Titus King, of Northampton, Massachusetts. Captured by Indians in 1755, King had been brought to Montreal only a few months before Lincoln's arrival and "was sold to the French for an 120 livere." Captain John Shepard, who later escaped and brought the first word about Lincoln and the other survivors, spent a month in prison before he was "Enlarged and went to Work for his bread." Lincoln, an officer (although a junior one), was probably not held long before he was given "Liberty to work for his Living."[14]

What sort of work did Lincoln do? No trade appears next to his name on his company roster, but if a town history written a century and half later is correct, Lincoln the "gentleman" in fact had some experience at blacksmithing, and it is easy to imagine such skilled labor being in high demand in wartime Montreal.[15] Robert Eastburn, a shipwright captured in March 1756, recalled working with an English smith in a shop "opposite to the General's Door"; Lincoln could well have taken Eastburn's place when the latter was transferred to Quebec the next year.[16] In fact, New England captives had an impressive variety of experiences in trades, as even a sample as small as the survivors of Hodges' Scout reveals. Joseph Abbot was a joiner, Jonathan Barnes a blacksmith, and Peleg Stevens a barber. James Archibald, captured the previous April near the Lake George Narrows, "was permitted to go to montreal to work for my living . . . where I workt at my Trade which is a Cordwainer."[17] Even those identified as "husbandman," "farmer," and "laborer" had experience with agriculture and would be eagerly sought by short-handed Canadian farmers.[18] The Hôpital Général, just outside the city walls, run by the Sisters of Charity (known locally as *les grises,* or the Grey Sisters), also needed workers "in simple but strenuous menial tasks," especially to build a seven-foot-high stone wall around the sisters' fourteen-acre property. According to William Henry Foster, the hospital's records show that certainly one captive, "and probably all of them at one time or another, [had] 'worked on our walls and kept our grounds.'"[19] In short, labor in the city was scarce, and the inhabitants were more than willing to tap windfall sources such as Anglo-American prisoners to make up the deficiency.

Canadian masters and mistresses wanted value for their money. No one knew how long the war might last, so purchases of prisoners were made with an eye toward the political future: if peace came too soon, with the prisoners set free as a matter of course, the investor in captive labor might be out of pocket. The typical price of two hundred livres for a captive was roughly equivalent to a common laborer's wages for fourteen months, so a captive had to work at least that long for the master to break even. After that the labor began to pay dividends, for there was no set "term" for the service, as was the case with contracted, or indentured, servants. Indeed, "the bondservant status of captives was open-ended"; as long as the situation suited the master or mistress, it "might last indefinitely." While "no one imagined *permanent* Anglo-American slaves," if there were a lengthy war or the breakdown of prisoner exchange or less formal ransom attempts, prisoners might be in the custody of Canadian inhabitants for the duration of the conflict. That would be the fate of several of Hodges' survivors.[20]

The treatment of prisoners in such situations could vary widely. A kind master or mistress, decent living conditions, and employment in a transferable trade could make life as a prisoner of war more bearable. Simeon Cook, a carter taken captive between Albany and Halfmoon, was sold to a "Gentleman at mount Real who was very Kind to me and used me Well."[21] On the other hand, the opposite conditions could make laboring in Canada brutal, humiliating drudgery. The masters of bonded workers enjoyed broad discretion over their charges' assignments and discipline. It goes without saying that most prisoners went to work for their masters reluctantly, and only to avoid the awful experience of long imprisonment or because they were forced to do so by a government that did not want responsibility for them. Captive workers could be punished by their masters for any infractions or for sloth, and it seems that at least some French Canadians did not hesitate to do so, employing "extended deprivation of adequate food and clothing, and physical brutalization" to keep their new servants, who were slaves in all but name, in line.[22]

Stubborn or recalcitrant captives could be threatened with a return to prison; all were subject to being resold. At the Hôpital Général, where prisoners were building the Grey Sisters' wall, the records from October 1756 to October 1757 include "the receipt for the sale of a British prisoner." According to the document, the man had been "purchased" by the nuns, and when they apparently had no further use for him, they sold him for a tidy profit. In other words, the Grey Sisters were themselves fully engaged in the general trade in captives.[23] The impression one gets from returning prisoners' accounts, however, is that harsh coercion was rare and probably unnecessary. The surgeon Ammi Cutter, at Fort Edward, wrote that James Archibald had insisted "yt ye Prisoners taken at Oswego [then at Montreal] are well used, & have Liberty to walk with yr Swords," an obvious reference to officers but confirmed by another escapee who observed "a great Number of our People that were lately taken Prisoners at Oswego walking the streets of Montreal: that the Soldires in general were very well used."[24]

At any rate, Lincoln was soon able to take in a large portion of the town. Quebec, 150 miles downriver from Montreal, was Canada's bulwark against the outside world and the colony's vital link with the mother country. Nevertheless, Montreal was the nerve center for both military and economic operations in the interior, the great logistical hub, whether one ventured westward to the Great Lakes, southwest to the Ohio country and Louisiana, or southward toward the British colonies. Montreal controlled roughly 95 percent of the Canadian fur trade, the "single most important commercial activity" in the colony, generating "more than half of the export revenues under the French regime." The local economy grew from this trade, and then from supplying and defending the supporting outposts. Military and provincial contracts went to merchants based in the town, who in turn hired tradesmen and voyageurs and attracted the farmers to feed them all. Missionaries in the seventeenth century, following closely in the wake of the traders, established headquarters in the town and helped to cement relations with Native nations. Montreal was also a market town, a port, a judicial and administrative seat, a production center, and a military depot. And it was growing. As many as half of the city's artisans were in the building trade, though some of them were far away, building forts where only recently there had been wilderness.[25] Thus Montreal's strategic importance was obvious to both British and French: it supplied the far-flung trading outposts, without which the colony could not be economically viable; it made possible French claims to the Ohio country by supporting its chain of forts, arming Native allies, and suppressing Native enemies; it was the base from which fortified strongholds trailed south, up the Champlain valley, ending at Fort Carillon. On the other hand, the loss of Montreal would be akin to slashing a tree at its base: the branches would quickly wither. It simply had to be defended at all costs; if Quebec was the front door of French Canada, Montreal was the equally important back door.

Going about his work, perhaps running errands for his master and employer, Lincoln would have become familiar with the city's layout and neighborhoods. Montreal took the shape of a rectangle nearly a mile long, about a quarter mile wide at its west end, and about half that width at the east end. Within that walled perimeter the ground rose steadily from the water's edge, creating more or less distinct "upper" and "lower" parts of town. There were three male religious orders in the city: the Recollets near the west gate, Sulpicians nearer the center of town, and Jesuits (soon to be suppressed in

France) toward the east end. There were also two female orders in addition to the Sisters of Charity mentioned earlier—the Religieuses hospitalieres at the Hôtel-Dieu and the Congregation of Notre Dame. The religious orders alone, with their spacious, walled-in properties and gardens, accounted for a fifth of the space within the walls and helped to separate the parts of town.[26] Rue Notre Dame ran most of the length of the upper town, which had more freestanding houses, while in the lower town, near the busy waterfront and served by Rue St. Paul, attached buildings lined the streets. The long walls of these buildings typically were parallel to and hugged the street line, and they had courtyards behind "for commercial, artisanal, or household use."[27]

Much of what Lincoln saw was the result of building reforms following disastrous fires. In 1721 a wind-driven blaze had consumed the Hôtel-Dieu and more than 130 houses. After that, wood-framed or half-timbered buildings were prohibited, and new houses were required to be built of stone. "Until such time as tile and slate is available," the ordinance demanded, the usual steeply pitched roofs were to be double-planked instead of covered with thin wood shingles (an exception was made for dormers), and chimneys were to project four *pieds* (ca. 4.5 feet) above the roofline. The result by the 1750s was a "typical" Montreal house of about one thousand square *pieds,* with a "massive two or three-*pied* thick gable wall" that incorporated chimney flues and rose above the roofline. The most common house of this pattern was two stories high, while some rose to three stories. Such was the standard for *new* buildings, but that still left many older, wooden houses in town; another forty-five of these in the lower town had gone up in flames in the infamous fire of 1734, allegedly started by the slave Angelique. Most of these had been rebuilt in the new style by the time of Lincoln's captivity, and the streets straightened and widened to at least thirty *pieds* to better facilitate firefighting. Lastly, each roof had, or was supposed to have, a ladder hooked over the ridge to aid firefighters.[28]

At the east end of the city, where Lincoln probably did not often venture, was the military and administrative quarter. On a small hill was an unimposing redoubt, presumably guarding the *magazin du roi* (storehouse) and the boatyard below. Nearby, the governor and the *intendant* for the colony kept houses for when they were in town. These were imposing buildings indeed, especially the governor's house. Two stories of cut stone (unlike the rough-split fieldstone of most Montreal houses) rose above a high basement floor, with a hipped roof of slate (no vulgar wood here) and a grand circular stairway entrance. Behind the house, which "resembled a traditional seventeenth-century French palace," were extensive and meticulously maintained gardens. If Lincoln did walk by this edifice on his way to the prison, he would certainly have remembered it, as there was nothing quite like it in New England.[29] One thing he might have noticed was that in a town so obviously dependent on the military for its protection and economy there were no barracks. The city did not normally contain a garrison of more than 250 men, even in wartime, and these were billeted by the inhabitants.[30]

At some point Lincoln must have passed through the marketplace, toward the southwest end. This busy area in the lower town, with its own gate leading to the river, was the site of formal markets on Tuesdays and Fridays and executions when there was occasion. With the religious orders taking up so much space within the walls, three *faubourgs,* or suburbs, had grown up outside of them for those who could not find space, or could not afford it, within. And once Lincoln got over his initial wonder at seeing a walled city, he would have become less impressed with the fortifications themselves. These were constructed in the wake of Queen Anne's War, and while they looked impressive (the French, Lincoln may have concluded, seemed to like building with stone), they were only four feet thick, expected only to withstand assaults by infantry. This in fact made some sense; the obvious threat to Montreal would come from the British colonies to the south, and the assumption guiding the engineer Gaspard-Joseph Chaussegros de Lery, who designed the walls, was that the British were unlikely to make use of heavy artillery—there was too great a distance, and there were too many geographic obstacles, including the wide St. Lawrence River itself, in between. Fort St. Frederick, at Crown Point, built during the same period, would be an additional check against an invader. So a conventional artillery siege was unlikely; a direct assault from the more numerous American colonists and their Native allies was a more reasonable scenario. The wall along the river that had greeted Lincoln when he first entered Montreal was in all more than two miles in length, with combinations of bastions and curtain walls pierced by embrasures and loopholes. A dry ditch eight feet deep on the landward sides added effective height to the wall. To attacking infantry without cannon, Montreal might indeed have been a hard nut to crack.[31]

But the relatively thin masonry walls of Montreal could not stand an hour's bombardment from artillery of even moderate caliber. Four years before Lincoln's arrival, another French engineer had declared that the recently finished wall (a project that had taken thirty years to complete) could "resist only a surprise attack or escalade, and no attack at all if it be with cannon." Another officer thought Montreal's fortifications "no more imposing than a garden wall," while Captain de Bougainville described the city as "badly fortified with a crenellated wall." Such information as returning captives could give of this situation would be of great value to Anglo-American strategists.[32]

"One could not understand how frightful this country is"

By the time Lincoln was released to work in the city, it was apparent to him that Montreal was already feeling the effects of the war, not six months old officially. Winter came early, compared with what he had become accustomed to in New England; although the autumn weather had been comfortable enough thus far, by mid-October de Bougainville noticed that the land seemed to be "setting into snow and cold." A week later he was complaining that "the cold has been very sharp these days. It has frozen quite hard the last two nights."[33] With winter fast approaching, the campaign season for both sides had reached its practical end, and after leaving adequate garrisons at their frontier forts, the bulk of the French forces began to pull back toward the St. Lawrence settlements to find winter quarters. Inevitably, some of these soldiers ended up in Montreal and its environs, bringing an unwelcome garrison-town atmosphere to the city. This war marked the first time that such large numbers of French regular troops had been committed to America. The presence of thousands of soldiers put immediate stress on Canadian food, firewood, and housing resources.

Food quickly became the most difficult need to satisfy. With its short growing season, Canada rarely produced agricultural surplus, and any number of unlucky weather conditions—a delayed spring, a wet summer—could mean below-par harvests. Canadian colonists frequently experienced grain shortages, which then raised prices for bread, that staple of life. Seventeen fifty-six had been a particularly hard year for the harvest, doubtless made worse by the absence of men employed on military projects. By early November bakers were being forced to mix oats with wheat flour in their bread—a healthful-sounding option to modern readers but somewhat scandalous in the eighteenth century, when oats were considered food for horses. Two weeks later even oats were unavailable, and recourse was made to a half-and-half mixture of wheat flour and peas. Even so, with so many more mouths to feed and less food with which to do it, bread quickly became scarce. The Guyenne battalion, returning from Carillon to winter quarters in Montreal, "found no bread at either St. Jean, Chambly, or Trois Rivières." In the cities, bread eventually had to be rationed. Officials in Quebec ruled that bread would be distributed to the public only in the afternoons, and only to citizens showing an appropriate ticket. De Bougainville decided to see for himself how this system played out. It proved a disturbing sight. "It presents the image of a famine," he observed. "Those who cannot get near hold out their permits on the end of a stick. It is a sight to keep away from." Especially, it was a scene to conceal from all those English prisoners about town, "who come every day to look on and who do not fail to draw their conclusions from it."[34] Lincoln certainly drew the obvious conclusions from similar shortages in Montreal. And this was before the long winter had set in fully.

That came soon enough. After Lincoln had been in Montreal for a month, traveling even to Quebec had become difficult, the ground already covered with snow and the rivers frozen at their edges. And with the winter came Canada's annual exile, as the St. Lawrence River inexorably froze shut against the outside world. "No vessel can winter here," reported de Bougainville, "the ice does not allow it." The last vessels to leave Quebec left their quays before mid-November, and that was pressing their luck; ahead lay a weeks-long voyage down the river, racing the frigid temperatures and bitter winds as the ice closed in behind them.[35] There would be no vessels from France— no food, supplies, or even news—until April or May, after the ice broke up. French officers like Montcalm and de Bougainville, new to the country, wrote with mounting disbelief and alarm at the winter conditions, unknown in their native land. Writing shortly after the last ships had sailed, de Bougainville reported that "all day there has been a very strong northwest wind, which brought with it thirteen inches of snow." On November 20 the daytime temperature was fifteen degrees Fahrenheit; the next day it was seven degrees. "There has been an astonishing amount of snow," General Montcalm wrote later that winter to friends at home, "the thermometer being many times down to twenty-seven, often eighteen to twenty, and nearly always from ten to fifteen, *minus*."[36] De Bougainville, usually a chatty diarist, over the course of his first Canadian winter often included for the day's entry simply a line recording what was falling from the sky, from what direction, its velocity, and the temperature. On January 18 he described "clear and frightfully cold weather. . . . Minus twenty-four degrees [−29°F]." The cold and snow were frequently lethal. De Bougainville wrote of the danger of going anywhere amid the fine, powdered snow, which, driven by the wind, "envelops you, blinds you, and leads one astray who knows the way very well. . . . There are instances of people who in the night, a hundred paces from their houses, have perished without being able to reach them." Unless one lived in a village or town, human company could be minimal, for "the roads are impassable." De Bougainville concluded, and Anglo-American prisoners would undoubtedly have agreed, that "one could not understand how frightful this country is if he has not been here. . . . It is impossible to conceive of a viler sort of weather."[37]

In practically his next line, however, de Bougainville wrote of attending a "great ball and faro [card game] at the Intendant's house." For the French officers, as for the cities' social elite, relief from the winter's boredom came in "a general succession of balls, receptions, & dinners." Writing from Montreal in late November, General Montcalm described how he and his officers, captive and exotic additions to the city's night life, were eagerly sought by the local grandees:

> M. le Chevalier (de Levis) passes the time socially at Madame de Pénissault's house. He has been to a great supper party at M. Martel's. As for myself I play at backgammon, or I have a hand at whist with my general, Madame Varin occasionally, or Madame d'Eschambault. . . . Quebec has appeared to me as a town of very high tone; I do not believe that in France there are a dozen surpassing Quebec in society.

Montcalm clearly enjoyed the attentions of the ladies of Montreal and Quebec, finding them "witty, courteous, and pious." Excessive gaming, he confessed, was the order of the day, though he did not say whether he played for high stakes. And of course the general was happy to reciprocate; indeed, as he was a gentleman the rules of society demanded it. By the following February he was reporting that

> Since being here I pass my time giving big dinners to parties of fifteen or sixteen persons and sometimes supper. . . . Sunday, I gathered together the ladies from France. . . . Wednesday, a gathering at the house of Madame Varin; Thursday, a ball at that of the Chevalier de Levis, who had invited sixty-five "dames or dem-

oiselles." Thirty would have been enough, so many men being away in the war. The hall was brilliantly illuminated. . . . [There was] much ceremony and attentive hospitality, refreshments in abundance, all the night, of every kind and species, and the party did not leave until seven o'clock in the morning.

Montcalm wrote that he, however, had retired early, for he "had had . . . the same day, a supper for eight ladies, in honour of Madame Varin. Tomorrow I shall give another for half a dozen." It seems that one of his staff acted as his social secretary, for he confessed that regarding the next day's supper, "I do not know yet to whom it is to be given."[38]

In contrast with the warm, well-fed, well-lubricated lives of Canada's upper crust over the winter, markedly rougher were those of the *habitants* and soldiers, to say nothing of the Anglo-American prisoners, many of whom likely shared garret quarters with servants, sleeping on pallets or heaped straw, shivering in the unwonted cold, and very likely hungry. In these conditions, sickness seemed likely to spread from the army, which had withdrawn for the winter to the settlements after marching through grim November weather. The men of the Guyenne battalion, starved for bread on their return, also were forced "to bivouac at night in the midst of ice and snow. They arrived . . . almost all with colds, wasted and emaciated." Nor had Lincoln escaped the dangers of smallpox, if he had not had the disease already. De Bougainville reported that smallpox had "reigned" in Canada throughout the year, opining that it was "the Acadians and British prisoners who have brought it"—a very plausible scenario.[39]

At least the prisoners were not subjected to systematic pressure to renounce their Protestant "heresy" and convert to Catholicism, as many had been led to expect. Doubtless the sheer number of captives in French hands made any expectations of mass conversions unrealistic. In past conflicts (or even when there was no official war on), captive English colonists had come a few at a time, or at most in dozens, allowing priests and nuns of the several orders to sift through the exhausted, terrified unfortunates to select those most likely to make the conversion, who were largely children and young women. Whole garrisons of prisoners such as those from Oswego—grown men, many of whom had trades, farms, and families at home—were much less persuadable, and as prisoners of war they were subject to sudden departure owing to ransom, return, and exchange. For these and other reasons, according to William Henry Foster, by the time of the Seven Years War in America the religious houses in Canada were not very eager for Anglo-American converts. For example, even though English-speaking prisoners had been "acquired" by the Grey Sisters, there are no records indicating that any of them converted or even that any concerted effort was made to bring about such an event. Further, "in Montreal, young captive Protestant females, who in earlier wars would have been eagerly sought out by the religious communities, languished and sometimes died in filthy jails just steps from convent walls. Young men who would have been considered subjects for adoption and resettlement died in the same prisons."[40] On the other hand, captives displaying any willingness or interest in conversion "could be treated as the most welcome of guests." One Thomas Brown, captured in January 1757, used this conversion zeal to his advantage. The farm family with which he had been placed "often endeavoured to persuade me to be of their Religion, making many fair promises if I would." Brown eventually took them up on it, demanding—and getting—decent clothing in exchange for going to Sunday Mass and receiving instruction. He was even allowed to ride to church with the family's two daughters (which may also have influenced his decision to "convert"). When Brown later attempted to escape and was returned, his master (and daughters), understandably, felt duped and betrayed.[41]

There is no evidence that Lincoln attempted any such thing in order to ameliorate his own situation, and Brown's rural hosts seem to have been particularly naïve. But the life of a prisoner in wartime Montreal was not an easy one, even if he was spared the prison. The inhabitants' resentment toward enemies, who at least indirectly had brought about their steadily deteriorating state, was often palpable. They occasionally, perhaps even frequently, vented their anger and frustration on helpless prisoners. Their abuse did not have to take physical form. It came in the stares and smiles directed at the men as they went about their work; in the catcalls and insults of children, who knew that they could behave so to *these* adults; in their being treated like the servants they were; in the appropriation of their labor, so highly valued at home, by people who despised them. One captive in the city witnessed prisoners from Oswego being brought in "and the French rejoicing at our downfall, and mocking us poor Prisoners, in our Exile and Extremity."[42] "The sight of captured men working for nuns," observed William Foster, became "one of the most favored spectacles in Montreal." The Grey Sisters made good use of their captives' labors, "but in the meantime the gaze and mockery of the audience must have mortified the workers."[43] One such prisoner reported that "ye french officers much Ridicule our officers for giving up Oswego so Soon."[44]

Bold Plans

At some point Lincoln began to think seriously about escaping his captivity. He must have fantasized about it on his journey north, but as the miles fell away behind him he must have seen how difficult, if not impossible, that would be. If he spent any time in Montreal's prison, he likely thought that a prisoner exchange was his best and perhaps only way out, and as an officer he could hold out reasonable hope there. Once released, however, and once he had settled into something of a routine and his master's initial vigilance had waned, the prospects for escape had improved.

Nevertheless, those prospects were still daunting. Lincoln would have had an idea of the distance to be covered from his own travels, but if he had more accurate information, he would have known that his nearest refuge, Fort William Henry, was more than 180 miles away, and he could hardly return the way he had come. There could be no question of using the La Prairie–St. Jean road—"abominable" as it may have been, it was too well traveled—and boats to speed him the length of Lake Champlain would not be at his command. It would be a long walk through mountainous forest if he was to succeed. And pursuit of some sort was practically assured. But even before that, there was the wide St. Lawrence to cross. Montreal was an island; the river that was a vital artery for the city's trade and for troop movement was also a swift-flowing moat that made Montreal a prison without bars. It is small wonder that the French allowed enemy captives a limited run of the town. Most sensible captives accepted their hard fate owing to a very reasonable fear of "something worse. Suppose they succeeded in escaping. . . . Then what? The Saint Lawrence Valley crawled with armed French soldiers and Canadian militia, and at least a hundred miles of forest separated them from home—a forest inhabited by a considerable number of French-allied Indians. Recapture—if they had avoided starvation—would certainly mean greater hardship, if not death, among the Indians, or back in Canadian prison."[45]

But escape was not impossible. As early as 1705 Joseph Petty and three other men taken in raids on Deerfield, Massachusetts, and held in Montreal stole a canoe and crossed the river. Traveling mostly on foot, they made their way halfway up Lake Champlain, across the Green Mountains, and down the Connecticut River, reaching Deerfield after three and a half weeks, "more dead than alive from hunger and fatigue."[46] In the very week that Lincoln arrived in Montreal, James Archibald and John Vela left it, reaching Fort William Henry after seventeen days' travel. On October 10, Captain John Shepard, of New Hampshire, and four others made their bid for freedom and were picked up two weeks later by boats on Lake George. Lincoln almost certainly heard of these daring escapes once he was at liberty in the town, and as days and weeks passed without the escapees being returned to captivity, others would be encouraged to try.

On the other hand, success, while possible, was still quite problematic. At least one attempted escape in 1759 ended in failure, cannibalism, and return to captivity. Thomas Brown and one other prisoner, "an English Lad," fled Montreal, but despite Brown's experience as a scout, they were twenty-two days in the woods, probably lost. Brown's companion died of starvation, and Brown cut as much meat as remained from the poor youth's corpse and carried it in a handkerchief. He then managed to kill some partridges, but the report of his musket drew the attention of Canadian scouts or hunters, and Brown was sent back to Montreal, where his master "called me a fool, for attempting a thing so impossible." Later, when he wrote of his experiences, Brown claimed to have been unable to eat the meat of his companion, but one wonders whether he was being entirely truthful to his readers.[47] Brown's ordeal would have been unknown to Lincoln, of course, but so would the fates of Archibald, Vela, and Shepard; for all that Montreal's inhabitants knew, their not returning might simply have meant that they had died in their vain attempts.

At any rate, there was no opportunity for Lincoln to make such an escape for the time being. Every escape made inhabitants more vigilant, more watchful of prisoners' activities, and even if he could have overcome the logistical difficulties outlined above, winter was setting in, as de Bougainville had noted, with hard frosts and threats of snow. Those countrymen of his who had left early in October had made their move at nearly the last reasonably safe moment: as we have seen, heavy snows and bitterly cold temperatures came in November. To make such a long journey without the right equipment, sufficient food, and adequate clothing was suicidal, and tracks in the snow would point the way for pursuers like a finger. Along with distance, and the St. Lawrence River, winter was Canada's jailer. So Lincoln and hundreds of other prisoners had no choice but to endure the privation, the cold, and the even frostier indifference of Montreal's citizenry.

Over the winter, then, or in the spring at the latest, Lincoln found fellow captives who were willing to accept the considerable risks involved in escaping their captivity. In this, at least, the long winter may have been helpful, for it had provided time and the opportunity to become acquainted with other prisoners and to sound them out on the question of escape. Lincoln could not be too careful in the selection of his comrades for an endeavor such as this. For one needed comrades. There were any number of difficulties that would be better overcome by a group, from manhandling boats or canoes to helping in the case of injury and keeping watch while others got vital sleep. No one escaping from Montreal tried it alone. And one's companions would have to be physically able and temperamentally prepared for the demanding trek. A prisoner with even the slightest limp or a persistent cough would have to be rejected as too great a risk, and a determined character or mental toughness would be necessary when inevitable setbacks threatened despair. Members of the group would have to trust one another's grit and endurance.

Someone who knew the way would also be necessary. Those captives from the surrender of Oswego could not be counted upon for this; those taken on the Lake George front constituted a likelier pool from which to find dependable guides.[48] As noted earlier, the easier route, by road and lake, was not a smart option, so runaways would be making most of their way through wilderness. An experienced woodsman was needed to navigate the trackless forest; it is significant that James Archibald and Captain Shepard, who made it home, were both rangers. Even so, experience was no guarantee of success: Thomas Brown had been one of Robert Rogers' famous partisans.

The group could not be too large or too small. A few men could meet to make plans oftener and more surreptitiously than could a half dozen or more. Petty, as we have seen, traveled with three companions. Shepard did likewise; three more were to rendezvous with him after they were over the river. Archibald left with only one, and that, as Thomas Brown discovered, was overly risky. The accounts of escaped prisoners, however, make clear that they kept their plans strictly among themselves, wisely not risking word of their designs leaking out. The fewer who knew of their plans, the better.[49]

Eventually, Lincoln conspired with three other men to make the attempt. One was a soldier taken at Oswego; neither he nor Lincoln could have been the all-important guide, however, so the identity of the guide and the fourth man remains a mystery. How did they come together and decide on their desperate undertaking? They may have worked together (perhaps on the Grey Sisters' wall) or managed to meet discreetly on Sundays,[50] when nearly the whole Catholic population was at Mass. Sadly, Lincoln goes into no such detail. But they clearly were no longer willing to wait for events or to endure another year in captivity. Over a series of clandestine meetings, we may safely imagine, they worked out solutions as best they could to the obstacles that lay in their path. Having settled on their group's members and found their guide, securing a boat to carry out the initial departure from their island prison must have been high on the conspirators' agenda. There was certainly no lack of water conveyance on the island; the trick would be to find one adequate to their numbers that they knew they could steal with minimal risk of discovery. Any alarm given in making off with a boat or canoe would scotch their plans at the outset and doubtless return them to worse circumstances than they had left.

Of those escapees mentioned above, only Joseph Petty described how it might have been done. Petty worked at Pointe-aux-Trembles, nine miles downriver from the city, and he and his companions took a canoe he knew to be nearby. It would be much easier to leave unnoticed from a point well outside Montreal; perhaps one of Lincoln's fellows had an arrangement similar to Petty's.[51] The fact that other escapees do not dwell on this part of the operation suggests that it turned out not to be the most difficult part, though surely it was the most critical and held the greatest risk of discovery. In any case, it required stealth, and darkness. The runaways would have to coordinate their movements and contrive to sneak away from the houses where they boarded to meet at the boat at the appointed time. Crossing the river in darkness was a hazard in itself, but necessary. They would have to cross and land unnoticed and put as much distance between themselves and pursuit as possible before their absence was discovered.

As for when to leave, that was in large part dictated by the season. Springtime would be the earliest time they could make their attempt, but that was still a difficult time. Just as winter came early to Canada, spring came late. Snow and ice remained on the ground well into April, and crossing the St. Lawrence before the ice had finished breaking up and passed downriver would invite additional hazards. Snow melt and rain conspired to make much of the countryside from La Prairie to St. Jean a freezing, forbidding marsh. For the best chance of success escapees would have to wait until May or June. Within that time frame, additional factors could help determine the best time for departure. Thomas Brown and his companion left Montreal before sunrise on a Sunday, when they could be confident that most of the population would be in church. In Joseph Petty's case, the decisive factor may have been the phase of the moon; he left on a Monday morning, the day before the new moon. Whether that was the consideration for Lincoln's party a half century later, on the date they chose for departure—June 17—there was also a new moon.

Even the best-laid plans are subject to chance factors; when all was said and done the escapees would need luck on their side, and a good deal of it. Each man would have to somehow evade detection as he left his billet and made his way either through the town (how they would get through the city's gates is a mystery) or along suburban lanes toward their rendezvous. An alert *habitant*, a challenge from anyone in the dark streets, a barking dog—any of these and more could end a runaway's flight before it was well begun and perhaps doom the enterprise for all. They would have to cross the river unseen and without mishap, make it past the settlements on the other side undetected as well, and strike off into the forest before they could even begin to feel reasonably safe. There was the strong possibility of pursuit by men who knew that business or of a chance encounter with hunters, Native or Canadian. Inclement weather could dangerously slow their progress; one or more of them could become ill; someone could twist an ankle over the long journey. But these were risks inherent in the plan, and Lincoln and his mates doubtless worked to mitigate their possibility as much as was possible. Of one thing they could be certain, however: they would not be able to bring enough food.

Starvation was the greatest threat to would-be escapees: they faced a demanding march of more than 180 miles over rough terrain, which under even the best conditions might require two weeks and would assuredly require more sustenance than was available to them in their captivity. As we have seen, there were no food surpluses in Montreal, and Anglo-American captives had only what was provided to them by their jailers or masters or what they could otherwise acquire or steal. Thomas Brown and his fellow conspirator agreed to run away, "but how to get Provisions for the Way," he recalled, "we Knew not." A partial solution arose, however, when Brown's master allowed him the use of a musket to kill pigeons for the family. "I shot a number," he remembered, "split and dried them, and concealed [some of them] in the Woods."[52]

Joseph Petty refers to some "provision" that he and his fellows took with them, but all escapee accounts agree that what they could take was never enough. Between the difficulty of collecting the food in the first place, hiding it until needed, and transporting it without being noticed, provisioning the escape was problematic at best. Petty and his companions used up their provisions (probably strictly rationed) after only six days; Brown made his last only a day longer. Lincoln would later give us the most detailed provisions list of any previous escapees: when he and his fellows left Montreal they carried "13 Bisket & thre[e] Pounds of Pork each," which they had managed to save or scrounge.[53] It would not be enough, and the deficit would have to be made up somehow along the way. That Lincoln and others were willing to take such a chance testifies to one further requirement for those attempting escape: faith—faith that the food would be there and faith in their ability to find it.

Escape

The runaways put Montreal behind them on June 17, apparently without incident, and made it past the French settlements on the south bank of the river. They had to cross one of the roads leading to St. Jean, but this they probably accomplished at night. Getting away from the road as soon as possible was likely their aim, for the way had become active again with French soldiers moving south for the year's campaign. Indians from the Great Lakes region had also begun to show up at Montreal and might move in the same direction. Keeping close to the road and, later, to the west side of Lake Champlain was the surest means of finding their way, but it also ran the greatest risk of discovery. From what Lincoln later told of their journey, it appears that they had determined to avoid that busy area and set a course through the woods toward Crown Point; from there they could take their bearings and make for the west side of Lake George.[54] If they could get to the Narrows—near to the place, in fact, where Lincoln had been taken— they stood a good chance of getting the attention of patrol boats from Fort William Henry or of encountering a scout from there. If not, at least Lincoln would know the rest of the way.

As they must have expected, the food gave out all too soon. The "Bisket" to which Lincoln referred was likely of the sort made famous (or infamous) by the navies of the period: a mixture of medium-ground flour, water, and salt worked into a thick dough, cut into 3- to 4-inch circles, baked and allowed to dry thoroughly. Their virtue lay in their portability and the fact that if they were kept dry they could last indefinitely. To eat them required either breaking them into bits with a rock or gun butt (they were too hard to bite) or soaking them in water, preferably some sort of soup. At least they were filling. The men also had three pounds of pork apiece, presumably salted and dried. The meat would likewise be nearly inedible if not rinsed or soaked in water. At perhaps 200 calories per biscuit, and 930 calories per pound of pork, each man carried food that amounted to between 5,000 and 5,500 calories, enough for only two or three days for a sedentary adult male at the modern rate. Lincoln and his companions were anything but sedentary, covering on average eleven miles of rough country each day. Even if the men carefully rationed their portions (Lincoln's language suggests that they had divided their gleanings evenly among them), the provisions they had brought would not have lasted very long.

Did they stop to look for food? Lincoln's timetable suggests that if they did, it could not have been for very long. Unlike Thomas Brown, Lincoln's party did not have a gun with which to hunt for game. Even if they had had a gun, it would have been dangerous to use it: Brown was discovered and returned to captivity after shooting at a partridge. Success at hunting was problematic at any rate, and a day lost in hopes of bagging some game was another day without food, another day in which they might be discovered. Trapping game was another possibility, and a more silent option, but it was no more sure than hunting and again threatened fatal delay. Fishing in the ponds along the way might yield better results (Petty and his comrades sustained themselves at least partly in this way), but Lincoln mentions no hooks and line in his account. In any case, cooking whatever they caught would be out of the question, as the smoke from a fire might be seen, or sniffed, from a considerable distance.

The men quickly lost weight, as their bodies began to self-consume. Given the food situation in Montreal, the men were likely already lean when they started out. Without much fat from which to draw, their bodies began to deplete muscle tissue. They became increasingly weak. They must have subsisted on whatever they could find to eat, and people in their situation are not terribly fussy. Thomas Brown wrote that he was twenty-two days on the run, "15 of which we had no Provision except Roots, Worms, and such like." Joseph Petty and his companions at one point resorted to "the leg of a tortoise and a small hook fish which we brought along a little way." Toward the end of the war, another escapee said he had survived on roots and wild strawberries.[55] Any or all of these, and perhaps some others, Lincoln's party may have eaten; he does not say, but their recourse must have been similar.

The crisis came when, famished and weak after almost two weeks of travel, they reached Crown Point. From the slope of a mountain (perhaps the one Rogers had used to make his intelligence reports) they could easily see the French fort below. There was activity there—and food. Having come so far, they still had nearly fifty miles to go, and two of them decided that they simply could not make it. Desperately hungry, dispirited, and broken down from their forced march, "Two not being Able to bear the hardships of so long a March Attended with Pinching Hunger . . . Proposed to Resign them selves unto the Enemy Again." Perhaps Lincoln and the fourth man, determined to continue, tried to talk them out of it: it was not much farther, they could argue, a few days at most. Just as likely, the two broken men had reached their physical and psychological limits. Starvation not only produces bodily atrophy but affects temperament as well, introducing irritability and impulsive behavior. Perhaps they had already begun to slow the party down; those who went on would make better time without them, and all of them knew it. We can imagine a final conference: the surrendering men would have to persuade their captors that there were just the two of them, perhaps saying that the party had split up to find food days earlier and that they had lost their way in the woods. If the French suspected otherwise, they might set out in pursuit of Lincoln and the fourth man or notify the forces gathering at Carillon to send out scouts to intercept them. There were farewells and wishes for good luck, and then the runaways parted company.[56]

Either there was no pursuit or Lincoln and his remaining companion manage to evade it, for sixteen days after leaving Montreal they were back at Fort William Henry. They had accomplished what only a handful of men had done so far, or would do for the rest of the war. And at least for the moment, they possessed the most up-to-date impressions of the disposition of French forces in that theater. In his interview with British and American officers, Lincoln divulged what information he had managed to gather at the time of his escape. Most of it was hearsay and rumor, but it could still be valuable if confirmed in some way. Three thousand reinforcements were supposedly bound from France for Canada; there were some 6,000 French regulars there already, part of a total force of at least 10,000, including Canadians, but only 5,000 could be spared for any attack southward because they felt that their Ohio posts were threatened by the activities of a certain Colonel Washington. Lincoln also knew of 300 regulars and 400 Indians who, five days before his escape, had left for Fort Carillon (good reason for Lincoln's party to have avoided the road from Montreal), but no more than that. The French, he informed, had been in a state of paralysis over rumors (which were false) of an Anglo-American expedition making its way up the St. Lawrence River. He could report from firsthand experience that "Provisions were extremely scarce at Montreal," which was certainly useful intelligence in its own right. Lastly, asked whether he had seen any further defensive works being built at Crown Point, Lincoln said he had seen none.[57]

No doubt Lincoln was eager to go home to Hingham. After some days' rest and a restorative diet, he was strong enough to travel, first to Fort Edward—one hopes he was able to ride that far or at least to get a boat from there down the Hudson River for part of the trip. He made his way through the Wilderness Woods again (they probably did not seem so intimidating now), making good time the way he had come the year before now that he was not tied to a slow-moving army. He had probably borrowed money to make the trip, staying at inns and taverns along the way. He reached Boston on July 13, shortly after which notices of his escape and remarkable journey appeared in the Boston newspapers. He may have returned to his hometown the next day, no doubt to joyous and relieved family and friends. His companion, who had shared the ordeal, had a "family" reunion of a different sort, for when they reached Fort Edward, he "was stop'd by General Webb, as he was one of the Regulars taken at Oswego," and returned to duty.[58]

Lincoln's intelligence had been critically wrong in one respect, however. French movements toward the Champlain theater had been delayed, not by rumors of invasion, but by logistical difficulties, especially regarding food. Once these were adequately addressed, Governor Vaudreuil and General Montcalm put their plans for the destruction of Fort William Henry into effect with dispatch. Even as Lincoln and his fellow escapees were slogging their way toward Crown Point, eight thousand French regulars, *troupes de la marine*, Canadian militia, and Indians from as far away as the western Great Lakes had begun moving toward Fort Carillon, the jump-off point for the operation. It was as well that Lincoln did not wait for the next new moon or linger at Fort William Henry upon his return. In either case he might well have been trapped with the rest of the garrison when, in the first days of August, the French and Indian army surrounded the fort. If he had survived the subsequent siege and the famous massacre that followed, he might well have become a prisoner again.

The Peregrinations of Peleg Stevens

Guests of the Seven Nations

In a statement that has since become famous, the eighteenth-century literary critic Samuel Johnson opined that "no man will be a sailor who has contrivance enough to get himself into a jail; for being in a ship is being in jail—with the chance of being drowned." Furthermore, he concluded, "a man in jail has more room, better food, and commonly better company."[1] Peleg Stevens, the twenty-one-year-old barber from Dartmouth, got the opportunity to test Dr. Johnson's hypothesis in the course of his long journey home. In the process, he spent time in no fewer than four prisons and crossed the Atlantic Ocean twice. He experienced what very few young men of his background did: foreign travel, though hardly under favorable circumstances. Stevens' odyssey began on the land, however, as a prisoner among Natives of the St. Lawrence River settlements.

Having undergone the same interrogations as Ensign Lincoln, and probably also hopeful of his redemption by the French, Stevens was returned to the custody of his captors "and held in Captivity by them about thirteen months Passing thro' all the Dangers, hardships and Difficultys to which those of our nation are Exposed who are so unhappy as to fall into the hands of that savage and Barbarous crew."[2] The survivors of Hodges' Scout learned the hard way that those captured by French-allied Indians did not have the status of prisoners of war. They became the absolute property of their Indian captors, and the French, dependent as they were on their allies, made no attempt to challenge that right. Indeed, as Lincoln discovered, French officers or Canadians could offer to purchase captives from Indians, but they could not force them to sell. And if those inhabitants of New France made such a purchase from Natives, the right of ownership passed to them. English captives became, as one official put it, "slaves fairly sold," and the government "could not legally force masters to give them up, as could be done with prisoners of war." The persistent need for bound labor in Canada was so great that it created a trade in captives, even in peacetime, and incidentally contributed significantly to saving the lives of Stevens and his fellows, as Indians had economic incentives to take prisoners rather than scalps. A New Hampshire captive at the beginning of the war explained that Indians "cannot make Money half so fast any other Way, as by taking Englishmen, and selling them for Slaves; and the French are very ready to buy them; for when they buy a Man, or Woman for 3 or 400 Livres, they pay in Paper Money or Goods, and they will ask double in Silver; and they make 'em work like Negro's, till they pay just what they ask."[3]

De Bougainville referred to "Iroquois" involved in the destruction of Hodges' Scout; these were members of the Seven Nations Iroquois, French-allied and Catholic-influenced branches of the parent Iroquois confederation of what is today New York State.[4] The original confederacy—Mohawk, Oneida, Onondaga, Cayuga, Seneca, and later Tuscarora peoples—though powerful, had suffered as well as benefited in the previous century from their strategic position between French and English colonies. Able to trade with either side, they nevertheless had aligned with Dutch, then English interests when the French in Canada saw them as troublesome competitors in the fur trade. French raids on Iroquois towns in the late 1660s and the failure of English colonial support during King William's War left the confederation Iroquois feeling vulnerable and disenchanted with their English allies. They embarked on a policy of neutrality, staying largely uncommitted in Queen Anne's and King George's Wars, while they recovered from their losses in war and from frequent epidemic events. In the meantime, French missionaries made converts among members of the confederation. With encouragement from Quebec and Montreal, the priests persuaded them to move to mission towns with easy access to those trade centers. These villages, from Lorette, near Quebec, to Oswegatchie (present-day Ogdensburg, New York), far upriver, became multinational in character, offering homes to varieties of Native peoples displaced by war, captured and assimilated enemies (including some English men and women), and French missionaries and traders. From the confederation, Mohawk and Onondaga people were particularly well represented in the St. Lawrence towns of Kahnawake and Oswegatchie. Considering the kinship networks that persisted among converted and nonconverted families, the ease of communication between the river and lake peoples, and the confederation's official neutral policy, there was considerable interaction between the Seven Nations and original-confederation Iroquois despite differences in religion, politics, and lifestyle.[5]

Into their hands came at least six of the survivors, and perhaps more. Joseph Abbot, the joiner; Jonathan Barnes, the nineteen-year-old blacksmith; John Erwin or Arwin, with the "poor and aged" mother; William Merry, now a three-time survivor of combat; Ebenezer Pratt, a young servant; and Peleg Stevens all began their captivity in the hybrid societies of the Seven Nations towns.[6] English captives might fare better on several levels among Seven Nations peoples than those made captive by more remote Native groups, as we will see in the next chapter. Still, the experience could be a punishing one, certainly initially. First, as de Bougainville related, it was the Iroquois contingent that took the casualties in crushing Hodges' command, and so it was they who decided which of their prisoners were subsequently executed. Conversion to Catholicism did not necessarily suppress age-old practices with regard to war, nor did French missionaries always work hard to eliminate them. While some traditions, such as ritual cannibalism and torture, were greatly reduced as a result of efforts by French priests, the taking of scalps and certain "purging" rituals, such as the gauntlet, were largely uncontested. As for Native warriors dispatching prisoners in the aftermath of combat or in the rush for honors or trophies, clergymen found it useless, and imprudent, to attempt intervention. At the Battle of Lake George earlier in the war, Seven Nations Iroquois from Kahnawake had grabbed some English prisoners, but "irritated to have lost several men" of their own, they had killed them on the spot. For Native warriors, even of the "Christianized" variety, combat was, as one of them explained, "an opportunity of distinguishing ourselves, and of getting some prisoners and scalps to show our people that we had been at war."[7] Having survived that fate, though probably made to watch the deaths of the others, Stevens and his associates were bundled off from the camp at Fort Carillon after a few days, separated so that "but few could Converse together." They must have hoped for a stop at a French settlement along the way, where they might plead for intercession, but this was from "not knowing the Manner of the Indians, who do not make any Stops among the French, in their return from War, till they get home."[8] They followed much the same route as had Lincoln before them, only instead of embarking for Montreal at La Prairie, they continued for another eight miles or so to Kahnawake.

Kahnawake had been established in the previous century, after some three hundred Iroquois converts were gathered at La Prairie. Needing more land for its community, the mission moved to a spot near the Lachine Rapids, above Montreal. The village attracted more families from the Iroquois, especially from the Mohawks, doubling its population in a decade. When Stevens and the other captives arrived, they saw a well-established town, complete with church, houses built with a fusion of Native and European techniques, extensive fields, and farm animals. If it all looked somewhat familiar, their welcome was familiar too: they were made to run a gauntlet. Robert Eastburn, who also had been "initiated" at Kahnawake, recalled that this included hurled stones and clumps of dirt. The bombardment ended when the captives reached the door of a lodge pointed out to them by their captors. Some of the captives were then moved on to Oswegatchie, a new settlement one hundred miles upriver that was both mission town and trade center, with a palisaded fort and French garrison, "a chapel, a storehouse, a barn, a stable, ovens, a sawmill, broad fields of corn and beans, and three villages of Iroquois."[9] There they again had to face a gauntlet, this time, according to Eastburn, with a rare variation: the Indians pummeled the captives with their fists.[10] William Merry almost certainly spent his captivity at Oswegatchie.

That winter the captives worked for the families to which they were assigned. They may have been kept by the families of the returning captors or, as was the case with John Erwin, "given away to an Indian," probably to replace a lost family member.[11] In the early spring they may have worked "with the Indians [and] Squaws," making sugar from maple sap and later preparing ground for planting. Those without exploitable trades—Erwin, Merry, Pratt—were given their masters' fields to work. It was meant to be demeaning labor, work generally done by women in Native societies, but that attempt at humiliation may not have succeeded with European men, for whom agricultural labor was the norm. Titus King recalled, with almost a touch of pride, that he had "tended a piece of Corne" at Kahnawake, "more than half an Acre which was in a flourishing Condition when I Left it."[12] Joseph Abbot, with his woodworking talents, and perhaps even Stevens the barber may have had some short-leash liberty to exercise their trades. While he was a prisoner at Kahnawake, Robert Eastburn was allowed "to work with a French Smith, for six Livers and five Souse per Week, which the Captain let me have to myself." Jonathan Barnes was a blacksmith also, but as he later reported, his master did not stay long in the town and took Barnes with him. Abbot and Stevens likely remained in Kahnawake. If they pleaded with the French there to be taken into custody and sent to Quebec as the Oswego prisoners had been, they would have received the same answer as did Eastburn, who wrote that "the Interpreter replied, that I was an Indian Prisoner, and the General would not suffer it, till the Indians were satisfied."[13]

In August 1757, with an influx of new prisoners came the word of a fresh disaster for Anglo-American arms and, for Stevens and Abbot at least, an opportunity to escape their Indian captivity. On August 9 Fort William Henry, over which Stevens and thousands of others had labored so long, had surrendered to a besieging force of French regulars, Canadians, and more than a thousand Native warriors. Worse, there had been a serious outbreak of violence after the capitulation. The Anglo-American defenders had been granted the "honors of war," permitting them to march out of the fort with unloaded arms and with flags flying, back to Albany, in return for their parole: an agreement not to take up arms again in this theater of the war. They were also allowed to retain much of their baggage. Such generous terms made sense to the French, who did not fancy having to tend and feed thousands of prisoners in Canada, which was already facing serious shortages. But to the Native allies, many of whom had come from the western Great Lakes for the campaign, the terms constituted little more than treachery, depriving them of the scalps, loot, and prisoners they considered their due, without which it would be a dishonor to return home. Ignoring what they thought were ridiculous stipulations, many of the Natives began plundering the Anglo-American wagons as they rolled from the camp. Those who resisted the determined Natives were struck down, initiating a brief but bloody frenzy of looting, killing, and kidnapping before the riot could be brought under control. Nearly seventy, mostly provincials, were killed, and hundreds taken captive, in what would be embellished in newspapers as a horrible "massacre" involving hundreds more victims, the inspiration for the central event in James Fenimore Cooper's *Last of the Mohicans*.[14] Anglo-American hopes for victory on the Lake Champlain front were again thwarted by audacious French-Indian spoiling attacks.

The opportunity for Stevens and Abbot came with the French generals' and officials' horror at having the honors of war so spectacularly violated, which they rightly feared would both reflect upon themselves and hand the enemy a colossal propaganda victory. They quickly set about to redeem, at great cost, as many of the Fort William Henry prisoners as they could persuade their Indian owners to part with, gather them in Quebec, and return them via cartel ships to the British base at Halifax, Nova Scotia. More than three hundred redeemed prisoners left Quebec's wharves on September 27. The flood of English prisoners that had come into Canada from the debacle at Oswego the year before, from the disaster at Fort William Henry, and from relatively minor catastrophes in between (e.g., Hodges' Scout) was an embarrassment of riches for their hosts. There were nowhere near as many French or Canadian prisoners of war in English hands in North America, and they simply could not be accommodated in Canada. Governor Vaudreuil was keen to get as many of them out of the country as possible, as quickly as possible, before winter closed the river. Fortunately for him, there was another outlet for prisoners held in Canada: Europe, where they could be exchanged for French prisoners in the Continental war. Vaudreuil reported sending 1,320 prisoners there by November.[15] The urgency to mitigate the damage of the Fort William Henry fiasco, combined with the hurry to rid Canada of extra mouths to feed, meant that French officials were not overly careful to send specific groups of captives to specific places. Prisoners from Oswego, Fort William Henry parolees, and captives redeemed in other ways found themselves incarcerated briefly and then bundled aboard ships bound for the Atlantic.

The Dauphine Bastion

It was at this time, in this seller's-market atmosphere of haste, that Stevens, and probably Abbot, was "bought by the french and Carried to Quebeck." They would have been transported down the river, running the rapids where possible, to Montreal. After that there were no falls to navigate, and one could make the downriver trip in two days. Quebec's outstanding geographic feature was its location on a cliff high above the St. Lawrence, below which, at river level, lay the Lower Town. This latter area held the wharves, warehouses, and related facilities where France and Canada met. Passengers, soldiers, sailors, and governors, whose feet had last touched land more than three thousand sea miles to the east, alighted again on French soil after a passage of two to three months. Stevens likely debarked at the common landing area, between the Royal and Dauphin Batteries in the Lower Town.

Here came also the clothing, manufactures, luxuries for the fortunate, food-stuffs, and trade goods without which the people of New France could not long subsist. Merchants favored living in the Lower Town for its ready access to the harbor and their warehouses. So did ship captains and seamen, domestics and artisans, who lived in multistory stone houses. By this time nearly 40 percent of the city's population of more than seventy-two hundred was crowded into the space between the river and the cliffs, so only a fifth of the houses in the Lower Town were still single-story dwellings.[16] None of the streets were paved, so in heavy rains or during the spring thaws the ways were "quagmires of mud, stagnant water and a juicy hodgepodge of living and dead animals piled up."[17] The city's inhabitants were accustomed to disposing of refuse in the streets, ordinances to the contrary notwithstanding, especially in winter, when the going was particularly difficult. People in the Lower Town were supposed to cast their trash, food scraps, and "night-soil" into the river, but the ordinance was often ignored. The unsanitary conditions, familiar enough in urban centers throughout Europe, doubtless contributed to another "European" characteristic of Quebec: its high mortality rate, especially for working people. Despite a young population overall, Quebec was hard on children, two out of three of whom did not live to see their fifteenth birthday.[18]

Stevens was led away from the docks and climbed a steep street (today's Côte de la Montagne), the only access to the Upper Town. Up there, on the plateau commanding the river, lived the socially prominent, along with the religious and military establishments. The way led between Fort St. Louis on the left, presiding over the Lower Town, and the Bishop's Palace on the right. Stevens could see that he was in a walled city, similar in intent to what Lincoln had seen in Montreal, but much more substantial and impressive. The steep cliffs, impossible for soldiers to climb, protected much of the northeast part of the Upper Town, but bastioned stone walls ringed it on the landward side, mounting artillery to repel attacks from the fields that would soon become famous as the Plains of Abraham. Most of the city's population lived in the Upper Town, where even within the walls there was more space than in the Lower Town, and it showed in the houses about him. Unlike those about the waterfront, three-quarters of the houses here were one-story dwellings, mostly built of stone. Many of these had vegetable gardens in back, another amenity of having space to spare. As in Montreal, religious orders—Jesuits, Recollets, Hospitalières, and Ursuline nuns—occupied disproportionate space, added to which was the seminary and the Bishop's Palace. The older, wealthier families had long lived in the Upper Town, although the religious establishments occasionally sold off some of their extensive lands, giving opportunities for some young artisan families to move up from the Lower Town—much to the distress of the upper crust.[19]

The prisoner was escorted to a long, three-story stone building in the northwest part of the Upper Town. Begun as a barracks for the city's garrison more than forty years earlier, it had recently been integrated into supplemental defenses for Quebec. Recognizing flaws in the original design of the walls, engineers had erected a series of fortified strongpoints, called redoubts, inside the perimeter, which would provide greater safety for the soldiers during bombardment and help repulse an enemy who managed to breach the walls. The old barracks, still preserved, formed the rear of the Dauphine Redoubt. Designed as it was to accommodate large numbers of men year-round, the barracks could be pressed into service as a reasonably commodious space for prisoners of war, of which Quebec now had its fill. On the side of the building opposite the redoubt, French workmen constructed a palisade of wooden pickets, creating a makeshift prison yard for the inmates' exercise. A prisoner held there the previous year described it as "A Grand long Stone Barrack of 3 Stories, divided into Convenient Rooms with Cabbins and Straw Beds, and in the 2 lower Stories fire Places. Our lot was an Upper Story in which was no fire Place."[20] The rooms were originally designed to hold perhaps a dozen soldiers, but that density undoubtedly increased with the glut of prisoners. The "cabbins" were likely bunks, either partly enclosed or with blankets for curtains, affording some warmth and privacy. The fireplaces kept the building reasonably warm during the frigid winters, and there was no shortage of firewood from the countryside.

Stevens testified that he was "Closely Confined about Two months" at Quebec, which conjures an image of shackles and solitary confinement. In fact, for a prison the redoubt was as humane an establishment as prisoners of war could expect. Certainly none wrote nostalgically of their Indian captivity in comparison. The food was adequate, if monotonous. Stephen Cross, captured at Oswego, was initially dismayed when he arrived at the prison and was "Served only Some Bread," but inmates assured him that "they had been Served with Provisions Sufficient for Comfortable Support, which was Great Satisfaction to us who were in Such a hungry State." So it proved: every two days he and his fellow prisoners received "2^{lb} of fresh Beef a man and two large loves of Good Bread for 3 men which was our allowance the whole time we Continued here." It was not very different from an ordinary laborer's diet in New France, though as a Catholic he would have had fish twice per week. Cross thought his treatment as a prisoner pretty fair in general, "Especially by the Old Gentleman who was the Keeper of the Prison who Conducted toward us more like a Father than an Enemy." Prison routine was likewise calculated to keep inmates in good health while maintaining security. Prisoners were confined to their rooms from sunset to eight or nine o'clock in the morning, "when we all let out into A large Yard" for exercise. At one o'clock they were confined again for an hour, then let out again until sunset. The regimen gave time for rooms, clothing, and blankets to be aired, the sick to be separated, and the prisoners to be counted. Razors and knives were forbidden, for obvious reasons, but officers and those who could pool their meager resources might hire someone from the city to shave them and cut their hair. Some had done this in the previous war, engaging a barber to come every Thursday to keep them minimally well groomed. It is possible that Stevens, a barber himself, assisted in this regard. "We were generally Healthy while here," remembered Cross. "Some few had Sickness which were Carryd to the Hospital and on Recovery were returned to us."[21]

All the same, it was a prison, and in 1757, with a surplus of captured soldiers, pinching shortages, and smallpox becoming widespread in Canada, conditions in the prison could be grim. Those who wrote of it in any detail considered any more than 250 inmates to be excessive, and one who was there at the same time as Stevens and Abbot reckoned that there were "more than 300 prisoners in Jail at once."[22] Such close confines made the prison a dangerous place if infectious disease broke out: over a seventeen-month period in the previous war seventy-seven people had died in the prison.[23] Smallpox threatened to make that mortality rate climb significantly. Prisoners showing symptoms of the dreaded disease were quarantined somewhere outside the prison; Titus King came down with a relatively mild case of it and was tended by a widow in the city, whom he paid two livres per day for his care with borrowed money.[24] Those who did not survive their stay in prison could expect to be "Carried out In ye Box, y^t was made for ye first y^t Died, which was made about 6 feet, In Length, 2 foot Broad 1½ foot high or Deep, and four handles like a hand barrow." They could not expect burial in any of the consecrated ground of Quebec's churchyards, and being mostly Protestant, they would not have wanted that anyway. They were apparently buried somewhere outside the city walls, but just where "we Never Could Learn, But they Usualy Return^d with ye Box in a Verey Short Time."[25]

Less deadly but torturous in its own way was a fairly common condition known simply as "itch," today known as scabies. Caused by tiny mites that burrowed under the flesh and caused painful itching and ugly rashes, it was spread by skin contact or by shared blankets or clothing—all but impossible to avoid in prison conditions. As with all eighteenth-century maladies, treatment was dubious, but in this case quarantine was used also: when seventeen men contracted "ye Itch" in the prison in 1745, wrote a captive sea captain, they were "put into ye Chamb^r over us to be Cured." Anyone who complained too loudly about deteriorating circumstances, or became too personal about assigning blame for it, could find himself in a very uncomfortable place indeed. One, "for saying y^t m^r Lorain [the prison keeper] was D^h [Death?]" was "Sent to ye Cashet or Dungion," where he received the clichéd bread-and-water diet and there was "no Day Light but what Enters at 3 Inch holes in a plate of Iron of 4 Inches Square."[26]

The Cartel Ship

At some point, no later than early November, Stevens received word that he was to be transported to France.[27] If there had been significant numbers of French prisoners in New England to exchange, he might have reached home in a matter of weeks. Owing to the failure of the Anglo-American efforts in this theater, however, prisoners were being sent to France to exchange for captured French soldiers in Europe. We cannot know just how Stevens felt about this. True, he would be getting out of Quebec, but he faced a lengthy and difficult alternative. Just how ambivalent prisoners might be to learn of their voyage is suggested by the prisoner Stephen Cross, who had made the trip the previous year. One hundred sixty of the prisoners at the Dauphine Redoubt were to go in one ship being readied for sail. When the French authorities called on the prisoners to sign up for the passage, only half the requisite number of volunteers came forward. The balance was made up by a draft, "Greatly to our Sorrow," Cross lamented, "as we had flatered our selves we Should be sent to Boston."[28]

Whether it was his choice or someone else's, Stevens was scheduled to go. His fellow survivor John Abbot stayed behind. We cannot be sure why, but the evidence suggests that he had become ill. No one wanted to send sick men on a lengthy sea voyage; the conditions would be too favorable for an on-board epidemic that could affect the crew as well as the passengers. Volunteers and draftees alike had to pass muster with medical personnel or be left behind to try again when (or if) they were sufficiently recovered. Eighteenth-century medicine being what it was, the procedure was superficial enough; one who made the crossing described it thus: "Yᵉ Doctor Came . . . to feel all of yᵉ mens pulses to See who was fit to Go." Perhaps to maintain a minimum of professional credibility, "Several was Rejected and thought not proper to Send."[29] Titus King was lucky. He left about the same time as did Stevens but got a berth on a cartel ship bound for England instead of France. Having survived his bout with smallpox, he bid his landlady adieu, gratefully paying what he owed for her care and kindness. He had learned some French, or she some English, for they were able to banter playfully at parting: she asked him "whither if She Should be taken in our Contray I would Kill her I told her I should rather mary to her."[30]

On the appointed day, Stevens and his fellow passengers were collected, searched (prisoners were not allowed to carry letters),[31] and marched to the Lower Town docks, guarded by a file of soldiers. Sadly, Stevens left us no description of his passage, but Stephen Cross made the journey at the same time of year as did Stevens, and there is no better chronicler of the prisoner's transatlantic experience; Stevens assuredly underwent something very similar. Cross boarded a ship he estimated at about 500 tons[32] that was well armed with eighteen cannon.[33] He and his fellow prisoners, 140 in all, were sent belowdecks to a space specially prepared for them. Under the lowest deck, and over the water casks in the hold, was laid a crude platform offering no more than four feet of headroom "and so small that we had not room for us all to lydow[n] Except lying Partly one on the other." The only way in or out of their compartment was through the main hatch, and this was boarded in to restrict upward access. Other hatches were mostly covered, only partially open to allow some ventilation. "This Dreary Place," remembered Cross, "was our abode for the Passage," though they were not fully confined to it just yet.[34] The wind on deck was often "Eastwardly and Cold," but ten or eleven days' sailing brought them down the St. Lawrence River to Anticosti Island, and in two more days they cleared the Strait of Belle Isle, a mere twelve-mile passage between Newfoundland and the Labrador coast. That the ship's captain took this route strongly suggests that he considered interception by Royal Navy vessels operating from Halifax to be the greater risk.

Entering the North Atlantic, the prisoners had to give up what very limited freedom they may have had to move about the ship. They were, wrote Cross, "Confined to our dark and wretched hole below decks, only allowed to Come on deck twice A day." On these occasions they were brought out in three "messes" of ten men each to receive "our Poor and Scanty allowance of Provisions." This consisted of "Bread Sufficient but Much Mouldy and Many Worms in it." Four days a week they were given beef, "but verry Poor A Great part of it is the Cattles heads and but little of that." The remaining days of the week, instead of beef they got "Hors Beens Boiled with Some of the Slush (taken from the top of the Copper in which the Ships Companys Meat is Boiled) put into them." Cutting their meat into ten equal portions was a problem, since having been deprived of anything sharp, they were "Unprovided to divide the little Meat they allowed us" and were forced to tear the meat as best they could or to borrow a knife from a sympathetic sailor. They had half an hour to eat and get some fresh air, after which time they were again sent below and another party brought up. The only other times prisoners could be on deck was for "necessary occasions [i.e., to use the ship's head] when two or three might be up at A time for A Short Space." Of course, prisoners were closely guarded while on deck.

All this security was understandable: the prisoners outnumbered the crew, and "if they had Given us more liberty their own [liberty] as well as their lives would have been in Danger as we had in Contemplation to Rise Upon them if any favourable Opertunity should give any Chance of Success." Such things were known to happen; at sea the prison was simultaneously the means of escape, so prudent captains kept their charges on a short leash. Cross, at least, understood his jailers' concern, and "therefore we Could not Blame them for our Close Confinement." Within these strictures, however, ships' officers could be reasonable and even sympathetic to the prisoners. Once, when they noticed that their allowance of beans seemed short, the prisoners sent a complaint to the captain. He then ordered an officer to stand by at their next mess to make sure they got their full share and admonished the cook "that in future we should not be Scanted." Cross had to admit that "as to our treatment from the officers and crew of the Ship we had not much Reason to Complain all things Considered."

But such minimal considerations could not alter the general misery of a five-week ocean crossing under the conditions prisoners faced. Their makeshift cell was always crowded, never comfortable. Those prisoners who had been fortunate enough to have two blankets when they boarded could make hammocks from them. This maritime expedient for saving space helped somewhat, but "being so Many of us in so small A place the Air was verry Bad and warm." Moreover, "the lice was not Scarce." These omnipresent companions of eighteenth-century peoples had shipped out with the prisoners from Quebec and in their present conditions positively flourished. The only space where the prisoners had sufficient light to find and kill them was near the hatch, which was "Generall[y] Crowded with Persons waiting for their turn to git on deck to Relieve nature." Any sort of personal hygiene was difficult, "and as for our Beards," lamented Cross, "they Must Grow until we can find means to get rid of them."

In foul weather—and virtually every North Atlantic crossing encountered some—the hatches were shut and covered with tarpaulins, plunging the inmates in darkness and sickening motion, "almost stifled for want of fresh Air." Added to this was the terror of "not being able to see what the danger was which we were in," especially for the great majority who had had no previous experience at sea, "nor any Communication with any one on Board." Seawater inevitably dripped or poured in from above, adding constant dampness to their concerns. The claustrophobic conditions "Rendered our Situation verry disagreeable," Cross concluded, "being in A Perfect Dungeon." One can easily imagine Dr. Johnson nodding sagely at the comparison.

Such an ordeal might be better tolerated with agreeable companionship, but there was no guarantee of this either, despite the adage about all being in the same boat. Owing to the way the cartels were organized, provincials found themselves thrust in with regular soldiers, sailors taken from captured vessels, and civilians taken from their farms. Ethnic prejudices did not help: on Cross' voyage, half of the 140 prisoners were "Soldiers of Shirlies Regiment," many of whom were of Scottish, Irish, and English extraction, "and by their manners and behavior we Suppose[d] were Convicts." Intermingled when they first came on board, they quickly sorted themselves, "these Soldiers taking one Side of the Ship and the Carpenters and Sailors the other . . . and neither of these two Parties allowed to go on the other Side on any Pretence." The hatchway necessarily was common ground, "but even in this we had many Contests and Sometimes Came to blows." Long confinement, fear, foul conditions, and animosity inexorably bred mental anguish that caused a few to snap. A young New Jersey man who had left a wife and child to go to war "was so overborn in his Mind with our danger that his reason gave way and he became delirious." During storms, when the prisoners were "Entombed," he "would Suddenly Start at a heavy Surge of the Sea and cry out the Ship was Sinking and our friends would never Know our unhappy fate." The effect of outbursts such as this on the other prisoners can be easily imagined. The poor man's mental state deteriorated steadily during the crossing, and by the time they reached France he had "lost his Reason totally and went raving distracted."

Cross' vessel reached the port of Brest without serious incident, either avoiding or facing down any British naval cruisers lurking off the Brittany coast. This major coastal city, France's premier port and naval base on the Atlantic coast, was very likely the terminal port for Peleg Stevens as well. In the itinerary Stevens wrote after his return from captivity, he remembered being "there Imprisoned in three separate Prisons in about the space of three months." Cross had the same experience, and we can trace his movements precisely, thanks to his faithful journal keeping. Cross, Stevens, and thousands of Anglo-American prisoners from the Atlantic rim entered a prisoner-exchange system that was still struggling for order and was hampered by international suspicion. Although exchanges rarely went without hitches, and mutual complaints and recriminations were rife, by the mid-eighteenth century the major European powers had worked out a series of practices that kept the flow of returning prisoners moving fairly regularly. Upon reaching Brest, prisoners were transferred in a series of marches inland to Dinan, from whence they could be easily sent to the regular cartel port of St. Malo, on the Channel coast (fig. 8.1).[35]

Brest Castle was the first stop for the prisoners, and the first prison to house them. A medieval fortress guarding the ancient anchorage, it was modernized by the famous French engineer Sébastien Le Prestre, Seigneur de Vauban, in the late seventeenth century. It remains today, having escaped obliteration during the Allied bombings of World War II. During the Seven Years War it was being used to hold prisoners; some three hundred were already in residence there when Cross and his fellow prisoners arrived, instantly swelling the prison population by nearly 50 percent. Similar to their treatment at Quebec, they were closely confined at night but had the liberty of the castle yard by day. Despite the awful conditions they had endured on the passage, according to Cross, the prisoners remained "Generally healthy the whole voyage," and among their first activities upon reaching Brest was to try to ensure that they stayed that way. They were "now busily employed

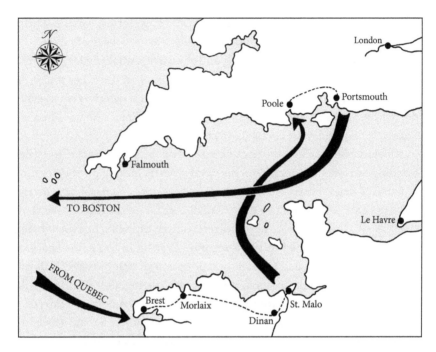

Figure 8.1. Peleg Stevens' Long Way Home. Map by Die Hoxie

in Washing Shaveing and killing lice," since they had had "no opportunity of doing Either for four Weeks" aboard the ship. Prisoners coming ashore "had Much of this work to do," admitted Cross, especially hunting lice, an activity "we continued from day to day until we had some Reduced our Stock."[36]

John Abbot's Release

Back in Quebec, John Abbot and the other prisoners who did not make the crossing passed the time as best they could manage. The more conniving among them may have been able to wheedle some additional comforts from their French hosts. Taking advantage of the charity demanded by the season, a Captain William Pote and his roommates "wrote a Letter to yᵉ Entendant [the *intendant* for New France lived nearby] and wishᵈ him a happy and merrey Chrismass &c." The hustle worked: the *intendant* "Sent us a Cagg of Clerett Containing about 3 Gallons."[37] One hopes they remembered to drink his health. Since this happened in the 1740s and not in the late 1750s, Pote and his friends were able to score a second time a week and a half later. Until 1755 France and England used calendars that differed by eleven days; the result was that Christmas—one French and one English—came twice for the prisoners. By the time of Abbot's imprisonment, however, England had synchronized its calendar with those of France and the rest of Europe. Ordinarily, alcoholic beverages or luxuries of any sort were to be had only for money. After unsuccessfully attempting to procure wine once the holiday season had passed, Captain Pote ruefully remarked, "Since we have no money to Get Drunk they are Determined we Shall be Sober."[38]

Their jailers were not entirely heartless, however. The men were allowed to earn some drinking money, as when "Several of yᵉ Prisoners . . . was Imployed by. . . yᵉ Prison Keeper, to through [throw] yᵉ Snow out of yᵉ Yard, over yᵉ piquets."[39] And Quebec had a great deal of snow to shovel. It is small wonder, though, that some prisoners sought escape from the tedium and danger of disease by accepting French offers of the opportunity to join work gangs. In October 1755 Stephen Cross recorded, "Some persons Come and made Proposals to tak A Number out Provided they were willing to go to work in the Countery 30 league distance." To this offer, "22 of our Soldiers Accepted . . . and went," incidentally easing the overcrowding of the prison.[40] John Abbot, if he was not ill, might have accepted such an offer or agreed to work in town. But that seems unlikely, for "sometime in Jan. 1758" he "dyed in prison at Quebeck . . . in his 24th y." His body was placed in the handbarrow box and carried to an anonymous grave outside the city walls.[41]

Imprisoned in France

For Peleg Stevens and his shipmates prison routine resumed. Aboard ship there had been no need to count the prisoners daily as there was no likelihood of a prisoner going "over the wall" in the middle of the Atlantic, but at Brest the practice began again, with head counts every morning. Escapes did occur, but unless the men spoke very good French (such as inhabitants of the British Channel Islands), there was little point, as they would be quickly found out and recaptured. No Americans appear to have been successful at least. Objections to prison food resumed as well. Prisoners objected that the bread they were given was mostly or all of barley meal "and verry full of Grit which we Supposed was Sand put in by the Baker," a common cheat to bring the bread to the regulation weight. As for their meat, Cross complained, no doubt with justification, that it was "of the Meanest

Pieces such as hocks Shins Shoulder pieces &c," so that very little meat was actually gleaned.[42] The quality and adequacy of prison food was the subject of most complaints made by prisoners on both sides of the English Channel despite assurances from officials that provisions were both ample and wholesome. For example, in response to complaints of repatriated British prisoners concerning Brest Castle, a French official insisted,

> They have the same food as the men on the Royal ships: 8 ounces of meat, a small measure but equal to the English prison ration; the same wine as on the Royal ships, which is incomparably superior to the small beer of England. Every day an examination of the prisoners is made by the Commissioner of the Prison, an interpreter and a representative of the prisoners. Bedding straw is changed every fifteen days, exactly as in the Royal Barracks.

Compelled to respond to complaints, the French bureaucrat did as his British counterparts did in like situations: rather than reporting the reality, he simply stated what was regulation—"a formal piece of humbug," as a later historian remarked.[43] In the system of prisoner exchange, as in government bureaucracy everywhere in the eighteenth century, there was plenty of opportunity for fraud and profiteering, and it is unlikely that prisoners of war regularly received all they were due. Cross, however, conceded that when they caught their cooks and bakers holding back on them, their complaints to French officers yielded quick rectification.

Cross was confined in Brest Castle for nearly a month, when in mid-December "all the Quebeck Prisoners [were] Drafted to March" 130 miles inland to Dinan. They were given some additional clothing, as it was winter, and they set out surrounded by a guard of fifty soldiers with fixed bayonets. The first day it rained, so at the end of the day's march the prisoners, soaking wet, were given a stable in which to sleep. They were also allowed 6¾ sous per day (approximately 3p in British currency) with which to purchase food from the locals, of which there were always some about. The locals brought "Bread and other victuals Ready Cooked" to sell, and they charged the limit of what the market would bear. Those prisoners who "had any article which they Could Possibly do without"—including clothing, buttons, and belt or shoe buckles—"Sold them for what they Could git for them." Some of the captive soldiers that Cross had found so odious "instead of buying victuals bought Brandy" and, without food in their stomachs, soon became pugnaciously drunk and sought to settle old grudges. And so it went, on an itinerary easily traceable today: from Brest to "Landeno" (Landerneau), then to "Landewiz" (Landiviseau) and to their second prison at "Murlex" (Morlaix). This was not their ultimate destination, however; they set out the next day for "Bellisle" (Belle-Isle-en-Terre), "Ginggong" (Guingamp), and finally, after ten days, Dinan.

A popular tourist town today, Dinan retains much of its medieval architecture. Cross accurately described it as "A Small Walled Town built on the brink of A Steep Presipace" overlooking La Rance River. From the high wall projected nine "castles" (tall rounded bastions), all but four in various stages of dilapidation. The largest of these, on the southeastern portion of the wall, was the "Shotto" (Chateau). Today a museum, in 1757 it was the prison, and here Cross and presumably Stevens spent the remainder of their time in confinement. Four large rooms on two floors each housed seventy to eighty men, but according to Cross, the prison held as many as fourteen hundred prisoners by the spring, no doubt stuffed into as many available spaces as could be found. At least the men could get dry; each room had two large windows and a fireplace, though with twenty-foot-high ceilings it could hardly have heated the entire space. Bedding was simplicity itself: each man was given eleven pounds of straw to spread on the stone floor, and of course they had blankets. Between each room was "A Necessary," an unlighted room with latrine facilities.

Spartan it was, but Cross, true to form, accepted what could not be helped and did not complain overmuch. He allowed that the march had been a hard one but said that the guards (who were changed every two days) "in General Used us very well," even procuring wagons to carry the increasing number of lame and sick. As if to give the lie to some accounts of hard usage in the prison, Cross wrote that close confinement in the dungeon and short rations were the worst treatment that he saw, and that was for breaking parole, failed escapes, and similar breaches of honor or security. The food seems to have been considerably better than at Brest Castle, and the prisoners even had liberty to explore, within limits, the walls, the castle roof (with its splendid view), and the grounds. Men like Stevens had perforce become acquainted with the principles of military engineering and concluded (correctly) that the town "by the Manner of its fortifications was walled and fortifyed before the Use of Cannon was found out." Some curious prisoners even descended a well in the Chateau yard and found at its bottom a passage "which went Quite under the Castle" but alas permitted no possibility of escape. For those who could afford it, there was a "Canteen Room" in the castle run by an old woman who sold small luxuries—butter, milk, brandy, sausages, candy—to the English, Irish, Scots, and "Yankeys as we Americans were Called."

As in Quebec, sickness broke out and spread rapidly among the inmates, and deaths mounted. In an October 1758 edition of the *Boston Gazette* a returning captive named Israel Calkins supplied a list of men who had come to a bad end as prisoners of the French in the space of a few months. Captured in August 1757 and sent in a cartel ship to France, Calkins kept a record of prison deaths up to February 16, 1758, when presumably he was repatriated. Thus he was imprisoned in France during the same period as was Stevens. Supporting Cross' claims regarding the general health during the Atlantic crossing, Calkins counted only four men who died aboard ship, out of what we must assume was a typically large proportion of passengers—it is quite possible, in fact, that Stevens was aboard Calkins' ship.[44] In contrast, forty men died in prison in France in about three months, and fourteen were left behind, too sick to travel when the others were sent to England.[45] In response to complaints of prison mortality at Dinan, a French official protested that sick men were sent to regular service hospitals, where they received the same treatment that French patients received, for whatever that was worth in practical terms. Officers were given an allowance of thirty sous (equal to 1s. 3d.) per day and new clothing as needed; ordinary patients were guaranteed a clean shirt upon entering the hospital, but there was no mention of extra allowance.[46] Nevertheless, the prison's graveyard became a busy place. This was an acre-size piece of land donated, along with some monetary support, to the prisoners by a local widow of an admiral of France. Since the "Popish Clergy allows none but Papists to be Buried" in the town's consecrated churchyards, this small plot had to serve for the many Protestants who died in Catholic France. By the time Stephen Cross left Dinan, the field was "almost dug over."

Redemption

Peleg Stevens was precise about the date he arrived in England: March 27, 1758. Once his turn came to cross the English Channel, his exit from France was quick. St. Malo, on the coast, was only fifteen miles downriver, a day's march from the Chateau at Dinan. The prisoners would be sent only when a cartel vessel was available, so Stevens and his fellow prisoners may have gone aboard the same evening so as to be ready to sail with the first favorable wind and tide. Keeping the islands of Jersey and Guernsey well to starboard, then bearing north-northeast, the ship could cross the Channel in a day, making for the English cartel port of Poole, on the Dorset coast. Known for its Newfoundland fishing industry—and for smuggling— Poole was a prosperous port, though difficult to approach because of shifting sands and a narrow harbor mouth. Portsmouth would have been easier to use in this regard, but being a major Royal Navy base, it would not do to have captains of an enemy nation snooping about on the pretense of prisoner exchange.[47] The main facilities for prisoners, however, were located in that famous port, and the redeemed ex-prisoners went there for processing, care, and to arrange repatriation. Stevens was a free man at last but still dependent and still far from home. To aid the thousands of men from the British Isles and the colonies in similar straits, the Naval Office had established, earlier in the century, the "Commissioners for taking care of sick and wounded seamen and for exchanging Prisoners of War," known more simply as the "Sick and Hurt Office." It was the commissioners' business to look after wounded seamen and returning prisoners, to disburse monies for their maintenance until they got home, and "in all things to act as their judgements and the necessities of the service should require."[48]

Stevens was in England for upwards of four months, during which time he "Lived upon his Majesty's Royal Bounty untill an oppertunity presented for your Petiti[r] to be sent home to New England." We know something of that royal bounty thanks to Titus King, who had left Portsmouth for home just two months before Stevens' arrival. According to King's journal, when he first arrived at Portsmouth "his majesty King George 2[d] gave 2 Guineas worth of Clothing to the Indians prisoners and allowed us Six pince p[r] day (a gracious King)."[49] What did Stevens do with his time in the "home" country? Six pence was less than the daily wage of an ordinary footman, and would do little more than keep body and soul together. It is possible that redeemed prisoners took up some day laboring to augment their stipend, but there is little evidence of this, and the resident laborers would have resented it, probably forcibly. Nevertheless, especially clever or frugal recipients of the king's bounty who had time on their hands and no inclination to drink away their money (as some did) could make their allowance stretch farther. London, that great center of empire of which colonists had heard all their lives, was only seventy-five miles away. Titus King and a friend "got a pass to go to London for 14 days," which, allowing for travel time, gave them a whole week in the city. We can only imagine the impact of such a trip on American provincials experiencing it for the first time. London was one of the biggest cities in the world, with massive, soaring architecture, evidence of fabulous wealth and wretched poverty, bustling businesses everywhere, and strange sights, smells, customs, and accents. Did Stevens, like King, make the London tour? His brief statement to the Massachusetts legislature months later does not signify as much. But he certainly had the time to do so, and he must have known he would be unlikely to have another such opportunity. And it was not the sort of material one would include in a humble petition for support.

At any rate, by the end of the summer he was on his way home at last, on board a vessel in an escorted convoy of some forty sail. Stevens arrived in Boston on September 18, 1758—two years to the day from when he had left Fort William Henry.[50] Perhaps, like some returning with Titus King, he "then Kissed the ground for Joy," as well he might, having escaped one final danger of the return voyage. That danger, ironically, arose from British armed forces in America, supposedly the brothers-in-arms of those like Stevens. With the expansion of Crown military operations in the theater, both the British army and, especially, the navy were in need of men. Titus King's vessel was bound for New York. Upon reaching the anchorage at Sandy Hook the repatriates were set ashore on Staten Island. There they were told that naval press gangs were operating in New York City. They learned that the previous year redcoat soldiers and seamen had cooperated in carrying off the biggest press sweep ever seen in America, with seven hundred to eight hundred men swept up in a single day, of whom four hundred were "retained in the service."[51] Despite protests, impressment continued. King prudently took a detour through Elizabethtown, New Jersey, on his way home to Northampton.[52] Abner Keyes, another returning prisoner, was less fortunate. Keyes took ship from England aboard a troop transport; when it reached New York, "the Kings Agent of the Transports . . . refused to put him & the other Prisoners on shore, and told them if they would not go into his Majesty's Regular Service on shore that [they] would be put on board the men of War." Essentially kidnapped, and helpless to resist, they were placed in a different sort of captivity that ended only with the war.[53] Stevens missed the real possibility of such an extended captivity by chance: his vessel brought him to Boston, where the Crown's forces were much less in evidence.

There were no bands or patriotic crowds on hand to welcome Stevens home and wish him well; these belong to another time. In fact, Stevens may not have felt very welcome at all. Robert Eastburn, arriving in Boston in similar circumstances the previous year, destitute and shoeless, had been "directed to a tavern, but found cold Entertainment there, the Master of the House seeing a ragged and lowsy Company turned us out to Wander in the Dark; he was suspicious of us, and feared we had come from Halifax, where the Small-Pox then was, and told us, he was ordered not to receive such as came from thence."[54]

The news of the war was dramatic, if mixed. While Stevens was en route home, ships going the other way carried word that in July 1758 a British land and naval force, with some provincial auxiliaries, had taken the fortress town of Louisbourg, this time for good. On the Lake Champlain front, however, the news was as bleak as ever. The long-awaited assault on Fort Carillon had finally been made on July 8, and it had been an utter shambles. Despite having more than twelve thousand men at his command—the largest Anglo-American army ever assembled in America—General James Abercromby still could not punch his way past the defenses at Fort Carillon. Led once more by the Marquis de Montcalm, French defenders, with only a quarter of Abercromby's strength, held stubbornly against repeated attacks for at least five hours. Abercromby withdrew his army the next day. The great push down the lakes to Montreal, begun three years earlier, had progressed no farther than it had been when Stevens was captured. Now there would have to be yet another campaign, in 1759. Stevens may also have learned eventually of the fate of his prison inmate, Joseph Abbot, buried somewhere outside the walls of Quebec.

Stevens returned to Dartmouth briefly, but there is evidence that he moved to Plymouth shortly thereafter. He had survived the massacre of Hodges' Scout, avoided being executed by his captors, and spent a year as a prisoner at Kahnawake. It had taken him, from the time he was redeemed by the French, another year just to get home. He had crossed the Atlantic, seen something of the Old World in France and England, and crossed the ocean again. Thin, undernourished, and ragged, he had nevertheless escaped disease and death aboard ship and in four different prisons in Canada and France. He was a lucky man, though he might not have felt that way; he certainly had next to nothing to show for his trials. He even had to petition his colony government for the pay that was due him from the 1756 campaign. But he seems to have kept a sense of humor about him: after outlining his itinerary as a prisoner of war, and the "Dangers, hardships and Difficultys" he had undergone, he regretted that he had been "incapacitated for serving his King, his Country, or himself, anymore than [by] Consuming a small portion of Provision [intended] for his Majestys Enemies."

Isaac Foster at the Edges of Empire

"Unhappy Fate"

Apart from Ensign Lincoln, who returned to the safety and comforts of home after ten months' captivity, the remaining survivors of Hodges' Scout endured some period of bondage with Native captors. Some of these were brief, lasting only until they could be taken to Montreal for redemption, as was apparently the case with the captive John Walklate. John Con spent six months with his Wabenaki master before he too was "sold to the French." Peleg Stevens, as we have seen, was with the Iroquois for about a year. In contrast to these, Isaac Foster, of Andover, almost disappeared into the vast North American interior. Of those survivors who lived to tell their stories, Foster experienced one of the longest captivities among Indians, almost certainly the loneliest and most isolated.

Foster's ordeal began in the immediate aftermath of the slaughter of September 19. Frightful apparitions, painted in red or black, laid violent hands on him after he had thrown down his musket in surrender. One Indian seemed to take particular charge of him, pushing him to the ground and pinioning his arms behind him with a few practiced strokes. Foster had prayed he might be spared, and perhaps now he began to hope, for it seemed he was not to be killed outright at least. Yanked to his feet, Foster then felt a thin but strong noose slipped over his head and tightened around his neck. Was he to be strangled, then, after all? But no, this was a specially prepared choke collar the warrior had brought with him for just such an occasion as this. It was a decorated halter, crafted with care by female hands more than a thousand miles away, with leads ten feet long. Presented with this gift, the warrior had been tasked with bringing a captive back to his village, led or pulled along by this simple yet effective device. Without it, a prisoner was a potentially dangerous burden for a warrior to bring home alive. With his hands tied and one of these around his neck, however, the prisoner was utterly helpless.[1]

It was Foster's "unhappy Fate," he wrote years later, to be among those who fell into the hands of "barbarous Indians called Ottawaws." These, as de Bougainville described, were among those of the raiding party most demanding action, and they had gotten their wish almost immediately. Now jubilant with their victory, they set to, scalping the dead and stripping them of anything valuable. At least four of them secured prisoners, Foster among them, and after tying their arms securely, began kicking and pushing them northward, but not before Foster's captor had "riffled his Pockits," finding the four dollars he had kept there, ironically, for safekeeping. The captives, constrained as they were, were made to run to the landing where the marauders had left their canoes. This was the typical and prudent practice following a raid, to put as much distance as possible between the attackers and any pursuit, but there was probably no great fear of pursuit in this case. Nevertheless, there were forms to be followed, and captives needed to begin experiencing the abuse and fear that would characterize their new status. The practice also may have served another practical purpose. The badly wounded had already been killed out of hand, but those less seriously wounded, or sick, or older, though initially spared, could be quickly weeded out. If they fell and could not rise, or could not keep up, they were hatcheted and scalped.[2] This may account for that lone corpse found weeks later by Captain Wooster's men, miles from the massacre site.

After Lincoln's departure from Fort Carillon, Foster and three others—William Bradbury, Benjamin Gushe, and Henry Partridge—were the first of the captives to be taken away.[3] Early the morning of September 21, de Bougainville recorded in his journal, the Ottawa warriors, "having four prisoners and about five hundred leagues to go to get home," slipped away without fanfare. It is likely that they indeed had an eye on the season: despite the unusual heat of that day, they knew that winter would come soon, and the return trip to their homeland would take at least two months. Foster and his fellow captives could not have known this initially, so perhaps they hoped, as they were forced to paddle their canoe northward down Lake Champlain, that they were to be handed over to French authorities at Montreal or at one of the French forts in between. Alternatively, they may have dreaded that they were being hustled off to a more remote spot, away from disapproving French eyes, where they would be tortured to death, for such had been the stuff of New England nightmares for a century and a half. Neither was to be their fate, at least not yet. What was in store for Foster, and likely for the others, was a life of slavery.

Modern readers are unaccustomed to thinking of Indian captivity in quite that way. This is largely because of a general, and understandable, association with the race-based, lifelong African bondage that played such a central role in New World colonial development. Slavery in America is normally considered in terms of an imported system of bondage, a hybrid of Western, Eastern, and African practices, and inevitably linked to a brutal, capitalist system of labor exploitation.[4] In recent decades, however, ethnologists and historians making more careful studies of Native American captive practices have challenged traditional assumptions that slavery cannot flourish in the absence of capitalist motivation.[5] They have found, in fact, that whether one considers Algonquian, Iroquois, Mississippian, or Great Lakes cultures, in the words of Christina Snyder, "captivity & its most exploitative form—slavery—was indigenous to North America, it was widespread, and it took many forms." Brett Rushforth agrees, maintaining that "Native slavery predominated in New France throughout the colony's first century."[6]

Earlier studies of Native American captivity focused on the phenomenon of "white Indians," mainly English captives who chose to remain with their adopted Indian families.[7] The most successful adoptions were of children and young women captured during raids on frontier settlements. Since the purpose of many such raids was to acquire replacements for losses sustained by a Native community, the candidates, although taken against their will, were gradually weaned from their former identities as English colonists. This *transculturation* was accomplished through a program of ritual cleansing of the former self, reclothing and renaming, and new "family" associations made through a largely noncoercive indoctrination.[8] The captives took the places of tribal members lost to warfare or disease or age and filled the role of the missing family member, becoming virtual kin. Writing later of their experiences, many praised the lifestyle they had come to know and the many kindnesses shown them by their Native families.

But such treatment was reserved largely for easily molded youth, taken to recover the vitality of a tribe or village. The experience of young men taken in arms as prisoners of war, however, was generally rather different. Those who experienced captivity under such circumstances had no doubts as to their status or whether the term *slave* was appropriate. For them, Indian captivity was a fearful and traumatic experience.

Of all the trophies a warrior brought home, the most impressive, most prestigious, and most appreciated by his family and community were live captives. What made the feat impressive at its most basic level was the sheer difficulty of the task. Raiders, often deep within unfriendly territory and with limited supplies, would find themselves "hard-pressed to control, feed, or otherwise care for a large party of captives"; indeed, they would be "dangerously encumbered" if those captives included vigorous young men of fighting age bent on escape. Thus it was that until the French began to offer rewards for captives turned over to them, and even afterwards, "the majority of persons captured in warfare were not enslaved but were disposed of in other ways, including immediate massacre or torture and sacrifice."[9] Nevertheless, prisoners of war were highly prized. The Jesuit missionary Sebastian Rale, referring to the Wabenaki people he served, wrote that "when a savage returns to his own country with many scalps, he is received with great honor, but he is at the height of his glory when he takes prisoners and brings them home alive." Such a feat made him "truly a man."[10] Likewise, Daniel Richter has shown that bringing captives home to Iroquoia bestowed recognition and status on young Five Nations Iroquois men and was in fact fundamental to the purpose of their "mourning wars."[11]

Some captives were brought back to be ritually slaughtered; the rest, it was assumed, were "adopted" into the tribe. But exactly "what captive adoption meant in Native societies is elusive at best," and what some have taken to be a process of inclusion, of truly transforming an outsider into a tribal member with all the benefits appertaining thereto, may well have been misinterpreted. The persistent position has been

> that adoption, and thus population replacement, is purely and exclusively a motivation for or by-product of warfare and ultimately acts as an extension of kinship. There is little else involved. . . . Herein lies the problem. To modern Westerners, the use of such a kindred metaphor suggests and is believed to reflect genuine nurturing and closeness; however, in Africa and elsewhere it conveys an

entirely different meaning: authority and subordination. . . . [In fact,] the form which has drawn the attention of scholars more precisely functioned as a method of enslavement.[12]

Why did Native American peoples practice slavery? Slaves provided welcome labor for the captor's household but also were objects of prestige, both for the captor and for his community. "No honor," argues Brett Rushforth, "was more important to a young man than capturing slaves." Living trophies, slaves were the means to social prominence and leadership roles, as well as to the acquisition of trade goods. For Native Americans, there was no moral stigma attached to holding people in bondage. Far from accepting the notion of human brotherhood, "Native people doubted that outsiders were fully human, and they certainly did not believe that all people were endowed with natural rights." Christina Snyder observes that Native peoples' origin sagas "typically focus on their own group, not on the origins of all Indians or of all humanity." For them, "kin were real people; others were something less."[13]

For Foster and his fellow captives (he does not say for how long they traveled together), their capture and the long journey to the Ottawa homeland marked the first phase of their Indian captivity. During this phase they experienced the first of three "constituent elements" of slavery, wherever practiced: their utter powerlessness.[14] It began the moment they dropped or lost their weapons. It was reinforced when their arms were tied and the halters put about their necks. It would be certified over the course of the next few weeks. Their powerlessness, they knew, was a bargain, forced on them but accepted nevertheless, representing a substitute for what otherwise would have been a violent death.[15] They had little choice but to bear their captors' abuse and comply with their captors' wishes, and for the moment those wishes were aimed at getting home as soon as possible. Indeed, captives were made to aid in this, forced to paddle canoes and carry heavy burdens, all the while threatened daily with death and, as one former captive put it, "enduring hunger, thirst, and a thousand outrages."[16] The most constant reminder of their powerlessness was the halter, which they wore whenever and for as long as their new masters felt necessary and which, according to one who knew, was "more painful than one can imagine."[17]

As long as escape was a remote possibility, or resistance a concern, Native warriors customarily trussed up their captives for the night, sometimes forcing each of them to lie bound between two of their captors. A long cord was laid across the captive's body and under the Indians on either side of him; if the captive moved, especially if he tried to get up, the sleeping Indians would be wakened. Titus King, a Massachusetts man captured in 1755, recalled that when night fell on the day he was taken, his captors had made camp, eaten (King was denied food), and then "they bou[nd] me Fast & made me Lye between two Indians tye[d] the End of the tomp [tumpline] to Each of their Feets." King admitted that he had "Sleept Very Lettel this night," for, as he asked, "Who Can Sleep that Leys Bound between Two Indians."[18] Foster might actually have appreciated that arrangement as autumn turned quickly to winter; he had been dressed for a hot day when captured and would have to shiver in his shirt unless his captors gave him at least a blanket, which they must have done to prevent him from freezing. At least the season spared Foster one torture: according to a French observer, the worst time for prisoners "was at night, when they found themselves at the mercy of gnats, blackflies, and mosquitoes."[19]

To the *Pays d'en Haut*

The way home for Foster's captors lay west-northwest from Montreal, up the Ottawa River—thus named by the French, but Kitchi-sippi (Great River) to the Algonkian people, who had used it from time out of mind. The river cuts through a section of the Canadian Shield, the vast shelf of volcanic rock scraped low by the glaciers of the Ice Age and stretching into the Arctic. Over this unrelenting plateau of rock is a thin soil that supports mostly conifer trees. The river offered the only practicable route to the northern Great Lakes through this barrier (fig. 9.1). French *coureurs de bois* (woodsmen and fur traders) had used this route for more than a hundred years, bringing back the wealth of furs from the *pays d'en haut*—the upper country—that had made Montreal what it was. The river had brought these Ottawa warriors eastward for the 1756 campaign and now would bring them home, bearing, in addition to the scalps they carried, the living proofs of their success.

It was not an easy route, however. The three hundred or so miles from Lachine, above the falls near Montreal, to Mattawa, where they would take up the next leg of their journey, was upriver, and in places the current was strong. The change in elevation from Montreal to Lake Huron by this route was more than five hundred feet. To make progress against the current, paddlers would have to maintain about fifty-five strokes per minute, the pace

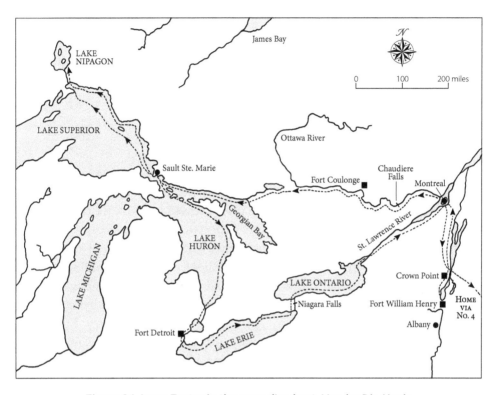

Figure 9.1. Isaac Foster in the *pays d'en haut.* Map by Die Hoxie

required of the famed voyageurs. Samuel de Champlain explored the Ottawa River in 1613 and reported places where "the water runs with great velocity. We had to get into the water and drag our canoes along the shore with a rope." Some rapids could be negotiated with skill and strenuous paddling. Champlain recalled that at one point "we passed another little fall by rowing, which makes one sweat. Great skill is required in passing these falls, in order to avoid the eddies and surf, in which they abound."[20] The captives' shoulders and backs ached painfully from this unaccustomed labor. Early on, however, Foster's party came to falls at which there was simply no choice but to debark, unload the canoes, and carry all, probably in several trips, to the upper side of the falls, reload the equipment, and set out again. Some of these portages stretched for miles. Most of the actual work was given to the captives in their capacity as slaves, driven relentlessly by their masters. Foster would repeat this process forty-one times before they left the river.

One hundred twenty-four miles into the voyage they came to a set of falls they could hear long before they saw it. At the Chaudiere Falls, in present-day Ottawa, "the water falls in one place with such force upon a rock that it has hollowed out in course of time a large and deep basin, in which the water has a circular motion and forms large eddies in the middle, so that the savages call it Asticou, which signifies boiler. This cataract produces such a noise in this basin that it is heard for more than two leagues."[21] Some sixty miles above the Chaudiere Falls was the old trading post of Fort Coulonge; after that point there would be little evidence of French occupation until they reached the Great Lakes. Foster must have wondered often how much farther they would go; he would have been distressed to know the truth. At Mattawa (Meeting of the Rivers), where the Ottawa begins its turn to the northeast, and where they took the left fork into the Petite River, they had come less than a third of the way. And still they went on, through what had become an increasingly cold and snowy landscape. The party went by Nipissing Lake to the French River, which empties out into Georgian Bay. From there it was another 217 water miles to Sault Ste. Marie, where Father Jacques Marquette in 1688 had established a mission among the Ojibwa people. As often happened, the mission was joined soon after by a trading post. And still they had not reached their ultimate destination.

It seems likely that Foster's party stopped to wait out the winter somewhere along this route. As we have seen, the ground even around Montreal was frozen hard by mid-October, with knee-deep snow and daytime temperatures in the single digits a month later. Allowing for days on which the travelers hunted for food, for stops at French posts and Native settlements on the way, and for days when travel was simply impracticable, it is difficult to imagine Foster's party making it as far as Sault Ste. Marie by the end of 1756, though it would have been possible. Fort Coulonge and Mattawa, which had Native communities nearby, were plausible stopovers, the latter being more firmly in traditional Ottawa territory. At any rate, while the captives would not have the incessant paddling to perform until May, when the river and lake ice broke up, their situation may not have been that much more pleasant. For one thing, they were kept perpetually hungry, probably at the edge of starvation, and this was done on purpose, to keep the prisoners weak and dependent on their captors.[22] In addition to this, along with the constant verbal and physical abuse to which the prisoners were subjected, was the ritual running of the gauntlet whenever they came to a Native village (which they had probably experienced shortly after their capture, when they had returned to the French advance camp near Fort Carillon): being forced to pass between two lines of warriors armed with sticks, with which they beat the bound prisoners as they went by. Tripping was allowed, so that some could get in additional blows while the hapless victims tried to escape. It was not the purpose to kill or seriously maim the captive—he was, after all, valuable property—but it could be a punishing experience all the same. Wherever the returning warriors stopped with their prisoners, provided there were sufficient Native people nearby to take part, the prisoner could be made to run the gauntlet again, this time pummeled by women and children as well.

Like all rituals, this one had a purpose, with roles for all involved. The captor gained recognition of his prowess and respect for his deeds. Those doing the pummeling got to share vicariously in the victory and to assert their superiority over their enemies as represented by the victim. The captive was reminded of the powerlessness of his position and of the loss of his personal honor—the second "constituent element" of slavery. The degradation suffered in the gauntlet and in other acts of disgrace was meant to strip prisoners of their former identities and to transform their status from that of men to that of domesticated animals. That transformation was reinforced in language. Native captives had no interest in learning the names of their prisoners, or in giving them new ones, unless they were ultimately adopted into a family; they were simply "dogs," no doubt introduced as such wherever they went. Rushforth notes that in Great Lakes languages "the verb to enslave . . . literally meant to make someone a dog. . . . 'I make him my slave' was to say 'I make him my dog.' . . . [or] 'I make him my little dog / puppy.'" *Slave* was hardly an endearing term: "simply calling someone a slave in any of the Algonquian or Siouxan languages was considered a great offense, a universal 'term of contempt.'" Willam Starna and Ralph Watkins established much the same for Iroqouian speakers, for whom "the expression for capturing and taming an animal, or for keeping it as a pet, is also the one used for taking a prisoner and making him a slave." Likewise, the phrase used for raising a domesticated animal, "is the same one used for 'mistreating or abusing' a person."[23] The hated choke halter was reapplied at these public rituals, reinforcing the "domesticated" status of the humiliated captive.

Over the winter, wherever he spent it, Foster would come to know what cold meant. New England winters could certainly be severe, but they hardly compared to the Arctic-like conditions of the Upper Country. Even today, temperatures during the coldest months there frequently dip into the double digits below zero Fahrenheit, with well over one hundred inches of snow considered normal. In such conditions, exposed flesh could suffer frostbite in minutes. The only warmth to be found was in the Natives' lodges; fortunately, of course, there was plenty of wood to burn. Customarily, women and children had the necessary but unpleasant task of gathering wood and water for the families (adult men never did this), but with slaves like Foster on hand, it was they who did the honors. Foster probably learned to walk on snowshoes his first winter as a captive—it would have been nigh impossible to perform his chores without them—and he must have been given marginally sufficient clothing to survive.

Communication was an obvious difficulty. Since the European captive/slave knew nothing of the language that was spoken all about him, and the Ottawas likewise knew nothing of his, he could not convey his thoughts or interact verbally—if that was even encouraged or allowed, given his "dog" status. Orders were given him accompanied by a gesture, a mime, or a blow. He must have learned some words perforce, but he was long past the years of childhood, when new languages come more easily. Utterly friendless and despised, robbed of freedom, manhood, human comfort, and even his name, Foster surely experienced the blackest despair. He did not even know what was to be his ultimate fate; no one in his former world knew where he was—*he* probably did not know himself—and it was by now clear to him that a slave's future was entirely in the hands of his master. Foster could be traded, sold, worked to death, or killed at any time.

It would not have comforted him to know that Natives captured by Anglo-Americans fared no better as a rule. Whites had no prisoner-taking ethos comparable to those of many Native American groups. More than a century of intermittent war had left colonists especially with a pronounced racial antipathy that was frequently and openly expressed even in times of peace. Live Native captives—most often women and children taken in raids on villages—were usually sold into slavery, but scalp bounties (as much as £300 in Massachusetts money) sometimes militated against their survival. Few Native soldiers surrendered in battle, and Europeans and colonists were often uninterested in sparing them: their scalps represented a more immediate and more practical reward. While some deplored the practice of killing or enslaving Native women and children especially, inhabitants of the frontier settlements saw little problem with the indiscriminate slaughter or enslavement of America's Native population. There was brutality enough to go around in this war.[24]

As isolated as Foster undoubtedly felt, he was in fact in the midst of a busy intercultural trade zone. Whether he understood it or not, his "Ottawa" captors were not members of a distinct, politically unified tribe but part of a "collection of closely allied villages" that included Ojibwa and Pottawatomie peoples. There were five such "core clusters" in the *pays d'en haut,* each "linked by geographical proximity, intermarriage, language, and culture more than political unity." The Ojibwa-Ottawa-Pottawatomie cluster was bound in a "regional political economy," cooperating in matters of trade and diplomacy, and their location in the north-central Great Lakes country placed them in an ideal situation to benefit from French commercial pursuits.[25] Every May, canoe fleets from Montreal made their way up the same river as had Foster, bound for Lake Superior and points northwest. There they traded French goods for the furs gathered over the previous season by Native and Canadian trappers, shuttling them back the way they had come before the winter closed in. It is likely that Foster had seen some of these bale-laden canoes racing the other way, some of the more daring ones shooting the rapids rather than face the delay and backbreaking work of portaging their cargoes. Just as Michilimackinac was the gateway to the Lake Michigan, Green Bay, and upper Mississippi fur sources, Sault Ste. Marie opened the way to Lake Superior and its hinterlands. The men who had captured Foster belonged to Native peoples who had long occupied and controlled these vital passages and were among New France's most important trading partners.

When the long winter ended and the lakes were sufficiently clear of ice, Foster was made to load his master's canoe once more and strike out on the last leg of his journey. Their destination, he would learn, was Lake Nipagon, a hundred miles north of Lake Superior and four hundred feet higher in elevation (more portages). In all, Foster would later claim, he had come "(as the French say) eleven Hundred Miles from Montreal."[26] Lake Nipagon, high in the Canadian Shield, is a favorite of sport fishermen today, but only in summer—mid-June to early September. The region is free of frost for only a quarter of the year. The mean temperature at the height of summer is 59 degrees Fahrenheit (average high temperatures in the low 70s). And it was even colder in 1757, with the Northern Hemisphere still in the grip of the

Little Ice Age. There was, and is, no significant agriculture of any kind in the area; the Ottawa and Nipissing people lived chiefly by hunting and fishing. Though still part of the Great Lakes trade network and a nexus also drawing trade from Hudson's Bay, Lake Nipagon must have seemed like the end of the earth to the young man from temperate, coastal Massachusetts.

Upon reaching his master's village at last, the uncertainty of Foster's destiny returned, as some long-deferred capture rituals could now be performed. More humiliation awaited him: stripped, painted, and forced once more to wear the halter, he endured yet again the gauntlet, was perhaps forced to dance and sing a song taught him by his master for this very occasion, and was taunted and degraded at every turn. There followed a more solemn ceremony, in which all eyes turned to the warrior who had captured and brought from so great a distance this "dog." With Foster seated prominently, his master began a seminarrated dance in which he and other members of his party acted out the massacre of Hodges' command, the taking of scalps, and Foster's capture. With calumet or tomahawk in hand, they mimed the fighting in a choreographed, theatrical performance that Father Marquette, who had witnessed a similar ritual, had said "might pass for a very fine opening of a ballet in France."[27] The dance, a vital ceremony for the returning warrior, was both a necessary affirmation of his masculinity and a much-anticipated entertainment for his people. The warrior's family beamed with pride, while other young men burned to win similar honors.

Then came the decision of what to do with the captive. In one sense Foster had already served his purpose and was dispensable. Through his own shame and degradation he had brought public honors and fame to his master, a function he could never perform again. He could now be ritually slaughtered, tortured to death for the further empowering and entertainment of his captor's village. Or he could continue in his enslavement, perhaps given to an older woman or a family in need of labor. It appears, however, that Foster's master decided to keep him, adopting him into his own family, and that the community honored his decision. As we have seen, however, "adoption" does not necessarily confer actual, familial status to an outsider who has had his honor stripped from him. One French trader familiar with the practices of Anishinaabe people (west of Lake Superior) affirmed that "adopted" captives "never lie in their Masters' Huts." The Indian master was to his captives "a feigned parent." These "adopted slaves," then, "were bound to a household of fictive kin, occupying the physical and metaphorical place of a child but constantly aware that they were not actual relatives."[28] Foster was undoubtedly given a new name, probably a demeaning one, and this was vital to the third constituent element of his slavery: "natal aliena- tion." Powerless, without honor, and "socially dead," his renaming was an almost universally utilized symbolic rite in which his former identity was stripped away.[29] One final incorporative ritual might have been visited upon him: Natives often marked their slaves in some way, a visible sign that sig- nified their status (or nonstatus). Iroquois masters, for example, tradition- ally severed a finger or two or inflicted some other mutilation.[30] Did Foster suffer dismemberment or some other disfiguring marking? He does not say so in the petition he made upon his eventual return, which suggests that he did not, or at least that it was not debilitating in any serious way.

Spared his life, at least for the moment, Foster settled into the routine that he must have feared would be his fate for the rest of his days. He may have been given a familial name, but he was never treated like family. He would have to earn his keep, but he was expected to do more: to keep his master's family in better ease and comfort than they had experienced pre- viously. He was given work that was normally the province of women and children: a French soldier observed that "slaves have to do the most menial work, such as cutting firewood, cultivating the fields, harvesting, pound- ing Indian corn or maize to make sagamité, cooking, mending the hunters' shoes, carrying their game, and, in general, anything that the women do. The women are in charge of the slaves, and deny them food if they are lazy."[31] They might deny them food as a matter of policy: Rushforth concluded that to keep the slave dependent and unable to escape or resist, his masters gave him "only 5–6 meals per week, just enough to keep him alive."[32]

For the slave, especially for a male slave, being at the mercy and the command of women was the most galling constant of his captivity, and it was meant to be. Native women had the responsibility for managing slaves, not only to exploit their labor but, according to the anthropologist Roland Viau, "to derive a sense of superiority by deliberately and publicly shaming defeated and captured men. . . . They humiliated their male slaves by restrict- ing them to generally female tasks." Women relished this responsibility, of- fering as it did the opportunity, along with adoption and torture rituals, to "play their part in the customs of war by reenacting a daily humiliation that dramatized the captives' loss of honor." Indeed, "Iroquois and Algonquian women recognized that their authority rested in part on rituals of unmanning directed at captured enemies."[33] The slave's function was to be a constant reminder of his new "family"'s standing, part of which involved being able to exploit the enemy's labor for their own uses, which meant keeping the slave tame and domesticated. Physical abuse, to which the slave dared not respond, and "a sophisticated language of dominion and ridicule" aided the process. So did "the perpetual threat of violence and murder." Because in fact slaves had no actual relatives in the village, they "lived outside the kinship system" and so were "liminal, even liminally human." They were almost never acknowledged as anything else, so that even if they served their masters for years, "a recalcitrant captive could expect a quick and unceremonious death."[34]

"A French Place called Detroit"

"With these savages," Foster recalled, "he was detained two Years." At that point, probably in the late summer of 1758, Foster's luck took a turn for the marginally better. His master was going on a trip that would take him far to the south and would require several weeks to complete. The destination was a place Foster may have heard of by this time, a French fort and settlement between two of the Great Lakes. In any case, he wrote, he was "permitted by his Indian owner to accompany him down the Lake to a French Place called Detroit." The word *permitted* is suggestive. Did Foster, seeing the trip as a chance to escape his emasculated life, beseech his master to take him with him? He might have viewed any change as opportunity to alter his condition, perhaps by escape. Or did his master, considering the distance he had to travel, naturally think of his slave? Whatever the case, Foster was again on the Great Lakes, paddling or sailing the more than 650 miles to where the waters of Lake Huron flowed, via Lake Ste. Claire and the Detroit River, into Lake Erie.[35]

Detroit was the brainchild of Antoine Laumet, Sieur de Cadillac, in 1702. It was conceived as a settlement not only for Canadian traders and their families but also for allied Indians seeking ready access to French trading goods. There was no doubt as to the strategic importance of the position; the problem was that Cadillac's Native trading partners had frequently been at odds with one another for generations beforehand. Inviting them into close proximity, with competition and with new jealousies to rekindle old rivalries, invited trouble. Cadillac stumbled into near-disastrous wars in 1706 with Ottawas on the one hand and Miamis on the other, and there was trouble again, this time with the Fox, in 1712.[36] During the War of the Austrian Succession (1740–1748), French officials in Canada worried about the "tepid commitment" of Indians in the Detroit area, fearing that they favored English takeover of the post. In the years immediately following the war, however, French and Canadian irregular troops reasserted their authority and largely recovered the Natives' allegiance and respect.[37] Detroit had water communication with Montreal via Lakes Erie and Ontario, but settlers, supplies, and soldiers were at the mercy of the winds: it could take from four to seven weeks for any of these to reach either end of the line. To hold on to this vital western post, Detroit would have to become more self-sufficient. The cost of keeping it adequately supplied from Montreal was especially high in time of war. Authorities in Quebec and Montreal offered encouragement for settlers to move there, hoping not only to make Detroit produce enough foodstuffs to supply the fort there but to make it the bread-basket for the upper Great Lakes.[38]

As their canoe approached the settlement from Lake Ste. Claire, Foster's heart must have soared to see so much evidence of a European footprint on the land (fig. 9.2). To his left was the Isle aux Couchons (today's Belle Isle), where the settlers put livestock to roam freely, protected from predators. On the right bank were large, cleared stretches where the inhabitants had their long and narrow farm lots, with the short sides on the river so that the houses would not be too far apart. About two miles from the first houses, and on the same side, was the fort. Unlike what Foster had seen of French fortifications thus far, this was a much simpler affair of upright timbers with small towers at the corners. But the space within was sufficiently expansive to hold many of the settlement's better houses, along with barracks and a church, arranged on four streets. Around the fort was an open field of fire five arpents wide (nearly 1,000 feet), though inhabitants attempted to encroach on this space from time to time. It was really more of a fortified village, combining the functions of defense, residence, trade, and administration. Although timber construction dominated, Foster saw evidence that the French penchant for building with stone was taking hold even here. Large boats with both sails and oars, loaded with stone from Isle Pierre, further downriver, could come to anchor a hundred yards from the fort, where smaller boats could shuttle the stone ashore for new building.[39]

A quarter mile or so before reaching the fort, just past the western tip of Isle aux Couchons, Foster's master turned their canoe to the southern shore,

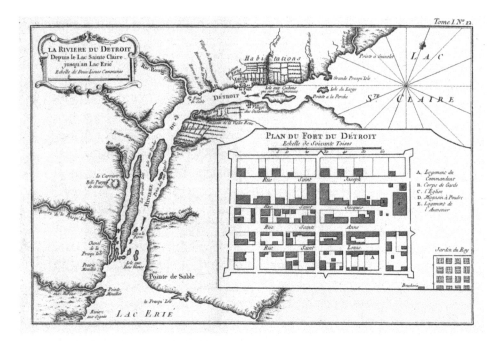

Figure 9.2. "La Riviere du Détroit: Depuis le Lac Sainte Claire jusqu'au Lac Erie." Published by N. Bellin, Paris, 1764. Map Collection, Yale University Library

where Foster could see near the shore a large Ottawa village with some ninety "Houses or Indian Cabbins," as another American captive, Charles Stuart, had described it earlier that year. Foster learned soon enough that within sight of Detroit were two more Native villages, where representative communities of some of New France's closest Native allies lived. Two miles from the fort, where the river bent slightly to the south, was a Huron village of sixty to seventy dwellings. At the upriver end of the village was a Catholic church and the "Priests House Garden and Plantation" (the Ottawa village had no such facilities, Stuart concluded, as they "are a Heathen Nation not Proselyted to the Roman Catholic Religion"). Across the river and a mile and a half from the fort was a Pottawatomie village, similar in size to the others. Foster does not say what his master's reason was for making this trip, but as he later related, soon after reaching Detroit Foster "interceded with a Frenchman to ransom him, which he accordingly effected for three Hund[rd]: Livers."[40]

Surely it was not that simple. Foster could hardly have "effected" his release from slavery without his Native master's consent. It is far more likely that his master arranged the transaction, for Detroit at that time trafficked in captive labor. Like new communities everywhere, Detroit needed workers to cut timber, clear fields, and construct housing. Unlike in the English colonies, however, there was no large and growing white population from which to draw sufficient indentured labor, and unlike on the French West Indies plantations (and, again, in the English Atlantic colonies), there was no ready access to African slave labor. Instead, the French at Detroit relied on Native slaves captured by their allies and sold to those who could afford them. It was generally regarded as a necessary practice if the settlement at the narrows was to achieve the aspirations of New France's strategic planners. Locally, owning slaves was recognized as the way to prosperity. According to a census of Detroit inhabitants in 1750, more than one-quarter of the ninety-six French householders owned slaves. Slaveholding families cultivated nearly three times as much land and produced more than twice as much European grain—wheat and oats—as families without slaves. Slaveholding families could also tend more cattle, pigs, and chickens, and so they likewise raised at least twice as many farm animals as non-slaveholding families. Altogether, that one-quarter of the population with slaves produced "about half of the town's wheat, oats, and beef" and thus became the most important suppliers for the fort's garrison.[41] In short, "the slave trade served the interests of the state by allowing Detroit's settlers to pursue agricultural and commercial interests simultaneously."[42] The increased productivity enjoyed by slaveholders permitted some economic diversification, such as the stone quarrying and transport already mentioned or the sawmill built on a creek about a mile from the fort, which sent cut planks to town on sawn-timber rafts.[43] All of this depended on human labor, and while free, white, family labor provided most of it, it was enslaved labor that helped move the settlement beyond mere subsistence to something like growth. Captive labor was very welcome at Detroit.

Foster's master surely knew this, and in fact Foster may have been, in large part, the reason for the long trip. Foster's value to his master as a war trophy faded over time; there would be no more great ceremonies or boastful retellings of his capture, especially as more prisoners came along after the capture of Fort William Henry.[44] Foster was now just a slave, and perhaps not a very useful one at that. Natives generally regarded female captives as preferable in the long run, for their procreative potential and their greater range of domestic skills. In the case of male captives especially, "once [they] had been dominated and domesticated, they had fulfilled their most important purpose."[45] Foster could simply have been killed, but he was valuable in another way: as a commodity.

And Detroit was the place to make the exchange, for there lived men like Pierre Chesne dit Labutte. Labutte, a longtime resident of Detroit, was an especially successful commercial farmer and trader. He had twice married a Métis woman (of French and Native parents) and with the help of those connections had procured Native slaves when he needed them. His ability to speak Miami, Ottawa, and Pottawatomie hugely facilitated his trade and his status in the settlement as an interpreter and negotiator. He had at least eighty-five acres under cultivation by the time Foster arrived, more than twice as much as the average slaveholder and six times as much as the average non-slaveholder. Not for him the three-by-forty-arpent landholding granted to newcomers below the Huron village. Labutte's house was among the better ones in the town, and his "plantation" opposite the fort was one of only three so designated and close to the Ottawa village, with which he had connections by marriage.[46] Labutte is in fact the likeliest candidate as the "Frenchman" who redeemed Foster from his Indian slavery. Few prospective buyers could have paid the three-hundred-livre price, which was equal to a Detroit laborer's wages for two years or the worth of three good cows. In terms of his notoriety, wealth, family connections, and the proximity of his land to the Ottawa village, the choice of Labutte makes the most sense; it is a pity that Foster did not name his benefactor. The American slave may have met Labutte in some chance encounter and "interceded" with him to buy him, or he may have added his voice to his master's in negotiating the purchase, but in any case, Isaac Foster's Indian bondage was at last over.[47]

This is not to say that Foster was now a free man; far from it. He was no longer a slave—the French did not normally enslave whites—but he would have to work off the three hundred livres he had begged his new French master to pay for him. The arrangement would be a more familiar one, at least: Foster would be acquainted with the indentured bondage customary in his own colony, which specified a date of termination for service. Also, unlike the situation in Montreal, white captives in Detroit were not held indefinitely. Foster may have heard of the example of Charles Stuart, who with his wife had been captured by Indians in western Pennsylvania and redeemed at Detroit only the previous year. The two priests who had purchased them in June 1756 had allowed them to repay the ransom with their labor, which they had accomplished by the following March.[48] Foster would have to work longer than that, but the terms were still generous: while a common laborer might earn the ransom amount in two years, Foster's master canceled the debt in one.

Foster's condition was more agreeable in a number of other ways. He no longer lived under the threat of being killed upon a whim, or of suffering punishment, so long, in the latter case, as he did what was required of him. He recovered his name, no longer being called simply "dog," and must have rejoiced even in hearing the French pronunciation of it. The food, both in its variety—beef, pork, poultry, vegetables, fruit (even grapes for wine)— and in its quantity, was restoring to his body and his spirit. Most of all, he knew that the work he did was, indirectly at least, for himself; he worked toward the goal of his freedom, now something more than a desperate hope. And the work he performed was more familiar, and to his mind more rewarding. Labutte and those of similar station had made their wealth through farming and breeding livestock, as did many in New England. On the south side of the river, in present-day Windsor, Ontario, where the largest plantations lay, the land was "bordered by prairies in such a way that the inhabitants have no wood to cut in order to clear their fields and sow their grain." Clearing and sowing were tasks Foster had performed in his native Andover, and there were animals to tend as well. Unusually for him, there were "large numbers of starlings," which ate the grain after sowing if it was not protected, and "people are needed to watch them," a simple but vital task to which Foster may occasionally have been assigned.[49] Across the river, on the fort side, the land was more thickly wooded, supplying the raw material for the sawmill; he may also have been set to work felling and hauling trees. It was hardly ideal, and some things could not be helped—he was still an enemy captive, and a Protestant—but this last period of bondage was the beginning of his reclamation of himself. A slave no longer, with liberty in his near future a growing certainty, Foster recovered something of his pride, certainly of his humanity, and his sense of manhood.

Return of the Captive

In the fall of 1759 Foster was released from his service and became at last a prisoner of war of the French. With what few personal belongings he had managed to acquire, he was sent to Montreal "With the Indians. . . On a Tradeing voyage" for exchange. To be journeying with Natives once again, but this time in the capacity of a fellow traveler, must have been a surreal experience for him. Whether they made the journey by canoe or on board a French vessel is not clear; if the latter, it may well have been Foster's first time on a sailing craft. In either case, the party probably kept the north shore of the lake in view until they reached the Niagara River. There Foster and the others disembarked, following the road that led past the spectacular falls (another wonder he could describe back home) and embarking again at the entrance to Lake Ontario for the passage to Fort Frontenac.[50]

Or rather, what was left of it. We cannot know how much news of the war Foster may have heard while in Detroit, but if he passed through the anchorage in what is modern Kingston, he might have heard, and seen, something of what had happened there the year before. After the long-awaited Anglo-American thrust against Fort Carillon in the summer of 1758 ended in another disaster, Colonel John Bradstreet and an army of provincial soldiers had salvaged something from the campaign. In a quick advance made in whaleboats up the Mohawk River to the blackened remains of the forts at Oswego, Bradstreet's raiders had then rowed across Lake Ontario with supplies and cannon and taken Fort Frontenac, a vital French installation on the lake, after a short siege. They had stayed long enough to knock down the walls, take or burn the vessels trapped there, and burn all else they could not carry away—and they carried away a great deal. It was one of the most daring and successful operations of the war—small wonder if the French did not want to tell Foster very much about it.[51]

Foster was escorted in due course to Montreal, and to a very different world. Quebec had surrendered on September 18 to a British army. Both the Marquis de Montcalm and James Wolfe, the general whose army had defeated Montcalm, were dead, mortally wounded on the Plains of Abraham, and the French forces that remained in that theater were at Trois-Rivières and around Montreal. Many of the Native allies of the French had since abandoned them. The situation for the French was grim indeed. Unless the British could be forced out of Quebec or a French fleet came in the spring to trap them, there was very little the remaining French troops could do but await the end. In the meantime, refugees came to Montreal, and harvests had continued bad: serious shortages for the coming winter were a virtual certainty. If previously there had been reluctance to hold numbers of Anglo-American prisoners in the city, there was understandably more now; the best thing to do was get rid of them by exchange. Accordingly, in November 1759 Isaac Foster was sent home in one of a series of prisoner exchanges that season. With the St. Lawrence blocked, the prisoners were finally being sent via Lake Champlain, the short route home. Perhaps Foster was at that time reunited with a fellow survivor of Hodges' Scout, Ebenezer Pratt. A seventeen-year-old servant from Bridgewater when he was taken, Pratt had lived at Kahnawake until he was redeemed by the French the previous May. Put in the prison in Montreal, he was released and exchanged at or about the same time as Foster.[52] It would have been interesting to hear them compare notes on their lengthy captivities among very different Indian peoples.

Foster got to see Crown Point again, but this time with a British flag flying over it. That summer's campaign, the fifth, had finally succeeded in ousting the French from Fort Carillon, and with that strongpoint lost, the French had abandoned their antiquated fort at Crown Point. Foster witnessed a hive of activity there, as the British general Jeffrey Amherst had set his victorious army to building a new, much larger fort as a base for the final push in the spring of 1760. From Crown Point, Foster, Pratt, and a party of other former captives traveled southeast along the new road that had been cut through the Green Mountains to Fort No. Four (today's Charlestown, New Hampshire), on the Connecticut River. There, in the last days of November, they paused to recoup after their miserable trek over the Green Mountains (the "road" was little more than a rugged path for long stretches) and have their statements taken by the authorities at the fort. Eight men in the party, two of them in a "Dangerous" condition, remained at No. Four under a doctor's care, but Foster and Pratt were both well enough to proceed on their way home. Foster was back in Andover by New Year's, having been absent, as he calculated, "from the day he was taken, three Years & two Months."[53]

In the petition he wrote days later, he told his readers that during his captivity he had "sufferd inconceivable hardships."[54] When appealing to colony authorities for aid in this way, petitioners occasionally resorted to hyperbolic language. In Foster's case, however, we may take him at his word. Systematically beaten and humiliated for two years, metaphorically emasculated, worked and threatened relentlessly, starved, and subjected to physical conditions that could easily have been lethal, he can be excused for summarizing his experience in a few vague, prescribed but truthful words. He may even have borne the marks of his captivity, in frostbitten toes or fingers—perhaps one of these was missing, cut away at far-off Lake Nipagon to mark his slave status. Also missing, and apparently forever, were the three other survivors who had gone with Foster into captivity among the Ottawas. William Bradbury, Benjamin Gushe, and Henry Partridge appear no more in surviving records. Traded, killed, dying in captivity, or adopted—whatever that meant—they were swallowed in the vastness of the continent and are lost to history. More fortunate than them, Isaac Foster had been to the western edges of France's North American empire and had returned.

10

Homecomings

War's End

The campaign that brought the war in North America to a virtual close was almost anticlimactic and can be quickly told. There would be no grand battles in 1760 such as those at Fort Carillon or Quebec, and there was only one real objective for the Anglo-American forces preparing to move against the enemy: Montreal. With Louisbourg taken in 1758, Quebec in hand since the autumn of 1759, and Britannia ruling the waves, British generals could afford to plan carefully and toward a common objective without fear of serious distractions or diversionary attacks elsewhere. The plan for the year was for three army groups—southwestward from Quebec, northeastward from reoccupied Oswego, and northward from Crown Point—to converge on Montreal simultaneously. Moving slowly and methodically, the three columns encountered weak resistance along the way. They had little to fear now from France's Indian allies, who had suffered terribly from smallpox epidemics since the start of the war, losing hundreds of warriors to the disease.[1] They could clearly see how the wind was blowing and wisely stayed neutral, or at least kept out of the way. Jeffrey Amherst's army from Oswego reached Lachine, at the west end of Montreal Island, on September 6. He was met there the next morning by a delegation from Governor Vaudreuil under a flag of truce. The chief of the delegation was none other than Louis Antoine de Bougainville, who four years earlier had helped interrogate the survivors of Captain Hodges' shattered command. De Bougainville came with a proposal of capitulation from the governor. Unwilling to subject the city—with its thin walls, few defenders, and throngs of civilians, refugees, and invalids—to certain destruction, Vaudreuil hoped for, and in the event received, generous terms from Amherst. The only condition that rankled proud European officers like de Bougainville was that they were not permitted the honors of war in making their surrender; their troops would have to lay down their arms and surrender their regimental flags.[2]

For our purposes, this final campaign and the capitulation of Montreal meant the release of almost all of the remaining survivors of Hodges' Scout still in the custody of the French or their Seven Nations allies. John Erwin, eighteen years old when captured, had been taken to Kahnawake and "given away to an Indian . . . with whom he lived until the surrender of Montreal." John Con, the seventeen-year-old servant, was twenty-one now; after his capture he had been "Carried to St Francway & about six months after sold to the French & by Them Imprisoned for some Time." He soon found a Canadian buyer, however, and "remained a servant till Montreal was Resined to His Britanick Majestye." John Walklate, of Gloucester, now twenty-six, "was taken and detained Prisoner"—he does not say with whom—"till Mont Real was taken and Canada surrendered to Generall Amherst."[3] Moses Emerson left no surviving record of his captivity, but he too appears to have returned home after the capitulation. A fifth captive held at Oswegatchie, the old soldier William Merry, heard of Amherst's advance in the summer of 1760 and decided that there would be no better opportunity for escape. Rather than risk being dragged off in the evacuation of the Indian town, he slipped away and, undetected, made the 115-mile trek to Oswego and safety with Amherst's army.[4]

It was getting late in the year for the freed captives, but to a man, they did not want to spend another winter in Canada; they just wanted to go home. That was easier wished for than done. They had nothing but the clothes on their backs, a few meager possessions, and whatever they could borrow in the way of supplies and money to help them on their way.[5] Additionally, they could not leave until they had official passes, documents that would allow them to travel through British lines and from town to town without being taken for deserters. One such document, addressed "To All whom it may Concern," survives in the Massachusetts Archives. It required the reader to permit John Erwin and two others, "being all Prisoners redeemed from Canada, to pass unmolested, being in their way home." The pass was signed by Sir William Johnson, who had accompanied Amherst's army and was now a baronet and superintendent of Indian affairs in North America.[6] One hopes that the signature of so illustrious a person, the hero of the 1755 Battle of Lake George, eased Erwin's return home, procuring for him accommodations at taverns along the way, or at least a dry barn in which to sleep.

Captives at Home

Meanwhile, how had the families of the dead and missing fared in their absence? The notification "kill'd or taken," however it was sent or received, considerably complicated the response of those concerned at home, making them "captives" in another sense. Some seemed sure of their soldier's decease, which suggests that more of the bodies found at Lake George had been identified and the sad news passed on. John Lewis' brother-in-law filed for, and was granted, administration of Lewis' estate, such as it was, within five months of the massacre. Azor Roundy, a "miner" (minor) servant from Beverly killed in his eighteenth year, was likewise treated as "Decd." by May 1757.[7] Four others were listed as "kill'd" outright. On the other hand, at least seven families, thanks to Ensign Lincoln's daring escape, received word after nearly a year of uncertainty that their loved ones were still alive and thus could hold out hope for the survivors' return. John Stacy's brother could write with confidence in 1758 of John's survival, for he had been "in formd By a Captive that Escaped from Canady that he saw ye aboves^d John Stacey near M^{t}Real." Samuel Emerson likewise related that his brother Moses had been captured by Indians "and is since been heard of to be in Captivity with them." The families of William Merry, Benjamin Gushe, Henry Partridge, and Thomas Woodward received similar good news. Initially, Joseph Abbot had been reported dead; it must have been a relieved father who later wrote, based on Lincoln's report, "I heare that he is among the Indians above Moriall." His hopes were to be dashed, however: Joseph would not return, dying a prisoner in the Dauphine Bastion. In addition to Abbot, three other survivors were erroneously declared dead on their company rosters. Moses Emerson's status was elevated after Lincoln's return, as was John Stacy's. Peleg Stevens' homecoming after two years' absence, however, may have been a complete surprise to family and friends, who had heard he was "kill'd with Hodges."[8]

The remaining families—those whose loved ones were either "kill'd or taken"—had to continue living with the uncertainty, and this imposed real hardships. Quite apart from the anxiety of those imagining friends or relations suffering captivity, there was the financial burden that had to be borne.

Households in Massachusetts had expected, indeed counted upon, the wages due the men who had gone upon the colony's, and the king's, business. Recognizing in 1757 that "many Private Soldiers of this Province Who Went upon the Last Crown Point Expedition Were Killed or Died in the service leaving no Real Estate and but Little more of personal Estates then their Wages," the Massachusetts legislature resolved that "in Every such Case the Widow of such Deceased Soldier or the next of Kin to said Intestate shall and hereby is impowered to Receive such Wages Without taking Letters of Administration."[9] Such consideration would substantially speed the process of relief for soldiers' families, but there was a catch: the subject had to be certainly dead, and the designation "kill'd or taken" alongside at least twenty-five names in the muster rolls in no way conveyed such certainty. The mother of John Erwin, "a very poor & and aged" widow "& never expecting to hear of your Petitioner's being a live," found herself in such straits that she was willing to declare her son dead in order to receive his wages.[10] Ebenezer Pratt's mother, also a widow, did not go so far but had few or no relations to help her and was "not able to earn her own Living."[11] She had expected Pratt to be home at the end of the 1756 campaign.

The legislature's resolve did not apply to the majority category of single men missing in action; their wages could be in limbo indefinitely. Thomas Woodward was a seventeen-year-old farm laborer when he set off into the woods with Captain Hodges' command. No one at home could be sure whether he was dead or alive, but his wages were stopped on September 19, 1756. Woodward was due "Eight Pounds twelve shillings and seven pence Lawful money," but he was in no position to collect it, and apparently neither was anyone else. More than two years after Thomas' absence, his brother Benjamin explained to authorities that "there is not any Person legally authorized to receive the same Wages, (the s^d. Thomas not having any Guardian) neither can any Person be authorized to receive the same, without the Aid of this Court, it being uncertain whether the s^d. Thomas is now living or dead, the Treasurer of the s^d. Province refusing to pay the same Wages." Benjamin argued that "it would be for the Advantage of the s^d. Thomas in case he be living & shall return home again" for his wages to be released to someone who could at least "place the same out at Interest" for Thomas' benefit. The General Court granted the request, but Thomas never came home.[12]

The hardship was especially great, as it always is, for the wives and children of the missing. Wives were left to wonder whether they were widows, and until they knew for certain, their options were fairly limited; they could not, for instance, remarry without a court's permission, and that usually required a spouse's absence of seven years. The status of William Merry, who was the only married man to survive the massacre of Hodges' Scout, would not be known for the better part of a year. His wife, Sarah, was left to care for his three minor children, none of whom was old enough to perform any work that would sustain the family. That the Merrys lived close to poverty is suggested by the action of the freeholders of Norton, the town in which they lived. In 1755, while her husband was away with William Johnson's army in the first year of the war, Sarah became sufficiently ill to require a doctor's attention. Dr. George Wheaton submitted the bill for "a visit and medicines" amounting to 12s. 6d. to the town selectmen, a practice usually only permitted when a patient was clearly unable to pay. The freeholders eventually voted to cover the doctor's expenses.[13] In the 1756 campaign year, both Sarah's son Henry (from a previous marriage) and her husband went off to war, so of course the labor of both men was lost for the year. Neither of them returned at the end of the season; Henry was captured with the garrison at Oswego, and little more than a month later William was reported captured or killed. She would not see her husband for another four years; it is unclear whether her son ever came home. The difficulties she experienced in keeping her remaining children housed, clothed, and fed all that time must have been legion.

Even if wives or other next of kin could access their missing soldiers' wages, there was often an unexpected deduction. Most Massachusetts soldiers, as we have seen, were issued arms purchased by the colony government, and the recipients were responsible for their return at the end of the campaign. Weapons lost for any reason, even in combat, were still charged to the soldier's account and subtracted from his wages. The colony normally assessed these at £4, which in the case of the killed and missing of Hodges' command amounted to nearly half of what they were otherwise due—a substantial loss. Typical of the petitions sent to the legislature for redress was that of Elizabeth Philips, of Malden, whose husband, James, had died on campaign. As often happened, his gun was not returned, probably pilfered by another soldier. "Now your Petitioner cannot Draw her said Husbands wages," she complained, "without the Deduction of four pounds for the said Gun and your Petitioner (without the Interposition of your Hon[rs]) must be a Sufferer for neglecting that which it was never in her power to perform."[14] Isaac Foster's father was able to collect his son's wages in his absence, but as a consequence of Isaac's being "either killed by the Enemy or taken Captive," his gun could hardly have been returned. "Yet," wrote the elder Foster, "there is kept back out of his wages from your Petitioner for said Gun the sum of four pounds," which he understandably thought was unjust, not to say mean-spirited.[15] Joseph Abbot's father, Thomas, also sought to collect his missing son's wages but asked that the penalty for the lost weapon be waived, given the circumstances.[16] In almost all cases, petitioners received the £4, but this often involved a filing fee and additional delay.

Men of means who had families were wise to make sure they had up-to-date wills before marching off to war. Such a one was thirty-seven-year-old Gideon Basset, also of Norton. He did not die with Hodges, apparently succumbing to illness not long after his neighbor's violent demise. Basset's oldest son was only ten, so he bequeathed to his "Dearly Beloved" wife, Bathsheba, all his real and personal estate, worth £178 6s. 8d. To his son Gideon he left £93 "Lawfull money," to be "Layed out to him in Learnin & to provide Cloaths. . . . And it is my will that my son shall have a Liberal Education," along with one-third of his father's books and "my best gun & sword." Basset and his wife were still sexually vigorous enough for him to provide for another offspring, "if it Do so prove that my wife is now with child so that she has a living child born of her Body." With will in hand, his widow was able to begin managing the estate immediately and to settle her husband's accounts within a couple of months of his death.[17]

Failure to leave a will saddled a family with, at the least, additional fees, inconvenience, and oversight from the court of probate. Someone would have to be appointed executor (often this was the wife, if she felt able to do it), make an inventory of the deceased's real and moveable estate, and then divide the estate as equally as possible according to law and custom. Every step in the process had to be approved by the court. Obadiah Eddy died at Lake George possessed of an estate worth about half that of Gideon Basset, but without a will. His widow, Lois, had to make frequent applications for allowance of money from the estate to cover expenses, such as "Necessaries for housekeeping £2. 5.," "time & Care in Lying in of a Child after my sd husband Deceased £4," "Allowance for an Old Great Coat Cut for ye Children," and "a day at the Judges." Since she was well into middle age and poor, with five children, remarriage was not in the cards, and she was forced to bind out several of her young ones to other families for their care; that too required fees. Whatever her husband's wishes might have been, his estate was divided, after all debts and fees were subtracted, so that his children, all minors when he died, received legacies of a mere £3 13s., the eldest getting a double share.[18] John Lewis, who was among the slain of Hodges' command, also did not have a will, but he had next to nothing to bequeath in any case. Even counting his soldier's wages, he died insolvent, and when two court-appointed commissioners collected claims for debt against his estate, they amounted to nearly a third more than it was worth. His wife and children were left nothing but their meager possessions.[19]

It is easier to gain an impression of the economic cost to families dealing with loss, or presumed loss, of fathers, sons, and brothers than it is to assess the emotional impact of that altered reality. When the elder John Con was struck with his final illness in late 1758, he made out his will. His namesake son was a prisoner in Montreal by then and would remain so until the end of the war, but the father only knew that he was among the missing. Con bequeathed to John and his younger brother, George, "all my lands and Buildings in Groton . . . provided my said son John shall come or send to New England himself to Receive his part . . . within Seven Years next after my Decease." In the necessarily careful and formulaic language of Con's will, we may be reading simply the customary concern with keeping legal loose ends firmly tied. Imagine the awkwardness of the younger Con's return, having been unjustifiably left out of his father's will, not to mention the lawsuits that would follow. But it is almost impossible not to see in this provision of Con's will a father's anxiety and care for the elder son he would never see again. In this case the father's faith was justified: the young soldier returned home two years later to better circumstances than those facing most other survivors.[20]

A clearer and more poignant example of personal loss is evident in the case of John Lewis. As stated earlier, his brother-in-law moved quickly to become administrator of Lewis' estate, assumedly for the benefit of the widow and children—there was certainly little of material value to be gained from the thankless task. Lewis' aged mother, Hannah, however, refused to give up on him, writing him into the will she made out in June 1757. To her "Beloved Son John Lewis if he be living" she bequeathed "Fifty pound, old Tenor"—more than his estate was worth—and "in Case of his Decease I will the same unto his two Children . . . to be equally divided between them."[21] More than a year later, with the court of probate proceeding on the assumption of John's decease, Hannah insisted to the Massachusetts legislature that "I had a Son John Lewis [who] went out in the year fifty six . . . and was taken at the Lake in Cap Hodges Scout."[22] One wonders whether she was ever able to accept her son's death before she went to her own grave four years later.

Hannah Titus was also a grieving mother. Her husband had died early in 1756, leaving her little estate. The court appointed a guardian for her youngest son, Benjamin, "a minor . . . aged seventeen years," but the lad must have prevailed upon him and his mother to allow him to go for a soldier that year. He enlisted in the same company as his older brother Noah, and together they set off for Lake George. Perhaps Hannah took some comfort in thinking they would be able to look out for each other. If so, her hopes turned to ashes, as Benjamin was killed with Captain Hodges, and Noah sickened shortly after and never recovered. By the end of December Hannah Titus was pleading with the judge of probate to have her son Benjamin's former guardian named administrator for the estates of Benjamin, Noah, and their spinster sister, Hepzibah, who also had died that year. Now bereft of husband and children after a year of unrelenting loss, Hannah understandably felt "not able to do such business myself."[23]

Picking Up the Pieces

Those survivors of Hodges' Scout who returned home did so possessed of few resources with which they might start over. None of them had much in the way of a personal estate, and none (with the exception of John Con, through inheritance) possessed land. Most had been, as Con described his own experience, "for four years in hard Servis & but very poor provisions." Forced labor and inadequate nutrition contributed to Ebenezer Pratt's difficulties also. A robust, seventeen-year-old farm laborer when he left Bridgewater, his long Indian captivity, capped by half a year in Montreal "close confined," wrought a marked change in him. He "came Home almost naked, and at present in a weakly state, not able to labour." All of them must have feared at some point that they would never return, as did William Merry, who "Despared of Ever seeing Norton my native place." Merry returned, as he admitted, especially "poor and Necessitous," for unlike the others, he had "a wife & Three children all needy."[24]

Poverty faced all who returned initially. Pratt had "no Estate, and no Relation able to do for him." His former company captain supported his bid for assistance, assuring Massachusetts authorities that Pratt's "Circumstances in the world are as low as can be, having not one Penny of Estate." John Erwin summed up the situation for most of them, to one degree or another: "Besides the loss of that time in the prime of his life," he explained, he had "returned home almost naked and nothing to cloath him with or support him, but only his Labour." He did not begrudge his mother drawing his wages, she being a "very poor & an aged person, & never expecting to hear of [his] being a live," but it meant that he had now "not one farthing at his Return to receive, towards his support & his said Mother's, &c."[25]

Among the first actions the returnees took toward easing their situations was to petition the Massachusetts government for relief, citing lost wages, lost time, suffering, or some combination of all three. The right to petition authority for redress and to have those petitions heard and considered was an ancient and fiercely guarded English privilege, and English colonists made sure that that birthright crossed the Atlantic with them. The Massachusetts Archives has extensive collections of these petitions, and it is largely from such documents that the stories of Hodges' soldiers have been recovered. While the language of the petitions varied, the structure was formulaic. First, there had to be some hardship, damage, or injustice done to the petitioner (or the clear prospect of such) for which the colony authorities were at least partly responsible, morally or actually. Second, there had to be a means of remedy available to the authorities, usually suggested by the petitioner. Third, the document had to be written in a respectful, supplicating voice if it was to reach sympathetic ears. Fourth, the petitioner, or an acceptable proxy, had to appear in person to present the petition. In the case of Hodges' returning survivors, the least disputable "damage" done them was in the nature of the wages they had not received for their time in the 1756 campaign.

For this they had reference to the muster rolls, made out late in 1756 and adjusted as necessary over the ensuing months. The rolls listed the number of weeks and days served, the rate at which each soldier was paid, and what each man was due, after any deductions (such as for those missing weapons). The men probably contacted their old captains—certainly that would be easier than consulting the colony treasurer in Boston—who kept copies of the rolls they submitted. John Erwin petitioned for "the Wages due for his servis untill he was Captivated, which wages were Eight Pounds twelve shillings & seven pence." That was straightforward, but Erwin argued that he was due more, for "some of his fellow soldiers [i.e., those not captured] received fourteen Pounds ten shillings for their service the same year," reflecting their continued service through November or early December. Isaac Foster likewise pointed out that "whereas he has receiv'd pay no longer than till the Day of his Captivity he humbly begs your Excellency & Honours, would take his case under your wise consideration, & make him such other Allowance for his time &c: as in your great goodness & wisdom shall seem mete."[26]

Robert Wilson, the young man who had made that incredible half marathon back to Fort William Henry with a hole through his shoulder, was among the first of the survivors of Hodges' Scout to see home. He received his wages but also had to endure the "Grate pain and Expence" of his wound. Whether his initial recovery was at the fort or in an Albany hospital, he was back in Lexington by the end of October 1756. Luckily for him, his wages were continued until December 5, when his company was mustered out; he would need the money. Wilson initially "had nothing Given him to help himself with all but paied his own Expence hom," and after that "Remained Lowe with his wound all the winter." He boarded at the home of Andrew Munroe—perhaps his former employer—for nearly five months while his wound slowly healed. He was by then able to do some work, but "he has not the use of his showlder so well as he had nor fears he Ever shall." More than two years after he was shot, Wilson was awarded £6 "in full for his Service and Sufferings," but the once hardy young man, now a disabled veteran, would never be the same again.[27]

Those survivors, along with hundreds of others petitioning over the course of the war, generally got what they asked for, within certain limits. By the time of the Seven Years War the Massachusetts government had stopped the practice of awarding pensions to widows and wounded men, opting for the much less costly practice of one-time, lump-sum payments. The same practice applied to returning captives. In addition to their just wages, Hodges' survivors received little more by way of recompense for their "lost time," regardless of how long that had been. Thus, whatever the legislature's "great goodness and wisdom," its generosity usually extended only to about £10. John Erwin and John Con each received this amount, as did William Merry (plus an additional £2 for his lost gun). For some reason, Ebenezer

Pratt received only £8. The "winner" in this game was Jeremiah Lincoln, who after his daring escape boldly asked the colony government to "Consider his Sufferings, & Loss of Time so far as to Allow him his Wages from the 18th of September last the Time of his Captivity to the 16th day of July last the Time of his Return home together with his Extraordinary Expense." Apparently the government did consider, and whether it was because of Lincoln's officer status, his temporary celebrity, or some other reason, the legislature awarded him £24 4s. 9d. for his ten-month captivity.[28] The awards, except for Lincoln's, represented little more than the pay the men were due in any case; they were, as Steven Eames has rightly described them, "no more than a token acknowledgement of service provided and loss incurred."[29]

It was almost all the financial help they would get. The towns from which they had come had few resources of their own, and the taxpayers reasonably considered matters involving provincial soldiers to be the province's responsibility.[30] Churches in the towns were traditional and obvious sources of charity, but their charity was customarily available only to church members, as when Jonathan Smith, of Reading, in 1756 asked his fellow church members for a contribution after his house had been consumed by fire or when Thomas Hartshorn, also of Reading, eleven years later was "brot low by y[e] Dispensat[n] of Provid:." Help was often less forthcoming to nonmembers. The same Reading church that was willing to give aid to Smith and Hartshorn was less enthusiastic about "One Labary [who] was taken Captive by ye Indians last Augt. & Carryed to Canada." This was apparently Peter Labaree, who had been captured August 30, 1754, along with Susannah Johnson and her family, at Fort No. Four (Charlestown, New Hampshire). Labaree had "Earnestly Requested help of us in Order to his Redemption." After some discussion, the congregation agreed to take up a contribution the next Sunday but only days later reversed its decision on account of "Some Jealousy [suspicion] & Surmises whether Labarra w[d]. Ever Obtain y[e] Money."[31]

Petitioning their colony government had another function for returning captives, one that had less to do with repositioning themselves in civilian life and more to do with how they processed their experiences. They had spent years in degrading circumstances, either as prisoners of despised "savages" or as forced laborers for their enemies in religion. Their status as men, which some of them had only begun to experience as soldiers, had been taken from them, returning them to the condition of children, powerless and dependent. For the men who came home, "the act of putting pen to paper was the first step in claiming control of their intercultural encounter."[32] None of the survivors of Hodges' Scout published a captivity memoir—a popular tract of suffering, adventure, and redemption—though they certainly had stories to tell. Instead, the petition was their opportunity to write the narrative of their recent experiences, though in deference to the limited needs of their readers, these were usually trimmed to the essentials. Universally, they alluded to extraordinary adversity and privation: "Hunger and Cold"; "savage slavery"; "inconceivable hardships"; "many and great hardships." They had been "Cruely used" by "that savage and Barbarous crew" of Indians, subject to treatment that, in some cases at least, surely needed little exaggeration. William Merry made the strongest case for himself, using the word *suffering* four times in his petition, adding "pain," "Despare," and finishing with "my Great suffering and fateough [fatigue] naked ness and los[s]es."[33] If the veterans (for such they now were) could not boast of heroic deeds, they could tell of their sufferings in the service, which they argued gave them equal claim to their colony's compassion.

If it is true that the essence of being a soldier is not one's willingness to slay but one's willingness to be slain, not to inflict suffering but to be willing to endure it, then the petition-narratives of the captives' hardships, while incomplete and imprecise, are not formulaic hyperbole but necessary and important expressions of their sense of self and service. Through their petitions the men reclaimed their manhood by demonstrating their ability to withstand all that their captivities could throw at them in the service of king and country. Whatever their quality or standing, they had been soldiers of the empire, willing volunteers in a world war. John Erwin insisted that in joining a provincial regiment he had been "inlisted into his Majestys Service." Isaac Foster's father likewise referred to his missing son as "a Soldier in His Majestys service." Ebenezer Pratt's master (while trying to secure his servant's wages) assured the colony government that Pratt had enlisted "to serve his majesty." William Merry, who was unashamed to recount his sufferings and his prior service, swore that he had always been "a faithfull soldier to serve his King and Country. . . . And always was Determind to do any utmost endeavor to serve his majestie in his Just war against france."[34] We should not dismiss such claims merely as ingratiating language. There is every reason to believe that to one degree or another, and in combination with whatever additional motivating factors there surely were, provincial soldiers regarded their service as a patriotic exercise, as duty.

Writing their own narratives helped the returning survivors to re-remember their captivities in subtly restorative ways. In his recounting of his enslavement by Ottawas, Isaac Foster referred to his Indian master as his "owner"—a clinically accurate description that nevertheless refused to acknowledge a "master" and thus implicitly denied Foster's reduction to the status of a slave. John Erwin's oblique reference to "an Indian" at Kahnawake "with whom he lived" surely obscures the actual living arrangement. Joshua Perry, one of the few who escaped the carnage of Hodges' Scout, confessed to the loss of "his Blanket And two Garments and my hat which I was obliged to throw off in the fight"—or threw off in his flight, as appears more likely.[35] Did they look upon their experience in providential terms? Christian teaching emphasized suffering as an ultimately positive process, a tempering of the soul that strengthened it to do God's will. Perhaps oddly, considering the Congregationalist atmosphere in which these men were reared, only William Merry seemed willing to give credit where it was due when he wrote that following his period of despair, "by ye Divine Blessing of Almighty God" he "Got from the savage slavery and with much suffering Got to oswego."[36]

In recalling their experiences, our petitioners readily dismissed the time spent with their Native captors as a period of "Barbarous" captivity, but they revealed few clues as to how they regarded their encounters with the great power against which they had contended, the French in Canada. As we have seen, captives quickly came to see life with the Canadians, even as servants, as infinitely preferable to life with the Indians, and some were able to experience the people and culture of New France at close range for an extended period, at least in the environs of Montreal and Quebec. Language and religion were the two greatest hurdles to acclimating themselves to their conditions. The first could be overcome to some degree without prejudice to one's soul; the second was less negotiable, and none of Hodges' survivors converted to Catholicism. Still, their immersion in a Catholic country must have left impressions on them, and those impressions need not have been entirely negative. Robert Eastburn, deacon that he was, used his experiences as a captive to take his coreligionists at home to task. In a version of the classic New England jeremiad sermon, he did not so much condemn the French for the "falseness" of their religion as praise them for their sincerity in it:

Suffer me with Humility and Sorrow to observe that our Enemies make better Use of a bad Religion, than we of a good One; they rise up long before Day in

Winter, and go [to Mass] through the Snow in the Coldest Seasons. . . . The [converted] Indians are as Zealous in Religion, as the French, they oblige their Children to Pray Morning and Evening . . . are punctual in performing the stated Acts of Devotion themselves, are still and peaceable in their own Families, and among each other as Neighbors![37]

All of our survivors must have witnessed something similar. Did they, like Eastburn, draw lessons from their observations, encouragement to reject "popish" superstition but to emulate the discipline they saw during their captivity?

Returning to normalcy meant resuming their interrupted lives. Peleg Stevens moved from Dartmouth to nearby Plymouth, where he presumably plied his skills as a barber. William Merry went back to farm labor in Norton, while John Con learned the responsibilities of land ownership in Haverhill. Isaac Foster decided to return to normalcy via matrimony: he married in March 1761, at twenty-three, little more than a year after his return. Marriage was in the cards for three other survivors that year. Jeremiah Lincoln was wed in April and became a father six months later (somewhere between a quarter and a third of New England marriages at that time began in similar fashion). Ebenezer Pratt did not wait even as long as Foster; his August wedding followed his return to Bridgewater by only nine months.[38]

The hastiest courtship, however, and the most intriguing, belonged to Peleg Stevens. In late February 1759, within only five months of his homecoming, he and Sarah Wright, of Plymouth, registered their intention to marry. Sarah was the widow of Martin Wright, a "seafaring man," and was carrying his child; Martin must have died close to the time Peleg Stevens returned. Marriage usually followed the announcement of intention by a few weeks or months, but there seems to have been a problem, for the intention was "entered anew April 9th . . . by desire of said Peleg Stevens." The issue may have been the unborn child, who was entitled to a share of its father's estate unless the mother remarried, in which case the wife's property became that of the new husband. New England courts tended to defend and protect the interests of children in these circumstances. Perhaps one of Martin's relations raised a fuss on behalf of his child, or perhaps intense social pressure caused Peleg and Sarah to postpone the nuptials. At any rate, when the child, a daughter, was born in June, Martin's estate still was not settled. Finally, in early March 1760, more than a year after her husband's death, the court named Sarah the administrator; the fact that it took so long strongly suggests a contending claim. Sarah submitted an inventory of the estate and accounts to the court of probate on March 24. Three days later, with the daughter's legacy secured, she and Peleg married. Their first child together, Asa, was born seven months later.[39]

In no discernible way did the captives' return to civilian life differ markedly from the return of most other provincial soldiers. The records of everyday life in eighteenth-century, small-town New England are scant enough, to be sure, but there is no indication that these veterans had any inordinate difficulty in resuming the lives they had anticipated before extraordinary circumstances intervened—with one possible exception. In February 1763 Sarah Merry, "represented . . . to be an inhabitant of Norton," was "warned out" of the neighboring town of Bridgewater. Warning out was a common practice that informed nonresidents that they were not entitled to the rights of residency, which in many cases led to the forced removal of undesirables from town. At the time, Sarah was living at the house of Lieutenant Amos Keith, a locally prominent man. Keith was approaching sixty and childless, so Sarah may have been employed in domestic service, keeping house. But she was apparently living there without her young children (warnings out typically specified whether children were involved) little more than two years after her husband William's return from captivity. It is possible that the arrangement at Keith's house was simply an expedient—a way of bringing some much-needed money into the Merry household—but it was unusual for husband and wife to live apart in this way, and perhaps William's readjustment to "normal" life had not gone smoothly. In any case, it seems likely that there was considerable stress in this veteran's family, but whether it was induced by poverty, his emotional state, or longstanding marital circumstances, we are unlikely ever to know.[40]

Beyond what they revealed in their petitions, the former captives did not write of their experiences, or at least no such account has come to light, but did they at least speak of them? Some, like Jeremiah Lincoln, who had pulled off his daring escape from Montreal, must have enjoyed some degree of local celebrity for a time. Surely Isaac Foster must have been asked about his journey to the middle of the continent. Others had stories to tell if they wished to do so—of Montreal, of Quebec, of prison, of the Indians' strange ways or rough treatment. They may well have been the most widely traveled men in their respective towns. All of them could flaunt the French or Native dialects they had managed, perforce, to learn. Peleg Stevens could tell his customers about France as he dressed their hair and shaved them, or perhaps regale fellow taverngoers with anecdotes from his trip to London. Did they tell of adventures now lost to history, of natural wonders like the Great Lakes, the St. Lawrence rapids, Niagara Falls? Our subjects' terse accounts of their captivity surely conceal varied and complex experiences despite the difficulties they had all endured. They went to places, encountered people, and experienced circumstances that they could not have foreseen or imagined, and some of these may not have been as unpleasant, at least in memory, as the language of their semiscripted petitions implies.

Of the fifteen men who survived Hodges' Scout to enter captivity in Canada, we can account in some way for all. Jeremiah Lincoln escaped; Joseph Abbot died in prison; Isaac Foster and Ebenezer Pratt returned home in prisoner exchanges late in the war, and Peleg Stevens by way of transatlantic cartel. Three men—William Bradbury, Benjamin Gushe, and Henry Partridge—may never have escaped their captivity with the Ottawas, while a fourth, John Stacy, was last known to be "near Montreal." William Merry escaped to Amherst's army in the final stages of the war. The last to be released were John Erwin, John Con, John Walklate, and Moses Emerson, freed when Montreal capitulated. Three other known survivors of the massacre also escaped captivity. Lieutenant Ezekiel Webb, who may have left the fighting early, served in a different company in the 1757 campaign, but there is no further record of service for him. Marriage to a local Yarmouth girl may have been the decisive factor in his giving up his military career. He could better afford it than most, with his lieutenant's wages of £37. 10s. 9d. for the campaign, more than twice what a private would have earned.[41] Robert Wilson recovered from his wound, but it is not clear what happened to the partly disabled Irish immigrant after that. Joshua Perry, the man rescued at the lakeshore after the destruction of Hodges' Scout, survived the massacre but not the war. He enlisted for nearly every subsequent campaign, and it was the last one that killed him: he died in September 1760, barely a week after Montreal fell, probably a victim of disease while on garrison duty. He had attained the rank of sergeant.[42]

The reader may have noticed that only fourteen of the captives are identified above. There is one more to be accounted for. His fate was entirely unknown until a chance encounter months after the fighting ceased.

The Court-Martial of Jonathan Barnes

The Renegade

With the capitulation of Montreal, effective resistance to the British invasion of Canada came to an end. While French forces had been decisively beaten, however, the Native nations along the St. Lawrence River had not. A week after Montreal's surrender, representatives of the Seven Nations met with British and League Iroquois counterparts at Kahnawake to come to an understanding. The Seven Nations agreed to abandon their alliance with the French, to ally themselves instead with the British, and to be reconciled with the Iroquois of the Mohawk River valley–Finger Lakes region. They also agreed to liberate all Anglo-American captives still in their possession—those who wanted to be liberated, at least. In return, the people of the Seven Nations were promised a resumption of normal trade with Albany (denied, of course, during the war) and that Catholic Indians could retain their priests and not be disturbed in their faith.[1]

The new arrangements did not explicitly penalize the Indians of Canada for their former connection to Britain's enemy, but that does not mean that there was no pressure on the Seven Nations to come to the peace table. During the 1759 and 1760 campaigns, they had felt, for the first time in the war, the heavy hand of invasion by the British. In the late summer of 1760, as Jeffrey Amherst's army advanced inexorably upon Montreal from the upper St. Lawrence, Natives in its path abandoned their villages despite assurances from League Iroquois that they would not be harmed if they made no resistance. At one point in the campaign Amherst's force of ten thousand men was held up for a week besieging Fort Levis, an island strongpoint blocking the river route to Montreal. After a spirited defense, the French defenders surrendered to the British on August 25.

The siege had ruined the fort, but it had also indirectly devastated the nearby Seven Nations town of Oswegatchie, where William Merry probably had spent his captivity. The French, anticipating Amherst's invasion route, had negotiated with the town's leaders only the previous year for permission to build Fort Levis. The fort would protect both French and Indians, it was argued, by preventing an enemy thrust from the west. Instead, it had the opposite effect. If Fort Levis had not been there to block the way, Amherst's army would likely have bypassed the Indian town with hardly a backward glance. As it was, with its proximity to the fort, its cleared land, and its abandoned buildings, Oswegatchie was an ideal base of operations and temporary hospital for the British siege. If this were not sufficiently disruptive, after the siege and Montreal's capitulation, British detachments remained, "cutting and destroying the houses for firewood," until by early October "most of . . . the Indian houses [were] destroyed." When the British, and some French squatters, turned Oswegatchie back over to those Indians who could be persuaded to return, the former residents found mostly devastation and had to begin rebuilding their community. In the meantime, the British had set about rebuilding Fort Levis to house a garrison, renaming it Fort William Augustus.[2]

Thus it was that in mid-March 1761 Lieutenant Hugh Meredith, of the 80th Foot (known as Gage's Light Infantry), was at Oswegatchie, presumably on some official business, when he met a group of Wabanaki men recently come to town. Just why the Wabanakis were there is unclear; their homeland was far downriver, below Montreal, but the last years of the war had necessitated relocations. Odanack, or St. Francis, a large Wabanaki town, had been attacked and all but destroyed by Rogers' Rangers' famous raid in the fall of 1759. There were Wabanakis living at Akwesasne, some fifty miles downriver from Oswegatchie, so perhaps these had lived at the latter place before the British occupation. But what especially attracted Meredith's attention was that the Wabanakis had with them an interpreter, a young white man dressed very much like those with whom he moved.

By itself this was not strange, especially not in Canada. Meredith would have known by then that French men frequently married Native women, or had lived with Indians for years in the course of conducting the fur trade, or, certainly, had gone to war alongside Natives since the establishment of the first French settlements. But this man defied Meredith's expectations. It must have been when the man spoke that the lieutenant realized he was not Canadian but a native English speaker, and a colonial at that. His curiosity thoroughly aroused, Meredith engaged the interpreter concerning his circumstances. The Kahnawake treaty, now half a year old, stipulated that English and provincial prisoners held by Seven Nations Indians were to be immediately released. The exception to this term regarded those captives who, after years of living in their new environments and having accepted adoption into new families, chose not to return. Some of these even presented themselves to British officials to certify their choice, presumably so that they would not be taken for unwilling captives or so that their white families could be notified. Meredith would have known that it was important to discover into which category this white interpreter fit. If he was being held against his will, perhaps he had deliberately been kept ignorant of the fact that he could now leave his Indian masters. If so, now was his chance to do so with British protection. On the other hand, if he was one of those who had become a "white Indian," perhaps Meredith could talk him out of it. In any case, he later recalled, Meredith concluded by endeavoring to persuade the interpreter "to Quitt the Indians, & come down to Montreal, where he might get Livley hood."[3]

The interpreter's response was equivocal, and suspicious. Whatever he told Meredith at that time, Meredith noticed that the man "soon after wanted to screen himself among the Indians" and was "seemingly affrighted." There was something else: Meredith had the feeling that he had seen the man before. Perhaps the mysterious interpreter had recognized him too; if so, his furtive behavior was doubly questionable. It could not have been long before Meredith heard from some of the men in his detachment who were much more sure of their man. As it happened, some of the men of the 80th Foot now with Meredith had been with Major Rogers on his St. Francis raid and had been captured on their nightmare return march and brought to the French fort at Isle aux Noix, on the Richelieu River. There, they swore, they had seen the interpreter "Guilty of several Crueltys against some of Major Rogers's Party on their Return from St. Francis." Perhaps the mention of Isle aux Noix jogged Meredith's memory: he had been a prisoner himself at that place earlier in the same year and now recalled that he had seen the interpreter there—a British subject at a French fort, apparently unconfined. Satisfied that something was seriously wrong about the English-speaking interpreter, and no doubt fearing that he would escape, Meredith had him arrested and brought first to Fort William Augustus and soon after to Montreal, 110 miles downriver.

Eventually—the records do not say at what point—the prisoner gave or acknowledged his name. He was Jonathan Barnes, twenty-three, of Boston, "blacksmith" according to his 1756 muster record but at nineteen years old in that year surely not an independent, master artisan. It came out later that his father may have lived in Malden, a town ten miles from the bustling seaport, but whether that was the son's place of birth is not clear. Barnes had been "killed or taken wth Hodges" nearly four and a half years earlier, according to the company's roster, and his whereabouts had not been reported by any of those who had returned from their captivity.[4] And now, instead of British victory being his salvation, Barnes was to face a trial for his life, before one of the most intimidating institutions of justice in the English-speaking world, a British army court-martial. He was accused of nothing less that "being a Traytor to his Country, & being in Arms against it."

"This country is at present under a military government"

Considering the charge, a court-martial proceeding would hardly have been unusual, but in fact a military court was the lot of anyone accused of a crime under the occupation. When the British acquired Canada, they also had to accept the responsibility, according to the understood laws of war, for keeping order there. Armies were expected to control their soldiers, and of course it was in the interest of no one but the lawless to permit disorder among the inhabitants in occupied zones. Conquerors usually employed existing police machinery, at least in part, indulging local judicial procedures and sensibilities in ordinary civil matters among the inhabitants. But in Canada, where many of the judicial posts had been held by metropolitan French appointees, "all Justice ceased upon the Conquest, for every Court of Civil or Criminal Judicature left the Country" along with the French army.[5] To fill the judicial vacuum, General Amherst established three military governments: at Quebec, Montreal, and Trois-Rivières midway between. General Thomas Gage became military governor of the Montreal district within two weeks of the surrender, and two weeks after that he announced that "as this country is at present under a military government, courts-martial are to take cognisance of all persons and crimes brought against them."[6] Until such time as a regular civil administration could be constituted in the former French colonies—and that would not happen for another four years—all criminal charges were to be heard before courts-martial, while civil cases were to be adjudicated in each parish by Canadian militia captains and could be appealed to British authorities. Gage's military government also took over some of the mundane but vital civil responsibilities of the town of Montreal itself, such as fire prevention, constabulary duties, and trash disposal.[7]

In part, of course, courts-martial were intended to regulate the behavior of soldiers, both in combat (cowardice, disobedience) and in camp (mutiny, striking a superior, theft). Normal military discipline demanded it, but in civilian zones there was the additional necessity of preventing soldiers, whether from contempt of the conquered or an excess of "high spiritedness," from abusing the citizenry. British army regulations and general orders in Montreal betray this concern for preventing unhelpful incidents. Until the troops could be assigned quarters in or around the town (the winter would soon be upon them), they were forbidden from going into the town unless on specific duties, and they were additionally ordered "not to go into the suburbs." Only days after the surrender of Montreal, officers and soldiers alike were commanded to return all wagons, carts, and horses to the inhabitants to whom they belonged—indicating that these had been "detained" against the owners' will—and that "for the future no waggons, carts or horses [were] to be taken on any account from the inhabitants without application made to Col. Robertson."[8] The privations of the following winter drove up prices for commodities generally, with the result that some of the soldiers took to bullying shopkeepers. Inhabitants complained that redcoats "have taken provisions at the market" at whatever price the soldiers felt like paying. When the merchants protested, the soldiers brushed them off with the claim that General Gage himself had approved the practice—a bold-faced lie that could only make Gage seem the culprit. He responded by promising that "whoever is detected in such practices will undoubtedly be severely punished."[9]

The troops could hardly spend a Canadian winter in tents, however, and before long British soldiers were quartered in the inhabitants' homes in much the same way that French troops had been before the conquest. The much larger number of occupying troops, however, meant that many more of the Canadian householders were affected, and more intensely: in the protests that soon came before British administrators, some inhabitants complained that they were being forced to quarter as many as six soldiers.[10] The redcoats were issued army provisions but were expected to "mess with their landlords." Thus the food-strapped inhabitants were spared having to feed their charges, but they were still required to provide them firewood.[11] Such persistent, close contact, under circumstances that were, to say the least, awkward if not hostile, could be a recipe for trouble. Adding to the difficulty was the religious divide between the conquering and the conquered, which had the potential to become a serious issue if not dealt with promptly. For years the Protestants who made up virtually the entire conquering army, British and Americans, had been indulged and even encouraged in their antipapist vitriol directed at the Catholic French and Indians of Canada. All that had now to cease; soldiers were told that "the [Catholic] clergy are [to be] treated with proper respect and not insulted" and that "no soldiers [are] to go into the churches or other places of worship without pulling off their hatts, and they must behave with the greatest decency."[12]

But British soldiers were not the only ones inclined to, or capable of, causing trouble. Even without the abuses tacitly confessed in British order books, the *habitants* of Canada were unlikely to accept their defeated status with the best grace. They too had learned to hate and fear the Protestant British and their American colonists, moving the exasperated military governor of Quebec to observe that "His Majesty's new Subjects [are] already prejudiced against us by every popish Art."[13] Some of the inhabitants of Montreal immediately took to dumping their "dirt"—household refuse, animal and human manure—around the British sentry posts by the city gates. When they were ordered to "carry it out of town" as they had done under French rule, they took to disposing of their waste on and about the ramparts by night.[14] Others engaged in more serious subversion, encouraging soldiers to desert, "fencing" stolen British supplies, extorting other inhabitants while pretending to be working for the British, and publicly insulting British officers.[15] For these and more serious offences, courts-martial applied to the inhabitants as well.

Jonathan Barnes was lodged in the same Montreal prison where some of his fellow survivors had stayed, but he soon discovered that those facing charges before a court-martial did not need to fear the law's delay. Contemporary practice stipulated that "no confinement shall continue more than eight days, or till such time a court martial can be conveniently assembled."[16] Barnes' court-martial began on April 2, the extra week and a half since his arrest undoubtedly reflecting the time taken to get him to Montreal. Still, if his arrest occurred "about the middle of March," then his trial took place with what modern defendants would consider amazing—and alarming—dispatch. Procedures were prescribed, rigid, and without the labyrinth of motions, stays, and other protections granted in civilian criminal courts. There was a court president, always the highest-ranking officer on the court, and several junior officers. The proper number was thirteen; there could be fewer under extraordinary circumstances, but always an odd number—there would be no "hung" courts-martial. A judge advocate, usually a captain or even a lieutenant, prosecuted the case for the court. The operation of the court-martial was straightforward: the prisoner heard the charges against him, then made his plea, and the trial began immediately. The judge advocate presented his witnesses ("evidences," as they were called), who duly gave their testimonies, and then it was the defendant's turn to present evidence or witnesses in his favor. Once all testimony had been heard and arguments made, the members of the court proceeded to deliberation, reached a verdict, and either exonerated or condemned the prisoner. Punishment, if applicable, also was rarely delayed, usually meted out in a matter of a few days.

The court-martial was designed to provide a reasonable approximation of the British civil legal system in areas where the latter could not easily apply, but in a simplified, efficient form suited to nonspecialists at law. Most especially, there were generally no lawyers to muddy the waters and no juries to frustrate the sword of justice. A defendant could call his own witnesses and directly question those of the prosecution, but only rarely was he granted legal counsel; his defense depended on his own abilities and the strength of the evidence he could produce in that very short interval between arrest and arraignment. He was given no list of the witnesses against him and could not know what they would say until he met them in the court. Only the most clever, quick-thinking defendants would be able to formulate, on the fly, pertinent questions for a witness or refutations of his testimony. The court-martial was contrived to produce results, and quickly, for an institution whose primary function was not the perfection of justice or the protection of individual rights. Its makeup, its rules of play, and its seeming haste all favored the prosecution.

This does not mean that courts-martial were kangaroo courts, however, nor does it mean that justice was not dispensed more or less correctly. During the four years of occupation before the terms of the Treaty of Paris took effect, about one-third of all trials involving *habitants* brought before courts-martial ended in acquittal of the defendants, while the sentences of many condemned soldiers were reduced or commuted, if for no other reason than to preserve garrison strength. In one instance the previous December, two deserters condemned to be hanged on the town ramparts had been pardoned after being given time to contemplate the consequences of their actions. Not all were so lucky, of course; in March 1761 two soldiers of the 44th Foot were sentenced to hang for robbery. One was pardoned the day before the execution, but the other ended his life at the end of a rope. The court could also split the difference. Only the day before Barnes' trial, and before the same court, three soldiers of the 80th Foot were tried for desertion to the enemy sometime before the war's end half a year earlier. One was acquitted, a second condemned to death but pardoned the next day, and only the third went to the gallows. In accordance with military law, all three could have been executed, but the court again exhibited mercy and incidentally reclaimed two soldiers for their regiment.[17]

First Day of Trial

Nevertheless, when Barnes' trial began on April 2, it would have been difficult for him not to be apprehensive about his prospects. The rigid formality of the proceedings would have been unlike anything he had ever experienced. Even being in the presence, let alone in the power, of splendidly uniformed British officers must have been bewildering. He had seen few enough of these while stationed at Fort William Henry, and of course he had seen no others in the meantime, unless as helpless or half-stripped prisoners in Canada. The court observed the proper forms: Barnes was brought into the court without handcuffs or fetters "or any marks of ignominy or reproach." The reason for this was simply to maintain, at least symbolically, the presumption of innocence until proven guilty, and so that the defendant would be "under no [more] terror or uneasiness than what proceeds from a sense of his guilt, and the misfortune of his present circumstances." The only exception to this practice occurred when there was "some danger of an escape or rescue," which was unlikely in Barnes' case.[18]

As Barnes stood before the court, he would have had a few moments to take in his surroundings and to fight whatever terror or uneasiness he felt.[19] Certainly he would not have known the British officers before him. Seated at a table was the court president, Lieutenant Colonel Thomas Ord, wearing the dark blue coat and red facings of the Royal Regiment of Artillery (then a semiautonomous branch of the service). Ord had seen his share of hard campaigning. He had begun his military career in 1741 as a lieutenant, winning a captaincy five years later by distinguishing himself at the Battle of Fontenoy. His had been the first company of the Royal Artillery in America for the current war, and it had been nearly annihilated with Braddock's command on the Monongahela in 1755. His efforts at successfully rebuilding his company had caught the eye of General Amherst, who had promoted him to major for the 1759 campaign and to his present rank a year later. In another year he would be commanding the artillery at the capture of Martinique—a far cry from the frigid post where he now served.[20]

The names of other officer-judges of the court were not recorded, but at his own, smaller table sat Judge Advocate Thomas Falconer, who also kept the record of the court's proceedings. Falconer, in scarlet coat and yellow facings, was a captain in the 44th Foot. He was probably happy to have this detached duty just now, as his regiment was distinguishing itself during the occupation for unruly behavior and outrages against the civilian population. Posted at The Cedars, a settlement on the river near Kahnawake, some of the men of the 44th had been amusing themselves that winter at the expense of the Indians of that town, robbing, beating, and generally abusing them. Two soldiers, mentioned above, were convicted by a court-martial of robbery, and another, a grenadier, was actually executed for the same crime. Nor were the outrages confined to the rank and file. A lieutenant of the regiment assaulted several Kahnawakes with a stick, beating them severely in a fit of rage. When the Indians complained, the major of the regiment refused to do anything about the matter. Another lieutenant made the mistake of "calling out" his commanding officer—challenging him to a duel—and getting himself cashiered for his trouble.[21]

The trial began at nine o'clock in the morning with the reading of the charges. In a civil trial the accused stood and raised his right hand as the charges were read, but in a court-martial this "ceremony" was generally dispensed with.[22] With that, the prisoner then entered his plea. A number of options were available to Barnes, though it is unlikely he knew of them. If he had, he might have saved both the court and himself a good deal of trouble. As was the case with most any trial, the prisoner could confess his crime, plead not guilty, or say nothing at all, refusing to plead one way or the other. Confession, of course, would end the trial right there, and the court could proceed to sentencing. But apart from the obvious dangers of that option for a defendant, courts-martial were not encouraged to accept direct confession. If they suspected the defendant of confessing simply out of terror, or "menace, or duresse," or indeed if they thought physical or mental "weakness" or confusion affected his judgment, they could reject the guilty plea and enter one of not guilty instead. Standing mute was a ploy that had been used in some spectacular cases in England and North America, but it would not get a defendant at court-martial very far. According to law, a trial could not proceed until the defendant had made a plea. The court had ways, however, to prevent an accused from bringing a trial to a halt in this manner. Prisoners refusing to plead could be subjected to *peine fort et dure*—torturous confinement, or deprivation of food and water—if they stayed silent. Though this expedient was rarely used, the court had the power to deploy it to compel a plea. But in the end it was not necessary; courts-martial generally proceeded anyway, treating the silence the same as a not-guilty plea. Lastly, silence was simply not smart: unless the prisoner was incapable of speech, the court considered standing mute as "malice," disrespect to the court.[23]

A "plea to the jurisdiction" was an alternative that had more potential and arguably could have succeeded. For this to work, Barnes could plead that the court-martial was the improper venue for his case, that it in fact had no jurisdiction in the matter. True, Barnes had been arrested in the Montreal military district, but the crimes with which he was charged (as will appear) had occurred long before that jurisdiction existed, and in disputed territory.[24] Then there was the matter of Barnes' status when the alleged crimes took place. If he had been a soldier with the regular army, he would legally have continued to be so until death or discharge; any crimes attributed to him during his captivity would thus naturally have exposed him to trial by court-martial. But Barnes had been a provincial soldier. His 1756 enlistment was for that year's campaign only, after which time he would have reverted to civilian status. Certainly his pay ceased after September 19 in that year, so the commonwealth of Massachusetts tacitly agreed. The alleged facts charged against him had occurred three years after he could be considered a soldier in His Majesty's service. Both the Mutiny Act, which authorized British military law, and the Articles of War, directing military conduct, "expressly [directed], that any officer, non-commissioned officer, or soldier, who shall be accused of any capital crime, violence, or offence against the person, estate, or property of any of [His Majesty's] subjects, *which is pun-*

ishable by the laws of the land, shall be delivered over to the civil magistrate."[25] Not only were the physical boundaries of the military governments hazy but there was at least the possibility for some jurisdictional overlap as well. If the court trying Barnes had had any doubts concerning their jurisdiction, or if some legal counsel had been present to insist, they could have referred the case to New York, sent Barnes to Albany for trial, and washed their hands of the whole affair. Barnes' trial would have gone on, only now in a civil court, where there would have been more time to mount a defense, gather witnesses, perhaps have legal counsel (though this was unlikely), and be tried before a jury of nonuniformed Americans.

With the charges read and the not-guilty plea made, the prosecution could begin. The first of the witnesses (called "deponents" in the record) against Barnes was the man who had arrested him. Hugh Meredith had been commissioned a lieutenant in the 80th Foot in July 1758, shortly after the disastrous attack on Fort Carillon. His uniform brought an uncharacteristic drabness to the setting. The 80th had been the brainchild of General Gage himself, intended to be the Regular Army's answer (and rival) to Robert Rogers' famed Ranger corps, a light-infantry unit trained for woods fighting and irregular warfare. They wore unadorned brown coats, Indian-style leggings, and cut-down, "jockey"-like caps. Meredith, after being sworn in, was invited to relate the circumstances of the defendant's detention. He told how he had come to be at Oswegatchie and found Barnes among the Wabanakis and stated the reasons for his suspicions. He told the court how he, Meredith, had become a prisoner of the Indians in 1759 and recalled in more detail now his encounter with Barnes at Isle aux Noix. Meredith said that Barnes had told him "he was a British subject, which was this Deponent's reason for Confining the Prisoner."

The court—someone on the court—asked the lieutenant to elaborate, asking "what Conversation passed between them" at the island. Getting the exact words was important; judges were supposed to get witnesses to "relate the very fact that the prisoner did, or the very words he made use of." Paraphrasing would not do, for it was "no Evidence in any criminal case, that the defendant did so and so, or said so and so, or words to the like effect, because the court must know the very act or words, to judge of their force and effect."[26] Meredith clarified, answering that "the Prisoner said he was an English man." It was a point worth making: if the man before them had admitted in October 1759 to being "English" and "a British subject," then arguably he could not be one of those "white Indians" who had renounced their former identity and taken up the Wabanakis' way of life. In other words, if Barnes had said those words, then he considered himself "English," not Wabanaki.

There was more. Meredith testified that Barnes had told him at that time "that he was sorry St. Francis was destroyed, as they were always good to the English." It was the sort of statement calculated to make a British prisoner bristle and a New Englander gasp. For two generations the people of St. Francis had been white New Englanders' worst nightmare, blamed for countless raids on the northern English frontier and for the slaughter and capture of hundreds of settlers. To them, the destruction of St. Francis and its people at the hands of Rogers' Rangers (however costly that raid had been) had simply been long-delayed justice, the hand of God at last striking down the bloodthirsty heathen. Barnes' alleged remark had thus been a cruel taunt. Lastly, Meredith added that Barnes had seemed to be associating freely with the Wabanakis at Isle aux Noix, which Meredith thought suspicious, "as he had been informed [by whom?] that no English were Allowed" on the island "but such as go with the Indians against the English." If Barnes had had a lawyer at his side, Meredith's insinuating, hearsay statement would have drawn a swift objection. The prisoner, however, had no questions for the witness, and Meredith was dismissed.

Meredith's testimony was only the beginning of the judge advocate's attempt to create a meaningful narrative of events. His testimony introduced Barnes as a self-identified British subject in close association with Britain's enemies during the war, and not, apparently, in the role of a prisoner. At Oswegatchie he had acted like a guilty man, "affrightened" and trying to make himself scarce, and when Meredith was a prisoner Barnes had allegedly said something galling and hateful. But significantly, Meredith had not seen Barnes with a gun or any other weapon in his hands, nor had he seen the prisoner actually *do* anything criminal.

That was left for the next two witnesses. The first, Sergeant Robert Lewis, also of the 80th Foot, was a tough man—tough and lucky. He must have been, for during the war he had survived not only seven weeks of the most harrowing march ever made but capture by vengeful Indians as well.

Everyone in the room knew the story. In mid-September 1759, as Quebec fell to General Wolfe's army, Major Rogers and nearly 200 men had set out from Crown Point, on Lake Champlain, on their epic but Pyrrhic mission to destroy the Wabanaki town of St. Francis. To augment his corps of Rangers, Rogers took volunteers from the 80th and the 60th (Royal American) Regiment. Discovering the raiders' trail and guessing their target, French and Indian forces set out in pursuit. Detachments of sick and wounded raiders had to be sent back, but on October 4 the remaining 142 men of Rogers' party succeeded in surprising and destroying the village. With no time to rest or gather sufficient supplies, the raiders then faced a march of two hundred miles through trackless wilderness to the Connecticut River in order to escape their enraged pursuers. Uncommonly wet and cold conditions from the start of the operation, the lack of provisions, and the rugged geography through which they had to pass reduced the party to walking scarecrows. Facing starvation, Rogers yielded to the necessity of breaking his force into smaller bands of ten or twenty men in the hope that they would be able to forage and hunt for food with better success. Such a move meant that their pursuers would be unable to follow them all, but it ran the risk of slower or less fortunate bands being overwhelmed by their enemies. So it proved: Rogers and most of his men made it to the northernmost English settlement on the Connecticut River, but 19 were overtaken and killed or later tortured to death. Another 30 or so died of starvation and exposure. Only a few of those captured were spared.[27]

Lewis was one of the survivors, and it was at this point, as he related, that Jonathan Barnes entered the story. Lewis was part of a band headed by a Lieutenant Jenkins, which had made its way back toward the lake but was still far from British-held Crown Point. Jenkins succumbed to hunger and the elements; the rest of his band split into even smaller units of about three men apiece, in hopes of finding food. Lewis and two others were discovered and captured by Indians from the Mississquoi Bay area. They were being led toward the French fort at Isle aux Noix when they encountered another Indian band that included Barnes. Lewis noted "that the Prisoner was in Arms" at the time. Three more of the famished raiders were caught shortly thereafter, and all were taken to the fort for interrogation. The Indians ordered Barnes to tie the Rangers, which Lewis thought he did entirely too thoroughly, and in spite of another English prisoner (whom Lewis did not know) begging Barnes to go easy on them. The next day, after what must have been another bad night for the English, stripped as they were to their shirts and leggings, Barnes appeared and demanded the silver sleeve buttons from Lewis' shirt. Lewis was in no condition to resist this robbery, and the next day Barnes came again for Lewis' leggings. This time he was driven off by a French officer, but before he left he told Lewis "to be ready the next day, to Guide the Indians to go in Search of the Remainder of the Party the Sergt. had been in, for that his Father the Indian Captain, desired it." Lewis said he "feigned sickness" to avoid that treasonable duty—given his condition, probably not much acting was required.

Lewis' account placed Barnes in the company of armed enemy Indians, cooperating in the capture and abuse of British soldiers, and calling the Indian war captain his "Father." The next witness, Private James Brown, also of the 80th, confirmed and added damning detail to Lewis' testimony. Brown and two others had waited for Lewis' return with, they hoped, some food, so when they heard someone calling for them the next evening, they assumed it was their sergeant. Instead, it was Barnes and one other white man, who assured them that Lewis' party was "safe enough" but stated that Barnes and his companion "belonged to the Indians" and that it was "in vain for them to make any resistance, as there were 100 Indians round them." The weakened raiders were in no condition to either resist or run. Barnes demanded the men's packs, weapons, and most of their ragged clothing and only then "gave a Hollow" for the nearby Indians to come up. Brought back to the same fort where Sergeant Lewis was held, Brown saw Barnes go out the next day with another party of Indians in search of one more group, led by a sergeant named Delano. They found them soon enough and brought back these last three men to the island, but this time to a very different fate. Delano or one of his men had some meat in his pack—human meat.

When Rogers' raiders had made their return march from St. Francis, they took with them several white captives of the Wabanakis, as well a few Native children. Two of these, "an English Girl, who had been taken some time before by the Indians," and a Native boy, had been with Delano's party. At some point after the band had subdivided, Delano and two others, driven by maddening hunger, killed the boy, butchered his body for the meat, and ate it—but not all of it. Now the uneaten meat, identified by the English girl as originally belonging to the boy, was their death warrant. French officers at the fort might have foiled the Indians' vengeance, so the Indians made sure these prisoners did not reach the fort. One was slowly executed "in the most barbarous manner" and then scalped; the other two, who presumably were made to watch, were then also killed and scalped.

What made these particularly gruesome details relevant to the court-martial was the question of Barnes' participation in them. Private Brown did not witness the execution of Delano and his men, but he remembered very clearly that Barnes had returned to the fort with a dripping scalp in hand and had begun behaving like a madman. Brown said that Barnes had taken a stick and begun beating an English prisoner who had been forced to help find Delano's party, shouting that "it was his fault." When a Native woman had intervened, Barnes had turned on Brown, behaving "very insolently & Cruelly to him," telling him that the Indians had let him off too easily; that he would later scalp Brown too; that "he would get him sent to the French Guard, where he would Beat him, two or three times a day, as he could do no more to him there." As reprehensible as all this was, it was not what Barnes was on trial for, and neither Brown nor Lewis had seen Barnes torture or kill anyone. Yes, he allegedly had a scalp in hand, but did that prove he had taken it? Again someone on the court interrupted with a more pertinent question: had Brown seen Barnes armed? Yes, Brown answered emphatically, "the Prisoner was in Arms with the Enemy," but he had to admit that he had not seen Barnes actually *use* those arms. However, he added, in the evening he had seen him dressing the scalp he had carried earlier.

The last prosecution witness for the day was Samuel "Hinckey," "a Person from Boston." Actually it was Samuel Henche, whom we last saw at Fort William Henry in September 1756.[28] If the prisoner was not forthcoming about his identity when arrested, Henche had probably been the one to identify him as "Jonathan Barnes or Burns," the young man who had followed Timothy Ruggles' regiment to Lake George nearly five years earlier. As it happened, Henche had been a corporal in that regiment. The court in Montreal could not have had ready access to Massachusetts muster rolls for 1756, so Henche's evidence was critical, and his memory was good. He assured the court that he "knew the Prisoner," and he correctly placed him in Captain Larner's company. Henche recalled other details from that day, including watching Hodges' command, with Barnes, "March off the Parade" that fateful Sunday morning. He had not seen or heard of Barnes again until he identified him at the Provost's Guard in Montreal.

Finally, "The Prisoner being put upon his Defense," it was Barnes' turn to write the narrative, if he could.[29] He began by acknowledging that he was indeed the Jonathan Barnes captured on that day in September 1756 and that his own survival was perhaps a matter of an inch. In the fighting, the nineteen-year-old blacksmith was wounded twice, "in One of his Leggs & a finger"—perhaps he held up his hand to show the court. The leg wound meant that he was not going to be one of the lucky few who escaped the massacre, but a slight deviation in the bullet's path could also have been the death of him—not from blood loss or sepsis, though these were of course possible. Indians tended to kill wounded captives who could not travel, or could not travel quickly enough. Barnes must have been interrogated at Ticonderoga as the others were, but he did not mention it. Instead, he recalled being brought first to Kahnawake, then to "Canasadaga." This last was a mission village at the west end of the island of Montreal for Iroquois and Algonquians. It is likely that it was there that he was given or traded to some Wabanakis.

He had tried to escape, he said—twice. He had connived with some other English prisoners to run away, but on both occasions someone, probably motivated by fear of failure and its consequences, informed the Indians of the plans, and Barnes was threatened with death if he tried to leave. He did not deny being armed but said "that he, at no time, Carried Arms against his King & Country." Rather, he was occasionally given a gun with which to hunt game.

The actions he had taken to locate, help capture, and bind the unfortunate remnants of Sergeant Delano's party were all done at the order of his Indian masters, Barnes insisted. He had not even been involved in the capture of Sergeant Lewis' party (as Lewis himself had admitted); when he had encountered them, they were already being led back to Isle aux Noix in the custody of two Indians and another white captive, one Christopher Proudfoot. Subsequently compelled to go after the others—in the capacity of an interpreter—Barnes had persuaded the Indians with him not to open fire on Private Brown's helpless contingent. He explained that he had been sent to take part in the capture of the third (Delano's) group but that he had not been present, having stopped along the way to make a fire, "and went no further with them." The packs and other belongings he took from the captives were not for him; all loot had to be given to his masters. He did not remember taking Sergeant Lewis' buttons but did recall being sent to get his leggings, which order "he durst not refuse, as the Indians were then in Liquor."

As for the torture and execution of Delano and the two others, he had had no hand in them. When he had returned to the island where he had sat out the last search, it was to find the three men already dead and scalped; he denied having anything to do with dressing the scalp. But the Indians had seemed not to be done; they told him they were going to kill the others too and commanded Barnes to tell them so to terrify them. When Barnes had pleaded for the Englishmen, his masters had made him beat them with the stick. The abuse, the threats—all of it was by coercion.

Barnes' defense started as a straightforward narrative of the circumstances of his captivity and by itself might have been compelling stuff. He had been a captive for nearly five years, longer than any of the other survivors of Hodges' Scout, and in the hands of some of the most dreaded enemies of the English. Surely he could have been expected to adopt some of the survival strategies made use of by other captives, especially after two failed escape attempts. It was difficult to condemn a man for complying with his captors when death or worse was the alternative. Other former captives had told stories of hardship, incessant humiliation, torture, hard labor, attempted escapes, and hopelessness, some of which were already in print for the morbidly curious. Barnes' account of his own captivity would likely have had many of the same features, but the court either did not hear them or chose not to record them. Perhaps they even cut him off, urging him to speak to the charges against him, for his recorded testimony quickly changes from chronological narrative to an almost stream-of-consciousness series of denials.

The Vital Question

Was Barnes in fact a renegade, an English colonist who had chosen to join his enemies?[30] The testimonies at the court-martial, along with some circumstantial evidence, are all that we have, and all that the court had, to help determine this. It is possible from the record to imagine several scenarios to explain the actions of Jonathan Barnes in the last months of the war, each of them plausible. First is the possibility that Barnes was being truthful about the circumstances of his presence and behavior at Isle aux Noix. If, like other captives, he was little more than a slave to the Wabanakis, he would have had to go where they went, do what they wanted, even carry arms if they so ordered.[31] That he spoke English would have made him the obvious choice for locating and questioning English prisoners and for conveying to them the taunts and threats of their Indian captors. His being sent to steal from the prisoners, even to physically abuse them, was what one might expect of his Wabanaki masters, not only to plague the captives but to heap further anguish on Barnes. Forcing him to act against his own kind would have reinforced the Indians' power and authority over him and reminded him, if reminding were needed, of his own abject subjugation.[32] He would have tied the prisoners tightly because he dared not do otherwise, beat them and abused them because he dared not do otherwise; in short, he would have been a frightened and obedient slave, which, after all, was the object of his kind of captivity. The half-crazed behavior Private Brown witnessed, the odd-sounding "It is your fault!" as he beat a prisoner, makes sense if it was the cathartic cry of a despondent, thoroughly broken young man finally able to vent his misery on someone even more wretched and despised than he.[33]

A second possibility is that Barnes was everything that the charges said he was, "a Traytor to his Country." Unlike some of the more lurid and sensational (and suspect) of the captivity narratives that made such compelling reading, a few captives' narratives, as we have seen, described gentle treatment at the hands of Indians and more benign methods of persuasion directed at adopting the subject into a Native family or band. Some English were won over by the lifestyle and relative freedom of Indians and accepted their adoption, increasingly identifying with their adopted people at the expense of their former personas. The younger the subject, the better the process worked, and Barnes was an impressionable nineteen-year-old when captured, unmarried, and so with presumably less to look forward to if he returned to Boston. The fact that his captors had entrusted him with a gun and had employed him to help capture Englishmen suggests a level of trust beyond that given other captives, adopted but not given the means to turn on their captors. Lewis reported that Barnes had let slip the honorific "Father" in reference to his Indian captain, a further sign, perhaps, that he had been adopted by the Wabanakis and that he acknowledged this. His treatment of English prisoners was little better than the Indians' treatment of their enemies described by countless survivors.

It is also possible that Barnes was a victim of what is known today as Stockholm Syndrome. The term was coined in the 1970s to describe the curious reactions of bank-holdup hostages to an extended period of captivity. Some hostages formed a seemingly irrational concern for and identification with the criminals who had placed them in danger and repeatedly threatened them with death. Since then the concept's explanatory powers have earned it a fixed place in modern prisoner psychology.[34] It also might explain the words and behavior Barnes' accusers reported. Psychologists and law-enforcement agencies generally agree on four specific conditions that must exist for Stockholm Syndrome to develop. All of them clearly relate to the situations of Indian captives, whether targeted for adoption or for protracted bondage. First, the victim feels a degree of gratitude to the captor simply for not being killed. In effect, the captor, who has complete control over the victim, "gives life" to the prisoner by not taking it. This is especially effective if the victim has witnessed others being killed by his or her captors. Even before the European settlement in North America began in earnest, the Native peoples had a reputation, deserved or not, for fiendish cruelty. As early as 1619, one future colonist later recalled, some of his fellows had recoiled in fear of a place

> devoid of all civil inhabitants, where there are only savage and brutish men which range up and down, little otherwise than the beasts of the same. . . . savage people, who are cruel, barbarous, and most treacherous, being most furious in their rage and merciless where they overcome; not being content only to kill and take away life, but delight to torment men in the most bloody manner that may be; flaying some alive with the shells of fishes, cutting off the members and joints of others by piecemeal and broiling on the coals, eat the collops of their flesh in their sight whilst they live, with other cruelties horrible to be related.

In the century and a half after that time there was scarcely an improvement in the expectations of those imagining capture by Indians. Considering the undeniable evidence of torturous executions in some cases, their fears were fully justified, even if death was in fact no longer the most common fate of prisoners. In a number of printed captivity narratives, the authors recall terrifying moments at the time of capture and the seemingly random slaughter of companions, neighbors, or family. In each of these narratives there is a point at which the author realizes that he or she will be spared, at least for the time being, and the sense of relief, even gratitude (though usually this is directed to God), is palpable if not explicit.[35]

Second, while the victim is spared, the captor threatens him or her with death, and the victim believes the captor fully capable. Faced with this threat, the victim "judges it safer to align with the perpetrator, endure the hardship of captivity, and comply with the captor than to resist." Such, at least initially, was the option followed by all the other survivors of Hodges' command. The third condition is the prolonged isolation of the victim from persons outside the captor's group. This includes purposely being kept ignorant of events in the outside world and being deprived of contact with family, friends, or former associates. In this situation, the captive is kept dependent on the captor for information and thus has access only to the captor's perspective. Certainly this was the case for most European captives in eighteenth-century America, who were either discouraged or forbidden from communicating with other prisoners, especially new ones.

Lastly, and crucially, the victim receives some tokens of kindness, real or imagined, from the captor. The "kindness" may be nothing more than an absence of abuse but often includes tangible privileges, such as food, more comfortable conditions, or a loosening of restraints. Whatever the captor's motives may be—humanity, practicality, or the victim's further dependence on him or her—the extension of some form of favor is central to the phenomenon of Stockholm Syndrome. If the victim is treated with nothing but cruelty, the captive can only respond with hatred and fear. But if victims experience what they perceive as compassion from their captors, they will "submerge the anger they feel in response to the terror and concentrate on the captors' 'good side' to protect themselves." Captives of Indians who wrote of their experiences seldom failed to mention acts of kindness extended them, either by their immediate captors or by some other members of the "other side."[36] As we have seen, even the offer of years of servitude under Canadian masters or mistresses was regarded by English captives as an unalloyed blessing compared with Indian bondage.

The effects of these conditions on some English captives, as with modern-day victims of Stockholm Syndrome, was to produce in them "positive feelings for their captors," in some extreme cases actual identification with them.[37] Psychologists note that hostages and kidnap victims subjected to the above conditions will display fear, suspicion, and anger toward once-trusted authorities similar to their captors'. Famous American renegades such as Simon Girty, who fought with British-allied Indians during the Revolution, and William Wells, who joined his Miami captors in fighting against the United States in the 1790s, endured conditions very similar to those regarded by modern experts as producing the paradoxical behavior of Stockholm Syndrome.

Barnes' conduct seems best explained in light of now broadly accepted theories of hostage or prisoner psychology. Of all the survivors of Hodges' Scout, Barnes had experienced the longest and most intense isolation. If his captivity, particularly in its initial phases, had been at all typical, he must have experienced at least the same fear, disorientation, and physical duress reported by others. His frustrated escape attempts, assuming that he had even possessed the courage to try, would have taught him the relative security of staying put, waiting on events, and trying to make the best of a very bad situation. Once his captors were reasonably confident that he was adjusting himself to his situation, they may well have begun to show "kindness" in the form of better treatment, limited movement, and, tentatively, the use of a firearm. It was not necessary for him to be "won over" by his captors in order for him to move more freely in their circles; in fact, those called "renegades" only "rarely, if ever, completed the transfer of allegiance from one society to another," even if they were not systematically abused as was Barnes. His master (or masters, if he, like Henry Grace, was "owned" by several masters) retained ownership and control over their captive until they chose to sell him (Grace's masters did not agree to do so for years)—or kill him.[38] Such "freedom" as Barnes may have had was relative. Lacking any other company or any other perspective than those of his captors, Barnes over the course of years may have struggled mentally to survive by depending upon, and identifying with, his captors: "Confusion, not conversion, typified the renegade experience."[39] Thus his lament concerning the destruction of St. Francis, which before Rogers' raid had probably been his home; thus his reference to his Indian "Father"; thus his outbursts of anger toward his (former) countrymen—countrymen who had, from his perspective, forgotten him and done nothing to rescue him from his ordeal. And thus the contrariness evident in some of his actions, as when he beat one prisoner with a stick and cursed him with that cryptic "It is your fault!"

The Second Day

At any rate, Barnes had finished his defense, such as it was. According to customary practice in these proceedings, once the defendant had presented his case and his evidences, "here the altercation should cease." But as a contemporary observed a few years later, "Of late the Judge Advocate has been permitted to Reply to the Prisoners' Defense & bring other evidences," both to challenge the defense and to "strengthen the testimony of [the prosecution's] former witnesses."[40] Something, or rather someone, introduced in Barnes' own statement gave Judge Advocate Falconer an opportunity to do just that. Barnes had brought up Christopher Proudfoot, another white captive. Barnes claimed that Proudfoot had also taken part in the capture of Delano's detachment and that he, Barnes, had done no more than Proudfoot had done, both of them forced by the Indians. The court had heard evidence against Barnes that was surely damaging, but in many ways it was far from satisfactory. He had been seen in arms, but no one had seen him actually use them against British subjects. He had been seen carrying a scalp, but no one had seen him actually take it (and strictly speaking, carrying a scalp was not a crime). He had assaulted and verbally abused helpless prisoners, which was reprehensible, to be sure, but none had been killed or reported any serious injuries. The judge advocate may not have regarded Barnes' evidence to be as incontrovertible as he could have wished, or perhaps he even entertained doubts as to Barnes' guilt. But if this man Proudfoot were alive and could be found, he would be in a position to support or deny Barnes' claims of coercion and his contention that he had interposed to spare Private Brown's party from being fired upon. Proudfoot was not a common name; perhaps Captain Falconer or someone else in the court thought it familiar. Whatever the case, the judge advocate asked for, and was granted, an adjournment of the court until the next day "for want of further Evidences." Barnes may have been informed at this time that he retained the right to a rejoinder—the right to question new witnesses and make another statement—but this was considered "rather a matter of special favour than of right," and so far no one seemed to be doing Barnes any favors.[41]

Barnes' anguish at this turn of events might well be imagined. If he knew anything about trial sessions, he would most likely have expected this court-martial to follow the forms of civil courts, in which the prosecution generally did not present new witnesses after the defense had rested. So far, Barnes had not questioned any of the judge advocate's evidences, whether from sheer inability or from confusion over his role in the proceedings. And now, having just delivered as best he could the most important argument of his life and hoping it would be enough, he would realize that it might all have been for naught. For courts-martial differed from civilian criminal trials most especially in this regard: while their supporters claimed that courts-martial were "inclined to grant every reasonable indulgence to a prisoner,"[42] each court could decide what was reasonable. The inexperience of the judges, the denial of defense counsel, the lack of juries, and the procedures of the court all decidedly favored conviction. To a large degree, conviction—and example—was the whole point.

The next day, "the Evidence required, not being come to Town," the court adjourned for another day. Was the anticlimax an agony or a relief for the prisoner? On Saturday the fourth the trial recommenced, and Captain Falconer produced not one but two additional witnesses against Barnes. The first, whom Barnes had last seen as a bearded, ragged prisoner in November 1759, now strode into the room a very different-looking man. Christopher Proudfoot, clean and clean-shaven, hair cropped short and combed, wore the red regimentals and blue facings of the Fourth Battalion of the 60th Foot, the Royal American Regiment. The 60th was a new regiment, raised at the beginning of the war largely from men recruited in the colonies. Whereas most regiments were made up of one or perhaps two battalions, the Royal Americans had four by the middle of the conflict, and they served in virtually all the theaters of the war. The Fourth Battalion had been present at the capitulation, and as luck would have it—bad luck for Barnes—had remained in the Montreal area for the occupation. Thus, Proudfoot was conveniently nearby and had been summoned to town for the second round of evidences against the defendant. Proudfoot did not disappoint; he had reason to remember the defendant well. He had much to say, and his testimony corroborated that of the former witnesses, indeed adding fresh, damning detail.

Proudfoot had also volunteered for duty with Rogers' Rangers, and early in March 1759 he had participated in a raid on a woodcutting party near Fort Carillon that bagged some French prisoners. Pursued by Canadian irregulars and Indians, the raiders had conducted a fighting retreat, inflicting casualties and making off with their prisoners. Rogers later reported three killed and one wounded on his side.[43] Actually, two had been killed; Proudfoot was twice wounded in the skirmishing and left behind for dead. Captured and spared for questioning, he was taken to Fort St. Jean, on the Richelieu River north of Isle aux Noix. It was at St. Jean that he first encountered Barnes. Someone told him that Barnes "was an Englishman," so he turned to what he assumed was a fellow prisoner for help with his wound. Barnes in reply cursed him, saying "The Devil be your Doctor." Proudfoot was taken by his Indian captors to Mississquoi Bay, at the northeast end of Lake Champlain, no doubt enduring the usual hardships of a despised enemy captive. That July or August, he said, he saw Barnes again, this time "Armed

& Equipped for War in the Indian manner." Barnes on that occasion was accompanying a war party headed against Amherst's army, which was then descending on Forts Carillon and Crown Point, and Proudfoot later saw him return with the same group.

Leaping three months ahead to early November, Proudfoot related how he and his Indian captors were escorting Sergeant Lewis and his men to Isle aux Noix when they met Barnes and a large group of Indians, much as the witness Lewis had described two days earlier. Proudfoot said that it was he who had asked Barnes to "tye them Easy," at which "the Prisoner appear'd Angry, & said he would tye him too," accusing Proudfoot of wanting the famished prisoners "to rise in the Night, to kill him [Barnes], and the Indians"— not a bad idea, Proudfoot must have thought. The witness next described the second trio's capture, confirming that Barnes had indeed told the Indians that "the English were Incapable of making Resistance" but adding that it had been another prisoner who had told Barnes that, rather than Barnes making the plea out of his own humanity. Worse, Proudfoot testified that on the next day, when Sergeant Delano's party was caught, he saw Barnes actually in the act of taking off the scalp of one of the executed men. Barnes even told Proudfoot that he had been ordered to kill the man—at this point there was a question from the court—but no, Proudfoot had not witnessed Barnes actually killing the man; he was already dead by the time Barnes' knife was at work. Carrying the scalp back into the fort, Barnes then dashed the bloody trophy in a prisoner's face—much as may have been done to him on the day of his capture at Lake George.

Proudfoot endured the following Canadian winter in Montreal, but by the late spring of 1760 he had had enough. He and another ranger plotted to make their escape from the last French stronghold rather than wait for Amherst's advancing army, even boasting to a captive officer that they would soon be at Crown Point and offering to take back any messages. They made their break for it on June 7. Roughly following the route taken three years earlier by Ensign Lincoln, they were a mere six miles from their objective, on the west side of the lake, eleven days later. Although less than the distance Ensign Lincoln had had to cover for his freedom, the 140 miles between Montreal and Crown Point were still dangerous, a no man's land crisscrossed by scouting and raiding parties. And like Lincoln and his comrades, Proudfoot and his companion had been unable to take with them enough food for the journey, surviving for the last six days on wild strawberries and roots.

The refugees made a fire near the shore that night, probably hoping that it would be seen by security details from the fort. Sure enough, the next morning at sunrise, rescue in the form of three boats filled with men from the fort greeted them.[44] Proudfoot had made it back, doubtless to the surprise of his old comrades in arms, who like Rogers had assumed him dead. Five weeks after Proudfoot's return, Isle aux Noix was abandoned and left to the advancing British.

When last Proudfoot had seen the prisoner, Barnes had been "sick with the Indians." Asked by someone on the court whether he had approached Barnes about the possibility of escaping together, Proudfoot drove in one final nail. He replied that "he had not trusted the Prisoner with his Intention to make his Escape from the Indians, for fear he [Barnes] should have Discovered him," that is, ratted him out.

It was devastating testimony from a soldier whose exploits would have earned him hero status in a later age. Unlike the previous witnesses, Proudfoot had had repeated contacts with the defendant over the course of more than a year, and none of them very positive. He could recount details of the unfortunate rangers' capture and execution with accuracy, had witnessed and indeed been on the receiving end of Barnes' inhumanity. But more, Proudfoot had seen Barnes in arms with the enemy, and definitely not on a hunting trip. He testified that he had seen Barnes peel the scalp from the dead man's head and that he had heard Barnes boast that he had killed the man himself, and he finished his relation by concluding that Barnes would have betrayed him if he had been foolish enough to let him know that he meant to escape. The defendant, clearly made desperate by Proudfoot's story, finally roused himself to ask the witness a question: was Proudfoot "not sensible, That He, the Prisoner, was Obliged by the Indians' Orders, to take off the scalp" of the corpse? It was a blunder, clear evidence that Barnes was incapable of conducting his own defense. Instead of denying the witness' story, by his question Barnes in fact admitted that he had lied to the court. Two days earlier he had maintained that he had had no hand in either the taking or the dressing of the scalp. Proudfoot shrugged off the question: he had already testified as to Barnes' words, but since he had not been present when the man was killed, he could not say whether Barnes had *actually* been ordered to do it.

If Christopher Proudfoot had been eager to present his testimony against Barnes, the last witness was probably more reluctant to relive his part in the matter. Josiah Malone was now once more a civilian but "Late of Major Rogers' Rangers" and another survivor of the St. Francis raid. He had been captured about the same time as Sergeant Lewis' men and admitted to the court that the Indians had gotten from him that "there were some more of the English Party in their Neighborhood." He did not say whether he had been tortured, but clearly some form of coercion had been applied, and the powerless, starving ranger had quickly crumbled. His captors had then taken him "back to the place where he was taken Prisoner" by them and forced him to guide them to where the others were. This was the instance in which Barnes and Proudfoot were sent forward to secure Private Brown and his two comrades. After the slaughter of Delano's group, Malone testified, Barnes had come into the place where the other prisoners were kept and struck him in the head with a hoe, drawing blood; only the interposition of a Native woman had saved him from more of the same. Shortly afterwards Barnes had returned with a scalp in hand "& Dashed it in the Deponent's face," telling him "that if it had not been for the squaw, his scalp might have been off, too."[45] Barnes had then boasted that "he had stab'ed one of the English Prisoners with his Knife, & taken off his scalp."

Perhaps he had merely said so to further bully Malone, but what he reportedly said next placed the issue of that scalp at center stage, both for the court and for us. Barnes had crowed that with the dead ranger's scalp, "the Indians would trust him now to go, where before this Action, they would not have done." With this statement, Barnes had admitted that he was not fully integrated with his captors and not anywhere near fully trusted by them out of their sight. For Barnes, the scalp had meant gaining that trust, and the greater freedom and privilege that went with it. It is curious that the Delano party's executioners would leave one scalp for Barnes. Were the tracking, pursuit, capture, torture, and execution of the rangers in part a test of Barnes' indoctrination? It seems unlikely that he would have been allowed to scalp the fallen enemy, as he now admitted he did, if he had not taken some hand in his killing. Malone gives us more clues: later he had seen Barnes "Dress & paint the scalp, which he kept and Carried in his Canoe . . . that he afterwards may present of it to an Old Indian." His "Father," presumably?

Compared with Proudfoot, the twice-wounded, indomitable man of action, Malone may have felt conspicuous. True, his situation had been very different, but he had "cracked" under pressure, had led the enemy to his comrades, which in turn had led to the horrible fate of three of them. Afterwards he had still been the victim, unable to defend himself from Barnes' assaults and having to be rescued by a woman. He must have felt the shame and injured pride all prisoners feel, made that much worse by "survivor's guilt" and the knowledge of his own human frailty when the test had come. Probably the members of the court were sympathetic; surely they had known of this sort of thing before. Christopher Proudfoot himself had spoken supportively of Malone, though that may not have been much comfort. Nevertheless, Malone showed himself to be a curiously forgiving man. The last he had seen of Barnes was in a hospital in Montreal the previous June. The sickness that Proudfoot reported had befallen Barnes was serious enough to have him brought there, where coincidentally Malone also was lodged. It was the last campaign summer of the war, and Montreal was awaiting the end. Strapped for resources, French authorities were in the process of emptying their prisons through exchange; scores of English captives were scheduled to leave soon. Malone reported an extraordinary dialogue between himself and his former tormenter. Barnes, perhaps fearing death and wanting to make what amends he could, "Asked [Malone's] pardon for his Behaviour to him." Malone, perhaps in a similar state of mind, apparently forgave him, and also tried "to persuade the Prisoner to go home to his Friends, with the Prisoners then going to be sent home from Montreal." It was extraordinary advice: Go home. Forget all this. No one has to know. Your secret is safe with me. Perhaps Malone did not believe Barnes had actually killed anyone (and neither he nor Proudfoot could claim to have seen him do so), and as for the scalp—well, the man had been dead already.

And what had the prisoner said to that, someone asked the witness. Malone hesitated. "The Prisoner Answered, He Could not, as he had done such things as he durst not go home." Malone knew nothing more; the conversation with Barnes must have ended on that dark note.

As promised, Barnes was now "Asked by the Court, if he had anything further to Add to his Defense." What could he say? So many voices were against him, and he had nothing, no one, to counter them. He had asked only one question of the witnesses against him, and that had done more harm than good. Gone now was any pretense of denial; the terrifying ordeal that was a military court-martial, made almost more awful by the dispassionate, matter-of-fact manner of it all, had overwhelmed him. It had never been a fair contest; from a modern perspective, they never were. Barnes' final plea was for the court to consider his circumstances:

> The Prisoner Declares, he has Nothing further to say for himself, Only, that whatever can be Laid to his Charge, was the Effects of Compulsion, by the Indians, whom he durst not disobey, as his Life was at their Mercy, & that he was very Young, when he was taken, and Living so long among them, had entirely subjected him to them. That when he was Ordered by them to do any Act of Cruelty it was very much against his Inclination, & thro' fear of them & a desire to gain more of their Affections; & was in hope by that means to find an opportunity to Escape from them; And humbly submits himself to the Mercy of the Court.

Barnes' last hope was that the court would take pity on him; that he was as much a victim as any of the other witnesses, some of whom (including Proudfoot) had also done what the Indians had made them do. He could not have known it, but he had in fact introduced what one former judge advocate would characterize as circumstances the court *ought* to consider: "A man that is urged to do what his judgement disapproves, and what is presumed his will (if left to himself) would reject, may plead this in exculpation of himself."[46] If ever there was a case for pleading coercion, surely this was it. And if a modern "expert witness" had been present, he or she would have emphasized the factors Barnes urged, factors that sometimes had resulted in behavior that was an unconscious survival strategy: he had been young and isolated; he had been at his captors' mercy and feared for his life; he had been entirely bent to their will. A person in those circumstances might do anything to "gain more of their Affections" and ameliorate a hellish existence. And despite what the witnesses reported Barnes saying, still none of them had *seen* Barnes kill anyone or actually *use* arms against any of His Majesty's (living) subjects.

The prosecution enjoyed one last, blatant advantage over the defense in a court-martial. As the court deliberated in private, the judge advocate remained with them, to "elucidate and explain whatever may be doubtful or intricate."[47] No counsel for the defense, if there had been one, was permitted the same privilege. There is no indication that the court took long to reach its decision. Questions of jurisdiction or of the prisoner's status apparently did not trouble the court. If there had been reservations after the trial's first day concerning the lack of hard evidence regarding the charges, they were largely dispelled by the testimony of the second day, and in any case evidence beyond a shadow of doubt was not required. If "positive proof" were lacking, according to common practice, "*Circumstantial* evidence, or the doctrine of *presumption* must take place. For when the fact itself cannot be demonstratively evinced, that which comes nearest to the proof of the fact is the proof of circumstances, which either *necessarily* or usually attend such facts; and these are called *presumptions,* which are only to be relied on till the contrary be actually proved." Indeed, Falconer may have assured the court that "violent presumption is many times equal to full proof, for there those circumstances appear which necessarily attend the fact; and probable presumption, arising from such circumstances as usually attend the fact, hath also its due weight."[48]

In other words, Barnes could be convicted of a capital crime on the preponderance of circumstantial evidence alone. And the circumstances were decidedly against him. Witnesses had given remarkably complementary and unchallenged accounts of Barnes' depravity and violence against his own kind; nearly all had seen him in arms acting in concert with the enemy; he had lied to the court about that scalp. It was not even necessary to prove that he had killed anyone, or tried to, to brand him with treasonous behavior. Nothing material had been offered in the way of defense. And while others had indeed been forced to comply with their fearsome captors, none of the witnesses had been under the impression that Barnes acted under compulsion. Lastly, there was the dramatic counterexample of another captive, Christopher Proudfoot. Despite all the difficulties he had faced, Proudfoot had escaped, while Barnes, with many more advantages and with four years' worth of opportunities, had not.

The court found Barnes "Guilty of the Crimes Laid to his Charge." The judge advocate was forbidden to record how individual court members voted or even to write "unanimous" if that was the case, so we cannot know whether the vote was close. But it is unlikely that the court had much sympathy for the friendless, luckless provincial. Even if the verdict had been by a bare majority, sentencing procedure virtually guaranteed the harsh outcome for which courts-martial were notorious. None of the minority judges, assuming there were any, were permitted to take part in determining the sentence of the court, "for it cannot be supposed that those who have found him not guilty would assign him a punishment." Nor, consequently, would they be able to argue for any amelioration of that punishment. Thus the defendant's fate was in the hands of the judges least inclined to be lenient. Those charged with sentencing the condemned could indeed recommend mercy, in which case the sentence was referred to the commanding general.[49] But there is likewise no suggestion that that option was considered.

And anyway, General Gage wanted to make an example of Barnes. Desertion was always a problem for the British army, no less than for any other. Desertion to the enemy was particularly heinous, and desertion to enemy Indians inexcusable. White captives occasionally were able to straddle the cultural divide, living for long periods in more or less agreeable circumstances with Native peoples before returning. These captives became cultural brokers, immensely valuable to both Natives and Europeans as interpreters and negotiators. Some of those who were not captured but deserted the army found that life among the Indians was not what their imaginations had suggested. One group of British army deserters was reported as living among the Senecas "in a miserable way, strip'd of everything, & Slaves to the Savages, who watch them close & prevent their leaving the place they are in." Although these men were redeemed, they were presented to their fellow soldiers as objects of pity and derision.[50] One deserter, Henry Hamilton, who fled to the French during the siege of Quebec in 1759, was seen by a witness in the French lines wearing a white coat and later keeping company with the Wabanakis at St. Francis. Hamilton had a different story, of course, but admitted that he had been with the Wabanakis until July 1760. He came to a bad end; his desertion and service with the French would have been enough to condemn him, but voluntarily living with Indians unfriendly to the British undoubtedly added to the case against him.[51] British and colonial authorities had long experience with white renegades, men who not only had chosen a Native lifestyle but willingly fought against other whites, and they nursed a particularly vindictive grudge against them. As early as King Philip's War in 1675–76, one Joshua Tifte, of Rhode Island, "who larned indyn maryed a indan . . . shot 20 times" at English colonists in a major battle. Captured at Providence a month later, he was given a traitor's death: "after his Confesyn [he] was hanged drawn and Qartered."[52]

British authorities in Canada suspected that there were more such renegades hiding among the Indians, and Barnes' capture prompted Gage to announce in general orders that he had good reason "to believe that there are some British subjects among the Indians, and who come into town in their

Indian dresses." He ordered that "all officers and soldiers who shall meet with any of the above persons do apprehend them and send them to the guard."[53] Barnes was no deserter; in fact, he had been wounded in action against the enemy, as had Proudfoot, which made his actions all the more inexplicable to his judges.

"The effect of infamy"

The court had decided that Barnes should die, but the final decision was General Gage's. He had the power to issue a pardon or to commute the sentence, but he had no interest in doing either. The paperwork crossed his desk on April 6, and he appended to it the statement, "I Approve of the above sentence, & Order that the Prisoner Jonathan Barnes, al[s]. Burns, be Hanged by the neck, untill he is Dead." At last, and by way of the most despised of the men who made up that doomed company, Hodges' Scout had come to the attention of the very highest authority.

Gage also specified the manner of Barnes' death: not by firing squad, as a soldier might hope for, but by hanging. Although execution by shooting had become fairly common as firearms came to dominate Western armies, it was in part an expedient: armies on the move might not have time to erect a gallows, but there were always plenty of muskets available at short notice. And while death by firing squad was a gory business that mangled the body in one shocking, explosive moment, it was generally quick, and so many soldiers recognized it as preferable to the pain and humiliation of slowly strangling at the end of a rope. But "the inflicting of punishments," a contemporary admitted, was "more for example, and to prevent evils, than to punish." The death of the malefactor, in other words, was secondary to the intended effect his death would have on those who witnessed the execution. Judges were expected to consider the nature of the crime, the motives behind it, and any particular "circumstances attending the committing of it," for example, whether the crime had been committed out of premeditation, passion, or imprudence. Depending on all these factors, then, "death may be inflicted in a more or less disgraceful manner." Disgrace. Degrees of disgrace. Certain forms of execution had, and were supposed to have, "the effect of infamy." Hanging was common; shooting was an exclusive option of the military, and came to be acknowledged as a more fitting "soldier's death." To deny that option was to say that the condemned was not worthy of the "honor," literally not worth the bullets; that he would have to accept the more vulgar, disgraceful death—insult upon injury. Each execution, and especially the manner of it, was supposed to be an object lesson in just desserts, a sermon in pantomime, not for the condemned—his life was unimportant now—but for the audience. For there would be an audience. To a world before popular prison-reform movements, the execution was meaningless without people to observe and reflect on the sure and awful justice that awaited those like Barnes.

Perhaps mercifully, Barnes did not have very long to wait. On Tuesday, April 7, the day after Gage's authorization, Barnes went to the gallows. Sometime between ten and twelve o'clock in the morning, when the town was at its busiest, the condemned man, red-coated guards on each side and preceded by a drummer beating the "dead march," walked the short distance to the marketplace, long since the site of criminal executions.[54] Walking behind Barnes on his last journey was the Reverend John Ogilvie, chaplain to the Royal American Regiment. Ogilvie was a Yale graduate, class of 1748; rector of St. Peter's Church in Albany, and a missionary to the nearby Mohawk people. Unlike Gideon Hawley, chaplain to Barnes' original Massachusetts regiment, Ogilvie seems to have enjoyed a chaplain's work; he began his army commission in the same month that Hodges' Scout met its fate. Tall and hardworking, he was fluent in Mohawk and Dutch—when in Albany he instructed a hundred Dutch-speaking children. He would soon translate his army connections into a commercial enterprise, becoming an officer, along with Captain Falconer, in the St. John's River Society, a land-speculation company aiming to open up more than half a million acres of land in Nova Scotia for settlement. Two years before the American Revolution, John Singleton Copley would paint his portrait. He was more activist than academic, for he wrote nothing for print.[55]

So, sadly, he passed up this opportunity for a surefire quick-seller; one can imagine the sensational but cautionary pamphlet, or the dying-man's-confession broadside that Barnes' story easily could have generated. Ogilvie, in fact, had to be prodded by General Gage months after the execution to set down his recollection of that day, for "the confession of the wretch . . . I was not informed of, till after his execution; or I should have ordered Mr. Ogilvy who attended Him, to have taken it down verbatim in writing, as He spoke it." Gage was clearly peeved at this lost opportunity. He had subsequently heard that there had been French involvement in the killings of Delano and his men (about which no one had been asked or offered anything at the court-martial), and he wanted particularly to associate the French commander with a war crime. But Gage had only himself to blame: he ought to have thought of getting Barnes' confession when he signed the execution order.[56]

What Ogilvie remembered certainly confirmed what not only Gage but also the officers who decided Barnes' fate had suspected all along, and it almost answers for us Barnes' status as a "white Indian." Ogilvie may have visited the prisoner the night of the sixth to offer spiritual counsel and to urge Barnes to make a clean breast of it before he went to meet his Maker. His words, and the imminence of death, did their work, for the next morning, "a few minutes before his execution," as the minister wrote Gage, Barnes seemed at last to admit his guilt. "About the Time the Indians Corn was fit to be gathered," Barnes related in the Native idiom of marking time, he had been with the party that captured Delano's men. After bringing the prisoners to Isle aux Noix, "the Indians came to a Resolution to Sacrifice" the man with the human flesh in his pack. The unlucky man "was led out by the Indians, to a small Distance from the French encampment, and there tortured in the most barbarous Manner." According to Ogilvie, Barnes said "that he, the Sd Burns assisted in the shocking Murder," adding that a number of French had come out from the fort to witness the horrid spectacle. "This," Ogilvie reported, "he assured me, as a dying Man, was all true." Barnes had not so completely embraced Native ways that he had forgotten the Protestant training of his former life. He had done wrong; he felt guilt; guilt had to be faced and confessed.[57]

One would give a great deal to have the verbatim statement that Gage had wanted rather than Ogilvie's "Substance" of Barnes' story. Barnes might have said much more, but Ogilvie was giving Gage what he most wanted from the affair: implications of French officers condoning atrocities. One suspects that Barnes' admission of this detail (which one doubts was important to him) was prompted by Ogilvie. Missing from the digest of Barnes' confession was his acknowledgment of bearing arms against his country—of being a traitor—nor did he say that he had actually killed the suffering prisoner. Perhaps he felt that nothing in his disclosure altered the fact that he had done what he had done under a kind of compulsion. And perhaps, in his unimaginable desperation at the prospect of losing his young life, he had not yet surrendered all hope that he might yet be spared, that confession might yield a last-minute reprieve.

It was not to be. At the gallows in the marketplace, where curious soldiers and civilians gathered to watch, Barnes, his arms pinioned behind him, was helped up a ladder that rested against the gallows lintel. The executioner, very possibly another condemned soldier granted his life in return for performing the repulsive office, placed the noose over Barnes' head (perhaps he was given a hood as well), the knot slightly to the side, as the sentence of the court was read to the crowd. Reverend Ogilvie intoned a final prayer, while the miserable young man drew his last, rapid breaths, his heart pounding in his ears. Or was he stoic, resigned, eager to end it all? At an officer's nod, the executioner turned the ladder suddenly, tumbling Barnes off. A short drop, and then the long, kicking agony. At some executions, friends of the condemned were permitted to pull down on the hanging person's body in order to end the victim's suffering more quickly. Courts-martial did not allow such participation, however, and Barnes had no friends anyway. When the body had hung long enough for death to be assured, and the "example" adequately demonstrated, it was taken down and buried in an unmarked grave outside the town. It is not now possible to say whether Samuel Henche, who had identified Barnes as the young blacksmith who set out with Captain Hodges' men, spoke much about his involvement in the sad affair or whether Barnes' father, wherever he was, learned at last what had happened to his missing son.

12

Coda: William Merry's Tale

"An honest, simple-hearted man"

With Jonathan Barnes' execution, we account for almost every one
of the nearly fifty men who set out from Fort William Henry to take their
unlucky part in Hodges' Scout. They represent only a small proportion of
the men whose lives and experiences were swallowed up in this war. They
are largely lost to history, in that they are not, and of course cannot, all be
included in general histories of the conflict. But as we have seen, it is possible to reconstruct past lives, at least in part, from the limited and scattered
records that survive. From these reconstructions we have seen something
of the varied experiences awaiting those captured in eighteenth-century forest warfare. In the twenty-first century, international conventions of long
standing govern the handling and processing of prisoners and have shaped
our expectations in that regard. Those expectations include humane treatment, standard practices for prisoner confinement and repatriation, and
monitoring by a neutral authority, such as the Red Cross. In contrast, the
experiences of the survivors of Hodges' Scout were highly varied, dependent
on a combination of European and Native American laws, conventions, customs, circumstances, and luck—good or bad.

One would imagine that the nine men who returned from captivity to
their homes would have had enough of military life. Most came home too
late in the war, and were too physically compromised or economically strait-
ened, to consider reenlistment, even if they had been so inclined. Jeremiah
Lincoln and Peleg Stevens both returned early enough in the war to take
part in active campaigns, but they chose not to do so. This does not mean
that the survivors were done with military service, however. All of them

were liable for service in their town militias until age sixty. After his marriage, Lincoln became a dedicated family man, ultimately raising ten children in his hometown of Hingham. When British and Americans, allies no longer, clashed at Lexington and Concord in 1775, New England militias mustered to continue the armed resistance. Lincoln, then forty-one, answered the alarm but was not required to serve beyond the emergency. Ebenezer Pratt and John Walklate served in Massachusetts state companies early in the war. Walklate may have seen service in the Continental Army despite being well past his youth. Peleg Stevens had likewise reached middle age when the war began, but that did not deter him from enlisting, in 1777, for three years in the Continental Army. He served out his time but stayed on until discharged in September 1782, when the war was all but over. Despite his age, given variously as forty-eight, fifty-five, and fifty-nine years (the first is nearest the mark), the five-feet-seven Stevens still had dark hair, but his youth had otherwise left him: he was discharged because of "being old and worn out in the service."[1] William Merry's campaigning days were over, but at fifty-two he was still willing to enlist for short stints with Massachusetts state regiments, responding to alarms and reinforcing coastal defenses.[2]

It is Merry, that old soldier who had survived three firefights and a long captivity, who provides us, at a remove, with one last look at the destruction of Hodges' Scout in September 1756. Alone among the survivors of the massacre, he gave an eyewitness account, which survived to be recorded later, of the circumstances surrounding the ruin of his company. Unlike the others, Merry related important details of the events of that awful day, as well as some clues to the mysteries we have encountered surrounding it.

In October 1853 a Boston banker with the last name Hodges was preparing a volume tracing the genealogy and history of the Hodges family in New England. In that month he received a letter from a distant cousin, the Reverend Joseph Hodges, a minister in North Oxford, Massachusetts. A collateral descendant of Captain Joseph, Reverend Hodges supplied his banker cousin with copies of documents relevant to the slain ancestor, documents that ended up in the finished work and are referenced in early chapters of this book. In addition to the written material, Reverend Hodges transferred to paper a piece of oral family history nearly a century old.

"The circumstances of the death of Capt. Joseph Hodges," the minister-antiquarian began, "were given to his family by William Merry, who was a soldier under his command." Merry, as we have seen, returned to Norton, after his captivity and escape, to an impoverished and needy family. With few or no other prospects, he returned to work as a farm laborer or perhaps was able to lease some land. At some point—one imagines that it was not very long after his return—he met with members of the Hodges family and, presumably at their urging, told how Captain Joseph had come to die. No one else living nearby would have had such information, and so far no surviving account had revealed the captain's part in the fighting. We can imagine the scene: Merry, the struggling laborer, seated before a hearth in the Hodges' comfortable but modest house. It is unlikely that he had ever been there before. There would be polite salutations, offers of refreshment, perhaps an inquiry as to Merry's circumstances, some exchange of town talk and news. The captain's widow eventually would signal her readiness to turn the conversation to the matter at hand. The small talk would cease and in the rapt silence that followed, Merry would tell his story.

Hodges was not even supposed to go on that mission, Merry related. The officer originally assigned was sick, and Hodges volunteered to take the man's place. Merry affirmed that the fight was no meeting-engagement encounter; Hodges' men had been suddenly and devastatingly ambushed, with "firing from every quarter," which "convinced them they were surrounded." Merry assured his listeners that he was "by the side of his commander" and witnessed what happened next. Hodges shouted to his men to "fight for their lives" and, perhaps to encourage some who froze or cowered, "set his men an energetic example by the use of his own gun." At some point in the fighting—it is not clear from the narrative—the captain went down, a bullet shattering his ankle. Unable to stand, Hodges continued to load and fire from his knees and to "encourage his men." Resistance attracted more gunfire, however, and Hodges was next struck in the chest. Stanching the blood with one hand, he tried desperately to ward off his attackers, who apparently wanted him alive, until one finally shot him through the head. Merry said that he himself killed the Indian who had struck the fatal blow. Hodges' command "fought bravely," Merry insisted, "but were overpowered by numbers." Merry, Reverend Hodges wrote, lived a "quiet and humble life. He had the reputation of being an honest, simple-hearted man, and his statement may be relied on as faithful."[3]

Perhaps so. But the reader would be correct in treating Merry's tale with more skepticism than did the Reverend Hodges. One's immediate reaction, in fact, might be to dismiss the story, as it only survives today as a thirdhand account, a tale calculated to assuage a grieving family. Certainly the family approved the story, for it survived and was passed on, finally recorded nearly a century later. But some circumstances of the tale seem implausible, not the least being Merry's claim to have slain Captain Hodges' killer. If true, then Merry accounted for fully one-half of the Native fatalities that day; that's possible, but would his captors have then permitted him to live? We know that they later executed several survivors in their rage. If Merry in fact killed an Indian, then one of his fellow survivors paid the price. Perhaps Merry told the story the way he did for the sake of the Hodges family: certainly it would have been satisfying for them to believe that the "savage" who had killed their husband or father or brother had not lived to boast of it. But Reverend Hodges let slip that "it was Merry's custom to relate with pride, that he killed the Indian who aimed the last fatal shot at his commander," a statement that suggests that Merry told the tale often enough for it to become "custom." We can speculate that he indeed told his tale often, to various audiences, perhaps regaling tavern patrons with his adventures in the "Old French War" in exchange for drinks. He would hardly have been the first or the last old soldier to do so.

We are also faced here with the problem of trusting memories, and not simply those of William Merry. It is to be expected that his recollection would embellish some features of the encounter while diminishing, dismissing, or simply forgetting others; this is a problem confronted in examining eyewitnesses at all times. But we must also ask how much of the tale as related by Reverend Hodges in 1853 was still even Merry's. For all we know, Private Merry, "honest, simple-hearted man" that he was, may have told the assembled Hodges family the facts accurately, as he remembered them, with the melodramatic flourishes instead being added in retellings of the story among family members over three generations. We simply cannot take Reverend Hodges' version of the events at face value.

Remains

And yet, there may be something useful, even revealing in this family story. Something may yet remain of Merry's original tale, for while the reader may legitimately doubt elements of the surviving narrative, in its broad outlines and even in its details the story is plausible.

Merry recalled, and Reverend Hodges' letter preserves, incidental details that can be verified. Merry claimed that Captain Hodges had fought with a musket that day and had left his sword behind. True: as we saw at the beginning of this book, Hodges' £2 5s. hanger was inventoried at Fort William Henry after his death. Merry revealed that Hodges volunteered to command the scout in the place of a sick comrade. This also rings true, given what we have gleaned about Hodges' character and given the rampant sickness at the fort, which felled officers and privates alike. And as for Captain Hodges' "Davy Crockett" moment—whittled down to the point of helplessness but still defiant—there are plenty of similar examples from every war. There is no reason to think that someone in Hodges' situation might *not* fight to the bitter end; after all, there were no good alternatives for him. The moment he was shot in the ankle, Hodges must surely have known that he, at least, was unlikely to live through the event. In short, Merry's story fits the facts we do have, and it does not contradict other accounts.

Merry's is also the only surviving account that tells us of Hodges' actions that day. Depending on the sequence of events, which may be variously interpreted, we gain tentative impressions of his performance as commander and its possible effect on events. One way to read Merry's tale is to see Hodges as the man of action, telling his men to "fight for their lives" and setting an "energetic example" for his men by keeping up a brisk fire. The problem with this portrayal, properly heroic as it must have seemed to Hodges' family, is that it represents exactly the *wrong* thing for a company commander to have been doing in a firefight. Hodges' job was to direct the response to the ambush—giving orders to his subordinates, deploying his men, directing return fire, pushing the fearful into action, securing the wounded—*not* getting involved in the fighting himself. Whether the best response was to conduct a retreat, or to dig in, or even to charge, the decision was his to make, and making the proper choice required him to assess the situation quickly and impose control over his men. Hodges' "save yourself" command was no direction at all and in fact would likely have contributed to the already chaotic situation: it would have given the men discretion to act as they saw fit, and it may even have initiated a fatal running retreat.

Read another way, Merry's tale could support another scenario. In this visualization, Hodges was near the front when the firing erupted and received his crippling shot early on. Unable to direct the fighting, unable to move from his spot, he urged his men to "fight for their lives," which was apparently all the leadership he could offer them in his condition. But in either case, his words would likely have had the same effect. Those men who did not panic, some of the very men Hodges might have been able to direct had he attempted to do so, drew themselves around their stricken commander and were mostly killed with him, their mangled corpses found by the boatmen that evening.

And again we must acknowledge that it might not have occurred either way, that for whatever reason, Merry's tale contained more of James Fennimore Cooper than of fact. But Merry made one further addition to the story, or rather, he included a part of the story left out of the other accounts, perhaps because it seemed so trifling. And like those parts of Merry's account already discussed, it is tantalizingly plausible. Merry described what may have been a critical few minutes before the firing began and in so doing suggested how Hodges' Scout came to be ambushed instead of entering a meeting engagement, from which more of them might have escaped.

Merry reported that when the scout was near its destination opposite the Narrows, Hodges had called a halt for rest and "a party was despatched to the lake, with canteens, for water." This makes sense, for as we have seen, it was an oppressively hot day, and the men had just trudged ten miles. Merry's relation then indicates that the watering party "returned immediately, with the alarming news that they found on the shore of the lake hundreds of fresh tracks of Indians in the sand by the lake." Again, the discovery Merry related reflects what we know of French and Indian movements that day. These were undoubtedly the tracks of the raiding party described by de Bougainville, which had descended on a point they thought was occupied by provincial observers but turned out to be empty. The reader will recall that this party, headed by the experienced partisan leader Joseph Marin, had returned to their rendezvous point three or four miles distant but after a conference had headed back in Hodges' direction.[4]

As the historian John Demos famously put it, "Some things we have to imagine."[5] We can imagine the halt: the men sit; conversation; laughter; the clatter of canteens. The watering party spotted, exposed as they gawk at tracks along the lakeshore? One imagines a stop of ten or fifteen minutes at a minimum. And in that pause Captain Hodges has a decision to make: what ought he to do? He has detected the presence on his side of the lake of an enemy force likely superior in size to his own. But he has no certainty as to the whereabouts, direction, or intention of the enemy, who might well be nearby—who might even be watching them at this moment. He has, in fact, accomplished the chief purpose for which these scouts existed; surely his primary duty now was to alert General Winslow at Fort William Henry of this threat, and of this opportunity to finally turn the tables on their hated foe. Hodges could return with his command to the fort. At somewhat more risk, he could hole up in a good position somewhere and send for reinforcements, which would probably not reach him until evening at best, if they came by boat. At minimum, he could dispatch messengers to the fort to tell Winslow the situation.

In the event, Hodges did none of these things. According to Merry, "The order was immediately given to resume the march." There is no indication that Hodges even put out flankers, as he had done on previous occasions, to prevent surprise. One would give a great deal to know the reasons for Hodges' fatal choice. Perhaps the "hundreds" of fresh tracks was an exaggeration, a device later added to the story to lend a greater sense of foreboding. Perhaps, like General Winslow and Colonel Bagley, Hodges wanted to "give the shaberoons a Drubing" after months of frustration and humiliations and saw a chance to do so that might not come again. At any rate, minutes after his men resumed their march, the blow fell, and fell hard. The halt Merry describes would have provided all the time necessary for experienced woods fighters, advancing with scouts ahead, to discover their enemy and prepare their trap. Merry's tale, providentially recorded a century later, may answer the question what went wrong that day.

In a word: everything.

It is pointless to blame Captain Hodges alone for what happened to his command, and too easy. If he made bad choices that day, it was at least in part because he had no more training for what faced him than did his men, and this, as we have seen, was a problem inherent in provincial military practices. For all that New England's politicians, planners, officers, and soldiers were able to accomplish in this war—and they accomplished plenty—there were stark limits to what they could do. From generals to quartermasters to private soldiers, nearly all had to learn their jobs on the fly. Resources and monies were limited, especially early in the war, so offensive operations were delayed or curtailed, the initiative lost or squandered, soldiers turned into pick, axe, and shovel men. The men were malnourished, many of them sick and unfit for duty at times, and they did not receive the specialized instruction and conditioning needed for the kind of warfare they were most likely to face. They expected to return home at the end of the season in any event. They were not bad material for soldiers, but little in their culture or experience encouraged developing the skills or discipline of soldiers on anything more than an ad hoc basis. Almost nothing in the campaign of 1756 turned out well for their side. The causes for the destruction of Hodges' Scout are many and of course must include enemy actions and sheer bad fortune, neither of which were Hodges' to control.

Lastly, William Merry's tale may one day help archaeologists digging at the reconstructed Fort William Henry. The vast majority of visitors to that popular tourist site are unaware that they park their cars and vans over the original fort's burying ground, containing more than a thousand burials from the occupations of 1756 and 1757.[6] In the future, archaeologists may be able to excavate this area, adding immensely to our knowledge of life and death at Lake George during the last of the French and Indian wars. If they do, they may discover the remains of a man about forty years old at the time of his violent death, with gunshot trauma to the ankle, chest, and head and the telltale marks of scalping and mutilation. They will almost certainly have found the bones of Captain Joseph Hodges and, nearby, those of nine of the men who died with him.

Appendix A
The Roll of Hodges' Scout

Of the approximately 48 men of Hodges' Scout, 36 are identified by name in official records:

	Age*	Occupation	Residence	Company	Initial Status
COMPANY OFFICERS					
Capt. Joseph Hodges	42	—	Norton	Hodges	"Killed by the Enemy"
Lt. Ezekiel Webb	23	—	Yarmouth	Knowles	escaped the fighting
Ens. Jeremiah Lincoln	22	blacksmith	Hingham	Thaxter	"kill'd or taken"
Sgt. John Lewis	43	husbandman	Wilmington	Butterfield	"kill'd or taken"
Cpl. Joseph Abbot	21	joiner	Andover	Parker	"killed"
Cpl. Henry Partridge	23	laborer	Easton	Williams	"kill'd or Captivate"
Cpl. Peleg Stevens	21	barber	Dartmouth	Bradford	"kill'd with Hodges"
PRIVATES					
Andrew Allen	16	—	Gloucester	Thompson	"kill'd Sept. 19"
Jonathan Barnes	19	blacksmith	Boston	Learned	"kill'd or taken wth Hodges"
William Bradbury	20	husbandman	Dudley	White	"kill'd or taken wth Hodges"
Jonathan Childs	18	cordwainer	Worcester	Learned	"kill'd or taken wth Hodges"
John Con	17	servant	Haverhill	Parker	"Dead or Captivated"
Moses Emerson	18	husbandman	Haverhill	Frye	"killed"
John Erwin	18	laborer	Dunstable	Butterfield	"kill'd or taken"
Isaac Foster	19	—	Andover	Frye	"killed"
Benjamin Gushe	26	tanner	Raynham	Williams	"killed or taken wth Hodges"
John Hartshorn	17	mason	Newbury	Young	"killed"
Isaiah Lyon	19	miller	Walpole	Bacon	"killed or taken wth Hodges"
William Merry	33	laborer	Norton	Williams	"killed or taken wth Hodges"
Amos Morse/Moses	18	laborer	Sturbridge	Dalrymple	"killed or taken"
Nicholas Mulzer	18	laborer	Wrentham	Thwing	"killed or taken wth Hodges"
Joseph Nichols	18	farmer	Hardwicke	Robinson	"kill'd or taken"
John Nut	—	—	Hopkinton	Keen	"killed or taken wth Hodges"
Joshua Perry	—	—	Haverhill	Parker	escaped the fighting
Ebenezer Pratt	18	servant	Bridgewater	Bacon	"killed or taken wth Hodges"

	Age*	Occupation	Residence	Company	Initial Status
John Preston	18	laborer	Leicester	Nixon	"killed or taken wth Hodges"
William Proctor	23	farmer	Woburn	Lord	"killed or taken"
Thomas Pulling	18	laborer	Rochester	Doty	"killed or taken wth Hodges"
Azor Roundy	18	servant	Beverly	Plaisted	"kill'd Sept. 19"
Thomas Slauder	21	weaver	Hingham	Thaxter	"Killd"
John Stacy	20	servant	Danvers	Fuller	"killed or taken"
Jonas Tarbold/Tarbel	18	farmer	Lunenburg	Reed	"kill'd"
Benjamin Titus	17	husbandman	Douglas	White	"kill'd or taken"
John Walklate	25	—	Gloucester	Thompson	"killed or taken with Hodges"
Robert Wilson	22	farmer	Lexington	Lord	wounded, escaped the fighting
Thomas Woodward	17	laborer	Dunstable	Butterfield	"killed or taken"

OTHER PRIVATES POSSIBLY BELONGING ON THE LIST

Abner Abbe	19	—	Windham, CT	Starr	"Dead or Captivated" September 19
Daniel Collar	24	—	Hopkinton	—	reported taken "near Lake George," "In the year 1756"
Gideon Colton	25	husbandman	Springfield	Mosely	wages stopped Sept. 19, no explanation
James Nason	17	cordwainer	Biddeford	Lane	"taken Captive," before Oct. 11
Ebenezer Saviles	—	—	Greenwood	Burke	wages stopped Sept. 19, no explanation

Source: Muster Rolls, 1756, Massachusetts Archives, Vols. 94 and 95
Note: Two additional, unnamed men escaped the fighting and made it back to Fort William Henry.
*At time of enlistment, spring 1756.

Appendix B
The Captives

Captain de Bougainville indicates in his *Adventure in the Wilderness*, 41, that in addition to those named below, two or three more of Hodges' command were initially spared but executed later that day or during the following night.

	Age*	Initial Status	Terminal Status
Joseph Abbot	21	"killed"	died in prison, Quebec, January 1758
Jonathan Barnes	19	"kill'd or taken wth Hodges"	executed, Montreal, April 1761
William Bradbury	20	"kill'd or taken wth Hodges"	taken by Ottawas toward *pays d'en haut*, fate unknown
John Con	17	"Dead or Captivated"	liberated at fall of Montreal, September 1760
Moses Emerson	18	"killed"	home by end of war
John Erwin	18	"kill'd or taken"	liberated at fall of Montreal, September 1760
Isaac Foster	19	"killed"	returned in prisoner exchange, November 1759
Benjamin Gushee	26	"killed or taken wth Hodges"	taken by Ottawas toward *pays d'en haut*, fate unknown
Jeremiah Lincoln	22	"kill'd or taken"	escaped from Montreal, June 1757
William Merry	33	"killed or taken wth Hodges"	escaped Indian captivity, summer 1760
Henry Partridge	23	"kill'd or Captivate"	taken by Ottawas toward *pays d'en haut*, fate unknown
Ebenezer Pratt	18	"killed or taken wth Hodges"	returned in prisoner exchange, November 1759
John Stacy	20	"killed or taken"	lived among Indians near Quebec, fate unknown
Peleg Stevens	21	"kill'd with Hodges"	returned in prisoner exchange via France and England, September 1758
John Walklate	25	"killed or taken with Hodges"	liberated at fall of Montreal, September 1760

*At time of enlistment, spring 1756.

Appendix C
William Merry's Account, Recorded 1853

Excerpt, Rev. Joseph Hodges Jr. to A. D. Hodges, Esq., Washington Bank, Boston. Dated North Oxford, 4 October 1853. In *Genealogical Record of the Hodges Family in New England,* by Almon D. Hodges (Boston: Dutton & Wentworth, 1853), 16.

The circumstances of the death of Capt. Joseph Hodges were given to his family by William Merry, who was a soldier under his command at the time of the desperate conflict in which he was killed. It had fallen to the lot of another officer to go out on this service called a 'scout,' for the purpose of making discoveries of the enemy, and especially that part of the enemy composed of Indians, which it was most hazardous to meet in a service of this kind. In consequence of illness, this officer was excused. Capt. Hodges volunteered his services on this occasion, and those who accompanied him were volunteers. His command numbered 60 men. The company marched nearly to the point designated in the order given to Capt. Hodges, when he made a halt, for the purpose of refreshment. A party was despatched to the lake, with canteens, for water; they returned immediately, with the alarming information that they saw on the shore of the lake hundreds of fresh tracks of Indians in the sand by the lake. The order was immediately given to resume the march. The company had proceeded but a short distance, when the firing from every quarter convinced them they were surrounded by Indians. Capt. Hodges charged his men 'to fight for their lives;' he set his men an energetic example by the use of his own gun, which he carried on this occasion, instead of his sword. He and his men fought bravely, but were overpowered by numbers. Merry's testimony was, that he fought by the side of his commander, who was first wounded in the ankle by a musket ball, when he dropped on his knees, and continued to fire and encourage his men. Another ball struck him in the breast. Placing one hand on the wound, to check the flowing blood, with his musket in the other, he still kept the Indians at bay; one of whom reached forward to sever his scalp; foiled thus, the Indian leveled his gun and shot him through the head, when the brave captain fell. It was Merry's custom to relate with pride, that he killed the Indian who aimed the last fatal shot at his commander, of whose bravery and character he spoke in the highest terms. Merry was taken prisoner; nearly if not all of the rest of the company were slaughtered. After being a prisoner with the Indians five years, Merry made his escape and returned to Norton, where he passed the remainder of his days in a quiet and humble life. He had the reputation of being an honest, simple-hearted man, and his statement may be relied on as faithful."

Appendix D
Captain Hodges' Sword

Like the facts surrounding Hodges' Scout, the fate of Hodges' father's heirloom, silver-hilted sword becomes obscure with time. Captain Hodges left the sword at home, willing it to his eldest son, Joseph III. Almon D. Hodges, who compiled the family history in 1853, assured readers that the sword was "preserved as an heir-loom in the family." A half century later, however, his son Almon Jr. indicated that the branch of the family to which the sword had devolved had fallen on hard times, and the sword had become a victim of their poverty. Joseph III had bequeathed the sword to his eldest, yet another Joseph. Joseph IV "had an energetic, capable New England wife, who held the interests of her children paramount to all other interests. Hence it was that when some articles were needed for her home, and ready cash was not immediately available, the silver hilt of Major Joseph's sword was sacrificed by her for the sake of her family and, by the process of barter, was transmuted into silver spoons. The blade is still owned by her grandchildren, whose respect for their capable grandmother is tempered by sorrow for the loss of a priceless heirloom."[1] Which was probably putting it mildly.

---

1. Quotations from Almon D. Hodges Jr., ed., *Almon Danforth Hodges and his Neighbors: An Autobiographical Sketch of a Typical Old New Englander* (Boston: privately printed, 1909), 21–22.

Notes

Prologue. Recovering Lost Lives

1. So insisted Benjamin Franklin in 1766. Quoted in Gordon S. Wood, *The Americanization of Benjamin Franklin* (New York: Penguin Books, 2004), 122.

2. Jonathan Mayhew, quoted in *Crucible of War: The Seven Years' War and the Fate of Empire in British North America, 1754–1766,* by Fred Anderson (New York: Vintage Books, 2000), 375.

Chapter 1. "Kill'd or taken"

1. Samuel Greenleaf journal, 1756–1767, 19 September 1756, Massachusetts Historical Society (hereafter MHS).

2. Josiah Thacher diary, 1756–1757, 15–17 September 1756, MHS.

3. Gen. John Winslow to Lord Loudoun, 19 September 1756, John Winslow Journal, 1744–1757 (hereafter JWJ), 3:160, MHS; Samuel Greenleaf journal, 19 September 1756. The identity of the wounded man, not given in any of the immediate accounts, is revealed in a petition he wrote to the Massachusetts government more than a year later. Massachusetts Archives Collection, 78:58, Massachusetts Archives, Boston.

4. Winslow to Loudoun, 19 September 1756, JWJ, 3:160; Josiah Thacher diary, 19 September 1756.

5. Josiah Thacher diary, 19 September 1756; *Boston Gazette,* 7 October 1756.

6. Winslow to Loudoun, 19 September 1756, JWJ, 3:160; Winslow to Benning Wentworth, 20 September 1756, JWJ, 3:168.

7. Winslow to Wentworth, 20 September 1756, JWJ, 3:168; *Boston Globe,* 7 October 1756.

8. Winslow to Wentworth, 20 September 1756, JWJ, 3:168.

9. That is, paper money issued earlier by Massachusetts Bay, highly inflated at this time but still in circulation.

10. *Papers Relating to Captain Thomas Lawrence's Company, Raised in Groton, Massachusetts, during the French and Indian War, 1758, Remarks made before the Massachusetts Historical Society May 8, 1890 by Samuel Abbot Green, M.D.* (Cambridge, MA: John Wilson & Son, University Press, 1890), 7–11. The inventories ranged from a low of £5 7s. 6d. to a high of £9 2s., this last an adjusted total after subtracting an unusual "purs" containing £11 5s.

11. "An Inventory of Sundrys Belonging to the late Capt. Joseph Hodges, deceased," in *Genealogical Record of the Hodges Family in New England,* by Almon D. Hodges (Boston: Dutton & Wentworth, 1853), 19.

Chapter 2. Captain Hodges' Company

1. The lake had been called St. Sacrement by the French since the early seventeenth century. For consistency's sake it will be referred to hereafter by the name it bears today, Lake George.

2. At least *Ticonderoga* is one way the name was rendered in English.

3. So named because boats and goods could go no farther on the river and needed to be carried to the head of Lake George.

4. Ian K. Steele, *Betrayals: Fort William Henry and the "Massacre"* (New York: Oxford University Press, 1990), chap. 2.

5. Fred Anderson, *A People's Army: Massachusetts Soldiers and Society in the Seven Years' War* (New York: Norton, 1985), 27.

6. Anderson, *People's Army*, 55–58.

7. George Faber Clark, *A History of the Town of Norton, Bristol County, Massachusetts, From 1669 to 1859* (Boston: Crosby, Nichols, 1859), 215; Almon D. Hodges, *Genealogical Record of the Hodges Family in New England* (Boston: Dutton & Wentworth, 1853), 20–21.

8. Almon D. Hodges Jr., *Genealogical Record of the Hodges Family of New England, Ending December 31, 1894* (Boston: Frank H. Hodges, 1896), 123–24. Norton in 1765 had 295 houses for its 343 families and 1,942 inhabitants. J. M. Bumstead, "Religion, Finance, and Democracy in Massachusetts: The Town of Norton as a Case Study," *Journal of American History* 57, no. 4 (March 1971): 819.

9. Hodges, *Genealogical Record of the Hodges Family* (1853), 15–16.

10. Lack of military experience may not have been regarded as a great liability. One colonel reportedly advised a newly coined officer, "To be an officer, there is no Necessity of being inspired with supernatural Talents. Common sense, and Deportment of a Gentleman are sufficient. The knowledge of your Duty, and the Military Art, will come with Time and Experience, but a close Application to the Study, is Necessary." *Boston Gazette,* 28 February 1757.

11. See Anderson, *People's Army*, chap. 2.

12. Thomas Winslow to Gov. William Shirley, Harwich, 20 July 1756, Massachusetts Archives Collection (hereafter MAC), 94B:360, Massachusetts Archives, Boston. Something similar happened to Simeon Cary, of Bridgewater, who received a captain's commission in 1755 but was likewise unable to recruit sufficient men for the campaign. Not until 1758 was he able to earn his coveted commission. *Journals of the House of Representatives of Massachusetts,* vol. 32 (Boston: Massachusetts Historical Society, 1958), 390.

13. Hodges, *Genealogical Record of the Hodges Family* (1853), 19.

14. Anderson, *People's Army*, 38–39.

15. He is listed as a husbandman on his company roster (MAC, 95:61), but this is likely a generous characterization for an unmarried, landless youth.

16. MAC, 79:410.

17. MAC, 77:141, 78:743. The law regarding servants' service dated from the previous war, when the colony wished to tap large manpower resources for the attack on Louisbourg. See *The Acts and Resolves, Public and Private, of the Province of Massachusetts Bay . . . ,* vol. 13, *1741–1747* (Boston: Wright & Potter, 1905), 629.

18. Shirley to Provincial Council of Pennsylvania, 2 February 1756, in *Minutes of the Provincial Council of Pennsylvania, from the Origin to the Termination of the Proprietary Government* (Harrisburg, PA: Theo Fenn, 1851), 45.

19. *Essex Institute Historical Collections* 43 (1907): 121; Middlesex County Probate Court Records, MAC, 35:19.

20. Mary Cone, ed., *Life of Rufus Putnam with Extracts from his Journal* (Cleveland, OH: William W. Williams, 1886), 33.

21. The number in the next age group, 25–29, was only half the number of those aged 20–24; after 30, the numbers for subsequent five-year age groups drop precipitously. Anderson, *People's Army*, 231.

22. Essex County Probate Court Records, MAC, 332:552.

23. Samuel Sewall, *The History of Woburn, Middlesex County, Massachusetts, from the Grant of its Territory to Charleston, in 1640, to the year 1860* (Boston: Wiggin & Lunt, 1868), 348.

24. MAC, 77:686, 750.

25. Orderly Book of John Thomas's Regiment, March 26, 1759–February 2, 1760, [early spring 1759], John Thomas Papers, Massachusetts Historical Society (hereafter MHS).

26. Described as "best Musketts with hollow Bayonets and Leather scabbards London proved Barrels, Walnut stocks, double Bridle Locks neat brass furniture with swivels & Butt slings." Account of military supplies purchased by Massachusetts, 3 January 1756, Archives and Special Collections, Robert Frost Memorial Library, Amherst College, Amherst, MA.

27. John Winslow Journal, 1744–1757 (hereafter JWJ), 2:249, MHS. They also received blankets, cartridge boxes, powder horns, cleaning tools, flints, powder, and bullets. "Account of disbursements to Col. Gridley's Regiment, April 26–June 5, 1756," Archives and Special Collections, Robert Frost Memorial Library, Amherst College. Some recruits declined the offer; one John Stockwell "had a Gun belonging to the Province Delivered to him but by Reason of the Gun being too heavy to carry he chose to take his own Gun with him into Service." MAC, 76:497.

28. MAC, 94B:332; Archives and Special Collections, Robert Frost Memorial Library, Amherst College.

29. Court-martial minutes, JWJ, 3:63.

30. Anderson, *People's Army*, 41, 52.

31. Diary of Abner Barrows, 16 August 1757, Barrow Papers, Massachusetts Society of Mayflower Descendants Library, Hingham, MA.

32. MAC, 95:70.

33. Anderson, *People's Army*, 52. Anderson also thought that hired substitutes tended to be older, and that may be so, but both Barrows and Pulling were young men.

34. MAC, 94B:200. Hunter may have been of Native American extraction, given his surname and the fact that his birthplace, according to his muster roll, was vaguely expressed as the "Island Counties" (today's Martha's Vineyard, Nantucket, and the Elizabeth chain).

35. Hodges, *Genealogical Record of the Hodges Family* (1853), 21.

36. Ruth Story Devereux Eddy, *The Eddy Family in America* (Boston: T. O. Metcalf, 1930), 895; Plymouth County Probate Records, Plymouth, MA, 19:12.

37. See Anderson, *People's Army*, chap. 7. For a discussion of New England's crusading mentality in the previous war, see Francis D. Cogliano, "Nil Desperandum Christo Duce:

The New England Crusade against Louisbourg, 1745," *Essex Institute Historical Collections* 128, no. 3 (1992): 180–207.

38. For 1756 examples of such sermons, see Samuel Webster, *Soldiers, and others, directed and encouraged, when going on a just and important, tho' difficult, enterprize, against their enemies: A sermon preached, March 25th 1756, at Salisbury . . .* (Boston: Edes & Gill, 1756); John Mellen, *The duty of all to be ready for future impending events: A sermon delivered . . . in Lancaster; Occasioned by the general muster and inspection of arms on that day* (Boston: S. Kneeland, 1756); and John Ballantine, *The importance of God's presence with an army, going against the enemy; and the grounds on which it may be expected: Represented in a sermon preached at a lecture in Westfield, on Wednesday June 2, 1756. Just before Captain John Mosely, and his company, began their march towards Crown-Point; Made publick at the desire of the hearers* (Boston: Edes & Gill, 1756).

39. Gad Hitchcock, *A Sermon Preached in the Second Precinct on Pembroke, New England before a Company voluntarily formed, for The Revival of Military Skill, &c. October 10, 1757* (Boston: Edes & Gill, 1757), 12.

40. Seth Metcalf, *Diary and Journal (1755–1807) of Seth Metcalf* (Boston: History Records Survey, 1939), 3.

41. Diary of Abner Barrows, 20 May 1756.

42. Court-martial minutes, JWJ, 2:108.

43. Diary of Abner Barrows, 30 June 1756; diary of Seth Tinkham, in *History of Plymouth County, Massachusetts,* by D. Hamilton Hurd (Philadelphia, 1884), 995; MAC, 96:520.

44. Metcalf, *Diary and Journal,* 3; petition of Edward Cobb, 8 April 1757, MAC, 76:622; Cone, *Life of Rufus Putnam,* 27.

45. Diary of Abner Barrows, 12, 13 May 1756.

Chapter 3. General Winslow's Dilemma

1. *The Papers of Sir William Johnson,* ed. James Sullivan, 14 vols. (Albany: University of the State of New York, Division of Archives and History, 1921–65), 2:74.

2. Many of the private soldiers under Winslow's command could make similar claims.

3. Ian K. Steele, *Betrayals: Fort William Henry and the "Massacre"* (New York: Oxford University Press, 1990), 66.

4. Rene Chartrand, *The Forts of Colonial North America: British, Dutch, and Swedish Colonies* (New York: Osprey, 2011), 39; Steele, *Betrayals,* 58–59.

5. Early sketches and plans indicate that trees had been stripped from the landscape within a half mile of the fort.

6. John Winslow to Spencer Phipps, 26 May 1756, John Winslow Journal, 1744–1757 (hereafter JWJ), 2:62, Massachusetts Historical Society.

7. Winslow to Phipps, 26 May 1756, JWJ, 2:62.

8. Winslow to Phipps, 26 May 1756, JWJ, 2:62.

9. Jonathan Bagley to Winslow, 3 June 1756, JWJ, 2:116.

10. JWJ, 2:112.

11. JWJ, 2:166–67.

12. Winslow to Charles Hardy, Albany, 14 June 1756, JWJ, 2:141.

13. Winslow to Massachusetts Council of War, 20 June 1756, JWJ, 2:168.

14. Winslow to Hardy, 14 June 1756, JWJ, 2:141; Winslow to Massachusetts Council of War, 20 June 1756, JWJ, 2:168.

15. Massachusetts Council of War to Winslow, 28 June 1756, JWJ, 2:231–32.

16. Bagley to Winslow, 12 June 1756, JWJ, 2:145.

17. Winslow to John Choate, 28 June 1756, JWJ, 2:209; John Ashley to Winslow, 26 June 1756, JWJ, 2:195–96.

18. Bagley to Winslow, 3 June 1756, JWJ, 2:116; Winslow to Moses Emerson, 24 June 1756, JWJ, 2:184; Bagley to Winslow, 6 July 1756, JWJ, 2:241; Bagley to Winslow, 27 June 1756, JWJ, 2:220.

19. Bagley to Winslow, 2 July 1756, JWJ, 2:228.

20. Examination of Sergeant James Archibald, 5 October 1756, JWJ, 3:244; examination of Thomas St. Law, 25 July 1756, JWJ, 3:313. Through the end of July, Winslow's total troop strength, including the sick, never exceeded 6,800.

21. Ambush survivors routinely overestimated the numbers attacking them, often wildly.

22. Report of Nathan Whiting, 28 May 1756, JWJ, 2:77.

23. Bagley to Winslow, 29 May 1756, JWJ, 2:94.

24. Diary of Abner Barrows, 2–3 June 1756, Massachusetts Society of Mayflower Descendants Library, Hingham, MA.

25. John Foye to Winslow, 4 June 1756, JWJ, 2:104.

26. Eleazar Fitch to Winslow, 11 June 1756, JWJ, 2:128; "The Journal of Charlotte Brown, Matron of the General Hospital with the English Forces in America, 1754–1756," in *Colonial Captivities, Marches, and Journeys,* ed. Isabel M. Calder (Port Washington, NY: Kennik, 1967), 195.

27. Isaac Wyman to Winslow, 17 June 1756, JWJ, 2:149; report of Robert Rogers, 18 June 1756, JWJ, 2:179; Henry Babcock to Winslow, 1 July 1756, JWJ, 2:223.

28. Babcock to Winslow, 1, 8, 9 July 1756, JWJ, 2:223, 256, 264.

29. Bagley to Winslow, 3 June 1756, JWJ, 2:116; Jehosaphat Starr to Winslow, 16 June 1756, JWJ, 2:148.

30. Bagley to Winslow, 26 May 1756, JWJ, 2:94.

31. For the debate between Shirley and Winslow on this subject, see correspondence from 25 April to 1 June 1756, JWJ, 2:47–90. Winslow had a point regarding the greater cost of ranging companies: Rogers' men received roughly twice the wages of a provincial soldier.

32. Orders to Samuel Thaxter, 11 June 1756, JWJ, 2:131, 138.

33. Thaxter to Winslow, 18 June 1756, JWJ, 2:156–59.

34. Report of Nathan Whiting, 28 May 1756, JWJ, 2:77.

35. "A List of the Men on a Scout Under the Command of Major Samuel Thaxter," n.d., JWJ, 2:154.

36. Seth Hudson to Winslow, 28 June 1756, JWJ, 2:216; report of Capt. Jonathan Butterfield, 9 July 1756, JWJ, 2:257–60. See also the petition of Catherine Losh, the widow of a man killed by Indians in a raid, found with a tomahawk sticking out of his skull. Massachusetts Archives Collection, 77:129–30, Massachusetts Archives, Boston. There may have been more to the abandoned tomahawk than the finders appreciated. In the Ohio country a French soldier noticed a similar practice: "It is . . . customary, when they have

been victorious in war, for the chief of the war party to leave a tomahawk on the battlefield. The emblems of the tribe and the number of warriors he had with him are indicated on its handle. He does this as much to show his valor, as to defy his enemies to come and attack him." J.C.B., *Travels in New France,* ed. Sylvester K. Stevens, Donald H. Kent, and Emma Edith Woods (Harrisburg: Pennsylvania Historical Commission, 1941), 99.

37. David Wooster to Winslow, 16 June 1756, JWJ, 2:144.

38. Winslow to Hardy, 21 June 1756, JWJ, 2:171.

39. Robert Rogers, *The Annotated and Illustrated Journals of Major Robert Rogers,* ed. Timothy J. Todish, illus. Gary Zaboly (Fleischmanns, NY: Purple Mountain, 2002), 41–47.

40. Rogers, *Annotated and Illustrated Journals,* 44.

41. Winslow to Wooster and Timothy Ruggles, 9 July 1756, JWJ, 2:260.

42. Wooster and Ruggles to Winslow, 10 July 1756, JWJ, 2:265. Their explanation for the first scout's failure was "the want of Skillfull Pilots," a curious application of nautical parlance.

Chapter 4. "Ye very bane of New England Men"

1. Jonathan Bagley to John Winslow, 6, 15 July 1756, John Winslow Journal, 1744–1757 (hereafter JWJ), 2:241, 280, Massachusetts Historical Society (hereafter MHS).

2. Return of provincial soldiers, Crown Point expedition, JWJ, 2:166–67.

3. Bagley to Winslow, 22 July 1756, JWJ, 2:298; Phineas Lyman to Winslow, 31 July 1756, JWJ, 2:337; John Choate to Winslow, 31 July 1756, JWJ, 2:338; Winslow to William Shirley, 2 August 1756, JWJ, 2:350.

4. John Osborne to Winslow, 10 May 1756, JWJ, vol. 2:58.

5. Josiah Thacher diary, 1756–1757, 9 July 1756, MHS.

6. Jehosaphat Starr to Winslow, 16 June 1756, JWJ, 2:148; Bagley to Winslow, 27 June, 15 July 1756, JWJ, 2:220, 280.

7. Hezekiah Gates to Winslow, 22 July 1756, JWJ, 2:292.

8. Thomas Moody, *Diary of Thomas Moody,* ed. P. M. Woodwell (Berwick, ME: Chronicle Print Shop, 1974), 34.

9. Report of the Captain of the Guard, Fort William Henry, 2 August 1756, JWJ, 3:3–4; Winslow to Charles Hardy, 28 July 1756, JWJ, 2:325.

10. Minutes of court-martial, August 1756, JWJ, 3:62–63, 68, 89–90.

11. Minutes of court-martial, August 1756, JWJ, 3:68. Miller, at 36, was hardly young in years, however.

12. At the assumed rate of 100–125 grains of gunpowder per discharge, a company of sixty men would burn a pound of powder or more with each volley.

13. "Rules for Regulating the Camp," 30 May 1756, JWJ, 2:80; orders for a field day, 1 July 1756, JWJ, 2:221.

14. Henry Babcock to Winslow, 5 July 1756, JWJ, 2:238.

15. Much of the company-level training the men received was probably antiquated drill anyway. A provincial prisoner told his French captors in 1755, "Their mode of fighting is to place themselves three deep; after the first rank fires it falls in the rear, and so with the others." It was a form of firing more reminiscent of the European wars of the previous century; at the very least, its retrograde movement suggests a defensive character to the

training. *Documents Relative to the Colonial History of the State of New York, Volume 11* (Albany: State University of New York, 1923), 333.

16. Meeting minutes, 24 May 1756, JWJ, vol. 2; Starr to Winslow, 16 June 1756, JWJ, 2:148; Stephen Lee to Winslow, 20 June 1756, JWJ, 2:176.

17. Stephen Hopkins to Winslow, 9 July 1756, JWJ, 2:329; Thomas Hubbard to Winslow, 12 July 1756, JWJ, 2:300. Winslow insisted a week later, however, that he was sure of his figures.

18. Despite Sir William Johnson's endorsement of Rogers, the ranger captain did not have the confidence of others that he would later earn. In response to one of Rogers' reconnaissance reports, the deputy secretary of the province of New York told Johnson, "I may be in an Error but don't believe a syllable of Rogers's Information," pointing out that it ran contrary to intelligence extracted from five deserters and that Rogers had observed French forts from too far away. Goldsbrow Banyar to William Johnson, 27 October 1755, in *The Papers of Sir William Johnson,* ed. James Sullivan, 14 vols. (Albany: University of the State of New York, Division of Archives and History, 1921–65), 2:242.

19. William Hervey, *The Journals of the Hon. William Hervey in North America and Europe, 1755–1814; with Order Books at Montreal, 1760–1763,* Suffolk Green Books No. 14 (Bury St. Edmonds: Paul & Matthew, Butter Market, 1906), 22, 25. For the French prisoners' examinations, see JWJ, 2:288–90.

20. Hervey, *Journals,* 29. In his own journals, printed after the war, Rogers wrote that he had only estimated the numbers at Ticonderoga to be two thousand, "judged from the number of their fires" as he passed by in the night. Hervey may have received a garbled version of Rogers' actual figures, or perhaps there was a problem at the press when Hervey's journal was transcribed—or perhaps Rogers subsequently edited his clearly erroneous estimate before his journals went to press.

21. Hervey, *Journals,* 23, 25.

22. Hervey, *Journals,* 31. For the examinations of St. Law and Charles Armand, see JWJ, 2:313–16.

23. JWJ, 2:313–16. The conditions the deserters described undoubtedly played a role in their decision to desert.

24. Hervey, *Journals,* 31.

25. JWJ, 2:321; Winslow to James Abercromby, 27 July 1756, JWJ, 2:323; general order, 30 July 1756, JWJ, 2:333. Men could be lost on such unauthorized joyrides. Only days after this order was issued, "6 or 7 men a fishing Down by the islands . . . went a Shore and thay was all taken as thay supposed." Josiah Thacher diary, 10 August 1756.

26. Winslow to Hardy, 28 July 1756, JWJ, 2:324. After five days Winslow had to amend his timetable, telling Lord Loudoun that he expected to be "ready at Furthest in twenty days." Winslow to Loudoun, 3 August 1756, JWJ, 3:5.

27. Winslow to John Whiting, 1 August 1756, JWJ, 2:341; Winslow to Province Commissioners, 1 August 1756, JWJ, 2:339.

28. Hervey, *Journals,* 33.

29. Choate to Winslow, 31 July 1756, JWJ, 2:338.

30. Bagley to Winslow, 26 July 1756, JWJ, 2:318.

31. Bagley to Winslow, 15 June 1756, JWJ, 2:280. Biting insects were among the mis-

eries of scouting in the warmer months. Rufus Putnam was another "volunteer in the ranging service" in 1757 who, with two other neophytes, attempted to travel as light as their Native opponents. They suffered greatly from "having nothing to cover us from the gnats and mosquitoes (with which that country abounds beyond description) but a shirt and breechclout." Mary Cone, ed., *Life of Rufus Putnam with Extracts from his Journal* (Cleveland, OH: William W. Williams, 1886), 25.

32. Lyman to Winslow, 31 July 1756, JWJ, 2:337.

33. "The Journal of the Rev. John Graham, Chaplain to Connecticut Troops in the Expedition to Crown Point, 1756," in *The Magazine of American History, with Notes and Queries*, vol. 8 (Chicago: A. S. Barnes, 1882), 210.

34. Winslow to Loudoun, 22 August 1756, JWJ, 3:22; Hubbard to Winslow, 2 August 1756, JWJ, 3:20; Winslow to Hubbard, 22 August 1756, JWJ, 3:48.

35. Joseph Dwight to Israel Williams, 16 August 1756, Israel Williams Papers, MHS.

36. Gerald E. Bradfield, *Fort William Henry: Digging up History* (n.p., 2000), 39.

37. Thomas Williams to Israel Williams, 28 August 1756, Israel Williams Papers, MHS. Winslow agreed that the men's diet was terribly deficient, begging the commissioners in Albany to "send us a Quantity of Vegetables for the Army Especially for the sick, this is a thing Greatly Wanted." Winslow to Province Commissioners, 4 September 1756, JWJ, 3:103.

38. Bradfield, *Fort William Henry*, 39.

39. Fred Anderson, *A People's Army: Massachusetts Soldiers and Society in the Seven Years' War* (New York: Norton, 1985), 96.

40. Bradfield, *Fort William Henry*, 41.

41. Diary of Lieutenant John Frost, 11 July 1760, quoted in Moody, *Diary of Thomas Moody*, 19.

42. Loudoun to Winslow, 4 September 1756, JWJ, 3:114–15. Winslow subsequently gave orders for the men to strike their tents, air them, and dry the ground, to clean the camp streets, and to take other basic measures.

43. Shirley to Winslow, 10 August 1756, JWJ, 3:31. Shirley wrote from Boston, from where communication with Lake George generally took a week to ten days. Winslow replied on the twenty-first.

44. Winslow to Shirley, 21 August 1756, JWJ, 3:35.

45. Fred Anderson, *Crucible of War: The Seven Years' War and the Fate of Empire in British North America, 1754–1766* (New York: Vintage Books, 2000), 150–57.

46. "The Journal of Charlotte Brown, Matron of the General Hospital with the English Forces in America, 1754–1756," in *Colonial Captivities, Marches, and Journeys*, ed. Isabel M. Calder (Port Washington, NY: Kennik, 1967), 195.

47. Thomas Williams to Israel Williams, 28 August 1756, Israel Williams Papers, MHS.

48. Loudoun to the Duke of Cumberland, 20 August 1756, in *Military Affairs in North America, 1748–1765*, ed. Stanley Pargellis (1936; repr., Hamden, CT: Archon Books, 1969), 228–29.

49. William Williams to Israel Williams, 4 September 1756, Israel Williams Papers, MHS.

50. Loudoun to the Duke of Cumberland, 20 August 1756, in Pargellis, *Military Affairs in North America*, 223, 227; Loudoun to Winslow, 20 August 1756, JWJ, 3:41.

Chapter 5. Slaughter

1. John Winslow to Phineas Lyman, 23 August 1756, JWJ, 3:51.

2. Winslow to Lyman, 28 August 1756, JWJ, 3:70; Lyman to Winslow, 24 August 1756, JWJ, 3:52.

3. Timothy Ruggles and David Wooster to Winslow, 12 July 1756, JWJ, 2:274.

4. "A Journal of a Scout of Lieutenant Jacob of the Stockbridge Indians," 18 July 1756, JWJ, 3:21.

5. Stanley Pargellis, ed., *Military Affairs in North America, 1748-1765* (1936; repr., Hamden, CT: Archon Books, 1969), 227; Lord Loudoun to Winslow, 28 August 1756, JWJ, 3:75.

6. William Hervey, *Journals of the Hon. William Hervey in North America and Europe, 1755-1814; with Order Books at Montreal, 1760-1763,* Suffolk Green Books No. 14 (Bury St. Edmonds: Paul & Matthew, Butter Market, 1906), 38; Robert Rogers, *The Annotated and Illustrated Journals of Major Robert Rogers,* ed. Timothy J. Todish, illus. Gary Zaboly (Fleischmanns, NY: Purple Mountain, 2002), 53.

7. William Williams to Israel Williams, 4 September 1756, Israel Williams Papers, Massachusetts Historical Society (hereafter MHS).

8. Hervey, *Journals,* 37.

9. Winslow to Loudoun, 5 September 1756, JWJ, 3:99; Hervey, *Journals,* 38.

10. Loudoun to Winslow, 30 August 1756, JWJ, 3:85.

11. The numbers and makeup of these scouts varied slightly. Information about their composition and the description of their operation that follows are from the scout reports in the John Winslow Papers.

12. Sir William Johnson had employed a similar system of reconnaissance the year before: "I keep constantly out two parties on each side of the Lake of 50 men each who send out small Scouting Parties to discover any Motions of the Enemy so as to prevent a Surprize." William Johnson to Spencer Phips, 10 October 1755, in *The Papers of Sir William Johnson,* ed. James Sullivan, 14 vols. (Albany: University of the State of New York, Division of Archives and History, 1921–65), 2:166–67.

13. JWJ, 3:57. The report is not endorsed and shifts from third to first person, so it is not clear whether Darling was the author or even the competent tracker in the group; I have made the attribution based on context.

14. Hervey, *Journals,* 35.

15. Report of Robert Rogers, 18 June 1756, JWJ, 2:179; Rogers, *Annotated and Illustrated Journals,* 46. The fate of John Hammer is included in "A Muster Roll of Captain Robert Rogers Company of Rangers from July the 23^d. Till September the 27th 1756," doc. 2747, Loudoun Papers, Huntingdon Library, San Marino, CA.

16. Ralph Waldo, aide-de-camp, to Capts. Joseph Hodges and Nathaniel Fuller, 9 September 1756, JWJ, 3:117; "Fort William Henry a Return of a Scout Capt: Joseph Hodges Chief Commander," JWJ, 3:128.

17. Winslow to William Shirley, 9, 13 September 1756, JWJ, 3:119, 134; Winslow to Thomas Hubbard, 22 August 1756, JWJ, 3:48.

18. Winslow to Province Commissioners, 6 September 1756, JWJ, 3:103; John Calef to Winslow, 18 September 1756, JWJ, 3:159.

19. Moses Emerson to Winslow, received 10 October 1756, JWJ, 3:265. A *barrel* was a

unit of measurement varying widely in volume depending on the contents, but for this commodity, at this time, 40 gallons would be a reasonable size. If so, the commissary's ration works out to five quarts per man per month, or ca. 4.4 ounces daily.

20. Winslow to Ralph Burton, 19 September 1756, JWJ, 3:159.

21. We learn from Samuel Greenleaf that the officer who was to visit the east side of the lake was Captain Edmund Moores, of Haverhill. Samuel Greenleaf journal, 1756–1767, 20 September 1756, MHS.

22. Orders, 18 September 1756, JWJ, 3:157. Twenty rounds per man is mentioned elsewhere and appears to have been standard for these scouts. The rounds were presumably in the form of paper cartridges. Regarding Major Miller, see Winslow to Loudoun, 21 September 1756, JWJ, 3:177.

23. Petition of John Erwin, Massachusetts Archives Collection (hereafter MAC), 79: 410, Massachusetts Archives, Boston. Erwin's companions may have been Thomas Woodward and the middle-aged John Lewis, like Erwin members of Butterfield's company. Petition of Robert Wilson, December 1758, MAC, 78:58.

24. I have reconstructed the roster of Hodges' Scout from 1756 muster rolls at the Massachusetts Archives; see appendix A.

25. Historical reenacters have told me, however, that transporting such a weapon through forest is no more troublesome than carrying other kit.

26. Josiah Thacher diary, 1756–1757, 17 September 1756, MHS. My identification of Webb as Hodges' lieutenant for the scout is tentative, based on a remark in Thacher's diary that "Lieut Webb went out" on one of the two scouts on either side of the lake. While the passage is ambiguous, my impression is that he was referring to Hodges' scout; I reckon that there is at least a 50% chance that I am right.

27. Winslow's dispatches place Wilson's arrival at 3:00 p.m.; the entries for 19 September 1756 in Samuel Greenleaf's journal and Josiah Thacher's diary, MHS, both record the time as an hour earlier. I have opted for 3:00, partly on the presumption that Winslow and his staff would have been more likely to have access to the correct local time—some of his letters are dated to the hour—and partly to give the wounded runner more time to cover the twelve miles through the woods. Interestingly, a forced march of twelve miles in three hours, with weapon and full kit, is part of the qualification for the U.S. Army's Expert Infantry Badge. According to former U.S. Army captain Victor Duphily, "Many fit, young and motivated troops have real trouble making that time." Private Wilson was not so encumbered by gear, but even so, Captain Duphily characterized his cross-country performance in three hours as "exceptional," especially considering his wounded status. Victor Duphily, e-mail communication to the author, 29 June 2013.

28. Samuel Greenleaf journal, 19 September 1756; Josiah Thacher diary, 19 September 1756; Winslow to Loudoun, 19 September 1756, JWJ, 3:160. Wilson's name is nowhere mentioned in the most immediate accounts. His identity is established by the petition he sent to the Massachusetts government a year and a half later requesting compensation for expenses associated with his recovery; see chapter 10.

29. An accurate estimate, as we will see.

30. The lieutenant's story is culled from Winslow to Loudoun, 19 September 1756, JWJ, 3:160; Winslow to Benning Wentworth, 20 September 1756, JWJ, 3:168; and an anonymous account dated 20 September and appearing in the Boston Gazette on 7 October

1756, which appears to have been written by someone at the fort (I suspect Rev. Gideon Hawley; see below) and based upon the lieutenant's story.

31. Winslow's letter to Loudoun described the site thus, but by that time the lieutenant of the party had just come in, so it is not clear whether he or Private Wilson had mentioned the island landmark. Captain John Nixon, commanding the *Loudoun,* described the location as "Opposite the Lower End of Dear Island," possibly present-day Green Island. John Nixon to Winslow, [22?] September 1756, JWJ, 3:191.

32. Perry's identity is made clear by his petition, in 1757, for compensation for items he lost or cast away in his escape. Petition of Joshua Perry, 30 March 1757, MAC, 76:430.

33. Nixon to Winslow, [22?] September 1756, JWJ, 3:191; Samuel Greenleaf journal, 19 September 1756; Josiah Thacher diary, 19 September 1756; Hervey, *Journals,* 40; Gideon Hawley journal and letters, 1753–1806, bk. 2, 21 September 1756, Congregational Library, Boston.

34. Winslow to Wentworth, 20 September 1756, JWJ, 3:168; Winslow to Loudoun, 21 September 1756, JWJ, 3:177.

35. Winslow to Wentworth, 20 September 1756, JWJ, 3:168; Winslow to Loudoun, 21 September 1756, JWJ, 3:177. One would give a great deal to have a record of Winslow's inquiry; alas, I have found none, and Winslow makes no further mention of the matter in his military journal. Lieutenant Webb was discharged at the end of the campaign along with his company; there is no hint of reprimand or odium attached to him.

36. The following discussion is founded primarily on three classic works of military history: S. L. A. Marshall, *Men Against Fire: The Problem of Battle Command* (Norman: University of Oklahoma Press, 2000); John Keegan, *The Face of Battle: A Study of Agincourt, Waterloo, and the Somme* (New York: Penguin Books, 1983); and Dave Grossman, *On Killing: The Psychological Cost of Learning to Kill in War and Society* (Boston: Little, Brown, 1996).

37. Better training, Marshall concluded, had corrected this tendency somewhat by the time of the Korean War.

38. Seth Pomeroy, *The Journals and Papers of Seth Pomeroy: Sometime General in the Colonial Service,* ed. Louis Effingham De Forest (New Haven, CT: Tuttle, Morehouse & Taylor, 1926), 138.

39. Grossman, *On Killing,* 8.

40. Grossman refers to incidents that occurred during the 1864 Battle of the Wilderness. In the thick woods, "the yellers could not be seen, and a company could make itself sound like a regiment if it shouted loud enough. Men spoke later of various units on both sides being 'yelled' out of their positions." Grossman, *On Killing,* 7.

41. Clifford J. Rogers, "The Efficacy of the English Longbow: A Reply to Kelly DeVries," *War in Society* 5, no. 2 (April 1998): 235.

42. Grossman, *On Killing,* 127.

43. Joshua Perry all but admitted doing this in his petition.

44. Grossman, *On Killing,* 127.

45. Unless otherwise indicated, the account of the funeral and the events surrounding it are taken from the Gideon Hawley journal and letters, bk. 2. Hawley did not mention Emory by name; he is identified in the *Boston Gazette,* 7 October 1756.

46. Emory's errand and the sentries' problem with enemy identification is taken from Winslow to Wentworth, 20 September 1756, JWJ, 3:168.

47. Gideon Hawley journal and letters; Armand Francis Lucier, *French and Indian War Notices Abstracted from Colonial Newspapers*, vol. 2, *1756–1757* (1999; repr., Berwyn Heights, MD: Heritage Books, 2009), 149. In a case of shutting the barn door too late, a general order went out on 25 September that "for the Future no person assume to go out of the Lines without Armed Guards." JWJ, 3:204.

48. Winslow to Loudoun, 21 September 1756, JWJ, 3:177.

49. Winslow to Loudoun, 29 September 1756, JWJ, 3:218; Winslow to Loudoun, 21 September 1756, JWJ, 3:177.

50. Council of War Minutes, Fort William Henry, 22 September 1756, Loudoun Papers. Six colonels contributed $5 each; eight lieutenant colonels, $4 each; and 6 majors, $3 each. General Winslow kicked in $20 for the total. In November, as the provincial regiments were leaving, three colonels were delegated to determine—on what basis is not clear—who had "won" the contest. Council of War Minutes, Fort William Henry, 10 November 1756, JWJ, 3:384. I have been unable to learn the identity of the lucky winner(s).

51. Winslow to Samuel Willard, 3 November 1756, JWJ, 3:351.

52. Loudoun to Winslow, 21 October 1756, JWJ, 3:306. Loudoun complained that of this number, "there were above 40, who had not the Least reasonable Pretence, from sickness, from going home."

53. "A Trew List of the Company Under Capt Thacher in Colonel Richard Gridlys Regement of foot," Barrows Papers, Massachusetts Society of Mayflower Descendants Library, Hingham, MA.

54. Fred Anderson, *A People's Army: Massachusetts Soldiers and Society in the Seven Years' War* (New York: Norton, 1985), 99.

55. Winslow to Willard, 3 November 1756, JWJ, 3:351.

56. One would think the bodies could all have been identified by comrades once they reached Fort William Henry, but curiously, only Hodges is specifically named in any of the reports and accounts. Even if no roster of the scout was made initially, a list of the dead and missing would seem to be the minimum bureaucratic response. No such list has yet been found.

57. Benjamin Cutter, *A History of the Cutter Family of New England* (Boston: David Clapp & Son, 1871), 65; Hervey, *Journals*, 40.

58. William Williams to Israel Williams, 25 September 1756, Israel Williams Papers, MHS; *Boston Gazette*, 7 October 1756.

59. Report of David Wooster, 7 October 1756, JWJ, 3:250; "Extracts from the Diary and Note Book of Captain William Bacon—1756," in *The Dedication of a Monument to the Memory of the Men of Walpole and Vicinity who served in the French and Indian War, 1755–1763*, by George A. Plimpton (n.p., 1902), 6.

60. "Extracts from the Diary and Note Book of Captain William Bacon," 9. Curiously, the text of Shepard's debriefing, which is in the John Winslow Journal, MHS, does not mention captives from Hodges' Scout. Bacon's is the only reference I have found for this early word of survivors. The news does not appear to have gained any currency. Sadly, the manuscript of his diary appears to be lost.

Chapter 6. Captain de Bougainville's American Adventure

1. Louis Antoine de Bougainville, *Adventure in the Wilderness: The American Journals of Louis Antoine De Bougainville, 1756–1760*, trans. and ed. Edward P. Hamilton (Norman: University of Oklahoma Press, 1964), 36. The biographical details that follow are largely derived from Hamilton's introduction and from the biographical sketch by Étienne Taillemite in the *Dictionary of Canadian History Online*.

2. Students of French, Canadian, and maritime history know that years after his sojourn in America de Bougainville became a world-traveling explorer and French admiral. An island in Papua New Guinea is named for him (actually, he named it himself), as is a South American flower, *Bougainvillea*.

3. De Bougainville, *Adventure in the Wilderness*, 8–9.

4. De Bougainville, *Adventure in the Wilderness*, 36.

5. De Bougainville, unfamiliar at that time with local geography, does not name the spot at which they stopped, but Sabbath Day Point was a well-known, often used waypoint on the lake, suitable for sizeable encampments, and his description of its location conforms to that place, as well as to the timetable of events he describes.

6. De Bougainville, *Adventure in the Wilderness*, 37–39.

7. De Bougainville, *Adventure in the Wilderness*, 39.

8. From the top of Shelving Rock Mountain, one can see a prominent "point" jutting northward from Huddle Bay; this may be the point de Bougainville indicates, as it seems to fit the few other geographic references in the body of evidence.

9. De Bougainville, *Adventure in the Wilderness*, 40.

10. John Winslow, general orders, Fort William Henry, 30 July 1756, JWJ, 2:333.

11. De Bougainville, *Adventure in the Wilderness*, 40.

12. De Bougainville, *Adventure in the Wilderness*, 40.

13. De Bougainville, *Adventure in the Wilderness*, 41.

14. The scalp count was given by the Chevalier de Montreuil, Montcalm's assistant staff officer at Carillon, in a letter to Governor Vaudreuil. It was probably higher than this suspiciously round figure; the number of provincials killed with Hodges was at least thirty. Chevalier de Montreuil to the Marquis de Vaudreuil, 20 September 1756, in *Bulletin of the Fort Ticonderoga Museum* 1, no. 3 (January 1928): 3.

15. The manuscript copy of de Bougainville's journal, from which the English translation was made, reads, "Les Sauvages ont 17 prisionners. Ils on ont deja assones quelques-uns." See "Essay on Sources," De Bougainville journal, Francis Parkman Papers, Massachusetts Historical Society. This probably accounts for the remains Wooster's men found at the Northwest Bay landing, miles from the massacre site; see previous chapter.

16. Gideon Hawley journal and letters, 1753–1806, bk. 2, 21 September 1756, Congregational Library, Boston; JWJ, 2:77.

17. See the examples of both male and female genital mutilation in Jane T. Merritt, *At the Crossroads: Indians and Empires on a Mid-Atlantic Frontier, 1700–1765* (Chapel Hill: University of North Carolina Press, 2003), 178–79. Archaeological evidence from Fort William Henry itself indicates genital mutilation. At least three of the skeletons associated with the 1757 siege and massacre exhibited damage, some extensive, to the pubic area. Maria A. Liston and Brenda J. Baker, "Reconstructing the Massacre at Fort William Henry," *International Journal of Osteoarchaeology* 6 (1995): 35–36, 38.

18. Gideon Hawley journals and letters, 21 September 1756; De Bougainville, *Adventure in the Wilderness*, 41. As he predicted, de Bougainville himself became "contaminated." A year later, at the prospect of having three thousand Indians available to raid the English colonies, he confessed, "What a scourge! Humanity shudders at being obliged to make use of such monsters. But without them the match would be too much against us" (191).

19. De Bougainville, *Adventure in the Wilderness*, 41–42.

20. James Smith, "Prisoner of the Caughnawagas," in *Captured by the Indians: 15 Firsthand Accounts, 1750–1870*, ed. Frederick Drimmer (New York: Dover, 1961), 29.

21. Thomas Brown, *A Plain Narrative of the Uncommon Sufferings and Remarkable Deliverance of Thomas Brown* . . . (Boston: Fowle & Draper, 1760), reprinted in *The Magazine of History*, Extra No. 4 (New York: William Abbat, 1908), 213–15. For examples of both French and English prisoner interrogations, see JWJ, 2:288–90 and 313–15; and *Documents Relative to the Colonial History of the State of New York, Volume 11* (Albany: State University of New York, 1923), 331–32.

22. De Bougainville, *Adventure in the Wilderness*, 42.

23. See chapter 5.

24. Montcalm confirmed the two Indians killed and added the three wounded in a letter to Count d'Argenson dated 22 September 1756. *Documents Relative to the Colonial History of New York; Procured in Holland, England and France*, vol. 10 (Albany: Weed, Parsons, 1858), 488.

25. De Bougainville, *Adventure in the Wilderness*, 41.

26. De Bougainville, *Adventure in the Wilderness*, 40.

Chapter 7. Ensign Lincoln's Great Escape

1. Armand Francis Lucier, *French and Indian War Notices Abstracted from Colonial Newspapers*, vol. 2, 1756–1757 (Bowie, MD: Heritage Press, 1999), 270–71. Two hundred livres was a common price for captives redeemed from Indians by the French. A prisoner taken by Captain Rogers in July told of an English servant living at his house who had been purchased from Indians for the same amount. JWJ, 2:288. There was considerable fluctuation in purchase prices, however, depending on a range of circumstances.

2. Like the precise number of men under Hodges' command, the number of surviving captives remains hazy. Some observers offer approximations (de Bougainville's 17, minus "several" executed; Monteuil's "a dozen"); Lincoln on his return reported twelve besides himself; and Jonathan Barnes years later testified to only ten. I have accounted for fifteen, though for three of these the evidence is tenuous. My figure is supported by Captain Henry Bacon, who had heard from the escapee John Shepard in October 1756 that "insin Linkon and fourteen men" had been carried into Canada (see chapter 5).

3. See appendix B.

4. Louis Antoine de Bougainville, *Adventure in the Wilderness: The American Journals of Louis Antoine De Bougainville, 1756–1760*, trans. and ed. Edward P. Hamilton (Norman: University of Oklahoma Press, 1964), 33.

5. Examination of Thomas St. Law, 25 July 1756, JWJ, 2:314; *New-York Mercury*, 23 August 1756; Chevalier de Montreuil to the Marquis de Vaudreuil, 20 September 1756, in *Bulletin of the Fort Ticonderoga Museum* 1, no. 3 (January 1928): 4.

6. Petition of Jeremiah Lincoln, 16 August 1757, Massachusetts Archives Collection

(hereafter MAC), 77:195, Massachusetts Archives, Boston; De Bougainville, *Adventure in the Wilderness,* 44.

7. Lincoln recalled arriving in Montreal about the first of October, a week's journey. Petition of Jeremiah Lincoln, 16 August 1757. Someone in a hurry, however, could make the trip in three days, as did de Bougainville a few weeks later. De Bougainville, *Adventure in the Wilderness,* 64–65.

8. William Henry Foster, *The Captors' Narrative: Catholic Women and Their Puritan Men on the Early American Frontier* (Ithaca, NY: Cornell University Press, 2003), 14.

9. Phyllis Lambert and Alan Stewart, eds., *Opening the Gates of Eighteenth-Century Montreal* (Montreal: Canadian Centre for Architecture, 1992), 24–25.

10. For an excellent analysis of New Englanders' dread of this fate, see Ann M. Little, *Abraham in Arms: War and Gender in Colonial New England* (Philadelphia: University of Pennsylvania Press, 2007), esp. chap. 4.

11. William Henry Atherton, *Montreal, 1535–1914,* vol. 2, *Under British Rule, 1760–1914* (Montreal: S. J. Clarke, 1914), 415.

12. *Boston Gazette,* 18 October 1756.

13. Foster, *Captors' Narrative,* 15.

14. *Boston Gazette,* 18 July 1756; Titus King, *Narrative of Titus King of Northampton, Massachusetts: A Prisoner of the Indians in Canada, 1755–1758* (Hartford: Connecticut Historical Society, 1938), 20; JWJ, 3:323; Lucier, *French and Indian War Notices,* 2:270.

15. George Lincoln, *History of the Town of Hingham, Massachusetts,* 3 vols. (1893, repr., Somersworth, NH: New England History Press, 1982), 3:7.

16. Robert Eastburn, "A Faithful Narrative, of the many Dangers and Sufferings, as well as Wonderful Deliverances of Robert Eastburn . . . ," in *Held Captive by Indians: Selected Narratives, 1642–1836,* ed. Richard Van der Beets (Knoxville: University of Tennessee Press, 1973), 168.

17. Examination of Sergeant James Archibald, 5 October 1756, JWJ, 3:244. Archibald said that he had worked "next Door to the General who I think they Called Mount Calm."

18. Foster, *Captors' Narrative,* 18.

19. Foster, *Captors' Narrative,* 102.

20. Foster, *Captors' Narrative,* 15, 34.

21. Petition of Simeon Cook, 3 May 1758, MAC, 77:600.

22. Foster, *Captors' Narrative,* 15.

23. Foster, *Captors' Narrative,* 104–5. Apparently, the nuns had purchased the prisoner from Indians for 200 livres.

24. Benjamin Cutter, *A History of the Cutter Family of New England* (Boston: David Clapp & Son, 1871), 65; *Boston Gazette,* 18 October 1756.

25. Lambert and Stewart, *Opening the Gates,* 49–50.

26. Lambert and Stewart, *Opening the Gates,* 59, 76.

27. Lambert and Stewart, *Opening the Gates,* 69.

28. The description of Montreal housing comes largely from Lambert and Stewart, *Opening the Gates,* 71–74. A few such houses survive in the old city.

29. Lambert and Stewart, *Opening the Gates,* 31, 76–78. Sadly, this mansion was destroyed in yet another fire, in 1803.

30. Lambert and Stewart, *Opening the Gates,* 31, 76.

31. Lambert and Stewart, *Opening the Gates*, 19–25.

32. Lambert and Stewart, *Opening the Gates*, 28.

33. De Bougainville, *Adventure in the Wilderness*, 54, 61.

34. De Bougainville, *Adventure in the Wilderness*, 70–71. At the end of November the people of Montreal learned that about one hundred Five Nations Indians were also coming to spend the winter. "These guests would be more welcome," grumbled de Bougainville, "if it were not necessary to feed them, but they are ambassadors who come only for this" (73).

35. De Bougainville, *Adventure in the Wilderness*, 68–70.

36. The French at this time used the Réaumur scale, which set the freezing temperature of water at zero degrees and the boiling temperature at eighty degrees.

37. De Bougainville, *Adventure in the Wilderness*, 71, 75, 78–79; Atherton, *Montreal, 1535–1914*, 2:400.

38. Atherton, *Montreal, 1535–1914*, 2:399, 400.

39. De Bougainville, *Adventure in the Wilderness*, 70, 192.

40. Foster, *Captors' Narrative*, 101.

41. Thomas Brown, *A Plain Narrative of the Uncommon Sufferings and Remarkable Deliverance of Thomas Brown . . .* (Boston: Fowle & Draper, 1760), reprinted in *The Magazine of History*, Extra No. 4 (New York: William Abbat, 1908), 220; Foster, *Captors' Narrative*, 15.

42. Eastburn, "Faithful Narrative," 168.

43. Foster, *Captors' Narrative*, 104.

44. Col. Hinsdale to Israel Williams, 5 October 1756, Israel Williams Papers, Massachusetts Historical Society.

45. Foster, *Captors' Narrative*, 104.

46. The account of Petty's escape is in Evan Haefeli and Kevin Sweeney, *Captive Histories: English, French and Native Narratives of the 1704 Deerfield Raid* (Amherst: University of Massachusetts Press, 2006), 175–80.

47. Brown, *Plain Narrative*, 220.

48. James Archibald estimated that there were about 100 Oswego prisoners working in the city when he left; the others had been sent to Quebec or were shortly to go there. JWJ, 3:245.

49. For example, Archibald told only one other of his intention to escape, and this was a trusted acquaintance who helped supply him for the journey. JWJ, 3:245.

50. As did Joseph Petty and his fellow runaways, who had similarly used the occasion of the Feast of the Ascension, in May, when "we had liberty to go in and around the city of Montreal." Haefeli and Sweeney, *Captive Histories*, 178.

51. Haefeli and Sweeney, *Captive Histories*, 178–79.

52. Brown, *Plain Narrative*, 219.

53. Haefeli and Sweeney, *Captive Histories*, 178; Brown, *Plain Narrative*, 219; petition of Jeremiah Lincoln, 16 August 1757.

54. If the party's "navigator" was indeed a ranger, he might have had knowledge of the way from Crown Point to Lake George, as Rogers' men had been that way at least a half-dozen times.

55. Brown, *Plain Narrative*, 219; Haefeli and Sweeney, *Captive Histories*, 180. See also the testimony of Christopher Proudfoot in chapter 11.

56. Petition of Jeremiah Lincoln, 16 August 1757. I have been unable to discover what happened to the men who gave themselves up.

57. Armand Francis Lucier, *French and Indian War Notices Abstracted from Colonial News-papers,* vol. 2, *1756–1757* (Bowie, MD: Heritage Press, 1999), 270–71; *Boston Gazette,* 18 July 1757. Seth Metcalf, a provincial soldier at Fort Edward, heard a different but in some ways more accurate version of Lincoln's intelligence. He wrote that "two men maid their Escape from Canada and they inform us that an Army is Coming Against us Containing 8000." Seth Metcalf, *Diary and Journal (1755–1807) of Seth Metcalf* (Boston: History Records Survey, 1939), 3.

58. *Boston Gazette,* 18 July 1757.

Chapter 8. The Peregrinations of Peleg Stevens

1. Samuel Johnson, quoted in Marcus Rediker, "'Under the Banner of King Death': The Social World of Anglo-American Pirates, 1716–1726," *William and Mary Quarterly,* 3rd ser., 38, no. 2 (April 1981): 206.

2. Petition of Peleg Stevens, 9 December 1758, Massachusetts Archives Collection (hereafter MAC), 97:16, Massachusetts Archives, Boston, reprinted in *New England Historical and Genealogical Register* 15 (January 1861): 32.

3. Ian K. Steele, *Betrayals: Fort William Henry and the "Massacre"* (New York: Oxford University Press, 1990), 14.

4. Canadian historians are divided over whether there existed a Seven Nations consciousness in the 1750s comparable to that of the famous Six Nations confederacy. I use the term *Seven Nations* as a shorthand reference for the French-aligned, St. Lawrence River Native communities.

5. For a history of this complex relationship, see Daniel K. Richter, *The Ordeal of the Longhouse: The Peoples of the Iroquois League in the Era of European Colonization* (Chapel Hill: University of North Carolina Press, 1992).

6. Barnes, Erwin, Merry, and Pratt all mention having spent the early part of their captivity at Kahnawake; my inclusion of Stevens is based on the circumstances of his account of his travels.

7. D. Peter MacLeod, *The Canadian Iroquois and the Seven Years' War* (Toronto: Dundurn, 1996), 73, 26.

8. Observations on the captives' march from Robert Eastburn, "A Faithful Narrative, of the many Dangers and Sufferings, as well as Wonderful Deliverances of Robert Eastburn . . . ," in *Held Captive by Indians: Selected Narratives, 1642–1836,* ed. Richard Van der Beets (Knoxville: University of Tennessee Press, 1973), 157, 160.

9. Eastburn, "Faithful Narrative," 158.

10. Eastburn, "Faithful Narrative," 161–62.

11. On Iroquoian "mourning-war" practices, in which captives were made to take the place of deceased families, see Daniel K. Richter's classic "War and Culture: The Iroquois Experience," *William and Mary Quarterly,* 3rd ser., 40, no. 4 (1983): 528–59.

12. Titus King, *Narrative of Titus King of Northampton, Massachusetts: A Prisoner of the Indians in Canada, 1755–1758* (Hartford: Connecticut Historical Society, 1938), 20.

13. Eastburn, "Faithful Narrative," 167, 170.

14. Still the best treatment of this complex episode, its aftermath, and its popular memory is Ian Steele's *Betrayals*.

15. Steele, *Betrayals*, 138.

16. Yvon Desloges, *A Tenant's Town: Quebec in the 18th Century* (Ottawa: National Historic Sites Parks Service, 1991), 23, 57.

17. Desloges, *Tenant's Town*, 103.

18. Desloges, *Tenant's Town*, 40.

19. Desloges, *Tenant's Town*, 53–55.

20. "Journal of Stephen Cross of Newburyport, Entitled 'Up to Ontario': The Activities of Newburyport Shipbuilders in Canada in 1756," *Essex Institute Historical Collections* 76 (January 1940): 20.

21. "Journal of Stephen Cross," 20. For the barber, see William Pote, *The Journal of Captain William Pote, Jr., During his Captivity in the French and Indian War from May, 1745, to August, 1747* (New York: Dodd, Mead, 1895), 151.

22. Captain Pote frequently recorded the numbers of inmates held at the redoubt during his stay; they averaged 250–90 over a two-year period. Titus King gave the 300-plus estimate. Pote, *Journal of Captain William Pote*, 166; King, *Narrative of Titus King*, 20.

23. Pote, *Journal of Captain William Pote*, 165–67.

24. King, *Narrative of Titus King*, 20.

25. Pote, *Journal of Captain William Pote*, 105.

26. Pote, *Journal of Captain William Pote*, 113, 127–29.

27. Stevens' timetable of the events of his captivity cannot be reconciled if taken too literally. If he spent thirteen months as a captive of the Indians, as he claimed, then he was brought to Quebec in mid-October 1757. Two months' further confinement would have put him past the time that ships could leave Quebec that year. Since he claimed to have reached England by the end of March 1758, having spent three months in French prisons, then he must have arrived in France in mid- to late December. To accomplish that, he must have left Quebec with the last of the vessels for France in early November.

28. "Journal of Stephen Cross," 21.

29. Pote, *Journal of Captain William Pote*, 152.

30. King, *Narrative of Titus King*, 20.

31. Francis Abell, *Prisoners of War in Britain, 1756 to 1815: A Record of Their Lives, Their Romance and Their Sufferings* (London: Oxford University Press, 1914), 25.

32. That is, tons "burden," a measure not of weight but of volume.

33. Thus Cross' vessel was not technically a cartel ship; these were forbidden to carry cannon or other merchandize. Breach of either regulation rendered a vessel liable to legal seizure. Abell, *Prisoners of War in Britain*, 25.

34. Unless otherwise noted, all quoted material in the remainder of this section is from the "Journal of Stephen Cross," 21–25.

35. According to Abell, *Prisoners of War in Britain*, 25, the cartel ports in this period were Dover, Poole, and Falmouth in England; and Calais, St. Malo, Le Havre, and Morlaix in France.

36. "Journal of Stephen Cross," 27–42.

37. Pote, *Journal of Captain William Pote*, 106.

38. Pote, *Journal of Captain William Pote*, 129.

39. Pote, *Journal of Captain William Pote*, 106, 129, 111.

40. "Journal of Stephen Cross," 21.

41. The only record of Abbot's fate I have found is from the *Vital Records of Andover, Massachusetts, to the end of the year 1859* (Topsfield, MA: Topsfield Historical Society, 1912), 365.

42. Unless otherwise indicated, in this section the experience of prisoners while in France is taken from "Journal of Stephen Cross," 28.

43. Abell, *Prisoners of War in Britain*, 9.

44. For example, the last cartel ship to leave Quebec in 1757, as reported by de Bougainville, was the *Robuste*, on 5 November with 106 prisoners.

45. *Boston Gazette*, 9 October 1758.

46. Abell, *Prisoners of War in Britain*, 6.

47. The cartel ports on both sides of the Channel tended to be second-tier in strategic value, yet either difficult to enter or easily defended.

48. Abell, *Prisoners of War in Britain*, 3.

49. King, *Narrative of Titus King*, 20.

50. The *Boston News-Letter* of 21 September 1758 reported the arrival of the convoy, in which "Several Masters of Vessels, and others, who have been heretofore taken by the French, and been carried Prisoners to France, are returned."

51. Gary Nash, *The Urban Crucible: The Northern Seaports and the Origins of the American Revolution* (Cambridge, MA: Harvard University Press, 1986), 151.

52. King, *Narrative of Titus King*, 21.

53. Petition of Abner Keyes, 19 March 1760, MAC, 79:32. See also the petition of Wells Coverly, who upon his return from captivity in 1759 was pressed "into the King's Service among his Regulars" and as of January 1760 was "not yet discharg'd." MAC, 78:763.

54. Eastburn, "Faithful Narrative," 174. The selectmen of Boston had complained as early as May 1756 that "a very Malignant Fever prevails in Town brought here by the Soldiers belonging to the Province that came from Halifax, Several of the Inhabitants who Attended them being taken sick and died." They quickly took steps to stop all ships coming from there for inspection. *Selectmen's Minutes from 1754 through 1763: Record Commissioners of the City of Boston* (1887; repr., Bowie, MD: Heritage Books, 2000), 39.

Chapter 9. Isaac Foster at the Edges of Empire

1. Brett Rushforth offers a careful description and thoughtful discussion of a surviving example of a Great Lakes slave halter, "simultaneously a work of fine art and a tool of human cruelty," in his *Bonds of Alliance: Indigenous and Atlantic Slaveries in New France* (Chapel Hill: University of North Carolina Press, 2012), 3–4. My imagining of Foster's first minutes of captivity is based largely upon Rushforth's study of capture practices.

2. Rushforth, *Bonds of Alliance*, 40.

3. De Bougainville wrote that the Ottawas had four prisoners with them when they left. Of the fifteen survivors identified, only Bradbury, Gushe, and Partridge are otherwise unaccounted for; they are therefore the most likely, along with Foster, to have been taken by the Ottawa warriors.

4. William A. Starna and Ralph Watkins, "Northern Iroquois Slavery," *Ethnohistory* 38, no. 1 (Winter 1991): 36.

5. For a sampling of the new literature on Native American slavery, see Alvin H. Morrison, "Dawnland Dog-Feast: Wabenaki Warfare, c. 1600–1760," in *Papers of the Twenty-first Algonquian Conference,* ed. William Cowan (Ottawa: Carleton University, 1990), 258–78; Starna and Watkins, "Northern Iroquois Slavery"; Jane T. Merritt, *At the Crossroads: Indians and Empires on a Mid-Atlantic Frontier, 1700–1763* (Chapel Hill: University of North Carolina Press, 2003); Christina Snyder, *Slavery in Indian Country: The Changing Face of Captivity in Early America* (Cambridge, MA: Harvard University Press, 2010); and Rushforth, *Bonds of Alliance.*

6. Snyder, *Slavery in Indian Country,* 4; Rushforth, *Bonds of Alliance,* 10.

7. The classic study, focused largely on captives taken on the eighteenth-century Ohio frontier, is James Axtell's "The White Indians of Colonial America," *William and Mary Quarterly,* 3rd ser., 32, no. 1 (January 1975): 55–88.

8. Alden T. Vaughan and Daniel K. Richter define *transculturation* as "a virtually complete shift from one culture to another," as distinct from *acculturation,* meaning "a partial shift or blending of cultures." Alden T. Vaughan and Daniel K. Richter, "Crossing the Cultural Divide: Indians and New Englanders, 1605–1763," *Proceedings of the American Antiquarian Society* 90 (1980): 24.

9. Starna and Watkins, "Northern Iroquois Slavery," 39.

10. Sebastian Rale, quoted in Rushforth, *Bonds of Alliance,* 39.

11. Daniel Richter, "War and Culture: The Iroquois Experience," *William and Mary Quarterly,* 3d ser., 40, no. 4 (1983): 528–59.

12. Rushforth, *Bonds of Alliance,* 47; Starna and Watkins, "Northern Iroquois Slavery," 36.

13. Rushforth, *Bonds of Alliance,* 4; Snyder, *Slavery in Indian Country,* 7.

14. Starna and Watkins identify the three constituent elements in "Northern Iroquois Slavery," 37.

15. Starna and Watkins, "Northern Iroquois Slavery," 46.

16. Louis Hennepin (missionary), quoted in Rushforth, *Bonds of Alliance,* 16.

17. Hennepin, quoted in Rushforth, *Bonds of Alliance,* 3.

18. Titus King, *Narrative of Titus King of Northampton, Massachusetts: A Prisoner of the Indians in Canada, 1755–1758* (Hartford: Connecticut Historical Society, 1938), 6. Robert Eastburn experience similar sleeping arrangements; see Robert Eastburn, "A Faithful Narrative, of the many Dangers and Sufferings, as well as Wonderful Deliverances of Robert Eastburn . . . ," in *Held Captive by Indians: Selected Narratives, 1642–1836,* ed. Richard Van der Beets (Knoxville: University of Tennessee Press, 1973), 156.

19. Starna and Watkins, "Northern Iroquois Slavery," 46.

20. Claiborne A. Skinner, *The Upper Country: French Enterprise in the Colonial Great Lakes* (Baltimore: Johns Hopkins University Press, 2008), 37; Samuel de Champlain, *Voyages of Samuel de Champlain, 1604–1618,* ed. William Lawson Grant (New York: Charles Scribner's Sons, 1907), 237.

21. Champlain, *Voyages of Samuel de Champlain,* 240. The French name Chaudiere means "kettle."

22. Rushforth, *Bonds of Alliance,* 17.

23. Rushforth, *Bonds of Alliance,* 36–37, 67; Starna and Watkins, "Northern Iroquois

Slavery," 47–49. Perhaps most suggestive of the captive's status, Native domesticated dogs were ritually killed and eaten at war feasts.

24. On Indian enslavement in seventeenth- and eighteenth-century North America, see the essays in Allen Gallay, ed., *Indian Slavery in Colonial America* (Lincoln: University of Nebraska Press, 2010).

25. Rushforth, *Bonds of Alliance,* 20–28.

26. Petition of Isaac Foster, Massachusetts Archives Collection (hereafter MAC), 78:681, Massachusetts Archives, Boston. Foster rendered the pronunciation "Alnipagon." Eleven hundred miles is a fairly accurate estimate, especially given the many loops and turns in the rivers.

27. Father Jacques Marquette, quoted in Rushforth, *Bonds of Alliance,* 33, 56. The reader will recall that de Bougainville witnessed a version of this ritual in Montreal, performed by the Menominees.

28. Rushforth, *Bonds of Alliance,* 49.

29. Starna and Watkins, "Northern Iroquois Slavery," 41.

30. Starna and Watkins, "Northern Iroquois Slavery," 43–44.

31. J.C.B., *Travels in New France,* ed. Sylvester K. Stevens, Donald H. Kent, and Emma Edith Woods (Harrisburg: Pennsylvania Historical Commission, 1941), 100.

32. Rushforth, *Bonds of Alliance,* 17.

33. William Henry Foster, *The Captors' Narrative: Catholic Women and Their Puritan Men on the Early American Frontier* (Ithaca, NY: Cornell University Press, 2003), 8, 10.

34. Rushforth, *Bonds of Alliance,* 19, 58.

35. Petition of Isaac Foster, MAC, 78:681. An American captive in Detroit wrote that "one Day's Paddle of Canoes" was eighteen miles. If Foster and company paddled that far each day, they would cover the distance to Detroit in little more than five weeks. Ernest J. Lajeunesse, ed., *The Windsor Border Region: Canada's Southernmost Frontier* (Toronto: Champlain Society, 1960), 59.

36. Skinner, *Upper Country,* 94–98.

37. Rushforth, *Bonds of Alliance,* 278; Lajeunesse, *Windsor Border Region,* 46.

38. On 28 June 1757 in Montreal, de Bougainville received letters from Detroit dated 7 May 1757; in contrast, a French engineer made the trip in 1749 in only four weeks. Louis Antoine de Bougainville, *Adventure in the Wilderness: The American Journals of Louis Antoine De Bougainville, 1756–1760,* trans. and ed. Edward P. Hamilton (Norman: University of Oklahoma Press, 1964), 119; Lajeunesse, *Windsor Border Region,* 44; Rushforth, *Bonds of Alliance,* 276.

39. Unless otherwise noted, my impression of 1757 Detroit is derived from documents in Lajeunesse, *Windsor Border Region,* 38–61.

40. Petition of Isaac Foster, MAC, 78:681.

41. Rushforth, *Bonds of Alliance,* 276. The 1750 census is printed in Lajeunesse, *Windsor Border Region,* 54–56.

42. Rushforth, *Bonds of Alliance,* 285.

43. Lajeunesse, *Windsor Border Region,* 44.

44. More than six hundred Ottawas and Ojibwas were present for the fall of the fort in August 1757, when they made off with a large share of the prisoners. See Ian K.

Steele, *Betrayals: Fort William Henry and the "Massacre"* (New York: Oxford University Press, 1990).

45. Rushforth, *Bonds of Alliance*, 65.

46. Rushforth's profile of Labutte is in *Bonds of Alliance,* 278–82; Charles Stuart's reference to the "Three Plantations. . . Belonging to three French Merch^{ts} who live in Fort de Troit" is quoted in Lajeunesse, *Windsor Border Region,* 61.

47. Rushforth points out that among Natives, slaves could be traded or sold as "tokens of friendship," and Labutte would certainly have been seen by Foster's Ottawa master as a man of significance, a man whose friendship was worth cultivating. Sadly, as Rushforth discovered, no records of slave sales in Detroit survive. Rushforth, *Bonds of Alliance,* 290, 292.

48. Lajeunesse, *Windsor Border Region,* 61.

49. Lajeunesse, *Windsor Border Region,* 47.

50. This conjectural travelogue is based on a journey from Montreal to Detroit made by Joseph Gaspard Chaussegros de Lery in 1749. Lajeunesse, *Windsor Border Region,* 42–43.

51. For a concise account of Bradstreet's attack on Fort Frontenac, see Fred Anderson, *Crucible of War: The Seven Years' War and the Fate of Empire in British North America, 1754–1766* (New York: Vintage Books, 2000), chap. 27.

52. Petition of Ebenezer Pratt, 8 January 1760, MAC, 78:743.

53. "Examination of Captives belonging to the Province of the Massachusetts Bay on their Return home from Canada," MAC, 78:659. Foster and Pratt were both given £7 "Sterl" at Fort No. Four.

54. Petition of Isaac Foster, MAC, 78:681.

Chapter 10. Homecomings

1. D. Peter MacLeod, "Microbes and Muskets: Smallpox and the Participation of Amerindian Allies of New France in the Seven Years' War," *Ethnohistory* 39, no. 1 (Winter 1992): 42–64.

2. Resentful French officers and soldiers burned their flags rather than surrender them. Fred Anderson, *Crucible of War: The Seven Years' War and the Fate of Empire in British North America, 1754–1766* (New York: Vintage Books, 2000), 408.

3. Petition of John Erwin, 15 January 1760, Massachusetts Archives Collection (hereafter MAC), 79:410, Massachusetts Archives, Boston; petition of John Con, 18 December 1760, MAC, 79:333; petition of John Walklate, MAC, 79:369.

4. Petition of William Merry, 1760, MAC, 79:705.

5. Numerous petitions to the Massachusetts General Court attest to the costs attending travel home after soldiers were discharged, especially if they took sick and needed care along the way. Even Ensign Lincoln, who had so dramatically escaped from Montreal, was faced with "Extraordinary Expense" in getting back to Hingham.

6. MAC, 79:270. Johnson was in Albany by 10 October, so Erwin presumably passed that way rather than taking the road from Crown Point. *The Papers of Sir William Johnson,* ed. James Sullivan, 14 vols. (Albany: University of the State of New York, Division of Archives and History, 1921–65), 3:267. See also the pass for William Ross and his sons, returned from captivity in France, in MAC, 77:334.

7. Middlesex County Probate Court Records, MAC, 38:15; Essex County Probate Court Records, MAC, 334:371.

8. MAC, 77:714, 691; 95:161.

9. MAC, 76:334.

10. MAC, 79:410.

11. MAC, 78:743.

12. MAC, 78:73.

13. Record Book, 1725–1769, Town of Norton, Town Clerk's Office, Norton, MA, 94. The freeholders agreed to pay the doctor at a town meeting held only two weeks after the news of Hodges' disaster reached eastern Massachusetts. It is possible that sympathy for Sarah's loss prompted them finally to pay the bill a year after the services were rendered.

14. Petition of Elizabeth Philips, MAC, 76:579.

15. Petition of John Foster, 2 April 1757, MAC, 76:519.

16. Petition of Thomas Abbot, 4 April 1757, MAC, 76:526. Both the Abbots and the Fosters were from Andover and undoubtedly were acquainted. Their petitions regarding the lost weapons were written only two days apart and in almost identical language. The elders Abbot and Foster likely had the petitions drawn up by the same man.

17. Will and inventory of Gideon Basset, Bristol County Probate Records, 15:219, 249.

18. Bristol County Probate Records, 15:443, 18:191–93. See also the petition of the unfortunate Elizabeth Briggs, the widow of a sick soldier who made it home but died soon afterwards. He too had little estate and no will and left Elizabeth with five children to care for. MAC, 77:31.

19. Middlesex County Probate Court Records, MAC, 30:63, 35:19.

20. Middlesex County Probate Court Records, MAC, 30:63. There may be another explanation for the elder Con's language. Ann M. Little has shown that New England parents of captives in Canada made their missing children's inheritance contingent on their return, fearing that they might otherwise choose new lives among their French or Indian captors. This concern applied chiefly to female captives, however, and was not as pronounced during the Seven Years War. Ann M. Little, *Abraham in Arms: War and Gender in Colonial New England* (Philadelphia: University of Pennsylvania Press, 2007), chap. 4.

21. Middlesex County Probate Court Records, MAC, 27:278–79.

22. MAC, 77:757.

23. Worcester County Probate Records, 5:218–20, 6:84, 206:378.

24. Petition of John Con, 18 December 1760; petition of Ebenezer Pratt, 8 January 1760, MAC, 78:743; petition of William Merry, 1760, MAC, 79:379.

25. Petition of Ebenezer Pratt, 8 January 1760.

26. Petition of John Erwin, 15 January 1760; petition of Isaac Foster, MAC, 78:681.

27. Petition of Robert Wilson, December 1758, MAC, 78:58–59; *Journals of the House of Representatives of Massachusetts*, vol. 35 (Boston: Massachusetts Historical Society, 1963), 231; MAC, 94:442, 95:200.

28. Petition of Jeremiah Lincoln, 16 August 1757, MAC, 77:195.

29. Steven C. Eames, *Rustic Warriors: Warfare and the Provincial Soldier on the New England Frontier, 1689–1748* (New York: New York University Press, 2011), 231.

30. The entire annual budget for the town of Norton in 1761, for example, was only £110. Record Book, 1725–1769, Town of Norton, 216.

31. James F. Cooper and Kenneth P. Minkema, eds., *The Colonial Church Records of the First Church of Reading (Wakefield) and the First Church of Rumney Marsh (Revere)* (Boston:

Colonial Society of Massachusetts, 2006), 199, 203, 197. Labaree escaped on 7 May 1757 and made his own way home. For his story and that of the Johnsons, see *A Narrative of the Captivity of Mrs. Johnson, Together with A Narrative of James Johnson: Indian Captive of Charlestown, New Hampshire* (Bowie, MD: Heritage Press, 2009).

32. William Henry Foster, *The Captors' Narrative: Catholic Women and Their Puritan Men on the Early American Frontier* (Ithaca, NY: Cornell University Press, 2003), 3.

33. Petition of William Merry, 1760, MAC, 79:379.

34. Petition of John Erwin, 15 January 1761; petition of John Foster, 2 April 1757; petition of Benjamin Keith, 4 July 1757, MAC, 77:141; petition of William Merry, 1760, MAC, 79:379.

35. Petition of John Foster, 2 April 1757; petition of John Erwin, 15 January 1761; petition of Joshua Perry, 30 March 1757, MAC, 76:430. Perry could not claim to have suffered captivity as did other survivors, but that did not stop him from petitioning for recompense for his "lost" items. The colony government did not buy his story.

36. Petition of William Merry, 1760, MAC, 79:705.

37. Robert Eastburn, "A Faithful Narrative, of the many Dangers and Sufferings, as well as Wonderful Deliverances of Robert Eastburn . . . ," in *Held Captive by Indians: Selected Narratives, 1642–1836*, ed. Richard Van der Beets (Knoxville: University of Tennessee Press, 1973), 176.

38. *Vital Records of Tewksbury, Massachusetts, to the End of the Year 1849* (Salem, MA: Essex Institute 1912), 123; George Lincoln, *History of the Town of Hingham, Massachusetts,* 3 vols. (1893; repr., Somersworth, NH: New England History Press, 1982), 3:7; *Vital Records of Bridgewater, Massachusetts, to the end of the year 1850*, vol. 2 (Boston: New England Historical and Genealogical Society, 1916), 305.

39. The courtship and marriage of Peleg Stevens and Sarah Wright is derived from *Vital Records of Plymouth, Massachusetts to the Year 1850* (Camden, ME: Picton, 1993), 229, 248–49, 350; and from Plymouth County Probate Records, Plymouth, MA, 15:485, 514.

40. David Thomas Konig, ed., *Plymouth Court Records, 1686–1859*, vol. 3, *General Sessions of the Peace, 1748–1781* (Wilmington, DE: Michael Glazier, 1978), 106.

41. MAC, 94:316, 559.

42. From George Wingate Chase, *The History of Haverhill, Massachusetts, from its First Settlement, in 1640, to the Year 1860* (Haverhill, MA: printed by the author, 1861), 358.

Chapter 11. The Court-Martial of Jonathan Barnes

1. D. Peter MacLeod, *The Canadian Iroquois and the Seven Years' War* (Toronto: Dundurn, 1996), 177–79.

2. MacLeod, *Canadian Iroquois,* 169.

3. Unless otherwise noted, evidence and quoted material regarding the fate of Jonathan Barnes is taken from the minutes of his court-martial, WO 71/135, and from correspondence in WO 34/5, folios 194 and 196, at the National Archives / Public Record Office, London. I am immeasurably indebted to Stephen Brumwell, who generously shared his copies and notes of the proceedings with me.

4. Massachusetts Archives Collection, 94:492, Massachusetts Archives, Boston.

5. General Thomas Gage to Charles Gould, 10 April 1764, in *Civilians under Military*

Justice: British Practice since 1689, Especially in North America, by Frederick Bernays Wiener (Chicago: University of Chicago Press, 1967), 255.

6. Wiener, *Civilians under Military Justice,* 39–42.

7. William Henry Atherton, *Montreal, 1535–1914,* vol. 1, *Under the French Régime, 1535–1760* (Montreal: S. J. Clarke, 1914), 15.

8. William Hervey, *Journals of the Hon. William Hervey in North America and Europe, from 1755 to 1814; with Order Books at Montreal, 1760–1763,* Suffolk Green Books No. 14 (Bury St. Edmonds: Paul & Matthew, Butter Market, 1906), 126.

9. Hervey, *Journals,* 139.

10. Phyllis Lambert and Alan Stewart, eds., *Opening the Gates of Eighteenth-Century Montreal* (Montreal: Canadian Centre for Architecture, 1992), 40.

11. Hervey, *Journals,* 129–30.

12. Hervey, *Journals,* 129, 133.

13. Governor James Murray to Gould, 12 November 1763, in Wiener, *Civilians under Military Justice,* 252.

14. Hervey, *Journals,* 132, 133.

15. Wiener, *Civilians under Military Justice,* 44–45; William Henry Atherton, *Montreal, 1535–1914,* vol. 2, *Under British Rule, 1760–1914* (Montreal: S. J. Clarke, 1914), 17.

16. Stephen Payne Adye, *A Treatise on Courts Martial; Also an Essay on Punishments and Rewards,* 8th ed. (London: Vernon, Heard, et al., 1810), 127. This discussion of military law was first published in New York in 1769. Adye, a first lieutenant in the Royal Regiment of Artillery, had previously been a judge advocate, appointed by General Gage. Adye's *Treatise* went through a number of editions, each adding elaboration or observations as needed. Most of these in fact reflected common practice in 1761.

17. Wiener, *Civilians under Military Justice,* 46–47; Hervey, *Journals,* 137, 142, 144.

18. Stephen Payne Adye, *A Treatise on Courts Martial . . . To which is added an Essay on Punishments and Rewards* (New York: H. Gaine, 1769), 59–60; unless otherwise noted, I cite this edition.

19. The Chateau de Ramezay, preserved for the modern visitor, was the British headquarters during the occupation; courts-martial may have been conducted there.

20. W. H. Askwith, *List of Officers of the Royal Regiment of Artillery from the Year 1716 to the Year 1899,* 4th ed. (London: William Clomes & Sons, 1900), 228.

21. For the depredations of the regiment's men against the Natives, see MacLeod, *Canadian Iroquois,* 186–87. The other offenses are cited in Wiener, *Civilians under Military Justice,* 47; and Hervey, *Journals,* 137, 142.

22. Adye, *Treatise on Courts Martial,* 60.

23. Adye, *Treatise on Courts Martial,* 60–62. *Peine fort et dure* was abolished in 1772. Sylvia R. Frey, "Courts and Cats: British Military Justice in the Eighteenth Century," *Military Affairs* 43, no. 1 (1979): 7.

24. The northern New York border, at 45 degrees latitude, was not fixed until the Treaty of Paris was finalized in 1763.

25. Adye, *Treatise on Courts Martial* (1810), 143–45, emphasis added.

26. Adye, *Treatise on Courts Martial,* 96.

27. Robert Rogers, *The Annotated and Illustrated Journals of Major Robert Rogers,* ed.

Timothy J. Todish, illus. Gary Zaboly (Fleischmanns, NY: Purple Mountain, 2002), 186. For the St. Francis raid and its aftermath, see also Stephen Brumwell, *White Devil: A True Story of War, Savagery, and Vengeance in Colonial America* (Cambridge, MA: Da Capo, 2006).

28. See chapter 5.

29. Curiously, the judge advocate's official duty included helping the prisoner conduct his defense, just one more quirk of the court-martial system. Frey, "Courts and Cats," 6.

30. For a concise discussion of English colonial renegades, see Colin Calloway, "Neither White nor Red: White Renegades on the American Indian Frontier," *Western Historical Quarterly* 17, no. 1 (January 1986): 43–66.

31. For example, Henry Grace, captured in Nova Scotia during the previous war, was given a gun and made to shoot at the severed head of a comrade. James Smith, of Philadelphia, a laborer on Braddock's ill-fated expedition in 1755, was taken by Indians and after spending some time with them was entrusted with a gun to hunt for the family with whom he lived. So was Thomas Brown, of Charlestown, Massachusetts. Henry Grace, *The History of the Life and Sufferings of Henry Grace,* Garland Library of North American Indian Captivities, 10 (New York: Garland, 1977), 18; James Smith, "Prisoner of the Caughnawagas," in *Captured by the Indians: 15 Firsthand Accounts, 1750–1870,* ed. Frederick Drimmer (New York: Dover, 1961), 36, 49; Thomas Brown, *A Plain Narrative of the Uncommon Sufferings and Remarkable Deliverance of Thomas Brown* . . . (Boston: Fowle & Draper, 1760), reprinted in *The Magazine of History,* Extra No. 4 (New York: William Abbat, 1908), 219.

32. As Jane Merritt observes, "Indians used violence against or among captives to control those they wanted to adopt in their communities and to remind them of the treatment that nonkin could expect." Jane T. Merritt, *At the Crossroads: Indians and Empires on a Mid-Atlantic Frontier, 1700–1763* (Chapel Hill: University of North Carolina Press, 2003), 180.

33. The captive James Smith admitted to participating in beating an English prisoner forced to run the gauntlet, and Thomas Brown confessed to helping torture a fellow prisoner to death: "Love of Life obliged me to comply, for I could expect no better Treatment if I refus'd." Smith, "Prisoner of the Caughnawagas," 44; Brown, *Plain Narrative,* 12.

34. Except where otherwise noted, the following discussion of Stockholm Syndrome is based upon Nathalie de Fabrique, Stephen J. Romano, Gregory M. Vecchi, and Vincent B. Van, "Understanding Stockholm Syndrome," *FBI Law Enforcement Bulletin* 76, no. 7 (July 2007), accessed 20 August 2011, http://www.fbi.gov/publications/leb/2007/july2007/july 2007leb.htm.

35. See, e.g., the account of Alexander Henry in Drimmer, *Captured by the Indians,* 80. The quotation is from William Bradford, *Of Plymouth Plantation 1620–1647,* ed. Samuel Eliot Morison (New York: Alfred A. Knopf, 1984), 26.

36. For examples, see James Axtell's classic "The White Indians of Colonial America," *William and Mary Quarterly,* 3rd ser., 32, no. 1 (January 1975): 55–88; and, more recently, Merritt, *At the Crossroads,* 180–81.

37. The textbook modern American example, of course, is the California newspaper heiress Patty Hearst, kidnapped in 1974 (like Barnes, at age 19) and within months cooperating with her bank-robbing captors.

38. Grace, *History of the Life and Sufferings.*

39. Calloway, "Neither White nor Red," 44. Captives from New England, in particular, rarely made the leap to full "transculturation." See Alden T. Vaughan and Daniel K. Richter,

"Crossing the Cultural Divide: Indians and New Englanders, 1605–1763," *Proceedings of the American Antiquarian Society* 90 (1980): 23–99.

40. Adye, *Treatise on Courts Martial,* 97.

41. Adye, *Treatise on Courts Martial,* 99.

42. Adye, *Treatise on Courts Martial,* 99.

43. The operation is described in Rogers, *Annotated and Illustrated Journals,* 154–58.

44. Burt Garfield Loescher, *Genesis: Rogers' Rangers, the First Green Berets* (Bowie, MD: Heritage Books, 2000), 106–7; Samuel Jenks, *Diary of Captain Samuel Jenks during the French and Indian War, 1760* (Cambridge: John Wilson & Son, 1890), 6, reprinted from *Massachusetts Historical Society Proceedings,* March 1890. The very next day, 20 June, about 130 exchanged English captives arrived at Crown Point by boats from St. John's. Proudfoot had definitely done it the hard way.

45. Proudfoot recalled this incident differently, saying that Barnes had first struck a prisoner named Todd with the scalp. When Malone had protested, Barnes grabbed the hoe and struck him, and Proudfoot wrested the hoe from Barnes' hands. Most likely the woman and Proudfoot both intervened to save Malone.

46. Adye, *Treatise on Courts Martial* (1810), 183.

47. Adye, *Treatise on Courts Martial,* 99.

48. Adye, *Treatise on Courts Martial* (1810), 157.

49. Adye, *Treatise on Courts Martial,* 105–6, 109–10.

50. Stephen Brumwell, *Redcoats: The British Soldier and War in the Americas, 1755–1763* (Cambridge: Cambridge University Press, 2002), 174.

51. Brumwell, *Redcoats,* 176–77. Hamilton was brought before a court-martial in July 1761, a few months after Barnes' trial.

52. James Oliver to John Cotton Jr., 14 January 1676, in *The Correspondence of John Cotton, Junior,* ed. Sheila McIntyre and Len Travers (Boston: Colonial Society of Massachusetts, 2009), 130.

53. Hervey, *Journals,* 144. The order was made on 31 March 1761, shortly after Barnes arrived in Montreal and shortly before his trial.

54. Lambert and Stewart, *Opening the Gates,* 50. A French inhabitant found guilty of murder by the court-martial had been hanged in the marketplace only weeks earlier. Atherton, *Montreal, 1535–1914,* 2:17.

55. Franklin Bowditch Dexter, *Biographical Sketches of the Graduates of Yale College,* 6 vols. (New York: Holt, 1885–1912), 2:174–77; Alexander V. Campbell, *The Royal American Regiment: An Atlantic Microcosm* (Norman: University of Oklahoma Press, 2010), 196.

56. WO 34/5, folio 196, National Archives / Public Record Office, London.

57. WO 34/5, folio 194, National Archives / Public Record Office, London.

Chapter 12. Coda: William Merry's Tale

1. Massachusetts Secretary of the Commonwealth, *Massachusetts Soldiers and Sailors of the Revolutionary War,* 17 vols. (Boston: Wright & Potter, 1896–1908). For Ebenezer Pratt's service in the Revolutionary War, see 12:675; for John Walklate's, 16:488; for Peleg Stevens', 14:919, 978.

2. *Massachusetts Soldiers and Sailors of the Revolutionary War,* 10:655, 692.

3. Reverend Joseph Hodges Jr. to A. D. Hodges, Esq., 4 October 1853, in *Genealogical*

Record of the Hodges Family in New England, by Almon D. Hodges (Boston: Dutton & Wentworth, 1853), 16. See also appendix C.

4. See chapter 6.

5. John Demos, *The Unredeemed Captive: A Family Story from Early America* (New York: Knopf, 1994), 17.

6. Dr. Maria A. Liston, e-mail communication to the author, 4 December 2007.

Essay on Sources

Hodges' Scout

In the past two decades a number of new histories have been published on the Seven Years War in America, commonly known in the United States and Canada as the French and Indian War. Most of these histories are relatively short, straightforward treatments of specific events, campaigns, and personalities. For a comprehensive and thorough treatment of the conflict, including its causes, global context, and long-term effects, the reader can do no better than Fred Anderson's *Crucible of War: The Seven Years' War and the Fate of Empire in British North America, 1754–1766* (New York: Vintage Books, 2000). Anderson wrote an abridged version, *The War That Made America: A Short History of the French and Indian War,* for Penguin Books (2006), and in the meantime two additional compact narratives of the war have appeared: William M. Fowler's *Empires at War: The French and Indian War and the Struggle for North America, 1754–1763* (New York: Walker, 2005) and Walter R. Borneman's *The French and Indian War: Deciding the Fate of North America* (New York: HarperCollins, 2006). Often ignored or overlooked by Anglophone writers is the French perspective of the war; William R. Nester's recent work *The French and Indian War and the Conquest of New France* (Norman: University of Oklahoma Press, 2014) is thus a welcome addition to the literature, exploring the political thinking and calculations of France's leaders in what was for them a disastrous conflict not only in Canada but throughout their worldwide empire.

Since most, if not all, of the men in Hodges' Scout hailed from Massachusetts, the natural place to begin any discussion of their motives, recruiting, training, and experiences as soldiers in an imperial war is with Fred Anderson, *A People's Army: Massachusetts Soldiers and Society in the Seven Years' War* (New York: Norton, 1985). Anderson's revealing discussion is drawn most especially from the journals and diaries of veterans of the war, for many of whom this seems to have been the first and only time they kept such a record. Sadly, none of my subjects left any such records of their careers, forcing me to look to more oblique sources for clues concerning their particular circumstances. Most of the men who marched with Captain Hodges were young men, unmarried and without estates, yet Massachusetts' well-kept vital records of births, marriages, and deaths, along with probate records for the counties from which the men came, produced insights on the life stories of some of even the more humble among them. Petitions and statements from families and friends to the Massachusetts authorities, preserved for the historian at the Massachusetts Archives, at Columbia Point, Boston, also contributed materially to creating a prosopography of Hodges' command. For specific actions regarding war efforts, policies, soldiers' pay and supply, responses to petitions, and a host of related issues, see the pertinent volumes of the *Journals of the House of Representatives of Massachusetts,* 52 vols. (Boston: Massachusetts Historical Society, 1919–86), and *The Acts and Resolves, Public and Private, of the Province of Massachusetts Bay . . .* , 21 vols. (Boston: Wright & Potter, 1869–1922).

The 1756 Crown Point campaign usually gets short shrift in histories of the Seven Years War in America, except as a catalog of stalled Anglo-American efforts and military disappointments. Ian K. Steele provides perhaps the best account of the 1755 and 1756 campaigns in the Lake George–Champlain corridor in *Betrayals: Fort William Henry and the "Massacre"* (New York: Oxford University Press, 1990). Steele's narrative is particularly valuable for its portrayal of the often diverging motives and interests of the players involved: metropolitan French, Canadians, British, American colonists, and especially the many Indian nations. My understanding and reconstruction of the 1756 Anglo-American situation was enhanced greatly by the papers of General John Winslow (about which more below), as well as by *Documents Relative to the Colonial History of the State of New York, Volume 11* (Albany: State University of New York, 1923). *The Papers of Sir William Johnson,* ed. James Sullivan, 14 vols. (Albany: University of the State of New York, Division of Archives and History, 1921–65), especially volumes 2 and 3, offer the perspective of an important and very well informed Crown administrator, as do *The Journals of Hon. William Hervey in North America and Europe, 1755–1814, with Order Books at Montreal, 1760–1763,* Suffolk Green Books No. 14 (Bury St. Edmonds: Paul & Matthew, Butter Market, 1906). In contrast to the records of metropolitan and colonial bureaucrats, I have tried to introduce the point of view of more ordinary folk, who nevertheless contribute vital nuance and detail. "The Journal of Charlotte Brown, Matron of the General Hospital with the English Forces in America, 1754–1756," in

Colonial Captivities, Marches, and Journeys, ed. Isabel M. Calder (Port Washington, NY: Kennik, 1967) adds a rare female voice to the male-dominated accounts, while J.C.B.'s *Travels in New France,* ed. Sylvester K. Stevens, Donald H. Kent, and Emma Edith Woods (Harrisburg: Pennsylvania Historical Commission, 1941), performs a similar function from the point of view of a French soldier.

Chapters 3, 4, and 5 could hardly have been written as they were without the collection known as the John Winslow Journal, 1744–1757, at the Massachusetts Historical Society. Belying its catalog designation, this multivolume record set is not in fact a journal as commonly understood. Rather it is a compilation of letters, muster returns, supply statements, scouting reports, court-martial précis, and related military items for Winslow's campaigns of 1755–56. Most of the records are a secretary's copies of the original documents. Arranged chronologically as they are, the papers for 1756 do indeed form a kind of journal of the campaign, from which most of my characterization of Fort William Henry's squalid conditions, the persistent problems with personnel and supply, and the records of local patrols is taken. It is curious that so few historians have made much use of this invaluable collection, and I have by no means fathomed all of its possibilities here. These await, and will greatly reward, the attentions of future scholars and students.

The Massachusetts Historical Society also holds a treasure-trove of soldiers' diaries, journals, and memoirs. Fred Anderson cataloged all those he found in an appendix to *A People's Army.* Some of these have been published, such as *Life of Rufus Putnam with Extracts from his Journal,* ed. Mary Cone (Cleveland, OH: William W. Williams, 1886), while the journals of Samuel Greenleaf and Josiah Thacher, eyewitnesses to the activities at Fort William Henry, are only available to the researcher in manuscript form. At the Congregational Library, in Boston, are the Gideon Hawley journal and letters, 1753–1806, also still in manuscript. This regimental chaplain's journal entries for 1756 document details for the immediate aftermath of Captain Hodges' disaster found nowhere else.

The conditions at Fort William Henry described in the above sources are supported by archaeology; for a very readable, layman's introduction to this evidence, see two well-illustrated works by the archaeologist David R. Starbuck: *The Great Warpath: British Military Sites from Albany to Crown Point* (Hanover, NH: University Press of New England, 1999) and *Massacre at Fort William Henry* (Hanover, NH: University Press of New England, 2002).

My analysis of the destruction of Hodges' Scout, detailed in chapter 5, depends on General Winslow's after-action reports to Lord Loudoun, the petitions of survivors made in the following months and years to the Massachusetts General Court, and the works of military historians and psychologists. Since no detailed account of the action by any of the survivors has yet come to light, Winslow's "journal" and the brief recollections of Robert Wilson and Joshua Perry (these last at the Massachusetts Archives, at Columbia Point) identify the approximate location and time of the debacle and introduce the challenge of reconciling confused and contradictory reports from participants in the same event. To help the reader understand the behavior of men suddenly exposed to deadly combat, and to inform my alternative interpretations of what happened to Hodges' men, I have relied on three classic works of military history: S. L. A. Marshall, *Men Against Fire: The Problem of Battle Command* (Norman: University of Oklahoma Press, 2000); John Keegan, *The Face of Battle: A Study of Agincourt, Waterloo, and the Somme* (New York: Penguin Books, 1983); and Dave Grossman, *On Killing: The Psychological Cost of Learning to Kill in War and Society* (Boston: Little, Brown, 1996).

As explained in chapter 5, no roster of those under Hodges' command on September 19, if one was ever made, has yet surfaced. I have reconstructed 75–85 percent of the roster from 1756 muster rolls at the Massachusetts Archives (see appendix A). This list revealed the curious mix of men, from some twenty-five different companies and representing at least four regiments, who made up Hodges' Scout. This seemed unusual, to say the least; I discovered, however, that in fact this ad hoc mix of men was the norm for mounting patrols from Fort William Henry that year, and this prompted my discussion of this pattern as a factor in the destruction of Hodges' Scout.

Any student of the French and Indian War must read the journals of Louis Antoine de Bougainville, the chatty and refreshingly opinionated chronicler of the French and Canadian experience of the war. De Bougainville was present almost from the beginning of the war in America and at the very end, and his perspectives, while often jaundiced, are nevertheless invaluable. He provides most of what we know concerning Hodges' Indian and Canadian opponents, their movements, and even their appearance, and he furnishes us with the perspective of the "other" side in chapter 6. I first read the journals decades ago, in Edward P. Hamilton's classic translation, *Adventure in the Wilderness: The American Journals of Louis Antoine De Bougainville,*

1756–1760 (Norman: University of Oklahoma Press, 1964), so when I first learned of Hodges' Scout, I recalled that de Bougainville had been in the neighborhood about that time and so might have had something to say on the matter. To my disappointment, he seemed to be referring to another incident on that day, one in which "a detachment of thirteen English" were nearly all captured or killed. Yet, the location he described and other circumstances fit the facts I had concerning Hodges' men.

What followed was a textbook lesson in verifying historical sources. The French for *thirteen* could not possibly have been confused by Hamilton with any French term for *fifty* (the number of men in Hodges' Scout) or any number near it, so I could not assume that de Bougainville's detailed account referred to my subjects. Hamilton's introduction to his book identifies his source as the verbatim copy of a French manuscript, made in the nineteenth century by none other than Francis Parkman, in preparation for his classic works on the French and Indian War. As it happens, Parkman's copy of the manuscript is in the collection of the Massachusetts Historical Society in Boston. An afternoon spent with the manuscript (while struggling to recall my high-school French) brought me to the appropriate passage, where, sure enough, what appeared to be the numeral 13 refers to the unfortunate "English." It was curious, though: the "1" was not completely straight, but a sinuous line, almost like the "long *s*" familiar to readers of eighteenth-century script; and Hamilton had deviated from literal translation in *writing out* "thirteen," rather than using the numeral I was seeing in Parkman's hand. I then noticed that many of Parkman's dates, such as "1755" and "1756," employed the same sinuous character for the numeral 5. Parkman wrote his fives in one long stroke instead of the commonly-taught two; the result was that in the course of a tedious transcription, and perhaps suffering from writer's cramp, Parkman's hurried 5 morphed into a very plausible-looking 1. Hamilton had read what was in fact "53" in the manuscript as "13" and then compounded the error by writing out the (false) number. Hodges' Scout has in fact been "hiding in plain sight" for more than half a century and would almost surely have come to light before this but for Hamilton's mistaken transcription.

Captives

The petitions of survivors of Hodges' Scout, and of those grieving or otherwise affected by the disaster, form the outlines of the chapters in the second half of this book. These documents, also housed at the Massachu-setts Archives in Boston, were invaluable for revealing the varied itineraries and experiences of American captives in the French and Indian War. Peti-tions take the form of a request for help or compensation from the colony's government, generally for wages owed or other costs associated with re-turning home. Considering their purpose, they are often maddeningly short on the sort of detail historians would like, but the persistent reader can tease considerable information from them nonetheless. To imagine the Montreal of Jeremiah Lincoln's captivity in chapter 7, I found two sources particularly helpful: *Opening the Gates of Eighteenth-Century Montreal*, ed. Phyllis Lambert and Alan Stewart (Montreal: Canadian Centre for Architec-ture, 1992); and William Henry Atherton's *Montreal, 1535–1914*, vol. 1, *Under the French Regime, 1535–1760* (Montreal: S. J. Clarke, 1914). Two additional sources added valuable detail and color. *The Captors' Narrative: Catholic Women and Their Puritan Men on the Early American Frontier*, by Wil-liam Henry Foster (Ithaca, NY: Cornell University Press, 2003), has fasci-nating sections on the employment of captives by the religious orders in Montreal and Quebec. The ubiquitous de Bougainville provides vignettes of life in the winter-bound city that Lincoln surely would have appreciated. The experiences of other captives, especially Joseph Petty, Thomas Brown, and Robert Eastburn, helped inform the story of Lincoln's captivity and escape.

The story of Peleg Stevens' long journey home, chronicled in chapter 8, begins with his year-long stay in Kahnawake. For an understanding of the relationships among the Iroquois of the Northeast at this time, the student should begin with Daniel K. Richter's classic book *The Ordeal of the Long-house: The Peoples of the Iroquois League in the Era of European Colonization* (Chapel Hill: University of North Carolina Press, 1992) and D. Peter Mac-Leod, *The Canadian Iroquois and the Seven Years' War* (Toronto: Dundurn, 1996). Stevens, along with Joseph Abbot, was subsequently moved to the prison in Quebec; my portrayal of the colonial city is largely shaped by the excellent study *A Tenant's Town: Quebec in the 18th Century*, by Yvon Desloges (Ottawa: National Historic Sites Parks Service, 1991). Another cap-tivity journal, *The Journal of Captain William Pote, Jr., During his Captivity in the French and Indian War from May, 1745, to August, 1747* (New York: Dodd, Mead, 1895), helped me to envision the experience of imprisonment in the Dauphine Bastion. Stevens' voyages across the Atlantic and his experiences in three French prisons surely must have been very similar to those described in the wonderfully detailed "Journal of Stephen Cross of Newburyport, Entitled 'Up to Ontario': The Activities of Newburyport Shipbuilders in Canada in 1756," *Essex Institute Historical Collections* 76 (January 1940). As for prisoner-exchange practices, Francis Abell wrote a delightfully biased and self-serving examination of the system a century ago and of the "superiority" of British treatment of prisoners of war over that of other nations in *Prisoners of War in Britain, 1756–1815: A Record of Their Lives, Their Romance and Their Sufferings* (London: Oxford University Press, 1914). Despite its age and patriotic prejudice, it is not a bad place to start on this understudied facet of eighteenth-century warfare.

Isaac Foster's captivity in the *pays d'en haut* is briefly outlined in his petition to the Massachusetts government. Concerning the experiences of captives, one classic study is James Axtell's "The White Indians of Colonial America," *William and Mary Quarterly*, 3rd ser., 32, no. 1 (January 1975): 55–88. Axtell's analysis focuses largely on captives taken on the eighteenth-century Ohio frontier and offers a relatively benign interpretation of captivity, stressing the adoption of captives into Native societies. Alden T. Vaughan and Daniel K. Richter reported something rather different in "Crossing the Cultural Divide: Indians and New Englanders, 1605–1763," *Proceedings of the American Antiquarian Society* 90 (1980): 23–99. Their research revealed little evidence of "transculturation" in that part of the Northeast. More recently, new literature on Native American slavery demonstrates that the treatment of captives in much of Native North America could be very unpleasant indeed; see Alvin H. Morrison, "Dawnland Dog-Feast: Wabenaki Warfare, c. 1600–1760," in *Papers of the Twenty-first Algonquian Conference*, ed. William Cowan (Ottawa: Carleton University, 1990), 258–78; William A. Starna and Ralph Watkins, "Northern Iroquois Slavery," *Ethnohistory* 38, no. 1 (Winter 1991): 34–57; Jane T. Merritt, *At the Crossroads: Indians and Empires on a Mid-Atlantic Frontier, 1700–1763* (Chapel Hill: University of North Carolina Press, 2003); Christina Snyder, *Slavery in Indian Country: The Changing Face of Captivity in Early America* (Cambridge, MA: Harvard University Press, 2010); and Brett Rushforth, *Bonds of Alliance: Indigenous and Atlantic Slaveries in New France* (Chapel Hill: University of North Carolina Press, 2012).

The minutes of the court-martial of Jonathan Barnes and related correspondence are at The National Archives/Public Record Office, London, WO 71/135, WO 34/5, folios 194 and 196. For modern discussions of court-martial procedures at this time, see Frederick Bernays Wiener, *Civilians under Military Justice: British Practice since 1689, Especially in North America* (Chicago: University of Chicago Press, 1967), and Sylvia R. Frey, "Courts and Cats: British Military Justice in the Eighteenth Century," *Military Affairs* 43, no. 1 (1979): 5–11. To go to the source, see Stephen Payne Adye, *A Treatise on Courts Martial; Also an Essay on Punishments and Rewards,* first published in New York in 1769. Adye had previously been a judge advocate, appointed by General Gage, and his *Treatise* reflects practices in use at the time of Barnes' trial. For a concise discussion of white "renegades," see Colin Calloway, "Neither White nor Red: White Renegades on the American Indian Frontier," *Western Historical Quarterly* 17, no. 1 (January 1986): 43–66. My understanding of Stockholm Syndrome and my application of it in Barnes' case are based on law-enforcement literature, particularly Nathalie de Fabrique, Stephen J. Romano, Gregory M. Vecchi, and Vincent B. Van, "Understanding Stockholm Syndrome," *FBI Law Enforcement Bulletin* 76, no. 7 (July 2007), accessed 20 August 2011, http://www.fbi.gov/publications/leb/2007/july2007/july2007leb.htm. Jane T. Merritt examines the ways in which Natives used violence, or the threat of it, to control captives, whether or not they were being considered for adoption; see her *At the Crossroads: Indians and Empires on a Mid-Atlantic Frontier, 1700–1763* (Chapel Hill: University of North Carolina Press, 2003).

Index